THE
VOCABULARY
BUILDER

By the Author

THE COMMAND OF WORDS

THE VOCABULARY BUILDER
(formerly *How to Double Your Vocabulary*)

The
Vocabulary
Builder

S. Stephenson Smith

Thomas Y. Crowell Company

NEW YORK, ESTABLISHED 1834

Formerly published under the title
How to Double Your Vocabulary

Copyright 1947 by S. Stephenson Smith

Second Printing

Manufactured in the United States of America by the
Vail-Ballou Press, Binghamton, New York

TO

FRANK LOXLEY GRIFFIN

After thirty-three years

CONTENTS

"... *language such as men do use.*"

—BEN JONSON

THE
VOCABULARY
BUILDER

WORDPLAY

Anyone learning a new card game wants to know how to figure the odds: How often is a card likely to turn up, and what combinations pay off? You should ask the same questions about words. Which words turn up most often, in the range just beyond your vocabulary? When you run into a new word, is it worth adding to your stock? And where do these new words fit in, if you want to bring them into play—or put them to work? In short, how do you figure the odds on words?

In the long run a gambler with a hard-headed system will beat anyone who plays hit-or-miss. The word-game can do with a system, too. This holds whether you're playing for fun or money.

Maybe you want a ready, wide, and sure command of words to get ahead in business. Or you would like to travel, first through books, and then in fact, and you feel that out-of-the-way words go with out-of-the-way places. Or perhaps—best reason of all—you want a livelier, wittier, richer vocabulary to increase your enjoyment of life, and your awareness of what is happening in the world.

For whatever purpose you want a better vocabulary, this book will tell you the gambling odds on how often words new to you will turn up, and in what kind of reading you're likely to find them. The words printed in SMALL CAPITALS in this book are the utility group just beyond the range of the average American's vocabulary. They're the terms you're most likely to need for all-round use, in reading, writing, and talking. Included are a good many new terms from politics, business, labor, science, and technology.

You'll be surprised to find how few additional words you need in each of these fields, to get along quite well. Where you used to draw a blank on certain words, you'll be able to read right along. Adding the right fifty or a hundred terms will put you at ease with special subjects you've always passed up because you didn't like those four or five blackouts of meaning to a page. Even a tough subject like atomic energy will yield to a little directed homework on the jargon in which atomic physicists talk to engineers. (In talking at long range to each other, the nuclear physicists usually employ that concentrated short-hand, mathematics.)

MEMORY PEGS

It's a safe bet you've been thinking to yourself, "This is all very well, but how am I going to remember these new words?" The memorizing you'll have to do for yourself, but this book presents seven strong memory pegs to help you out:

1. *Tie many words into one.* In a list of synonyms, you're pretty sure to know at least one word in the group. Center the others on it. Distinguish the fine shades of difference in meaning. In doing so, you'll find you've mastered a handful of words in one operation.

2. *100 will get you 5000.* Learn the 100 Latin and Greek roots that among them yield 5000 derivatives. Once you know these stems, you can sight-read the literal meaning of words derived from them.

3. *Tie in to one package new words that belong to a given subject.*

4. *Keep an eye out for slang as language in the making.* It's an A-1 guide to the way words change meaning, as well as a key to the spirit of your own times.

5. *Run down the history of any interesting new word you meet.* Play detective on its trail, and you won't forget it. Do you know what a GOOGOL is? or a CHIMERA? or EXTRAPOLATION? Where is the original BEDLAM? Who first used the word PANDEMONIUM? When the girls in the backroom at *Vogue,* the fashion magazine, want to designate a woman's clothes as gaudy and MERETRICIOUS, what term do they use? Should LaGuardia have sued *Time* for coupling his name with the epithet STEATOPYGOUS? Do you know where the *juke* in *juke-box* comes from? Is it related in origin to the *Jukes* family often found in juke-joints? How did the word MORON, a TRANSLITERATION of the Greek word for "fool," acquire a different meaning by a majority vote? How did a good Old English word *walk* come to have a Greek trailer hitched on it to form *walkathon*? And how do perfectly proper words—*hot, lit, swell,* BUZZARD, *tomato,*—come down in the world, acquiring a slang or vulgar sense? (You'll find the answers later in the book.)

6. *Learn new words two ways.* In the dictionary way, where you tie the meaning in with the term; and vice versa, in crossword puzzle style, where you supply the word when the clue is given. Vice-versa quizzes

2

are found at the end of each section of this book, to help you turn the trick.

7. *Always remember the new key word in a joke*. By thus getting a humorous association with a new word, you'll find it will stick by you. Learn the tricks and turns of wordplay, and you won't need jokebooks.

This ends the sales talk, and there'll be no middle commercials.

Gags Have a Serious Side

The highest priced words you hear are ghost-written by gagmen who furnish the raw material for comedy over the air and on the screen. They have a word-lore all their own, which they practice for five to fifteen hundred dollars a week, or fifty dollars a gag at piece rates. That's SIZABLE pay for confounding ACRIMONY with MATRIMONY, or extracting ATTAR of roses from the otter.

Quite apart from the dollar sign on it, gagmen's word-lore is worth a close look, if you're given to the popular American pastime of playing with words—or if you're part of the forty per cent who make their living in the word-trades.

Gag writers' tricks with words point up the fact that we have two distinct levels of language: familiar, ordinary words that everybody knows; and more elaborate words that don't turn up so often, but many of which we need to know if we're to feel at home in listening and reading today.

To be sure, gagmen play hob with the big words, making not sense but fun of them. They keep on confusing BIGOTRY with BIGAMY, *illiterate* with ILLEGITIMATE, *monotony* with MONOGAMY, OSCULATION with OSCILLATION. They trade on the fact that for many of their listeners, these fancy terms linger in a twilight zone of meaning. It's their deliberate intent to make everybody feel cosy at hearing big words jumbled up or smacked down. After all, such words loom up as over-size in ordinary talk, so no wonder they get the bulldozer treatment from gagmen.

Their wrecking technique incidentally reveals our language as full of tricky words, some with nineteen different meanings, others which sound alike but differ in sense. To ring good punning changes, gag writers have to know their way around in the language. They don't get paid for ignorance, only for SIMULATING it.

Their trade is a hard one, and they regard it as serious business. They

3

never laugh at each other's jokes, rarely at their own. Like comedians, they are usually melancholy men in private life.

For anyone who doesn't have to be funny for a living, it's instructive to go behind the scenes and watch gag writers at work. Two or three of them get together, take off their coats, loosen up their ties—and consult a master file. For gagmen do not depend on their own unaided intellects. A gag file is a collection of stock jokes: Joe Millers, they're called in the trade, after the Englishman who put out what was allegedly the first modern joke book. Some of the famous files in the industry run to over a million entries, classified by subject. And many of the jokes are finally pegged on a single word.

Having decided on the general subject they want to play with, the gagmen fish a few jokes out of the file. With luck, one of these will furnish the skeleton structure for a new gag. Given this start, they begin batting the topic around. They try to put a new rattle on the old wheeze. Or they look for a "gimmick," the "twist" or "wrinkle" that will be the turning point of the joke. A *gimmick,* originally a magician's prop, is the device that will make an old gag new. It may be a dodge that will turn a piece of wordplay into an action gag. Any one of these shifts by which they work the transformation is called a "switcheroo."

The charge is repeatedly made that there are no new gags. This is really a libel on the gagmen. They improvise new variations on the old themes, at their best combining surprise with the charm of the familiar. It is true that the stock gag patterns are hand-me-downs from vaudeville and BURLESQUE. From these sources the gag writers also get their lingo and their craft tradition.

GAG WRITERS' LINGO

Fertile invention and ingenious fancy are required to clean up "blue" burlesque gags for radio use. These shady gags are theoretically TABOO on the air. However, a gag writer who can leave a faint trace of bluing when he launders the joke is all the more admired—and more highly paid.

A gag that keeps the blue tinge is called a "double-intender," Gagland jargon for *double entendre.* The double meaning makes the joke funny at two levels. Children and other innocents hearing the crack for the first time take it literally, laughing at the surface humor; listeners who

4

remember the original as they heard it in vaudeville or burlesque, laugh at the artfulness with which the blue tinge is disguised.

Another name for a double meaning of this sort is "insinuendo." This is a portmanteau word, or "combo," as the gagmen would label it, thus abbreviating *combination*. By telescoping INSINUATION and INNUENDO, they get *insinuendo,* on the principle of blend words brought into vogue by Lewis Carroll.

"Shock logic" is another favorite with gag writers. Supposedly a specialty of women comediennes, it is ILLOGICAL logic, more easily illustrated than defined. A high school girl has to turn down a boy's proposal. She writes:

Dear Jerry:
I'm sorry, but I can't get engaged to you. My mother thinks I am too young to be engaged, and besides I'm already engaged to another boy.

Yours regretfully,
Guess Who

Gag writers' lingo is consistently funnier than their gags. It should interest the slang-fancier. And like much vivid JARGON developed in specialized trades and sports, a few of the terms are making their way into general use. *Gimmick,* for instance, in the sense either of a trick device or the point of a joke, is creeping into the vocabulary of columnists and feature writers.

Even apart from their trade lingo, gagmen's maneuvers are of real concern to anyone who follows words with a fully awakened interest. For the very fact that gag writers often use a long and unusual word as the hinge of a joke, or as a peg for situation comedy, tells us something quite significant: they are well aware of the limitations of the average vocabulary and are quite willing to cash in on its shortcomings.

When Fred Allen's jokesmiths work out a fishing routine, they have Allen referring to the bait in his most arch and solemn tones: "I presume you mean the legless INVERTEBRATE." This is the old minstrel trick, using a long fancy term, instead of calling a worm a worm.

Chico Marx can stretch a pun over five hundred feet of film, making it funnier all the time, as he did when he worried the word VIADUCT, which he rendered "Why a duck?"

And even the highbrow radio writers have taken advantage of gagmen's technique. You might never expect to hear on the air such words as LEPIDOPTERIST and ENTOMOLOGIST. Both occur in a very famous radio play by Norman Corwin, "My Client Curley," about an unusual caterpillar which would dance to the tune of "Yes, sir, she's my baby" but remained inert to all other music. The dancing caterpillar was given a real New York build-up, which involved calling in the experts on butterflies and insects who travel under the learned names above. Corwin made mild fun of the fancy professional titles, at the same time explaining them UNOBTRUSIVELY.

There are many similar occasions where anyone working with words can turn gagmen's trade secrets to account. Just what words do they think outside the familiar range? How do they pick the words that they "kick around"? It's not hard to find out. Here are some specimens from a gag writer's file.

1. WHAT WORD WAS MURDERED?

1. The gentleman said he was a dramatic *cricket*.—Artemus Ward.
2. What is ACRIMONY? It's sometimes called holy, another name for marriage.—Manchester schoolboy.
3. Hashimura Togo deals with the question: Can a Japanese-American boy grow up to be president?
    "He must firstly obtain the consent of Hon. Roosevelt, who probably would not give it. . . . When inexperienced gentleman are called by White House to take job, must enjoy great agony trying to study Constitution, boat-building, Tuskagee (*sic*) and other racing problems necessary to ENCUMBRANCE of office."—Irwin, *Letters of a Japanese Schoolboy* (1906).
4. "An' when Mrs. Grubbs sez you wasn't no lidy, wot did yer say?"
    "I sez, 'two negatives means an INFIRMARY,' and knocks her down."
5. Sergeant O'Hara said, "It was like this. I found this man shot full of poisoned arrows. Naturally I had my first-aid kit with me. So what do you think I gave him?"
    Archie took the straw from his mouth and said, "An *anecdote?*"—Craig Rice, *Home Sweet* HOMICIDE.
6. At this time King Henry VIII walked with difficulty, having an *abbess* on his knee.—London schoolboy.
7. Mrs. Ruth Senseman went to Cleveland Saturday, where she will take up nursing at the *Home Pathetic* Hospital.—Adv. in the Covington, Ohio, *News*.
8. E . . . n triumphant. An inspirational RHAPSODY in seven cantos. Translated from the JOHNSONESE by W. W., poet LARIAT.—N. Y. Public Library catalogue entry.
9. "Do you come to Sunday School voluntarily, or because you are COERCED?" asked the pretty teacher.

'Voluntarily, I guess," replied little Edgar. "I thought they only had to get coerced if they was Baptists."

10. The inhabitants of London suffer from a high rate of *morality*.—London *Globe*.
11. No man is a hero to his *wallet*.—Wall Street Journal.
12. Esau wrote fables and sold his birthright for a bottle of POTASH.—Detroit schoolboy.
13. A kolleckshun is then taken up to buy overkoats for the *indignant* cullured people of Kanady.—Artemus Ward at Oberlin.
14. Captain Dum John (pseud.)—The *autobituary* of a West Pointer.—N. Y. Public Library catalogue entry.
15. I pleasure showing these without OBLIGATO.—Japanese landscape-gardener advertising fishponds for sale, in the Oakland Tribune.

COLUMNISTS COIN WORDS

Like the gag writers, Broadway, Hollywood and radio columnists are often credited with wrecking the language. They do take liberties with it. But they also add to its stock-in-trade.

Walter Winchell is the star contributor. Mostly he gives currency to his own coinages based on the slang and jargon of the amusement world: theaters, movies, night-clubs, carnivals, circuses, gambling joints and the divorce courts.

Dealing largely in personal gossip, he is particularly resourceful in inventing fancy wording for birth, actual or expected, courtship, marriage, and divorce. His couples do not merely have childen: they *blessed-event* or REDUPLICATE. The same event foretold is *infanticipate*—or be *baby-bound*. Couples in love are *that way, on fire*, or *uh-huh*, and later *on the merge* (engaged). They *middle-aisle it* one year and some time later turn up in the column as *Renovated*. He is fond of puns: a *Merry Magdalene* of *Two Times Square*, a *messer of ceremonies*.

Winchell has an advantage not enjoyed by most of the gossip-MONGERS: he doubles in brass by going on the air. But while he has a delivery that's peculiar to him, he uses far less Winchellese over the radio than in print.

Many of the Winchell tricks result from fast interplay between him and *Variety*, the chief trade publication of the amusement world. This journal is fond of clipped forms: *pic*, for moving picture—the plural is *pix; biz*, for business; *exec*, for executive; *exhib*, for an EXHIBITOR; *legit*, for legitimate. *Variety* writes *h.o.* for home office and *b.o.* for box office. A headline reads: "B'way's B.O. Hypo May Wind up in House Shortage." (The increase in Broadway box office receipts may result in a shortage of theaters.) *Hypo* (meaning "increase") shortened from HYPO- DERMIC suggesting a "hopped up" condition, is typical *Variety* imagery.

The editors of *Variety* relish fancy coinages of a PRETENTIOUS kind: They take the suffix *itis* from APPENDICITIS and arrive at *budgetitis,* a sudden affliction of ECONOMIZING that sometimes seizes a movie producer. The rewrite desk on the magazine likes vivid compounds: *spine-chiller, cliff-hanger* (a radio or movie serial MELODRAMA which leaves the heroine hanging to the cliff edge at the end of an instalment). There are lively phrases for a theatrical success: a *socko,* a *clickeroo* or a *bell-ringer;* and a richer list for failures: a *flopperoo,* a *turkey* and a *clambake* (particularly of a messed-up rehearsal); *poison* or *arsenic* in radio.

An amusing take-off on *Variety* style was heard on the New York night club circuit in 1939, when a group called The Revuers used an opening number, half-sung, half-spoken, in which they offered to translate *Variety* jargon: [1]

> Broadway is dead and the theatre's a flop
> Receipts at the box office start to drop
> Deep in despair the theatre is—
> Variety says—Show Bizz Fizz!
>
> You open a show in Buffalo
> You give out passes but business is slow
> You give out more passes till it's full enough—
> Variety says—Buff on Cuff!
>
> An opera opens at popular price
> But popular price does not suffice
> The opera decides to close up shop—
> Variety says—Pop Op Flop!
>
> You open a picture out of town
> The reviews come in—all thumbs down
> You open five more but none of them clicks—
> Variety says—Hix Nix Six Pix!

Variety and Winchell do not exhaust the columnists' bag of tricks. Earl Wilson, self-styled saloon editor of the New York *Post,* has a cunning way with a long or unusual word. He sneaks up to it, gives a preliminary cough to attract attention, then springs the word and adds a

[1] Copyright 1939 by The Revuers; quoted by permission. The Revuers: Betty Comden and Adolph Green, co-authors of *On the Town* and *Billion Dollar Baby;* Judy Holiday, lead actress in *Born Yesterday;* Al Hammer, dead-pan comic in the movies.

translation. He once said of La Guardia: "Butch is RESILIENT—(don't look it up—it means 'bouncy')."

What the Broadway and Hollywood gossip artists do for diversion, more serious columnists do in earnest. They put unusual words into circulation to convey new meanings, as *Time* did with "TYCOON." In this case they find rather than coin the words. Keeping a weather eye out for these novel terms is an ideal way to extend your own word range.

2. WORDS IN THE NEWS

1. In his speech at the Democratic Convention, in July, 1944, Henry A. Wallace called some of his conservative opponents TROGLODYTES. Nobody at the press and radio table knew what he meant. Do you?

2. In his column in the New York *Herald Tribune,* Sumner Welles, former Under-Secretary of State, sometimes uses the word PROTOCOL. Can you translate it?

3. Military commentators keep talking about LOGISTICS. Is there a simple equivalent? And does one say logistics *is* or logistics *are?*

4. An article in the *Partisan Review* by Arthur Koestler has the title, "*The* INTELLIGENTSIA." Who or what are they?

5. In Leonard Lyons' column in the New York *Post* for October 25, 1944, there was a squib as follows:

During the preliminary discussions on the forthcoming International Business Conference in which 46 nations will participate, Sylvia Porter, the financial columnist, asked the President of the National Association of Manufacturers: "Mr. Gaylord, would you say that one of the results of this conference will be an agreement on policy toward CARTELS?" . . . "I doubt it," Mr. Gaylord answered. "We'd be lucky if we agree on a definition of the word."

Do *you* know what a cartel is?

6. From the same source:

Last time he [Zero Mostel, the comedian] was in Hollywood, the papers extraed about wages being frozen, and according to Zero, a $100,000-a-year man dashed up to him breathlessly and said, "Look, Zero, you're a college man, aren't you?" "Yeah," said Zero. "Well, then, what does FISCAL mean?"

What does fiscal mean? And what about that verb "extraed"?

7. *The New Republic* "Bandwagon" in the issue of November 13, 1944 carried the following:—

9

At a rehearsal for WGN's fashion show, the *Tribune*'s Robert R. McCormick dropped by to have a look and promptly censored the word "DÉCOLLETAGE" from the script, saying he'd never heard of it, and "besides, it sounded too foreign."—*Dale Harrison in The Chicago Sun*.

Do you like décolletage? Would you know it if you heard it on the air?

8. The International Business Conference at Rye was snarled for a while, during the discussion on cartels, over the translation into the 51 other languages, of the word *"know-how."* The compromise effected was to substitute, instead of "know-how," the long phrase "technical information and important knowledge designed to etc., etc., . . ." Can you fill out the etceteras? And is *know-how* slang, COLLOQUIAL, or standard American? Also, is it good British English?

9. One sober radio man said of another: "His head is full of CHIMERAS." What is a chimera?

10. In the issue of October 9, 1944, the magazine *Time* used a fairly modest ration of PORTMANTEAU (blend) words: *cinemagnate, cinemactress, musicomedienne, musicomic, cinemadolescent, cinemadaptation.* Can you give ordinary SYNONYMS for these verbal potpies? In the same issue, *Time* also used the following coined words: *batoneers, argentinity, oofs,* and *glollog.* Can you sight-read those? *Time* also featured in this issue *Quis custodiet ipsos custodes?* (Who will guard the guards themselves?) There is an old popular song which recalls this Latin tag. Do you know it?

STORIES BEHIND WORDS

There is plenty of entertainment to be had from picking up new words through reading. A personal clipping service which culls out an amusing collection of novel and striking words, is a never-failing source of diversion. But a more systematic approach is required, if vocabulary-building is to be done within reasonable time limits. It is easier to get good returns from a rich lode, than to depend on picking up nuggets. That is why from this point on many groups of words are presented out of context. They are arranged, however, according to patterns that make sense and permit rapid learning.

One type of word that proves baffling is the allusive word: a proper name which carries a great deal of meaning for a reader who knows the story that lies behind it.

Sometimes names do more than make news. Proper names occasionally work their way into the language as terms for common objects, or as shorthand ways of describing characters or events. Often the dictionary record on such a word doesn't tell the juicier part of the story. Take these entries in the New Word List in the 1944 edition of Webster's Unabridged:

Annie Oakley. Slang. A complimentary ticket.
McCoy,—the *real McCoy*. Slang, U. S. The genuine article.

There's a picturesque story behind each of these CURT explanations. A COMPLIMENTARY ticket is punched full of holes. After Annie Oakley had shot at them, so were the playing cards thrown into the air as her targets. She was Buffalo Bill's star EXHIBITIONIST with a pistol. It took Webster quite a while to recognize her: she's been dead a quarter of a century.

Behind the term "the real McCoy" is a still more colorful story. Norman Selby, the MIDDLEWEIGHT boxer of the twenties, who fought under the *nom de guerre,* Kid McCoy, was an amiable, quiet sort of man who outside the ring didn't look like a tough fighter. One night, wearing evening dress, he went into a restaurant bar with friends. A quarrelsome drunk addressed offensive remarks to McCoy, and started to paw him. McCoy warned him, saying quietly that his name was McCoy, and it would be better to lay off him. The drunk said, "Aw, you're not McCoy." The fighter let him have a right to the jaw. When the drunk came to, several hours later, he found McCoy's card on his chest. "It was the real McCoy," he muttered.

That's how proper names start on the way to becoming common nouns —or adjectives. For a long time they remain allusions. Then the story behind the allusion is gradually forgotten. Finally a CHESTERFIELD is just a formal topcoat or a DIVAN—or, spelled with a capital, an elegantly mannered gentleman, left over from an earlier period. No longer does Chesterfield mean only the Fourth Earl of the name, writing letters to his DOLTISH son on ETIQUETTE and polite behavior, or telling the House of Lords why he was opposed to CENSORSHIP: "Wit, my lords, is the property of those who have it, often the only property they have. We, my lords, thank God, have other means of SUBSISTENCE."

And there's one North Carolina Congressman who added a word to the language, when he admitted his speech on the House floor was intended mainly for the benefit of the folks back home in Buncombe

County. His name is forgotten, but *buncombe* is still with us, though it's been shortened, first to *bunkum,* now to *bunk.*

For practical purposes, we do not need to know the history of common allusions. But there is a lot of satisfaction to be had from knowing the story behind the word: how some character, real or imagined, came to have his name become the symbol of something universal in human experience; or how some place or building had its name transferred to a whole class of objects, products, or ideas.

Here's a MEDLEY of these proper names which have become common. For how many can you give the story behind the word?

3. TRANSLATE—AND TELL THE STORY

In each group of ten onetime proper names that have become common words, put in the blank [ ] before the name in column 1 the letter of the equivalent term in column 2. For example:

51. [ ] MICAWBER   [a] self-righteous man
52. [ ] BABBITT   [b] PROCRASTINATOR
53. [ ] PHILISTINE   [c] booster
54. [ ] PHARISEE   [d] person of smug tastes

The letters in column 1 above should run: [b], [c], [d], [a].

1. [ ] AMPERE   [a] REACTIONARY
2. [ ] ANGORA   [b] merchant fleet
3. [ ] ARABESQUE   [c] thief
4. [ ] ARGOSY   [d] mad confusion
5. [ ] ARMADA   [e] ex-bachelor
6. [ ] BARABBAS   [f] sausage
7. [ ] BEDLAM   [g] battle-fleet
8. [ ] BENEDICK   [h] lacy FRETWORK
9. [ ] BOLOGNA   [i] goathair
10. [ ] BOURBON   [j] unit of current

11. [ ] BOYCOTT   [a] gas jet
12. [ ] BROUGHAM   [b] would-be tide-stopper
13. [ ] BUNSEN   [c] hot pepper
14. [ ] CABAL   [d] half-horse, half-man
15. [ ] CANUTE   [e] CONFIDANTE
16. [ ] CASSANDRA   [f] political plot or plotters
17. [ ] CAYENNE   [g] carriage
18. [ ] CENTAUR   [h] not having any
19. [ ] CHINOOK   [i] prophetess of doom
20. [ ] EGERIA   [j] gentle, warm wind

21. [ ] FABIAN	[a] knee pants
22. [ ] GALVANIC	[b] match
23. [ ] HELOT	[c] DEODORANT
24. [ ] JEHU	[d] slave
25. [ ] KNICKERBOCKER	[e] fast driver
26. [ ] LISTERINE	[f] execution without court action
27. [ ] LUCIFER	[g] delayer
28. [ ] LYNCH	[h] paving process
29. [ ] MACADAM	[i] responding to electrical stimulus
30. [ ] MADRAS	[j] fabric

31. [ ] MAUSOLEUM	[a] supreme personage
32. [ ] MECCA	[b] supreme goal
33. [ ] MOGUL	[c] APPEASEMENT
34. [ ] MUNICH	[d] SATIRIC SQUIB
35. [ ] NARCISSUS	[e] doom
36. [ ] NEMESIS	[f] large tomb-edifice
37. [ ] OHM	[g] catchall for all gods
38. [ ] PANTHEON	[h] parting shot
39. [ ] PARTHIAN	[i] unit of electrical resistance
40. [ ] PASQUINADE	[j] self-admirer

41. [ ] PHOENIX	[a] palace guard
42. [ ] PLATONIC	[b] tough customer
43. [ ] PRAETORIAN	[c] carriage
44. [ ] RUBICON	[d] king-maker
45. [ ] STOIC	[e] kind of boot
46. [ ] TARTAR	[f] non-carnal, idealistic
47. [ ] TITIAN	[g] resurrected itself from ashes
48. [ ] VICTORIA	[h] CRUCIAL, IRREVOCABLE step
49. [ ] WARWICK	[i] UNFLINCHING
50. [ ] WELLINGTON	[j] reddish-brown

IMPORTING FOREIGN WORDS

You might think the half million words, more or less, in our UNABRIDGED dictionaries would be enough for most purposes. But we keep up the ten-centuries old custom of importing alien terms into English, where they gradually become NATURALIZED. Hitler has just given us two. *Lebensraum* means "living space," and the *Luftwaffe*—the German "air force"—was to scare the rest of the world into providing the German people with plenty of room to expand.

Usually these foreign terms make their way in because English does not have exact equivalents. As a rule they encounter strong resistance, and many writers bar them. But a few such words get over the immigration barriers, because they can do special jobs. In time, they offset the antiforeign prejudice which they inevitably stir up in many readers.

The sensible course, when you encounter them, is to break these words up and find out why they've been allowed to take out first papers. Usually there's a reason.

Two journalists in the country on a holiday came on the word *Poltergeist.*

"I'ts an athletic ghost," said one, "it throws furniture around, drops things over the stair BANISTER, bangs away at the walls, and is generally a practical joker."

"I don't doubt it," said the other, "and I know that *Geist* means 'spirit' in German. But what's *Polter?*"

"This high school dictionary doesn't give the word *Poltergeist,* let alone tell what it comes from."

"Then the dictionary can't be much good."

"I don't see that follows. How often would the word *Poltergeist* turn up in student reading?"

"Not often.—But look up the derivation in the big Webster."

"That gives *Polter* as 'noise' or 'racket.'"

"Of course, it's a first cousin of our word 'pother.'"

"So a *Poltergeist* is just a noisy ghost?"

"That should settle it—even if it doesn't EXORCISE the ghost."

"A *Poltergeist* needs no exercise!"

"Sign off on that one—before it starts throwing things at you!"

4. FOREIGN WORDS AND PHRASES RECENTLY IN PRINT

In each group of ten foreign words or phrases, match the word with the proper clue in the right-hand column, thus:

21. [   ] WALPURGISNACHT
     [a] Hallowe'en
     [b] *Fortune* used it to describe the *wild, witch-like orgy* of German finance under Schacht
     [c] Christmas

The meaning [b] is right, so you put *b* in the blank between the brackets. Here are the twenty you're to match with their clues:

1. [ ] AGENT PROVOCATEUR
2. [ ] AD INFINITUM
3. [ ] ANNO DOMINI
4. [ ] PIÈCE DE RESISTANCE
5. [ ] AFFAIRE D'AMOUR
6. [ ] BLITZKRIEG
7. [ ] CORPUS DELICTI
8. [ ] COUP D'ÉTAT
9. [ ] PUTSCH
10. [ ] ANSCHLUSS

[a] a small-scale uprising
[b] main dish; chief attraction
[c] love affair
[d] lightning war
[e] a sudden stroke to change REGIMES
[f] and so on, without end
[g] in the year of our Lord
[h] a man planted to make trouble
[i] union
[j] basic facts of a crime; not necessarily the body!

11. [ ] ERSATZ

12. [ ] AIDE MEMOIRE
13. [ ] ZEITGEIST
14. [ ] WELTANSCHAUUNG

15. [ ] DOPPELGÄNGER
16. [ ] WANDERJAHR
17. [ ] AGIT-PROP

18. [ ] DAS EWIG-WEIBLICHE
19. [ ] SCHWÄRMEREI
20. [ ] DRANG NACH OSTEN

[a] your own ghost or divided personality
[b] longing revery
[c] year for wandering or traveling
[d] WPA "living newspaper" an example
[e] spirit of the Age
[f] substitute, usually ADULTERATED
[g] thrust toward the Orient or Near East
[h] way of looking at the world
[i] the eternal feminine
[j] diplomats send them to each other to be sure they both remember the conversation in the same sense

THE PACKRAT METHOD

All this wordplay adds up to a story. Words have their comedy—witness the gag writers and columnists. Packaged up in words we find the history of far off times and places, of characters real and imagined. New words making their way into the language give us the feel of the period we've just lived through. Sometimes these words creep in by the slang route, more often from the JARGONS of the various trades. Again, we get new coinages, or new meanings infused into old terms, through war, politics, science or invention—all four of which have been working on a mass production basis in the last ten years.

Many of these words we pick up as we read—the natural way to add to our stock-in-trade. But if we want to bring a little art to the aid of nature, and extend our word-range faster, there's a good deal to be said for importing a certain amount of system into the business. So long as we add words on a random basis, our collection will be slow in growing, and a bit scrappy. There are ways of improving on the PACKRAT method, of gathering only shiny odds and ends, and piling them up in a miscellaneous heap.

If we had all the time in the world, the hit-or-miss technique of acquiring words would do well enough. But there's one great drawback to it. It takes too long. Many of the words needed to build out a good working vocabulary don't turn up often enough in reading—yet we need to know them when they appear.

Throughout this book, for example, words beyond the average vocabulary of the commonest ten thousand words in the language are printed in SMALL CAPITALS. They are standard words you need to add to your vocabulary, if you don't already know them. If you glance back, you will see that in this chapter most of the words beyond the ten thousand level are found in the workouts on "What Word Was Murdered,"—"Words in the News," "Translate—and Tell the Story." If you read fairly rapidly for two hours a day, in a wide range of material, you would encounter the less frequent of these words—say those in the eighteenth and nineteenth thousands—less than five times in a year. That is not often enough to learn them by OSMOSIS—or SEEPAGE. Rather you'll have to seek them out, and make a frontal attack.

To help you plan your campaign strategy, the methods so far sampled in the guise of wordplay will be fully developed later on in the book. The comedy and history of words will be amply displayed. But it is important at the outset to carry in suspension in your mind some of the key approaches to word-study even though the systematic and full treatment of these methods will come later.

Word-Detection

It really takes the technique of a good detective to run down the secrets of words, and fit them into place in the scheme of things. Such word-DETECTION calls for a discerning ear and a sharp eye.

The magician Houdini trained his assistants by taking them past jewelers' shop-windows, allowing them to inspect the display first for three minutes—in later trials for only thirty seconds—then asking them to turn away and ITEMIZE the contents of the exhibit.

It takes just such a seeing eye to learn the ways of words. Recall the surroundings of a new word, and remember what it meant in its setting, and you'll have less trouble with it when you meet it again. You can PENETRATE its disguises, if it turns up in strange company. And you won't confuse it with words that are closely similar, any more than a detective will be fooled into mistaking a near double for the man he's shadowing.

A detective tries to find out all he can about anybody whom he is investigating. He checks the man's origin. He finds out about his habits. He wants to know what company he keeps, where his hideouts are. If there is any striking peculiarity about the person, he notes it, and tries to account for it. He is tireless in running down all the information he can get. You should approach new words in the same spirit.

Observation can take you only so far in word-detection, however. You have to know how to interpret and analyze the evidence. Sometimes you have to fall back on the files, using dictionaries and reference works which store up the lore of words.

And a good investigator trails his subject's record wherever he has worked. By the same token, there's no better resource for the word-detective than to examine *words at work*. That's the way to find out how people who work in the word-trades go about enlarging their stock; and what words they have to add

> to broaden their scope of reading,
> to sharpen their conversational wit,
> to point up their writing,
> to add to their income.

Quiz Keys for Chapter I

1. Page 6.

1. critic	6. abscess	11. valet	14. auto-, "self,"
2. matrimony	7. homeopathic	12. pottage (a mess,	blended with
3. incumbency	8. laureate	not a bottle)	obituary
4. affirmative	9. immersed	13. indigent	15. obligation
5. antidote	10. mortality		

2. Page 9.

1. cave-dwellers
2. diplomatic etiquette
3. art of organizing and administering service of supply, including quarters
4. Those with whom intellect is a passion.
5. See page 243.
6. financial (especially pertaining to public finance)

17

7. How far down the neckline comes.
8. See page 239.
9. An imaginary monster with a lion's head, a goat's body, and a serpent's tail; it breathed out fire. Now: any fantastic or absurd idea.
10. In order: producer, movie actress, soubrette, comedian, bobby-soxer, movie version. *Batoneers:* "baton-wielders" or "conductors." *Argentinity:* "essence of being Argentine." *Oofs,* jocose spelling for Fr. *oeufs* (eggs). *Glollog:* your guess is as good as mine. The old song: Who'll take care of the caretaker's daughter, when the caretaker's busy taking care? (See also page 256.)

3. Page 12.

1.	[j]	11.	[h]	21.	[g]	31.	[f]	41.	[g]
2.	[i]	12.	[g]	22.	[i]	32.	[b]	42.	[f]
3.	[h]	13.	[a]	23.	[d]	33.	[a]	43.	[a]
4.	[b]	14.	[f]	24.	[e]	34.	[c]	44.	[h]
5.	[g]	15.	[b]	25.	[a]	35.	[j]	45.	[i]
6.	[c]	16.	[i]	26.	[c]	36.	[e]	46.	[b]
7.	[d]	17.	[c]	27.	[b]	37.	[i]	47.	[j]
8.	[e]	18.	[d]	28.	[f]	38.	[g]	48.	[c]
9.	[f]	19.	[j]	29.	[h]	39.	[h]	49.	[d]
10.	[a]	20.	[e]	30.	[j]	40.	[d]	50.	[e]

4. Page 14.

1.	[h]	6.	[d]	11.	[f]	16.	[c]
2.	[f]	7.	[j]	12.	[j]	17.	[d]
3.	[g]	8.	[e]	13.	[e]	18.	[i]
4.	[b]	9.	[a]	14.	[h]	19.	[b]
5.	[c]	10.	[i]	15.	[a]	20.	[g]

You will want to familiarize yourself with the words you missed in these four quizzes. It stands to reason that it takes more than two quick looks—once at the word in the quiz, and again when you check it with the key—to fasten the new word in your memory, and turn it into part of your recognition vocabulary: words you know when you see or hear them. After you have done your homework on the words that were beyond your range, try your hand at the following Vice-Versa Quiz, twenty items picked at random from the 100 words involved. Vice-Versa, because now you're given only the clue. You're to recall the word—as if you were solving a cross-word puzzle.

VICE-VERSA QUIZ FOR CHAPTER I

1. In a well-known schoolboy boner, what word is confused with a synonym for marriage? —————

2. Of two candidates running for office, the man already holding the office is called the —————.
3. A cave-dweller (hence a "throw back" or reactionary) can be labelled a —————.
4. An imaginary monster that has come to stand for anything fantastic is a —————.
5. The unit of electrical current is an —————.
6. An agreement between two or more firms (countries, or trusts) to divide up the market, fix minimum prices at which they will sell, and limit production to keep prices up, is called a —————.
7. A fleet of large ships is sometimes called an —————.
8. Instead of *tycoon*, *Time* might have adopted the word ————— for a supreme personage in the business world.
9. The lacy fretwork of the Alhambra in Granada is called —————.
10. A mythological creature, half-horse, half man, is a —————.
11. A king-maker is called a —————, from the famous Earl of the name who made and unmade kings at the time of the Wars of the Roses.
12. A certain type of hard-surface road is called —————, from the inventor of this type of surfacing.
13. The fabled bird of antiquity which when burned would rise renewed from its ashes is called a —————. (The capital of Arizona)
14. A large tomb-edifice is called a ————— from the famous King of Caria who built the first one of the type, which was one of the seven wonders of the ancient world.
15. The slaves who did the menial work in Sparta were called —————.
16. On a certain pillar in medieval Rome, people used to post satiric squibs against their enemies, hence the term —————.
17. What is the term for that branch of military art covering transport and supply? —————
18. What is the Latin phrase for "the substantial and important fact (or facts) of a crime"? —————
19. World-outlook, or view of the world, in German is —————, and since we have no exactly equivalent single word in English, we often use the German term.
20. An athletic ghost is a —————.

Average Score *18* Your Score —

It is easier to master new words in a practical situation than it is where you are using them only to solve a puzzle. A word picked up to fill an immediate need, and put to real use right away, is much more readily remembered. That is why it is so valuable to watch *words at work*.

[II]

WORDS AT WORK

Anybody who walks into the PERSONNEL office of a big firm and asks for a job usually confronts—as the first HURDLE—a vocabulary check-up. "If there is time for only one test," says a famous PSYCHOLOGIST who conducts PLACEMENT examinations for such a firm, "I give the applicant a vocabulary test. It's the best single measure." And he doesn't make it easy.

It's no joke, trying to spot the right meaning out of four alternatives for each of a hundred words, all in twenty minutes. It takes quick wits and a sure sense of words to make a good score.

Try your hand on this test, which is only a thirty-word one. Go straight through it without stopping, then backtrack to the words that baffled you. But stop cold after *six minutes,* and check your score by the key on p. 35.

5. How Good Is Your Vocabulary—Under Stress?

Place in the brackets the number of the word or phrase closest in meaning to the initial word—for example:

1. [   ] ALLERGIC (1) lazy (2) friendly (3) adverse (4) adversely sensitive to

The right equivalent is [4], so you place that number in the bracket preceding allergic. (A proper use of the word: "The doctor found the patient allergic to egg proteins.")

1. [   ] bone [1] mistake [2] vertebrate [3] horn [4] element of SKELETAL structure
2. [   ] creep [1] hidden place [2] cry [3] crawl [4] sidle up to
3. [   ] affect [1] result [2] influence [3] cause [4] shortcoming
4. [   ] accord [1] notes in harmony [2] unit for measuring wood [3] agreement [4] bind up
5. [   ] apparel [1] seeming [2] clothing [3] endanger [4] act of removing skin
6. [   ] attest [1] dislike strongly [2] examine [3] bear witness [4] exactly on the point

20

7. [ ] behavior [1] wickedness [2] way of acting [3] school of PSYCHOL-
OGY [4] occasion for punishment
8. [ ] ally [1] to state as supposition [2] narrow lane [3] to label as false-
hood [4] fellow-BELLIGERENT
9. [ ] affront [1] precede [2] insult [3] ahead [4] beach
10. [ ] assassinate [1] jump on [2] make an assertion [3] kill [4] repeat
11. [ ] EDICT [1] banning of sacraments [2] UKASE [3] decision of jury
[4] tyranny
12. [ ] PROVOST [1] enraging [2] official [3] foresighted [4] a special kind
of ceremonial gown
13. [ ] NOISOME [1] clamorous [2] smelly [3] appalling [4] rascal
14. [ ] CANTO [1] half gallop [2] a singer [3] section of a long poem
[4] drinking room
15. [ ] OVERARCH [1] church POTENTATE [2] a kind of tree [3] meet above
in middle [4] COQUETTE
16. [ ] MODULATION [1] shyness [2] temperance [3] method of shifting
from one key to another [4] admiration
17. [ ] KINETIC [1] EGOTISTIC [2] wavy [3] pertaining to motion [4] attractive
18. [ ] IMMINENCE [1] quality of being outstanding [2] height [3] state of
threatening [4] edge of cliff
19. [ ] SUBTRAHEND [1] lower tendency [2] number to be taken away from
another [3] underground stream [4] drift below
20. [ ] ENZYME [1] commissioned officer in Navy [2] flag [3] gland-
produced CATALYTIC agent [4] a paste
21. [ ] AMBIVALENT [1] walking [2] tricky [3] double-valued [4] sym-
metrical
22. [ ] EMPATHY [1] lack of sympathy [2] DIVERGENCE [3] feeling into
[4] roundabout way
23. [ ] BOTULISM [1] turning rods [2] poisoning from bacterially spoiled
foods [3] improper canning [4] ALCOHOLISM
24. [ ] CATALYST [1] INVERT [2] one who classifies books [3] stone-
throwing device [4] reaction agent itself unchanged
25. [ ] IRREDENTA [1] UNRECLAIMED [2] water-ditch [3] GULLY [4] glit-
tering
26. [ ] NEUTRON [1] impartial [2] of intermediate gender [3] colorless
[4] uncharged particle
27. [ ] DYSGENIC [1] non-inheritable [2] unhealthy [3] kingly family
[4] REGENERATIVE
28. [ ] ENDOCRINE [1] HERETICAL doctrine [2] DUCTLESS gland [3] salty
[4] poisoned
29. [ ] MULTIVERSE [1] kind of TURBINE [2] plural worlds [3] universal
screw [4] extra stanza
30. [ ] PASQUINADE [1] volley of shots [2] ornament [3] SATIRIC verse
[4] column

This isn't a big enough sample to give any exact measure of your total vocabulary. But it's built on something more than guesswork. The first word is from the commonest thousand words used in print, No. 2 from the second commonest thousand, and so on up to No. 20, which is in the twentieth commonest thousand. (See p. 60 for a full explanation.) The last ten are unusual words, of a technical or special type, and are frankly bafflers.

Discounting for the shortness and spottiness of the test, you can, if you like, make a rough guess about your vocabulary range. If you got ten right, you probably have an average American vocabulary—the chances are you know the commonest ten thousand words in the language. Add another thousand for each additional word on which you scored correctly. If you got all thirty right, you can feel plenty superior.

After you've checked your answers, you may find it amusing to go through the list again, and see if you can figure out what words the test-COMPILER had in mind for the "confusions," as the wrong equivalents are called in a workout of this kind. The misleading definitions are for "confusion" words that closely resemble the main numbered word, but which have entirely different meanings. For No. 14, CANTO, [1] is a definition of CANTER; [2] of *cantor,* the singer in a Jewish synagogue; [3] is the right definition for CANTO; and [4] defines a CANTEEN.

If you fell for some of these confusions, put it down to the fact that English is full of tricky words. One of the first things anyone working in the word-trades has to learn is to be everlastingly on guard against confounding words that look or sound alike.

What does JIBE mean to you? *Jeer, agree,* or *flip a sail?* It means all three. There are three different words, all spelled alike and pronounced alike. They look like identical TRIPLETS. But they are not related at all. Their meanings are poles apart:

The Dodger fans jibed at the visiting team. ("Jeered")
For once, a politician's actions jibed with his words. ("Agreed")
We jibed to the north, and ducked the sail. (Here *jibed* means "shifted course so that the sail flipped over." Samuel Eliot Morison, in his life of Columbus, *Admiral of the Ocean Sea,* spells it "gybbed," pronouncing it evidently with the short "i" sound.)

Take another example. PAN was the Greek god, half-man, half-goat, who played the flute and represented universal nature as is. His name also gives us the prefix *pan-,* meaning "all," as in the compound *Pan-*

American. There is another word *pan,* meaning "a container or dish," quite unrelated to the Greek god. The slang sense of *pan,* meaning "to abuse vigorously," probably comes from the harsh scouring involved in gold-panning. Then there is still another slang sense of *pan:* "face," as in the compound *deadpan.*

Westerners learning Chinese complain that a single word spoken in that language may have five different meanings, depending on a slight variation in the pitch. *Pan* has that many meanings in English, without any pitch difference at all!

These few words spelled and pronounced alike, but with different meanings, are called HOMOGRAPHS. The only way you can tell homographs apart is by the company they're in. You have to know all the meanings, and pick the one that fits.

Then there are words that sound alike, but are spelled differently. *Sight, cite,* and *site,* for instance; *their, there,* and *they're.* These are called HOMONYMS. When it comes to writing them, they give trouble to the absent-minded, or to those with a bad hollow where their spelling bump should be. But real difficulty arises when homonyms are only heard, not seen.

HAZARDS OF STENOGRAPHY

Some of the most frequent errors made by stenographers are in fact due to confusing words that sound alike but have meanings at the poles asunder. Not long ago, in one of the top sales organizations of the country, a house-organ publication was sent out to encourage the women secretaries in the divisional offices. One sentence read: "The ideal secretary should *compliment* the work of the sales manager." No doubt telling the boss how good he is may be adroit secretarial strategy. But what the vice-president in charge of sales had dictated was "complement."

That sort of error comes easy when two words sound alike—HOMO-PHONES, as they're called. There's no way of telling from a lightline short-hand PHONETIC character which word is meant—except from the sense.

6. PICK THE RIGHT WORD

1. ANNALIST or ANALYST? He was an ——————— with the Du Pont Company.
2. AURICLE or oracle? The Delphic ——————— was in the heart of Greece.

3. Bass or base? Purcell liked a firm ground _____.
4. BOLL, BOLE, or bowl? The dry-rot was in the _____ of the tree.
5. Borough, burrow, or BURRO? Somebody beat up the _____ COUN-
CILLOR.
6. CARAT, CARET, or carrot? He marked the insert with a _____.
7. QUIRE or choir? They sold music paper by the _____.
8. Crews, cruise, or CRUSE? They brought in the _____ of holy oil.
9. Faker or FAKIR? This _____ was a holy man.
10. FANE, feign, or fain? How could he _____ illness well enough to
fool an army doctor?
11. Idol, idle, or IDYL? Their romance was a summer _____.
12. Literal or LITTORAL? They postponed attack on the Adriatic _____.
13. Raise, raze, or rays? They will _____ the fort on the island after
capturing it.
14. Right, write, rite, or -wright? It was a solemn _____.
15. LICHEN or liken? A _____ is similar to moss.
16. Vial, vile, or VIOL? He put the perfume in a small _____.

Then, to add to the PITFALLS, there are words that look or sound very
much alike, though one of the vowels may be different. *Affect* and
effect are the stock pair—but there are many others that are easily mis-
read from shorthand notes.

7. WHICH WORD WAS MEANT?

1. Adapt, adept, adopt. He was so _____ they called him in to
_____ the play for the movies.
2. ALLUSIVE, ELUSIVE, ILLUSIVE. I found the meaning very _____ because the writing was highly _____.
3. Ballad, BALLET, ballot. Let me write the _____ of a country, and I
care not who casts its _____.
4. BAZAAR, BIZARRE. There were a good many _____ hats donated to
the church _____.
5. Cannon, CANON, and canyon. They fired the salute according to the
_____ of military etiquette.
6. COMA, COMMA. He fell into a _____ from which he did not
recover.
7. Consul, council, counsel. The American _____ gave him good
_____ to get out fast.
8. Decent, descent, dissent. The motion was passed without _____.
9. Eminent, imminent, IMMANENT. An explosion was _____.
10. EPIGRAM, EPIGRAPH, epitaph. They took an impression of the
_____, which proved to be an _____ in the form of an
_____.
11. HYPERCRITICAL, HYPOCRITICAL. The book reviewer had no time to be
_____.

24

12. MAGNATE, magnet, maggot. He was a great iron ——————.
13. Spacious, SPECIOUS. 1. He gave a —————— reason.
14. Surplus, SURPLICE. They had an extra —————— for the visiting cleric.
15. VENAL, VENIAL. It does not pay a politician to be openly ——————.

A really topflight stenographer who wants to graduate into the secretary class must be able to mop up UNOBTRUSIVELY on the boss's errors, particularly if she's working for an executive in the amusement business. It's no myth that they are given to outdoing Amos and Andy at PERPETRATING MALAPROPISMS.

Here's a collection lovingly gathered over many years, of words confounded by one or another of these MOGULS, dictating over his head. The sentences given opposite are to test your ability to discriminate between the words. They're not the sentences in which the word was butchered.

8. PUT THE RIGHT WORD IN THE RIGHT SLOT

A

1. The law provided for —————— prices for basic crops.   PARODY
2. He wrote a —————— of a famous song.   PARAGON
3. A very —————— of fashion.   PARADOX
4. A most ingenious ——————.   PARITY

B

1. The choir sang a well known ——————.   CANTER
2. The horses went at a fast ——————.   CANTATA
3. The —————— sang the Kol Nidre.   CANTO
4. He talked a very smug ——————.   CANTOR
5. They got a drink in the ——————.   CANT
6. The third —————— of a Renaissance epic.   CANTEEN

C

1. They sang a well known sea ——————.   CHANTRY
2. It was a —————— venture altogether.   chant
3. Masses for the departed were sung in the ——————.   CHANTEY
4. A solemn Gregorian —————— was sung.   CHANCY

D

1. The —————— inhabitants were Indians.   abdominal
2. It was a severe —————— wound.   HEBDOMADA1
3. Hydrogen sulfide has an —————smell.   ABORIGINAL
4. A meeting of the —————— Council was held.   abominable

25

E

1. The Lewis and Clark ——————— Exposition.
2. Poe was interested in theories of vegetable ———————.
3. Richardson wrote ——————— novels.
4. Polonius uttered ——————— remarks.
5. He stood ——————— duty before the palace.
6. A ——————— being will respond to stimulus.
7. Clarissa was a woman of ———————.

sentiment
SENTENTIOUS
SENTIENT
sentimental
SENTIENCE
sentinel
CENTENNIAL

F

1. An exhaustive ——————— showed no arsenic.
2. There was one bad ——————— in that history.
3. Reasoning from ——————— often errs.
4. First aid work calls for some knowledge of ———————.

ANACHRONISM
ANALOGY
analysis
anatomy

G

1. He computed the ——————— between the extremes.
2. They invited him to ——————— between the conflicting claims.
3. Trial by ordeal was a ——————— custom.
4. Water is a good ——————— for transmitting sound.
5. Fewer persons now ——————— upon their sins.
6. NATUROPATHS do not ——————— as a rule.

medium
MEDIATE
MEDIAN
MEDIEVAL
meditate
MEDICATE

H

1. They brought out a ——————— horse for the child.
2. A ——————— approach to the problem will show the various stages of development.
3. ——————— is the possessive case.
4. The advertisement quite brazenly specified that only a ——————— need apply.
5. A ——————— instance is more conclusive than an ATYPICAL one.
6. His manner was bland and ———————.

gentile
genial
gentle
GENETIC
GENERIC
GENITIVE

I

1. We flushed a ——————— of partridges.
2. He gave her a ——————— glance.
3. Put back the ——————— on the jar.

cover
COVEY
COVERT

J

1. The canoe made a swift ——————— down the rapids.

decent

2. He was inclined to ———————— fully on his trip.   DESCANT
3. It happened in the last ———————— of the century. descent
4. He told him to ———————— four LITRES of the fluid. DECANT
5. Everything was done in ———————— and orderly decade
style.
6. The motion was passed without ————————.   dissent

K

1. He expressed a ———————— opinion.   DISSOLUTE
2. He tried to ———————— himself from his party on dissipate
questions of national defense.
3. MODERNIST music abounds in ———————— phrases. DISSONANT
4. He told them to ———————— the CADAVER. DISSOCIATE
5. It is unwise to ———————— one's energies before a DISSEMINATE
match, by too much practice play.
6. A thoroughly ———————— wretch. dissect

L

1. They quietly arranged a ———————— of his duties. RESURGENCE
2. The ———————— was due to a revival of interest in resurrection
the classics.
3. There was a ———————— of interest in the relics. RENAISSANCE
4. The ———————— of Lazarus was thought a miracle. RESUMPTION

M

1. The emperor had a magnificent ————————. RETENTION
2. His ———————— proved of great aid in diplomacy. RETICENCE
3. The lawyer accepted a large ————————. retinue
4. His memory showed unusual powers of ————————. RETAINER

N

1. One ———————— of the front was weak. SECTIONAL
2. The fanatic was an extreme ————————. SECTOR
3. The ———————— of the League at Geneva. secular
4. He was ———————— even for a diplomat. SECTARIAN
5. The ———————— dispute between North and South. SECRETARIAT
6. The dispute was over ————————, not religious SECRETIVE
issues.

THE HUNT FOR SYNONYMS

Next to the hazard of using the wrong word, comes a menace that
haunts everybody in the word-trades: the danger of overworking one
word. It's not only your friends who will tell you about it. The rewrite
man will protest, the copy desk will yell, the news editor will tell you to

find a new word for it, the script-producer will claim you're getting into a rut, and you'll begin to feel like a pariah. That's why everyone who works with words is on the alert for synonyms.

Headline Writer's Headaches

When a headline writer needs a synonym, he has to have it in a hurry. He has no time to look it up. His problem is severely practical. He has to have a word to fit a fixed space. How would you like to cudgel your wits to find a three-letter word meaning "depression," or a five-letter one for "consolidate"? You'd be as stymied as a poet trying to find a rhyme for "orange"—until you picked up the knack. The old hand at the game can usually shuffle around the words in the headline, if he has to. He knows the usable equivalents for most words that turn up often in the news. His synonym-finder has to be inside his head; and it had better work at adding-machine speed.

9. Headline Synonyms

These words occurred in the *key* passages of newspaper stories. The headline writer in each case wanted to use the word to convey the core of the story, but found he needed a shorter term. How fast can you furnish in each case the needed headline synonym, with the number of letters specified in the middle column?

Key Word in Story	Number of Letters in Synonym	Synonym?	Key Word in Story	Number of Letters in Synonym	Synonym?
1. ALLEGATION	5		14. level	4	
2. catastrophe	5		15. JEOPARDIZE	4	
3. IMPLICATE	7		16. narrative	5	
4. VINDICATE	5		17. CONFLAGRATION	4	
5. EXONERATE	5		18. congregate	6	
6. acknowledge	5		19. diminish	6	
7. facilitate	5		20. reduction	4	
8. irritate	4		21. HOLOCAUST	5	
9. EULOGIZE	6		22. INUNDATION	5	
10. apprehend	5		23. APPORTION	5	
11. ASPERSION	4		24. contribute	4	
12. DISCRIMINATION	4		25. SCRUTINIZE	4	
13. OSTENTATION	7				

10. More Headline Synonyms

Often the headline writer wants a more vigorous or telling synonym, even when he is not so cramped for space. Give short, expressive synonyms for each of the following 25 words found in the news:

1. admonish	9. secrete	17. upbraid
2. SUCCUMB	10. COMMANDEER	18. outlaw
3. GAINSAY	11. government	19. SCHISM
4. DONATE	12. surrender	20. consolidate
5. ALLOCATE	13. ASSEMBLAGE	21. transaction
6. investigation	14. congregate	22. PIGEONHOLE
7. endowment	15. EXPATRIATE	23. conspiracy
8. SWELTER	16. REPUDIATE	24. postponement
	25. CATECHIZE	

11. Long Words for Short in Headlines

Sometimes a headline writer needs a longer word to fill out a line. What are long synonyms for the following:

1. question	13. outcome
2. end	14. levy
3. ease	15. rush
4. lessen	16. revolt
5. bid	17. fray
6. charge	18. beat
7. hint	19. unfair
8. show	20. dried
9. start	21. fret
10. steal	22. tight
11. scare	23. build
12. end	24. burst
	25. rate

Trouble at the Rewrite Desk

A rewrite man on a newspaper or magazine has one chief duty: to make copy more readable. He's the sworn enemy of blackouts of meaning. Whatever will jar on a reader, or slow him down, the rewrite man must eliminate. This includes any harping repeatedly on a single word, which is as bad as a MONOTONE in singing.

To avoid this stumbling block to easy and effortless reading, a rewrite man needs a ready command of synonyms for words that turn up often in a given type of news. Otherwise the reader will be JUSTIFIABLY annoyed at the repetition, and will suspect Gertrude Stein's influence at work.

On a business page, for example, price rises and falls have figured every day for years. In talking of prices, rewrite men have hit on a number of equivalents for the word *increase*. It's a *hike, boost,* or *up*. These three synonyms are both verbs and nouns. If an "up" in prices sounds barbarous to the ear—and it is not exactly polite standard English—put it down to two factors: the EXIGENCIES of rewrite, and the ready INTERCHANGEABILITY of parts of speech in our language. A preposition is first transformed into a verb—"OPA 'upped' the price of shirts"—then into a noun: "an 'up' in prices."

Another part of the rewrite job is open war on fancy phrases and complicated sentences. Like Jiminy Cricket in Walt Disney's *Pinocchio,* the rewrite man is fond of the slogan, "Break it up, boys!" In recasting sentences that get lost in a maze, much of the trouble can be resolved by substituting simple words for PRETENTIOUS ones.

A standing grievance at the rewrite desk is that copy turned in by feature writers and critics with their own by-lines is not to be "improved." It must stand as written.

Pitts Sanborn, the music critic on the New York *World-Telegram* in the old days, once wrote:

The evening's only other magic issued from the leader's NECROMANTIC hands, whose baton-less paired sweep would have brushed desk and score into the void immense, had such mediocre IMPEDIMENTA ENCUMBERED the PODIUM.

No rewrite man was allowed to touch this piece of fancy VERBIAGE. Had he been turned loose on it, his first impulse would have been to throw it out, lock, stock and barrel. With capital punishment barred, he would probably have recast it to read:

Conducting without a BATON or score, the leader waved his hands around so that he would have knocked the music desk off the PODIUM—if there had been a desk, which there wasn't. As it was, he had enough magic in his hands to raise the dead.

A classic example of over-elaborate language is found in the following news story:

At a press conference March 10, 1942, President Roosevelt was reading out to reporters a letter which Dean Landis of Harvard Law School, Director of

Civilian Defense, had prepared for him to send to the Federal Works Agency on the subject of blacking out government buildings during air raids. The letter said:

"Such preparations shall be made as will completely obscure all Federal buildings and non-Federal buildings occupied by the Federal Government during an air raid for any period of time from VISIBILITY by means of internal or external illumination. Such OBSCURATION may be obtained either by blackout construction or by termination of the illumination.

"This will of course, require that in building areas in which production must continue during the blackout, construction must be provided that internal illumination must continue. Other areas, whether or not occupied by PERSONNEL, may be obscured by terminating the illumination."

" 'Obscuration,' " said the President, "is not my word, nor is 'termination of the illumination' my language."

Turning to his press secretary, he ordered a rewrite job.

"Tell them," he said, "that in buildings where they have to keep the work going, to put something across the window. In buildings where they can afford to stop work for awhile, turn out the lights. Stop there."

Goethe called such fancy official language "CHANCELLERY-style." Maury Maverick coined an American name for it: *gobbledygook*.

CONDENSING FOR SPACE AND SPEED

Magazines which reprint in condensed form articles from other sources, or which offer their readers cut-down versions of best-sellers, must boil down the material to the indispensable minimum. This means shorter, plainer synonyms, as a way of saving space and increasing readability.

12. SHORT WORDS FOR LONG

Give a short synonym for each of the following words:

1. precipitous	13. LIBIDINOUS
2. collapse	14. RELICT
3. commotion	15. PEDESTRIAN
4. EMACIATED	16. DEFUNCT
5. CONTORTED	17. PERSPICUOUS
6. SCINTILLATE	18. CALIBRATION
7. abominate	19. INTERROGATION
8. SOMNOLENT	20. DENIGRATE
9. LOQUACIOUS	21. INCULCATION
10. ERUBESCENCE	22. INDURATED
11. DOMICILE	23. ANATHEMA
12. EXPECTORATE	24. BENEFACTION

25. insinuate

The digest magazines sometimes use articles from semi-technical sources, or draw on the monthly magazines which use relatively high-brow diction. These condensations must be rewritten in simpler wording. Anybody translating into this simpler English needs a ready command of synonyms.

13. PLAIN WORDS FOR LEARNED

Suggest plain SYNONYMS for the following learned words:

1. CONCATENATION	13. GARGANTUAN
2. CONCUSSION	14. HERCULEAN
3. DISINTEGRATE	15. OPTIMISTIC
4. DEHYDRATE	16. SPORADIC
5. CIRCUITOUS	17. ARTICULATION
6. CORPOREAL	18. ERUDITION
7. ADULATION	19. VITUPERATION
8. EMULATION	20. VOLATILITY
9. EXPOSTULATE	21. RESILIENCE
10. PROGNOSTICATE	22. CIRCUMSCRIBE
11. MERETRICIOUS	23. LOCUM TENENS
12. GRATUITY	24. MUTATION
	25. APPELLATION

Immediately practical work with synonyms leads, sooner or later, to a strong interest in the theory of the subject: how do synonymous words come to develop fine shades of difference in meaning? You'll find this question answered at length in Chapter IX. But there are a good many tricks of the word-trades that are needed, fully to appreciate the finer points of synonym study. The problem of meaning is central—how words change meaning, and why. One way to lead up to this is to look closely at new words—which are not yet encrusted with history.

CHECKING ON EVERY WORD

A custom has grown up on the newsmagazines *Time* and *Newsweek* of attaching a "researcher" to every staff writer. *Fortune* and *Business Week* follow the same practice, and it is spreading to other magazines. The researcher digs up material, looks up references, and writes background reports on whatever topic the writer is pursuing. In addition, the researcher is responsible for checking the correctness of every fact—and word—in the story, once it's gone past the rewrite desk.

Not only do proper names and place names call for the researcher's constant vigilance; with new terms constantly turning up in science and TECHNOLOGY, and new coinages coming in from war, politics, and business, a researcher often has her work cut out for her, in AUTHENTICATING new TERMINOLOGY. Particularly is this true on *Time* and *Fortune*, which are more hospitable to new words than *Newsweek.*

The managing editor and senior editors on *Time* are INSISTENT that any new term that's to keep its place in the copy shall be explained, even if it takes a footnote. Preferably it should be translated in the story, as UNOBTRUSIVELY as *Time* style permits.

But above all, it must be correct, and the researcher must have the authority ready to prove it. If the word is too new to have found its way into the dictionaries or encyclopedias, this takes some tall rustling. And even if the dictionary has grudgingly admitted it, labeling it *slang, cant,* or *technical,* the entry often isn't full enough to give the feel, flavor and history of the word. For these the researcher has to get down and dig.

If you had access to the researchers' file entries on new words checked since *Time* began, you'd have pretty good clues to the history of the Jazz Age '20's, the troubled '30's, and the stormy '40's. Here are samples of the type they check (these are not actually from *Time* files), with ANNOTATIONS (not in *Time* style):

Ad lib, slang, verb and adverb. Polite equivalent: "to IMPROVISE"—to speak, sing, or play without a SCRIPT." This may have been used in theater circles before radio got going in the early twenties, but it had no wide currency. Now it slips out so naturally in radio studio talk that there's no dispensing with it.

Agit-prop, Theater cant. Bob-tailed form of AGITATION-PROPAGANDA, a compound formed on analogy with the Russian phrase. It is shorthand for a play—or theater—used as a vehicle for spreading propaganda. It conjures up the Russian revolution, the Group Theater of Clurman and Odets, and the Chinese revolutionary theater that followed the Eighth Route Army in its great retreat. The living newspaper form EVOLVED by the W.P.A. Federal Theater is the most notable American type.

AUTARKY. Economic self-containment. A country aims to produce and manufacture everything it uses, so that it will be (often militarily) independent of foreign sources. Suggests unpleasant memories of AUTARKIC Germany and other AUTARKIES of the thirties and forties. (There's a good deal of confusion between this word and *autarchy,* which is "self-rule"; some dictionaries have been so influenced by the pressure of popular

33

(though Greekless and illiterate) usage, that they allow autarchy to mean the same as autarky.

Crack down, slang. To come down hard on. Given wide vogue by General Hugh Johnson of the NRA.

Doghouse, colloq. This has graduated out of the slang category. How different a word from *kennel,* in its flavor and surrounding AURA.

MONTAGE.

1. Photography. COMPOSITE picture making.

2. Motion pictures. Literally, the *mounting* (after cutting) of alternating sequences from two strips of film having CONVERGING lines of action, so that the moment of highest excitement will be achieved when the two trains of events link up. The excitement *mounts,* too.

It happens that all the words in the foregoing have been admitted to the New Word List in the front matter of the 1944 edition of Webster's Unabridged. Not all of *Time's* candidates are so fortunate, particularly their coinages (see p. 70). The only blend word they've got into the language, in a quarter century of trying, is SOCIALITE. But in general, their use of slang is authentic. They've yet to be caught out applying a slang word in the wrong CONTEXT or period. And they're good pickers when it comes to the technical terms that have the best chance to make their way into general use.

GETTING WORD-WISE

What this all adds up to is that anybody working in the word-trades—stenographer, journalist, rewrite man, ad, SCRIPT, or gag writer, editor, or researcher—needs a ready, wide and sure command of words. Ready, because he's usually working against a deadline, and has to be able to summon up the needed words fast. Wide, for the sake of variety and fitness—the right word in the right place. Sure, to dodge the pitfalls offered by tricky words in the language.

Acquiring this command means keeping on the trail of new words, and clearing up the meaning of those only half known. Clearly it's an advantage to tackle words in a practical situation, as those working in the word-trades do of necessity. They learn them on the site, in relation to an immediate need. That way they don't forget them. Further, they acquire a feeling for the word, and a sense of what company it belongs in.

And judging by the evidence just given—of the trial and error methods used by stenographers, headline writers, rewrite men and researchers—those working in the word-trades enlarge their stock by

spotting the tricky ones,
word-detection,
hunting for synonyms,
haunting the dictionary.

QUIZ KEYS FOR CHAPTER II

5. Page 20.

1. [4]	6. [3]	11. [2]	16. [3]	21. [3]	26. [4]
2. [3]	7. [2]	12. [2]	17. [3]	22. [3]	27. [2]
3. [2]	8. [4]	13. [2]	18. [3]	23. [2]	28. [2]
4. [3]	9. [2]	14. [3]	19. [2]	24. [4]	29. [2]
5. [2]	10. [3]	15. [3]	20. [3]	25. [1]	30. [3]

6. Page 23.

1. analyst	5. borough	9. fakir	13. raze
2. oracle	6. caret	10. feign	14. rite
3. bass	7. quire	11. idyl	15. lichen
4. bole	8. cruse	12. littoral	16. vial

7. Page 24.

1. adept, adapt	5. canons	9. imminent	12. magnate
2. elusive, allusive	6. coma	10. epigraph, epitaph, epigram	13. specious
3. ballads, ballots	7. consul, counsel		14. surplice
4. bizarre, bazaar	8. dissent	11. hypercritical	15. venal

8. Page 25.

A	B	C	D
1. parity	1. cantata	1. chantey	1. aboriginal
2. parody	2. canter	2. chancy	2. abdominal
3. paragon	3. cantor	3. chantry	3. abominable
4. paradox	4. cant	4. chant	4. hebdomadal
	5. canteen		
	6. canto		

E	F	G	H
1. centennial	1. analysis	1. median	1. gentle
2. sentience	2. anachronism	2. mediate	2. genetic
3. sentimental	3. analogy	3. medieval	3. genitive
4. sententious	4. anatomy	4. medium	4. gentile
5. sentinel		5. meditate	5. generic
6. sentient		6. medicate	6. genial
7. sentiment			

I	J	K	L
1. covey	1. descent	1. disseminate	1. resumption
2. covert	2. descant	2. dissociate	2. Renaissance
3. cover	3. decade	3. dissonant	3. resurgence
	4. decant	4. dissect	4. resurrection
	5. decent	5. dissipate	
	6. dissent	6. dissolute	

M	N
1. retinue	1. sector
2. reticence	2. sectarian
3. retainer	3. secretariat
4. retention	4. secretive
	5. sectional
	6. secular

9. Page 28.

1. claim	7. speed	13. display	19. lessen
2. smash	8. fret	14. raze	20. drop
3. involve	9. praise	15. risk	21. blaze
4. clear	10. catch	16. story	22. flood
5. clear	11. slur	17. fire	23. share
6. admit	12. bias	18. gather	24. give

25. scan

10. Page 29.

1. warn	7. gift	13. meeting	19. split
2. die	8. bake	14. meet	20. merge
3. deny	9. hide	15. exile	21. deal
4. give	10. seize, take	16. disown	22. bury (in committee)
5. allot	11. regime	17. scold	
6. inquiry	12. yield	18. ban	23. plot

24. delay   25. question

11. Page 29.

1. interrogate	7. intimation	13. denouement	19. inequitable
2. abolish	8. demonstrate	14. assessment	20. dehydrated
3. alleviate	9. inception	15. stampede	21. bother
4. mitigate	10. defalcate	16. rebellion	22. constricted
5. invitation	11. frighten	17. fracas	23. construct
6. allegation	12. terminate	18. overwhelm	24. explode

25. estimate

12. Page 31.

1. steep	7. despise	13. lewd	19. question
2. fold	8. sleepy	14. widow	20. blacken
3. stir	9. talkative	15. walker	21. implanting
4. thin	10. blush	16. dead	22. hardened
5. twisted	11. house	17. clear	23. curse
6. sparkle	12. spit	18. scaling	24. aid

25. hint

13. Page 32.

1. chain	8. rivalry	13. huge	20. lightness
2. shock	9. object	14. difficult	21. bounce
3. break up	10. foretell	15. hopeful	22. limit
4. dry	11. false or fake	16. rare	23. substitute
5. roundabout	(lit. harlot-like)	17. joint	("stand-in")
6. bodily	12. gift (idiomati-	18. learning	24. change
7. flattery	cally, "tip")	19. cursing	25. name

Vice-Versa Quiz for Chapter II

1. A more polite synonym for *smelly* is ——————.
2. A single word for "gland-produced catalytic agent" is ——————.
3. The uncharged particles used to bombard U-235 atoms are called ——————.
4. A synonym for *jeer* is ——————.
5. Words spelled and pronounced alike but different in meaning are called ——————.
6. Words which sound alike but are spelled differently are called —————— or, in stenography, ——————. What pairs or triplets give you trouble?
7. A sacred shrine is also called a ——————.
8. A church official attached to a cathedral is called a ——————.
9. The near-synonym for *outstanding* is ——————.
10. Sins of a trifling nature are described as ——————.
11. Polonius was given to (sententious or sentimental?) sayings.
12. A "take-off" on a famous song or poem is called a ——————.
13. The Dark Ages are sometimes included as part of the —————— period.
14. One —————— (pours out) wine, but —————— (holds forth about) its fine flavor.
15. When the new volcano Paricutin flared up again after a period of quiescence, it was said to show a —————— of activity.
16. A lawyer's fee paid in advance to pre-empt his services for a given case is called a ——————.

17. A long word for *showiness* or *display* is ―――――.
18. A fire of great extent and destructiveness is called a ―――――.
19. A Biblical word for *deny* is ―――――.
20. A longer synonym for *lessen* is ―――――.
21. A solemn curse pronounced by a high religious authority or group is an ―――――.
22. A long synonym for *rivalry* is ―――――.
23. A long synonym for "foolish worship" is ―――――.
24. A clergyman going away on a long leave usually has to get a ―――――.
25. A play or a theater used for spreading propaganda is labeled ―――――.
26. Economic self-containment is ―――――. With what other word is this term often confused—even by some dictionaries?
27. Adverse sensitivity to some substance is called an ―――――.
28. A two-letter synonym in business for the noun *increase* is ―. What part of speech is it, normally?
29. A ten-letter word for "dried" is ―――――.
30. What famous painter's name is used as the adjective for "reddish-brown"?
31. What philosophic school has given its name to an "unflinching attitude"?
32. What river associated with Julius Caesar's career is used to mean a "crucial, irrevocable step"?
33. What fabled bird of antiquity was regularly resurrected from its own ashes?
34. What famous philosopher's name is used adjectivally to mean "idealistic" as opposed to carnal love?

III

USING THE DICTIONARY

A good dictionary is not a dull book. Many a hot argument has gone into making it. When does a word like *jazz* cease to be slang? And what senses of the word are still slang? Is *highbrow* slang, or has it now become good informal English? How soon will *beachhead*, coined by analogy with *bridgehead*, be accepted as standard English? In its proper sense, almost at once. But when a marine brags that he has established a "beachhead" with a girl on shore, everybody spots this as a slang use of the term—and rather neat slang at that.

In 1940 President Roosevelt used *razz* twice in his campaign speeches, and the New York *Times* printed it as it came in the handouts, without quotation marks. *Razz* is a bobtailed form of *raspberry,* from the slang expression "Give 'em the raspberry," which first appeared in print around 1920. *Razz* conveys a shade of meaning for which there is no other exact equivalent. "Deride," "HECKLE," "insult," or "BEDEVIL" will not replace it without a loss of flavor and sting.

Yet even though it is a part of White House American, *razz* is still not admitted to the King's English by the dictionary makers. Nobody would question it in comic dialogue. Gossip columnists use it without a second thought. It sounds natural in a radio serial. A political writer would spring it without quotation marks in *Collier's.* But the editor of a genteel magazine or a serious book would put quotation marks around it—if he let it by at all. So the dictionary makers play safe, and label it slang.

At least it has gained entry into the dictionary. Most slang never gets that far, rather it withers on the vine. But expressive, colorful, short slang words that fill a real need persist in getting into print, thanks to Damon Runyon, Walter Winchell, sports writers, radio, the movies, and novelists with an ear for spoken American—Sinclair Lewis, John Dos Passos, James M. Cain, Raymond Chandler, and company. Among them, they finally force the dictionary editors to record slang that has got into nationwide use. If it maintains its vogue, it may eventually

39

graduate into the COLLOQUIAL or *Informal* class—the halfway house between slang and standard English.

Gelett Burgess's coined word BLURB, to describe the puff that a publisher prints on the jacket of a new book, has now, after thirty years, had its dictionary label changed from *Slang* to *Informal*. It has made its way in England, too, and is recommended by a leading British authority on words, Ernest Weekley. In another few years, it may climb to the level of standard English.

When the dictionary puts *no label* after a word, it indicates by silence that the word is in general and current use—that it's standard—and will pass muster in formal writing and speaking.

But if you don't think there are many borderline cases that stir up argument in the editorial room of a dictionary, try your hand at sorting out a job-lot of words used in a single issue of a current magazine.

14. ARE YOU SURE YOU KNOW SLANG WHEN YOU SEE IT?

Of the following words from *Time,* October 9, 1944, which are (1) slang, which (2) colloquial, and which (3) standard? Check once $\sqrt{}$ for slang; twice for colloquial.

1. comeuppance	17. semaphoring	33. trap ("Keep my	48. henchmen
2. sideswipe	18. riposted	trap shut")	49. short snort
3. hubbub	19. lunge	34. hobo	50. bigwigs
4. haberdasher	20. trek	35. bust	51. butted
5. fracas	21. bugs	36. rabble-rouser	52. joker
6. dastardly	22. caitiff	37. phony	53. riffled
7. conking	23. midriff	38. full of beans	54. bedlam
8. zeroed	24. bordello	39. fiasco	55. lathery
9. cockade	25. Boche	40. tussle	56. hangovers
10. totting up	26. coup	41. eight ball	57. hijacking
11. bloc	27. chits	42. newshens	58. chary
12. stalemate	28. haggling	43. setup	59. drab
13. hodgepodge	29. leering	44. poncho	60. sexy
14. unleash	30. quipped	45. frazzled	61. flibbertigibbet
15. strafing	31. swatch	46. mascot	62. ersatz
16. nipped	32. jettisoned	47. leathernecks	63. rant

64. goons

FOR LIMITED CIRCULATION ONLY

Dictionary-makers have a good many other special labels for words, besides *Slang* and *Informal*. They run up warning signals for words that are in some way limited in their use:

Archaic —Found only in older English literature, from Chaucer through Milton: *jowke* (rest); *limbeck* (a pinch); *wonner* (for *dweller, inhabitant*).

Obsolete —No longer in common use, out of date; not in the fashion of our time: *laxy* (for *lax*); *witcrack* (Shakespearean for "wisecrack" —it should be revived).

Poetic —Used only in poetry—hence barred from present day prose as out of place: *eftsoons, aye* (for "always"), *yore*.

Dialect —Used only in certain districts or regions; not in nationwide use: *beasties, shindy* (a dance, noisy gathering, or a fight), *briggle-diggle* (to putter around, procrastinate).

U.S. —Used only in the United States; *graft* (illicit rake-off in connection with public business) is marked *U.S. Colloq.* by the Concise Oxford.

Brit. —Used only in Great Britain: *dustbin* (garbage can).

Scot. —Of Scottish origin: *loch* (lake).

Lat. —Latin. So also *Fr.* (French), *Germ.*, etc.

Technical—Properly used only in scientific or technical connections. Some dictionaries subdivide this category into *Geog.* (Geography), *Geol., Chem., Math., Electr., Naval, Mil., Med.*, etc.

Technical words are continually shuttling into wider use, in senses derived from their technical meaning. Hence they are a constant headache to dictionary editors. How soon are these FIGURATIVE and DERIVATIVE senses to be recognized as standard? ALLERGIC is a banner example. It's fast coming into common use, in such statements as "I'm allergic to crooners . . . singing commercials . . . soap operas." No doubt it's a politer LOCUTION than "a pain in the neck," but its proper English rendering would be "I'm ANTIPATHETIC to . . ." Somehow that sounds over-elaborate. Yet *allergic* is already so over-worked that it's setting up an ALLERGY against itself. It runs the risk of being labelled *Slang,* instead of making the shift from *Technical* to *Standard* in one jump.

DICTIONARY AS FIRST AID

Stenographers, proof-readers, printers, writers, and all the rest of us, when in doubt about the spelling of a word—or when we wonder how it's to be divided by a hyphen—turn to the dictionary. And we rely on it to settle arguments over pronunciation.

Now that radio has brought the spoken word into such sharp relief, these arguments are apt to be hot and heavy. The major networks employ speech consultants to cope with the problem. The *NBC Handbook of Pronunciation* (Thomas Y. Crowell Company, 432 Fourth Avenue,

New York City, 1944) by James F. Bender, is the result of careful inquiry into the actual problems of announcers and newscasters in dealing with disputed words. It deals also with the pronunciation of proper and place names in the news—especially foreign ones. CBS puts out a similar guide: *World Words,* by W. Cabell Greet.

The British Broadcasting Corporation has compiled a list of tricky words, many of them often mispronounced, the others in dispute. This list has been recorded (it is distributed by the Linguaphone Company) to indicate the standard pronunciations which the BBC requires of its staff, and of anybody else it puts on the air (Americans presumably excepted). Here's a selection from the list, omitting most of the words for which the British pronunciation differs from our usage (they pronounce *futile* "fewtyle," INTESTINAL "intestýnal," fertile "fertyle"), and leaving out also terms that are peculiarly British (See pp. 74–77).

15. AND DO YOU KNOW WHAT THEY MEAN?

First time through, cover up the right hand column, giving the key to pronunciation, and see how you score. Second time through, check to see how many of these nutcrackers you can define. This is a high ceiling list.

1. ACOUSTIC	acóostic
2. ACUMEN	akéwmen
3. ADHERENT	adhéerent
4. ADIEU	adéw
5. AERATED	áy-erayted
6. AERIAL	(a) noun—1st syllable to be pronounced air; (b) adjective, ay-éerial
7. ALTERCATE	awltercayt
8. amateur	ámaterr, final syllable rhymes with fur
9. AMENABLE	améenable
10. APPLICABLE	stress on first syllable
11. ASPIRANT	stress on second syllable, which is pronounced as *spire*
12. BARRAGE	bárraazh (Amer. barráazh)
13. BASALT	bássŏlt (Amer. also băsalt)
14. BEDIZEN	rhymes with *horizon*
15. BROCHURE	broshúre
16. BRUIT	as *brute*
17. BUFFET	(a) meaning a blow, búffet
	(b) meaning a refreshment bar—as in French (approx. boof-fay, stress evenly distributed)
18. BYZANTINE	Byzántyne (Amer. Bízanteen or Bizánteen

42

19.	CACIQUE	kasséek
20.	CANDELABRA	candeláabra
21.	CARILLON	caríllyon with the stress on *rill*
22.	CASUALTY	caz-ewalty, first *a* short
23.	CELTIC	initial *C* to be pronounced *s*, not *k*; but *k* pron. general in Wales
24.	CENOTAPH	sénnotaaf
25.	CENTENARY	sentéenary
26.	CENTRIFUGAL	sentríffewgal
27.	CERAMIC	serámmic
28.	CEREBRAL	sérrebral
29.	CHARGÉ	shárzhay
30.	CHAUFFEUR	shofer
31.	CHIMERICAL	kimmérical
32.	CHIROPODY	kyróppody
33.	CLANDESTINE	clan-déss-tin
34.	COGNIZANT	cógnizzant
35.	COMMANDANT	principal stress on last syllable, which is annt, not aant
36.	COMMUNIQUE	comméwnikay
37.	CONCERTO	conchérto
38.	CONCUPISCENCE	konkéwpisense
39.	CONDOLENCE	condólence
40.	CONJUGAL	stress on first syllable
41.	content	noun—cóntent
		verb and adjective—contént
42.	CONTUMELY	contéwmly
43.	conversant	stress on first syllable
44.	COXWAIN	kox'n
45.	CREDENCE	créedence
46.	CUL DE SAC	cul to rhyme with *full*—duh sack; preferably "blind alley" (!)
47.	CULINARY	kéwlinăry (Amer. is kewlinairy)
48.	CUNEIFORM	rhymes with *uniform*
49.	CURATOR	kewráytor
50.	DAIL	rhymes with *oil*
51.	DAIS	dáy-iss
52.	DAUPHIN	dawfin
53.	DECORUM	decōrum
54.	DESPICABLE	stress on first syllable
55.	DESULTORY	déssultŏry (Amer., ō)
56.	DIOCESAN	stress on second syllable, which is -oss-
57.	DISPUTABLE	dispéwtable (Amer. also díspewtable)
58.	DOCTRINAL	doctrýnal (Amer., dóctrĭnal)
59.	DYNAST	dinnast (Amer., dīnast)
60.	ELEEMOSYNARY	ellimóssinăry
61.	EMANATE	émmanayt

43

62.	EMANATION	emmanáyshon
63.	ENCLAVE	áhnklayv
64.	ENNUI	áhnwee
65.	ENSEMBLE	ahnsómble
66.	ENTOURAGE	ahntouráazh
67.	ENVIRONS	envýrons
68.	EPHEMERAL	effémmeral
69.	EPILOGUE	éppilog
70.	EQUABLE	1st syllable is *ek*, not eek
71.	EQUERRY	ékkwerry
72.	exquisite	éksquizzit
73.	FALCON	fawkon
74.	FANFARE	fánfair
75.	FETISH	feetish (Amer. also fettish)
76.	finance	finnánce
77.	FORECASTLE	főksle
78.	formidable	stress on 1st syllable
79.	GAELIC	gaylic
80.	GALA	gaala
81.	GHOUL	gool
82.	GRATIS	gráytis
83.	HAREM	hairem
84.	ILLUSTRATIVE	stress on 2nd syllable; but *illustrayted*
85.	IMPORTUNE	stress on 2nd syllable
86.	INHERENT	inhéerent
87.	IRREFUTABLE	irréffewtable
88.	IRREPARABLE	stress on 2nd syllable
89.	IRREVOCABLE	stress on 2nd syllable
90.	leisure	rhymes with measure (Amer. also leezhure)
91.	LEIT-MOTIF	líght-motéef
92.	MACHINATION	makkináyshun
93.	MALINGERER	hard *g* as in *go*, accent on *ling*
94.	MEDIEVAL	meddy-éeval (Amer. also meedy-éeval)
95.	MEMOIR	mémmwaar
96.	MINUTIAE	min-yéwshiee
97.	MOSLEM	mózlem (short *o*)
98.	NADIR	náydear
99.	OBLIGATORY	obblígatory (on the record, it sounds to an American ear like "obblig'try"; we say obbligatory, or ŏbligatory)
100.	OMNISCIENCE	omnísience
101.	OPUS	ópus
102.	PANACHE	pannásh
103.	PANEGYRIST	pannijírist
104.	PATHOS	páythos
105.	PEREMPTORY	stress on 2nd syllable
106.	PLEBISCITE	plébbissit

44

107. premature	prémmatewr (Amer. preematéwr)
108. PREMIER	premmier (Amer., préemier)
109. project	noun—prŏj′ect; verb—prō′ject
110. PROMULGATE	prómmulgate (Amer. also pro múl gate)
111. PROVOST	civic and academic—próvvost
	military—provvō (Amer. both o's long)
112. QUEUE	kew
113. ration	rhymes with fashion (Amer. prefers it to rhyme with nation)
114. RECONDITE	rekóndyte
115. RECONNAISSANCE	stress on con-: rekónisance
116. REMONSTRATE	stress on 2nd syllable
117. REPLICA	répplika
118. RESPITE	réspit (both vowels short)
119. RIBALD	ríbbald
120. romance	stress on 2nd syllable
121. route	root (Amer. also rowte)
122. SACERDOTAL	sasserdōtal
123. SACROSANCT	sáckrosanct
124. satire	sáttyre
125. satyr	satter (Amer. also sāter)
126. SCION	sýon
127. SHEIK	shayk (Amer. sheek only)
128. SONOROUS	sonōrous
129. Soviet	Soviet—o always long
130. SPA	spaa
131. STATUS	stáytus
132. SYNOD	sínnod
133. TENET	téenet
134. TOTALISATOR	tōtalyzaytor
135. TRIPARTITE	trypartyte; equal stress on 1st and 2nd syllables (Amer. hits the 2nd a little harder)
136. vehement	veéhement
137. VIANDS	výands
138. VILIFY	víllify

It would probably promote more Anglo-American DISHARMONY if this list—with the key covered up—were tried out on the staff announcers of American radio stations. They would wonder what screws were loose at the BBC; and how such sixty-four dollar words ever got by the SCRIPT editor and program director.

The explanation is that the BBC has an active board of experts on pronunciation and usage, including among its members Bernard Shaw and Daniel Jones, the PHONETICIAN. This board is no mere false front. It safeguards the standards of the language by barring COCKNEY and over-ripe Oxford accents, making sure that announcers know how to stand and deliver. And since the program authorities of the BBC favor LITER-ATE—even highbrow—programs, there is a real need for settling the pronunciation of these difficult words.

There is no need to go overseas, however, to find words often mispronounced. We have a notable list right here at home.

16. Can You Say It Right—and Define It?

First time through, see how many of these you can pronounce correctly. Second time through, check those you can define. Most of them are words you would run into only five or six times a year if you read for two hours a day in many different books and magazines.

1. ACCLIMATE	26. COGNOMEN	51. harass	76. salmon
2. ADEPT	27. CONJURE	52. HEINOUS	77. SALUTARY
3. ADOBE	28. conduit	53. HERCULEAN	78. SATIETY
4. AGGRANDIZE	29. CONJUGAL	54. HOLOCAUST	79. SAVANT
5. ALIAS	30. CONTUMELY	55. impious	80. SCENARIO
6. ALPACA	31. CREMATORY	56. impotent	81. SCHISM
7. AMENITIES	32. COURTESY	57. INCHOATE	82. series
8. ANCHOVY	33. CUPOLA	58. INCLEMENT	83. SILHOUETTE
9. APOTHEOSIS	34. data	59. incomparable	84. SINECURE
10. apparatus	35. DECADENCE	60. INDISSOLUBLE	85. SKELETAL
11. AERATED	36. DEFALCATE	61. INVEIGLE	86. SPECIE
12. ARBITER	37. DEFICIT	62. IRREMEDIABLE	87. species
13. arctic	38. DESICCATE	63. IRASCIBLE	88. SPECIOUS
14. ARMISTICE	39. DELIQUESCENT	64. IRRELEVANT	89. statistics
15. barbarous	40. DETONATE	65. LINEAMENT	90. STABILIZE
16. BESTIAL	41. DESUETUDE	66. MAUVE	91. STRATIFY
17. BIOGRAPHY	42. DISSOLUBLE	67. mischievous	92. STRATUM
18. BLACKGUARD	43. DOMICILE	68. OLEOMARGARINE	93. STRIATED
19. BLATANT	44. EXPONENT	69. PEONY	94. SUBJUGATE
20. bouquet	45. EXEMPLARY	70. PLAGIARISM	95. SUBPENA
21. CALLIOPE	46. fungi	71. PRECEDENCE	96. SUBTERFUGE
22. CEREBRUM	47. GENEALOGY	72. QUAY	97. SUTURE
23. CHAMELEON	48. GONDOLA	73. ROBUST	98. VAGARY
24. CINEMA	49. GARRULITY	74. romance	99. VAUDEVILLE
25. CHIMERA	50. GRIMACE	75. SACRILEGIOUS	100. XYLOPHONE

Mapping the Maze

The chief role of a dictionary is to serve as a storehouse of word-meanings. Anyone can open it. But it's an odd kind of DEPOSITORY, for

46

it's only after you've opened it, that you need the combination: the code in which a dictionary tells the story of each word. You must note the key to pronunciation; the method for showing the breaks between sylla- bles, if you have to HYPHENATE the word; the abbreviations employed to give the facts about it; and the system for showing its PEDIGREE or DERIVA- TION—ETYMOLOGY is the technical term. And as a matter of prime con- cern, what aid is offered for determining the right meaning of a word *in a given situation?* For you often have to pick out, from the dictionary entry, the particular meaning which fits.

A casual glance at any page will show that one out of every four or five English words has multiple meanings, anywhere from two to fifty —and some keep adding more. If you find in your reading a statement:

He knew enough German to follow the *tenor* of Goebbels' speeches com- ing over short wave . . .

a quick check will show you that *tenor* in this CONTEXT doesn't refer to the high pitch of the late German PROPAGANDA minister's voice; here it means rather the "drift" or "general PURPORT" of his speeches. And in the stock phrase "the even *tenor* of his ways," the word means "course" or "general tendency."

There's a story about an editor of the *Daily Worker* who pulled a yard of copy off the TELETYPE and threw it across the desk to his newest cub, saying

"Here, boy, class-*angle* these stories and mind you hew to the *line.*"

The *angle* here is not "the space between two intersecting lines or planes"; nor is it the "number of degrees of opening." And the *line* in- tended is not the "MATHEMATICAL track made by a moving point." What the editor is saying, spelled out, is "Re-slant these stories according to MARXIAN doctrines of class-conflict, and keep to the present 'Party line' in rewriting them."

You'll note of course that *tenor, angle,* and *line* are relatively simple cases of dual or triple meanings, which you can sight-read.

READING CHARACTER

Words describing some aspect of human nature, however, are likely to roll up a whole bundle of complex meanings. Take, for instance, the word *character.* Here is its entry in the *Concise Oxford Dictionary:*

character (k-), n. & v.t. Distinctive mark; (pl.) inscribed letters or figures; national writing-symbols (*in the German c.*) person's handwriting; characteristic (esp. of species &c. in Nat. Hist.); collective peculiarities, sort, style; person's or race's idiosyncracy, mental or moral nature; moral strength, backbone; reputation, good reputation; description of person's qualities; testimonial; status; known person (usu. *public c.*); imaginary person created by novelist or dramatist; actor's or hypocrite's part (*in, out of, c.,* appropriate to those or not, also more widely of actions that are in accord or not with person's c.); eccentric person (*c. actor,* who devotes himself to eccentricities). (Vb. poetic & archaic) inscribe; describe. [f. F. caractère f. L. f. Gk *kharaktēr* stamp (*kharattō* engrave)].

It's not hard to tell which meaning is involved in the lines

> Firm *character'd* in antique gold
> The head of Alexander, King of Macedon . . .

Here it is the literal, primary sense of the word: *stamped* or *engraved*. The head of the King is stamped on the old Greek coin—with perhaps a double meaning implied, that his temperament is revealed by the face. When Jeremy Taylor says in one of his sermons

> God hath writ His Commandements in so large *characters* . . .

he means "letters" or "symbols,"—which in the days of writing on wax, clay or stone, were stamped, INCISED, or carved. We carry this meaning over to describe any alphabet or set of symbols, written or printed. And *character* may also mean the "style of handwriting peculiar to an individual," since it was possible to recognize from his single letter strokes the CHIROGRAPHY of a particular scribe or copyist. Again, in a sense derived from this, *character* is used to mean a cipher or secret mode of writing peculiar to one man. All these meanings are pretty close to the literal.

In the stock phrase "inheritance of acquired *characters*" the word means "the distinguishing features of a species or GENUS,"—the "characteristics." In Macaulay's use of it in the following,

> He now tried to give to the war the *character* of a crusade . . .

it means "essential peculiarity or nature."

When we find a historian writing of Henry VIII

> Thorough selfishness formed the basis of Henry's *character* . . .

we recognize the principal present-day meaning of the word: "the sum of the mental and moral qualities which distinguish an individual or a race." This is the *stamp* of a man, the *brand* or IMPRINT left upon his nature by that sovereign instrument for marking, life itself. Derived from this is the common use of the word to mean "moral FIBER," as in "a man of strong *character.*"

In the passage

Henry James wrote a *character* for his servant in a style so elaborate that neither she nor any of her prospective employers could make out what it meant . . .

the meaning is "a formal TESTIMONIAL from an employer as to the reputation and efficiency of one who has been in his employ."

Familiar enough is the use of the word to mean "a person in a play or novel." From this use also comes the phrase "out of *character,*" meaning acting "contrary to the personality which an actor has assumed in the play." And the meaning "an odd or eccentric person" is at once clear to us in Goldsmith's lines

> A very impudent fellow this, but he's a
> *character* and I'll humor him . . .

From this use perhaps comes the recent DEROGATORY slang sense, found in "Are you bringing those *characters* to dinner again?"

These examples do not by any means exhaust the possibilities of the term (see p. 155). The *Oxford English Dictionary* gives twenty-four different meanings for *character,* nineteen as a noun and five as a verb; some of them are subdivided. And its latest citation is dated 1888. A lot of new shades of meaning have come in through the immense development of PSYCHOLOGY in the nearly sixty years that have elapsed.

It is doubtful, in fact, if even the main meaning of the word, quoted above, will fully convey the sense of the term as it is used in discussions of the PSYCHOLOGICAL novel and drama, in the phrase "development of *character.*" Since Goethe and Coleridge first called attention to the extraordinary significance of *the growth of character* in the modern scheme of things, the word has taken on great richness of meaning. Character, in this sense, connotes more than the *stamp* of a man. The time factor comes in. What a man has been, is taken as predicting what he is likely to become in the future. His "character" in this sense is a growing process. The term hints also at the judgment others form of his make-up. It includes his motives and probable future acts. *Character in this sense varies with time and the observer.* It becomes a matter of interpretation. How many readings there have been of the "character" of Hamlet!

17. Pick the Right Meaning

The following words dealing with aspects of human nature have a long history behind them. While they may not all have piled up as many meanings as *character,* each one can be taken in a good many different senses. For each of the sentences containing the word, jot down your notion of the meaning as it is used in this particular instance. Then check your definitions with the dictionary entry.

A. Wit

1. She relied on her mother *wit* to get her out of a tight spot.
2. He kept his *wits* about him.
3. True *wit* is Nature to advantage dressed,
   What oft was thought but ne'er so well expressed.
4. "We ought to get together. I'm a *wit* myself." "Half—or three-quarters?" (Does it have the same sense in the implied *half-wit?*)
5. "I am not only witty in myself, but the cause that *wit* is in other men." —Falstaff.

B. Humor

1. Every Man in His *Humour.* (British spelling in this title).
2. She was in a very bad *humor.*
3. A very happy mixture of the *humors.*
4. "Better *humor* him, Mac. He's a bad actor when he's lit."
5. Fred Allen's *humor,* while often including laughter at himself, is tempered by wit—and the wit is always at somebody else's expense, his favorite targets being the imbecilities of other radio programs. Jack Benny, on the other hand, is usually on the receiving end of the *humor* and wit in the jibes contrived by his own gagmen.

C. Temper

1. His *temper* got the better of him.
2. The Mayans were of more civilized *temper* than the Aztecs and Toltecs.
3. It takes vanadium alloy to give steel the right *temper* for the purpose.
4. *Temper* the wind to the shorn lamb.

D. Heart

1. "I have the body of a weak woman, but the *heart* and stomach of a prince."—Queen Elizabeth. (And what does *stomach* mean here?)
2. He went straight to the *heart* of the matter.
3. "Have a *heart,* bud, and give me one more beer."

50

4. The electrocardiogram showed grave irregularities in *heart* action.
5. Mackinder the Englishman anticipated the doctrines of Dr. Haushofer as to the importance of the *Heart*land of Eurasia; in fact, geopolitics may be said to be of British invention, not German.

E. Mind

1. "*Mind* the baby while I go to the attic, will you?"
2. He didn't *mind* the hubbub, in fact he was used to it from batting out his copy in the infernal din of a newspaper city room.
3. The splendid shadowy caverns of the *mind,*
   Illumined by the very fires of spirit.
4. Neurologists and experimental psychologists seem determined to break down the boundaries between *mind* and matter.
5. "I felt as if I were going out of my *mind*." "How could you tell?"
6. Do you think clairvoyance, clairaudience, telepathy, prevision and similar phenomena of parapsychology are matters of *mind* or of the senses? Or are both involved?
7. Time out of *mind*. (This is a tricky one.)
8. "I've spoken my *mind* too fully out."—Browning, *Soul's Progress,* i.207.
9. She knows her own *mind*—such as it is. (Double talk here.)
10. "The Papacy, under the guidance of her greatest *minds* . . ." Bryce.
11. He never saw that treasure except in his *mind's* eye, clouded over with the fumes of alcohol.
12. He went to a psychoanalyst for a *mind*-cure at twenty dollars a visit, when what he needed was some hard exercise and a good dose of physic.
13. "The blacksmith said to me the other day, that his 'prentice had no *mind* to his trade.'"—George Eliot, *Daniel Deronda,* lviii.

It pays to buckle down to the dictionary. It's not enough to consult it on the run. A few sessions of INTENSIVE use will convince you that *you can double your effective vocabulary by clearing up the meanings of words you only half know*. For this purpose you need to own a dictionary.

Choosing Your Dictionary

For handy desk use, there are five good dictionaries on the market, each with certain distinctive features.

The most recent in the field, the *American College Dictionary* (Random House, distributed also by Harper Bros.), is edited by the well known LEXICOGRAPHER, C. L. Barnhart, with the collaboration of 350 specialists. Sir William Craigie, last editor of the OED, and editor of the *Dictionary of American English,* appears as consultant on usage levels, as do Professors M. M. Mathews, Charles Fries, and Albert Baugh.

Dr. Kemp Malone prepared the rigorous and authoritative etymologies. Dr. Irving Lorge dealt with problems of SEMANTICS, making it feasible to arrange the definitions of multiple-meaning words in order of semantic frequency, with the commonest meaning first. W. Cabell Greet, editor of *American Speech,* is the authority for the pronunciations, which are in accord with actual American practice, with British variants indicated. The roster of the other experts in technical fields reads like a Who's Who of American scholarship.

As the title indicates, this is the first all-purpose desk dictionary prepared primarily in terms of the *American* language. As a CORRELATE, it has necessarily given fuller treatment to Briticisms, which are contributed by the leading authority in the field, Allen Walker Read.

The coverage of technical terms is very full; and the handling of TERMINOLOGY in grammar, rhetoric, and general LINGUISTICS—so important for the student of words—is in accord with the best present-day practice in these fields. The *American College Dictionary* also has high readability in both senses of the term: it is easy on the eyes, and its style of definition is plain, lucid, and well within the comprehension level of a senior high school student.

The *Thorndike-Century Senior Dictionary* is admirable for high school students and adult foreigners. It aims to define each word in terms simpler than the term defined. On the basis of Thorndike's word counts, it distinguishes, among its 50,000 entries, the 20,000 words most commonly used in print (see p. 60).

What Thorndike achieves by scientific word counts, the *Winston Simplified Dictionary,* long in the field, aims to reach by rule of thumb methods. It plays down LOGICAL, formal definition, in order to get easy INTELLIGIBILITY.

Funk & Wagnalls College Standard Dictionary is hospitable to new words and phrases and gives full coverage on slang and JARGON. Because it is up to the minute, many journalists prefer it.

Webster's Collegiate Dictionary is somewhat slower in admitting new words into the main vocabulary. But it has a kind of ante-room, the "New Word List" in the front which as we noted (p. 34) is convenient for the DEVOTEE of current social history. The *Collegiate* has a good measure of the conservatism on usage that naturally goes with the great authority and historical PRESTIGE of its parent, Webster's *New International Dictionary.* The definitions are given with logical rigor and precision, to stand up in a court of law or before a tribunal of scholars. If anybody has to keep on looking up the words in the definition, too, that doesn't worry the editors.

The *Concise Oxford Dictionary,* an ABRIDGEMENT of the great *Oxford English Dictionary,* is enlivened now and then by the quiet, SARDONIC wit of the Fowler brothers, who made the CONDENSATION. Even though there is a special American edition, there was no way to edit out the British flavor. Again, the work is longer on the literary and historical side than on the technical and scientific, in line with the Fowlers' conviction that a dictionary is concerned with words and word-usage, not with the things and processes for which words stand. They did not believe in making a LEXICON ENCYCLOPEDIC. But they created the *Concise Oxford* style, and once the user learns to watch for their higher mischief he enjoys a good deal of quiet amusement.

Of the pocket dictionaries, only one is worth having. This is also the work of the Fowlers: the *Pocket Oxford Dictionary of Current English.* It has been revised for American use by George Santvoord. Its 1050 close-packed but easily readable pages, 3½ inches by 6, contain a lot in small compass. The preface is a noble specimen of the Fowlers' wit. Here's one example:

. . . the reader . . . may fairly expect to be told not only the meaning of an ox, an icosahedron . . . a major-general . . . but also what are the words for the ox of various ages and sexes, and for *the other regular solids, army officers* . . . and so forth.

If you don't think the Fowlers intended that JUXTAPOSITION of army officers and other regular solids, ask Sad Sack, Bill Mauldin, or even Gertrude Stein's Brewsie and Willie. The Fowlers had just come out of the British Army when they wrote these lines.

Their *Pocket Oxford* also contains a valuable appendix giving pronunciations of foreign words and phrases, including both the usual Anglo-American APPROXIMATION and the actual pronunciation in the foreign language, indicated by the International PHONETIC Alphabet. Another appendix, by the late Lt.-Colonel Le Mesurier, gives words that have recently come into the language (up to 1934) and new meanings and uses of words listed in the main body of the lexicon. While the Fowlers say that this pocket work is not, like their *Concise Oxford,* intended for those who like to read the dictionary straight through, don't believe them. They have slipped in some quiet wit in this one, too.

18. Suppose You Were Writing a Dictionary

Just for fun, see how you'd make out compiling dictionary entries for the following words, all of which have multiple meanings. If you want to do it right, and start a collection for word-games and word-quizzes, make your entries on cards 4 x 6 inches. Put the word under treatment in the upper left-hand corner, and jot down the definitions for the different meanings in numbered order. Then check them with your desk dictionary. Keep the cards in alphabetical order, and as you run into the word in your reading, copy down the sentence in which it occurs—particularly if you find a lively or humorous use of the word.

Take, for example, the word caisson (pronounced, in America, "kaysen," in England "kassoon," with the accent on the "soon.") You'll think at once of the line from the song, "The caissons went rolling along." Here it means "a vehicle to carry ammunition." Then you think of men working under water, tunneling, who get the "bends" if they come out of the caissons too quickly, without depressurizing gradually. In this use, a caisson is "an airtight pressure chamber permitting men to work under water." Evidently sentences illustrating the word's use are very helpful in giving a full and precise sense of its varied meanings.

Try your hand at dictionary entries for these words:

1. ABSTRACT	6. CORRELATION	11. DYNAMICS	16. LEACH
2. ANTECEDENT	7. COSMOS	12. ENSEMBLE	17. MANIPULATE
3. CAPITALISM	8. DEDUCTION	13. EQUINOCTIAL	18. MEDIAN
4. CONSCRIPT	9. DUCTILE	14. INDUCTION	19. mode
5. RECONVERSION	10. DYNAMIC	15. JARGON	20. MOLLIFY

19. Fortune-Telling with a Dictionary

Here's a parlor game invented by a sardonic wit who said the one excuse for bridge is that it ends free speech for morons.

His favorite type of word-quiz is based on a method of fortune-telling that was in vogue in the late Middle Ages and the early Renaissance. The person who wanted to know his future was blindfolded, and handed a small pointer or stylus. He was then led to a table or lectern on which lay a copy of Vergil's *Aeneid*. He was expected to open it at random, and bring the pointer to rest on one line of the poem. The expert fortune-teller then interpreted this verse for him, as revealing his future destiny. This was called consulting the Vergilian lots, or STICHO-MANCY.

Try this method, using a dictionary instead of Vergil. When the word has been selected, go round the circle until you find someone who can define it correctly, not necessarily in the exact words of the dictionary, but near enough to convey the sense—or senses—of the term. A pleasant variation is to ask that the definer also use the word in a sentence, humorously if possible—with an added point for every laugh. (Serious players will promptly develop frozen faces.)

Keep score, devise appropriate penalties and rewards—and if anyone wants to gamble on his word-prowess, let his conscience be his guide.

It is to be made clear from the start that the words picked by the blind-folded person, taken in sequence as long as he does the picking, will be interpreted as his fortune by the most expert word-doctor in the room, as shown by the score.

This method of DIVINATION is no worse than any other. I just tried it, and turned up *faculty*—I was on one for fifteen years; INAUGURATION—I've attended a lot of them; *pennant,*—associated usually with college games, and I've coached a good many; *Spokane*—where I've been twice on business; and *unemployed*—which I hope is not prophetic. At least this gives faster action than a Ouija board, and it's more fun than ANA-GRAMS or the various modern VARIANTS of *bouts rimés*. And it makes the dictionary seem more sociable.

Court of Last Resort

Anybody, however, who wants to get primed for such games by reading a page of the lexicon every day, and learning the words which amuse him, should not rest content with a desk or pocket dictionary. A work is available that is much richer reading.

The greatest venture in the history of LEXICOGRAPHY is the *Oxford English Dictionary* (OED)—sometimes called the New English Dic-tionary, or Murray's, from its first editor. Begun in 1857, and completed only in 1932, this work treats words on historical principles. For each entry, instances of the use of the word were gathered, including wher-ever FEASIBLE its earliest use, and TRAVERSING its history through all its subsequent changes of meaning. Five million quotations in all were collected, of which two million were finally used in the thirteen huge folio volumes. So for each of the 215,000 main words, and the 200,000 subordinate word- and phrase-entries, not only are there definitions which show all the meanings that the word has had, but examples of the use in each sense are given.

The OED is therefore a great treasury of sentences from English literature, beginning with the eighth century, and coming down, in the last volume, to 1930. These illustrations, which give the word in CONTEXT—on the site where it was found, so to speak—are the best revelations of the actual significance which the word has had at different periods. To trace the successive meanings and uses of the word *humor,* or of the word *wit,* as recorded in the OED, is an exercise that will uncover much of the history of the English mind and of English social life during a thousand years.

A Dictionary of American English (DAE) has been made on the same principles, but the ILLUSTRATIVE sentences are predominantly from American literature before 1900, and slang is not treated at all. These limitations rule out the bulk of the saltier and more CHARACTERISTICALLY American expressions, so the DAE, useful though it is, is nothing like as entertaining reading as the OED.

Take, for example, the OED entry on the word *lousy.* It shows that the word was used as a VULGARISM as early as 1386. In this sense, the OED defines lousy as

dirty, filthy, obscene. Also as a general term of abuse: Mean, scurvy, sorry, vile, contemptible.

Then follows the annotation: *Now rare*—which was true only when it was written. But the really amusing part of the entry under *lousy* comes with the examples from the best authors:

1663 DRYDEN *Wild Gallant* l i And to discredit me before strangers, for a lousy, paltry sum of money?
1708 *Brit. Apollo* No. 38 2/1 Wicked Rhimes . . . sung to lowsey Tunes.
1893 STEVENSON *Catriona* 65 The lousiest, lowest, story to hand down to your namesakes in the future.

All these examples from standard authors do not make *lousy* anything but a slang vulgarism in present day usage, but they do show it has hung on a long time.

One of the most admirable features of the OED is the introductory article on the vocabulary of the English language. It contains one REVELATORY passage that brings into place with a sudden click that huge,

KALEIDOSCOPIC collection of words which the dictionary offers. In a flash we see an ordered picture of the English vocabulary, marked by strong and sure design:

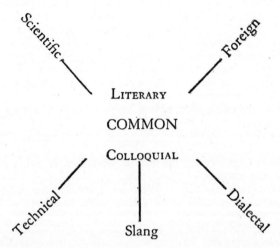

The center is occupied by the common words, in which literary and colloquial words meet. "Scientific" and "foreign" words enter the common language through literature; "slang" words ascend through colloquial use; the "technical" terms of crafts and processes, and the "dialect" words, blend with the common language both in speech and literature. Slang also touches on one side the technical vocabulary of trades and occupations, as in "nautical slang," "Public School slang," "the slang of the Stock Exchange," and on another passes into true dialect. Dialects, similarly, pass into foreign languages. Scientific terminology passes on one side into purely foreign words, on another it blends with the technical vocabulary of art and manufactures. It is not possible to fix the points at which the "English Language" stops, along any of these diverging lines.—OED, I, xxvii, note. (Quoted by permission of the Oxford University Press.)

Quiz Keys for Chapter III

14. Page 40. *Words not included here are standard.*

1. colloq.	25. slang, derogatory	36. slang	50. colloq.
7. slang	French word for	37. slang	56. slang
8. slang	"German"	38. slang	57. colloq.
10. colloq.	30. Standard as noun,	41. slang	60. slang
15. slang	colloq. as verb.	42. slang	64. slang
17. colloq.	33. slang	47. slang	
24. Italian, euphemism	35. slang	49. slang	

1. When carbonic acid gas is blown into water under pressure, the resulting mixture is called ——————— water.
2. The word in England is pronounced in two ways: if it's a noun referring to a radio antenna, it's pronounced ———————, with three syllables; if it's an adjective meaning 'of or pertaining to the air,' it's called ———————, with four syllables.
3. The adjective meaning of or pertaining to pottery is ———————.
4. A secret rendezvous between lovers is usually referred to as ———————.
5. Wedge-shaped characters incised into clay tablets are labelled ——————— writing.
6. A line of reasoning that cannot be successfully challenged is called ———————.
7. An even climate, free from extremes of heat and cold, is often called ———————.
8. A device for figuring out the odds at a big race, in very rapid time, as based on the actual bets laid, is called a ———————.
9. A popular special election to determine the will of the people, often on the question as to what country they prefer to belong to, is called a ———————.
10. A dragon fly's life is literally ———————, since it lives only one day.
11. A favorite slang term for false is ———————. It originally referred to paste jewels.
12. When President Truman ran a men's clothing store, he was, technically speaking, a ———————, but anybody who called him that was well advised to smile when he said it.
13. Part of technical know-how involves the elimination of ——————— in the end-product.
14. In Shanghai, in the old days, a man ordering drinks at his club signed a ——————— for them.
15. The aftermath of over-indulgence in alcohol is a ———————.

From Chapter I

16. Reddish-brown hair is called ———————, from a favorite color used by a great Venetian painter.
17. When you catch a ———————, the reference is to the wildness and fast riding speed of certain Asiatic tribesmen who invaded Europe.
18. A carriage named after the last Queen of England to rule in her own right is a ———————.
19. A party boss who handpicks candidates for high office, as Pendergast handpicked Truman for U.S. Senator from Missouri, is sometimes called a ———————, sometimes by less polite names.
20. A kind of high military boot worn by the conqueror in the Peninsular War against Napoleon is called by his name, a ——————— boot.

21. A fellow-belligerent is, briefly put, an ——————.
22. Words of identical sound but different meaning are called ——————.
23. When you mean 'advice' you spell the word ——————, 'el'; when you are referring to a town governing body, it's spelled ——————, with the 'il' ending.
24. An outcast dog is a ——————; so was Ishmael, son of Hagar.
25. The military force which seizes food or property forcibly is said to —————— it.

IV

ANALYSIS OF VOCABULARY

There are a good many ways of taking the vocabulary apart. One of the most rewarding might be called the gambler's system. How often does each word turn up, and in what combinations?

English is Scotch, in one respect. The small change in the language is important. Ten words, used over and over, make up a quarter of everything written or spoken:

the, of, and, to, a, in, that, it, is, I

Add forty more, and you have the fifty which make up half the total running words in all English and American writing:

the, of, and, it, to, was, is, will, at, we, he, dear, from, are, all, has, very, were, been, I, a, in, that, you, for, as, have, not, with, be, your, by, but, my, this, his, which, me, so, one, if, they, had, would, she, or, there, her, an

THE SCORE ON WORDS

Besides this small change, we now know which words are most commonly used in print, thanks to a lot of tedious work by E. L. Thorndike and his helpers. They counted ten million running words in books and magazines most widely read at grade, high school, and adult levels, to find out how often each word occurred (frequency), and in how many different kinds of material it was found (range). Taking account of these two CRITERIA, they grouped words by thousands, from the thousand most commonly and widely found (1), and so on up to the twentieth thousand (20), containing mostly long, hard words used now and then in highbrow writing. According to this system, *the higher the frequency number, the rarer the word.*

Thorndike's word-count determined the FREQUENCY and range of words only as used *in print*. So occasionally a word that frequently turns up in talk may not be included, or it will have quite a high number, because it is not often written. BOTCH, for example, which President Roosevelt used in his first political address in the 1944 campaign, is in the eighteenth thousand; yet it is a word every farm boy knows and uses. But it seems to find its way into print rather rarely, maybe because it sounds slangy—though it is indicated as standard English in dictionaries. The President even spelled it out, when he gave his speech on the air, perhaps to avoid confusion with a similar five-letter word, perhaps to emphasize its meaning. BOTCH is a fighting word, when applied to somebody else's technique.

There are not too many examples like this, in which the Thorndike number seems not to indicate the difficulty of the word. For the most part, the words in the lower brackets are easy, and the words in the higher thousands are hard, hence less apt to be familiar to the listener or reader with an average vocabulary.

Van, substantial, perpetual, fluid, and *novelty* are typical words in the fourth thousand, according to the Thorndike count.

When you reach the ninth thousand, some of the words are tougher going: *similitude, choleric, intricate, pre-eminence, regime.*

The words in the fourteenth thousand are distinctly not the familiar: OBDURATE, TURBID, UMBRAGE, FRUITION, MISAPPREHENSION, SYLLOGISM, are just a few. However, you also find in this range TAXICAB, QUOTA, and SCRIPT, all words which everybody knows. Apparently they were not so often found in print, when Thorndike made his count.

FLAWS IN THE FINDINGS

Many words listed have also come into wider use since the count was made twenty-five years ago. Two world wars have made a difference. Radio has shifted the word-SPECTRUM, making COLLOQUIAL language more important—and it's on this side that Thorndike's count is admittedly weakest. PSYCHOANALYSIS, PSYCHIATRY, ELECTRONICS, atom-splitting and various other technical branches have introduced many new words. And it's not only new words and new meanings that have upset the rank order.

20. WORDS YOU'LL SEE ONCE IN A MONTH OF SUNDAYS

Thorndike himself admits, on the basis of a careful statistical study of the reliability of his placement of words in the list, that about a thousand of those included would belong outside it—if the count were much extended.[1]

---

[1] This proved to be the case when Thorndike and Lorge prepared the *Teachers Word Book of 30,000 Words,* published in late 1944. The earlier book is the more readily usable by laymen, though statisticians will prefer the newer work, since it is based on a count of 18,000,000 running words.

Without benefit of statistics, and purely on the basis of one man's fancy, here are some candidates picked from the list that could well be replaced. The picker knew only thirty-two of them. How many do you know?

1. TRIVET	19. FITCH	37. LAPPET	53. SEBACEOUS
2. FELLOE	20. FLAGON	38. LIBBARD	54. SELVAGE
3. FERRET	21. FLITCH	39. LORN	55. SHENT
4. FERRULE	22. FUNK	40. LOUR	56. SILESIA
5. DARNEL	23. FURBELOW	41. MARQUISETTE	57. SPLAY
6. DACE	24. GALENA	42. NARD	58. STANCHION
7. COLE	25. GALLEON	43. PALID (sic,	59. STEAPSIN
8. COLLOP	26. GARBLE	probably a	60. STIPULE
9. CARPEL	27. GHOUL	misprint)	61. STOMA
10. AGARIC	28. GIBBER	44. PIMPERNEL	62. STOMATE
11. FRONTLET	29. GLOZE	45. PLUMULE	63. TENDANCE
12. HATCHMENT	30. GROAT	46. PURSUIVANT	64. THALLUS
13. FUSTIAN	31. GYVE	47. PYX	65. THRID
14. ALEXANDRINE	32. MESSALINE	48. RACEME	66. THRUM
15. FITTLE	33. MOIL	49. RAVIN	67. TRICOTINE
16. FIEF	34. MULLEIN	50. RIVE	68. TRYPSIN
17. FILLIP	35. JUSTLE	51. ROOD	69. TUSSAH
18. FINESSE	36. KIBE	52. RUNNEL	70. XYLEN

A Rough and Ready Gauge

After making all discounts and allowances, however, Thorndike's grouping of words by thousands is still a good rough-and-ready guide in estimating the difficulty of a word. If it's in the first ten thousand, the chances are the average reader will know it, though he may have to infer the meaning if it's used in a special, novel, or extended sense. If it's over ten, he may or may not know it.

To be sure, some of the words in the higher brackets are derived from shorter, easier words—which is lucky, because we can usually sight-read these, even if we haven't seen them before. But the bulk of the words above the ten thousand line are part of the learned vocabulary. Most of them are needed by anyone who wants to be a thoroughly literate reader or writer; and many of them are among the more expressive words in English.

For vocabulary-building, there is a question of practical interest involved. How many of these high-bracket words turn up per running hundred thousand words you read?

To get down to cases, it is interesting to see how Thorndike's count applies in this respect to *Newsweek* and *Time,* which together run a little under a hundred thousand words a week.

In the main, *Newsweek* is written in the commonest ten thousand words in the language. But a typical issue contains a sprinkling of words beyond this range, a very few new coinages, and an occasional word still classified as slang by the dictionaries.

21. Have You a Middlebrow Vocabulary?

Words Beyond the Commonest 10,000 in *Newsweek,*
October 2, 1944

(   ) the number in parentheses after each word so marked indicates in which of Thorndike's thousands it occurs

(over 20)   means beyond Thorndike's 20,000 count

(not in T)   means not in *Thorndike's Century Senior Dictionary* which in-cludes the 50,000 most necessary words

(Tech.)   technical term

(neol.)   NEOLOGISM: a new use of an old word; this new meaning not yet listed in the dictionaries

(inf.)   means *informal* or *colloquial* (according to Thorndike, *op. cit.*), not yet standard American, but out of the slang class.

(slang)   means a word so designated by the Thorndike dictionary (or, if it's not in the dictionaries yet, on the authority of the writer of this book.)

Check each word you can define in the various departments of *News-week:*

PERISCOPE:

BLACKLIST (over 20)	RECURRING (15)	BACKFIRED (over 20)
INOCULATIONS (18)	CHAOTIC (15)	REHABILITATE (19)
INSIGNE (over 20 [IN-SIGNIA is (13)])	OSTENSIBLY (11)	SYNTHETIC (11)
	DEMORALIZING (16)	LUCRATIVE (14)

"PERISCOPE" gives inside information and forecasts trends. It makes a guess at the news three or four weeks before it happens. It guesses right about 88% of the time, a high score for any prophet. The twelve words over the 10,000 range indicate the things most in the news: war, including economic warfare; post-war problems,—REHABILITATION; and wartime substitutes. A more recent word-count on this section shows fewer long, hard words, perhaps because the new editor in charge

63

is a former Associated Press man who keeps pretty well within the limits of the 10,000 commonest words.

WASHINGTON TRENDS:

RECONVERSION (neol., over 20)	DETERIORATION (15)	PRIORITY (14)
	SWATH (20)	PARADOXICAL (15)
TITANIC (18)	GUERILLA (over 20)	
INVENTORY (11)	DEFERMENT (over 20)	

"Washington Trends" gave advance news and inside information on wartime production problems. It now covers peacetime production as affected by government regulation.

FIGHTING FRONTS:

SECTOR (16)	SLITHERED (over 20)	BUFFOONS (14)
PINCERS (11)	ERODED (over 20)	SUBSISTENCE (15)
VULNERABLE (11)	BRIDGEHEADS (over 20)	INSIGNIA (13)
MANEUVER (11)	PONTOON (over 20)	DISRUPTED (20)
TENACITY (13)	CAVERNOUS (16)	TERRAIN (over 20)
DEMOLITIONS (16)	LUNAR (14)	EXPLETIVES (16)
QUAGMIRE (16)	FUTURIST (over 20)	

Notice the special vocabulary required to describe World War II.

WAR TIDES (Army):

STRATEGY (12)	AVALANCHE (11)	AUTOMATA (18)
ENTRANCED (over 21)	BARRAGE (16)	ADAPTABILITY (19)
CAULDRON (16)	MECHANIZED (20)	
HURLYBURLY (16)	MORALE (18)	

"Hurly-burly" is one of the few RHYMING RE-DUPLICATED compounds found in this issue of the magazine.

WAR TIDES (Navy):

GADFLIES (20)	OBJECTIVE (14)	CASUALTIES (13)
AMPHIBIOUS (16)	ENTAIL (11)	
STOLLS (over 20)	RECONNAISSANCE (over 20)	

The naval commentator gets on with even fewer long words and technical terms than his Army CONFRERE. This column aims at dealing with complicated naval strategy in simple, direct language.

64

NATIONAL AFFAIRS:

BARRAGE (16)
RANCOR (15)
PROVOCATIVE (17)
SATIRIC (15)
BOTCHED (18)
RECONVERSION (neol. over 20)
SERENITY (15)

MIGRANT (19)
"DEVIATED" (13 malapropism for devious)
MORALE (18)
PRIORITY (14)
URBANE (over 20)
CHARGE D'AFFAIRES (over 20)

PROTOCOL (over 20)
VORACIOUS (14)
DIALECTICS (over 20)
CALISTHENICS (over 20)
INACCESSIBILITY (over 20)
DISSIDENT (over 20)

You can tell from this list a good deal about the history of the United States in wartime. We were thrown out of KILTER by the war, and domestic issues were largely affected by what happened outside the country. Workers moved around (MIGRANTS), and were worried over what would happen to them when war orders stopped.

WASHINGTON TIDES—Lindley:

DEMILITARIZED (over 20)
SURVEILLANCE (14)

DRASTIC (13)
DELINEATION (15)

STRINGENT (13)

Ernest Lindley is considered to have as reliable inside information as any of the Washington columnists. He rarely if ever gets out on a limb. Since he prefers to interpret policies and events, rather than deal in personalities and anecdotes, he keeps to a plain, unvarnished style, and never raises his voice to accent a point. He uses few COLLOQUIALISMS and no slang, very few words beyond the 10,000 range.

FROM THE CAPITAL:

CASUALTY (13)

MORALE (18)

FOREIGN AFFAIRS:

ARMISTICE (14)
ONEROUS (15)
IMMINENCE (18)
PLEBISCITE (17)
FRATERNIZATION (over 20)
DISMEMBERMENT (over 20)
ORDNANCE (12)
BLOC (over 20)
INSOMNIAC (over 20)

PREREQUISITE (over 20)
BELEAGUERED (15)
LORGNETTE (20)
"DE FACTO" (over 20, Latin but practically anglicized)
REGIME (11)
DEMOBILIZE (over 20)
NEON (over 20)

bonzer (Australian slang)
FANFARE (over 20)
RETRIBUTION (13)
PRIMA-FACIE (Latin anglicized, over 20)
LEGALISTIC (over 20)
CARABINIERI (over 20)

Here, as in "Fighting Fronts," the war and its political bearings dominated the field. The language of diplomacy is in evidence.

CANADIAN WEEK:

Zombie (slang, over 20)   *brush-off* (slang)

Apparently slang has its innings even in a dominion that keeps closer to the King's English than we do.

PAN-AMERICAN WEEK:

EMANATED (15)   EMBEZZLEMENT (18)
INFLATION (18)   NEPOTISM (over 20)

These words tell a tale not unlike O. Henry's stories of banana republics at the turn of the century. Probably the occurrence of these words is accidental in the section: you could find instances of all these happenings here at home, too.

BUSINESS, LABOR, AGRICULTURE, AVIATION:

TENTATIVE (15)	RECONVERSION (not in	EXPOSE (over 20)
SYNCHRONIZE (over 20)	Thorndike, neol. over	REPERCUSSION (over 20)
SOLVENCY (over 20)	20)	DRUMMERS (coll. or inf.)
PRIORITY (14)	CUTBACKS (in Thorndike	IRONICALLY (12)
DISCRIMINATION (14)	in literal sense, here	AUTOMOTIVE (over 20)
PRECEDENCE (11)	neol.)	TECHNICIANS (over 20)
TERMINALS (13)	ADMINISTRATIVE (13)	BEARISH (over 20)
MUNICIPALITIES (16)	PRIORITIES (14)	IMPACT (13)
STRATEGIC (14)	OBJECTIVES (14)	PARITY (20)
BROCHURES (over 20)	*plugged* (press agent	AFFILIATE (13)
OMNIBUS (12)	slang)	TRANSOCEAN (over 20)

The words over the 10,000 level reflect the special conditions of industry, business, AVIATION, and labor in wartime.

BUSINESS TIDES:

WINDFALL (17)   RECONVERT (over 20)   CRUCIAL (17)

TRANSITION:
MAROONED (over 20)

"Transition" is *Newsweek's* column about names in the news: deaths, marriages, births, and ODDITIES,—the gossip section of the magazine. Apparently it takes few highbrow words to tell these stories of real life. This is the most-read section of the magazine, according to surveys of reader-interest. "Periscope" comes second.

FOURTH ESTATE (The Press):

VAGARIES (11)
BARBECUE (12)
MICROPHONE (has come into wide use since Thorndike's count, over 20)
PHOTOGENIC (coin., not in T)
COMPLIANT (19)

PHOBIA (over 20)
STICKLER (over 20)
damndest, corniest (quoted from press agent, both slang)
AVID (over 20)
PUEBLO (13)
CORONARY THROMBOSIS both tech., over 20)

TUBERCULOSIS (11)
toughies (slang)
FRAZZLE (inf., over 20)
griped (this sense not in T, slang)
MORALE (18)

This section deals with the news of newspapers and magazines. *Newsweek* has lately changed the name of this department to "The Press." Apparently shop talk in the profession requires more unusual words than some other sections of the magazine. It seems odd to find a *Time-Life* coinage, PHOTOGENIC, accepted by *Newsweek*, which usually avoids any tricks of style, diction, or phrasing invented by *Time*.

MEDICINE:

ANTIBODIES (over 20)
PHAGOCYTES (over 20)
PATHOLOGISTS (over 20)
ACIDITY (13)
MOLECULAR (over 20)
ULTRACENTRIFUGE (over 20)
INFECTIOUS (9)
MENINGITIS (13)
SULFA (neol. over 20)
PENICILLIN (neol. over 20)
PSYCHOANALYSIS (over 20)
PSYCHIATRY (over 20)
PSYCHOANALYST (over 20)

PSYCHOSOMATIC (over 20)
SEMINARS (over 20)
CLINICAL (15)
CONCEPTS (15)
SYMBOLIC (18)
"OEDIPUS COMPLEX" (tech. over 20)
HYSTERIA (19)
PEPTIC (over 20)
ULCERS (20)
COLITIS (over 20)
MIGRAINE (over 20)
BRONCHIAL ASTHMA (17)

CIRRHOSIS (over 20)
ALCOHOLISM (over 20)
SYPHILIS (19)
FIBROUS (11)
ATROPHY (15)
JAUNDICE (13)
ASCITES (20)
HEMORRHAGE (18)
INTRAVENOUSLY (over 20)
DISORIENTATION (not in T)
PARALYSIS (11)
NUTRITIONAL (over 20)

As you would expect, "Medicine," like the science section following, requires more technical terms than any other department. Some of these terms are translated in the text. Most of them are necessary short-hand, or INDISPENSABLE terms, for which no ordinary words would serve. Try to find synonyms to replace them and you will realize that technical writing, even though meant for the general reader, requires a good many special words. This column in *Newsweek* has very high standing with the medical profession.

SCIENCE:

HYDRA (12)	REGENERATION (12)	POSTAMPUTATION (over 20)
CHAMELEON (13)	EMBRYONIC (19)	FIBROUS (11)
ZOOLOGIST (17)	BLASTEMA (over 20)	CARTILAGE (11)

RADIO:

MICROPHONE (neol. over 20!)

This section deals chiefly with the program end of radio, including lively newsnotes on radio personalities. So technical JARGON is not needed. In the stories dealing with the technical or engineering side of radio, in other issues, necessary technical terms are used, but sparingly, always with UNOBTRUSIVE translation for the reader not familiar with them.

SPORT WEEK:

FLEDGLING (17)	CADDIE (over 20)	SPORADIC (19)
KIDS (inf.)	DEPILOUS (over 20)	

Newsweek's sport column avoids slang and jargon. Unusual words—"depilous" (for "bald") is a case in point—are used a little as the gag writers do, for comic effect.

SPORTS:

HEX (inf., over 20)	AUTOSUGGESTION (over 20)	HYPNOTISM (over 20)
HYPNOLOGIST (coin.)	HYPNOTIC (18)	PRESTIDIGITATED (over 20)
ELITE (over 20)	LEGERDEMAIN (over 20)	

Newsweek's regular reporting on sports avoids slang, but it runs to words drawn from PSEUDO-science and odd professions.

EDUCATION:

FAVORITISM (18)	FUSILLADE (20)	EFFIGY (11)

BOOKS:

DISPARAGEMENT (12)	APPRAISALS (20)	PRE-EMINENTLY (12)
CRYSTALLIZATION (over 20)	FAUNA (16)	DISINTEGRATION (17)
FELICITOUS (18)	IRREVOCABLY (14)	

The book review section on *Newsweek* follows newspaper reviewing methods. It rules out "literary" jargon, and avoids CLICHÉS and fancy words. The aim is to extract news from books selected for review. Bad books are given silent treatment. Notice how few long, hard words are needed—not more than two to a column.

THEATER:

STEREOTYPES (15)

No stage LINGO here.

MUSIC:

LOGICAL (12)

A welcome absence of technical jargon that can spoil music reviews for the non-musical reader.

MOVIES:

IDEALIST (18)   IDYL (14)   CINEMATIC (18)

The *Newsweek* movie reviewing is designed to tell what's in the picture, and to keep critical evaluation to a minimum. It has no need for fancy critical terms. Idyl is a good shorthand word; cinematic a necessary synonym.

PERSPECTIVE:

AVOIDANCE (14)   ENTANGLEMENTS (15)   INDOCTRINATE (over 20)
                       COMMITMENTS (over 20)

Run back through the *Newsweek* word list and count the number you checked which you could define. Multiply this figure by 40, add 10,000 to it, and you'll have a rough and ready measure of your total reading vocabulary.

Time-TICS

Time has always prided itself on a style at once COLLOQUIAL and condensed. Its *Time*-tried tricks are sometimes trying to persons on the receiving end. To the copy of the *Iliad* on its owner-editor's desk is attributed the magazine's addiction to compound Homeric EPITHETS. Homer would be surprised to find LaGuardia labeled as "duck-bottomed," an epithet which once alternated with a startling rival, STEATOPYGOUS. The boys in the political department hoarded this one up for six months, finally springing it on "Butch," as they called him, just before his campaign for re-election in 1942—probably the one time it was used in print outside of works in ANTHROPOLOGY.

69

Time-style shows a fondness for odd, startling, and unusual words—attention-catchers. Its PORTMANTEAU or blend words are a virtual trademark. ARCHAIC words are used in a slang sense. The C.I.O. gets a "blow to the MAZARD"—which means head. Dialect is sprinkled in for local color.

And the editors aren't a bit afraid to use learned words when they need to, in reviewing Toynbee's *Study of History,* or Northrup's *Meeting of East and West,* or new editions of Joyce and Proust. They're equally bold in tackling the jargon of science and TECHNOLOGY, and do a good job of translating it.

Time editors believe in keeping the reader on the jump, though perhaps they wouldn't go quite so far as the advertising agency head who used to greet his staff every morning with the slogan, "Boys, hit 'em in the eye, ear, nose and throat."

Evidently *Time's* DICTION has a good deal to offer the CONNOISSEUR of words. Anybody who can do a BREAK-DOWN of its vocabulary knows his way around the dictionary pretty well—and sometimes he'll have to go outside it.

22. HAVE YOU A HIGHBROW—AND LOWBROW—VOCABULARY?

How many of the following words from *Time,* October 9, 1944, can you label correctly, as slang, coinages, blends, foreign (giving the language), technical, informal, or standard? (All standard words included are beyond Thorndike's commonest 10,000. For once, these high-frequency words are not set in SMALL CAPITALS, since to do so would defeat the purpose of this quiz.)

You have already worked on sixty-four of these words in Word-Quiz 14.

Check also the words which you can define, as you did for the *Newsweek* list.

Miscellany:
[ ] comeuppance [ ] cinemagnate [ ] monogrammed [ ] mantises

U.S. at War:

[ ] sideswipe	[ ] hubbub	[ ] kaleidoscopic
[ ] conking	[ ] haberdasher	[ ] asperity
[ ] zeroed	[ ] fracas	[ ] synthetic
[ ] totting up	[ ] dastardly	[ ] mezzanine
[ ] play footie	[ ] cockade	[ ] punitive
[ ] bloc	[ ] aggravation	[ ] embargo

People:
[　] trap ("keep my   [　] cinemarmful   [　] racketeer
     trap shut")   [　] fascists   [　] faker
[　] cinemactress   [　] hobo   [　] fake
[　] nostalgia   [　] bust   [　] baton
[　] Isolationist   [　] rabble-rouser   [　] imbedding
[　] tirade   [　] phony   [　] taxied
[　] musicomedienne [　] full of beans   [　] souvenir
[　] exposé   [　] agents provocateurs

Art:
[　] decadent   [　] voluptuous   [　] sensuous
[　] portfolios   [　] exuberant   [　] cubism

Music:
[　] fiasco   [　] repertoir   [　] pennant   [　] prepped
[　] tussle   [　] batoneers   [　] clutch   [　] bugaboo
[　] beige   [　] economics   [　] rejuvenated [　] seductive
[　] repertory   [　] impresarios [　] perennial [　] bleachers
[　] eight ball   [　] anticlimax   [　] crucial

Science:
[　] radiation   [　] electrons   [　] electron   [　] vacuum
[　] radium   [　] cathode   [　] focal   [　] therapeutic
[　] Radiological [　] phenomenal [　] accelerating

Religion:
[　] agnosticism   [　] Evangelism   [　] autopsy
[　] Seminary   [　] evangelists

Education:
[　] psychology   [　] barbaros   [　] projectors
[　] psychological [　] Punica fides

The Press:
[　] aggressors   [　] furor   [　] argentinity [　] newshens

Army and Navy:
[　] minutemen   [　] mobilization [　] belligerent [　] poncho
[　] outmoded   [　] revulsion   [　] casualty   [　] frazzled
[　] incompetence [　] federalization [　] evacuate   [　] mascot
[　] mechanized   [　] pacifists   [　] setup   [　] leathernecks

Milestones:
[　] cinemadolescent [　] mercurial   [　] expatriate [　] henchmen
[　] swart   [　] plebiscite [　] strategy

Radio:
[　] short snort [　] farcical   [　] envisioning [　] encyclopedic
[　] microphone   [　] television [　] cinema

72

Business & Finance:

[ ] bigwigs	[ ] bedlam	[ ] expediency	[ ] chary
[ ] butted	[ ] lathery	[ ] socialization	[ ] stabilization
[ ] reconversion	[ ] automotive	[ ] nebulous	[ ] blueprinted
[ ] priorities	[ ] attrition	[ ] a-glimmering	[ ] devaluation
[ ] joker	[ ] hangovers	[ ] dictator	[ ] bilateral
[ ] riffled	[ ] hijacking	[ ] proximity	[ ] fiscal
[ ] salvaging	[ ] format	[ ] caviar	[ ] burgeoned
[ ] par	[ ] avalanche	[ ] enamored	[ ] autopsy
[ ] bloc	[ ] arbiter	[ ] subsidiaries	[ ] parity

Medicine:

[ ] pathologist	[ ] arcane	[ ] endemic	[ ] peritonitis
[ ] susceptibility	[ ] typhus	[ ] virulence	

Cinema:

[ ] cinemadaptation	[ ] titillated	[ ] flibbertigibbet
[ ] tarpon	[ ] noblesse	[ ] ersatz
[ ] cinemaddicts	[ ] domesticity	[ ] multimillion-heiress
[ ] drab	[ ] mannerisms	
[ ] sexy	[ ] spurious	[ ] clichés
[ ] oofs	[ ] glollog	[ ] musicomic
	[ ] musicomedienne	

Books:

[ ] rant	[ ] polemicists	[ ] rostrum
[ ] clichés	[ ] adjectival writing styles	[ ] lurid
[ ] liquidate		[ ] inferentially
[ ] illiteracy	[ ] indistinguishable	[ ] bestiality
[ ] goons	[ ] strident	[ ] polemical
[ ] rubles	[ ] propaganda	[ ] incisiveness
[ ] ideological	[ ] Agitka	[ ] synthetics
[ ] unobjectivity	[ ] indirection	[ ] bourgeois
[ ] polemic	[ ] pomposity	[ ] saboteurs
	[ ] platitudes	

Running back through the list, count the words you checked—those you could define. Multiply your score by 30, add 10,000, and you'll have another estimate of your total reading vocabulary. How does it compare with the score you made on the *Newsweek* list?

An actual count shows that *Time* in a typical issue uses 38 per cent more words outside the range of the commonest ten thousand than *Newsweek* does. The figures are: *Time*, 349. *Newsweek*, 254. But 44 of *Time's* 349 are coinages, blends, or slang; while *Newsweek* rations itself to 9 slang terms. Discounting the non-standard element, *Time* employs

21.7 per cent more standard words beyond the 10,000 commonest—a decidedly significant difference.

Time has, by legend, five levels of rewrite, each of which is supposed to ginger up copy and improve readability. *Newsweek* has only two levels of rewrite—really only one, besides the copy desk.

The magazines quite evidently have very different policies on diction. *Newsweek* editors come mostly from the big press associations; *Time's* editors from more varied backgrounds. The news editor on *Newsweek*, in whose head is to be found the style sheet of the magazine, was trained on the New York *Times*.

Whether the *Time* or *Newsweek* policy on word-choice is better, must be left to the reader to judge. *Newsweek* plays it safe. *Time* keeps much further ahead of the dictionary.

Time was founded a quarter of a century ago, shortly after Henry L. Mencken published the first edition of *The American Language*. Ring Lardner, Sinclair Lewis, Damon Runyon, and John Dos Passos were beginning to make serious (or comic) use of American LINGO in fiction. In the emancipated spirit of its beginnings, *Time* has always used a sprinkling of Americanisms, slightly fewer as it has grown older and spread its circulation to a world-wide Anglo-American audience.

Before the talkies gave the American IDIOM wide currency, Britishers and Australians needed footnotes to read *Time*—as they did for Sinclair Lewis's *Main Street,* which in 1922 was published in England with a GLOSSARY of eight hundred American words and phrases, translated into British. Now, thanks to talkie dialogue and the American armies, inhabitants of the British Isles and their Dominions can read *Time* with ease if not with entire comfort.

Time's extensive use of Americanisms raises, however, the problem of the differences between "American" and "British" English.

BRITISH VERSUS AMERICAN

Americans are not, as a rule, perfectly at home with British English. If an American junior executive goes to London, to work in the British branch of his firm, he finds that in a few respects business speaks a different language over there. He must learn to call bonds "DEBENTURES" and a payroll a "salary sheet." He doesn't get a raise in salary, but a "rise"—here the New York *Times* follows British usage. He finds that he has, not a white-collar job, but a "black-coat position." A soft snap is a "cushy job." A sit-down strike becomes a "stay-in" strike. A realtor is a "house and estate agent." A check stub is dignified as a "cheque COUNTERFOIL." And in the advertising field, a BILLBOARD becomes a "HOARDING."

There are novel words for items of ordinary living. The American must look not for an apartment but for a "service flat." He goes up not in an elevator, but in a "lift." If he looks around for a lunch counter, he'll find it under the sign of a "snack bar" (this term is now coming into use here). If he forgets the key to his "flat," it would do no good to try to climb in through the "TRANSOM," for in British NOMENCLATURE that means the horizontal bars across a door- or window-top; what we call a transom is a "FANLIGHT." An American porch-climber or second-story man is a "cat burglar." You ring not for the janitor, but for the "caretaker," to make repairs to the "tap" (our water-faucet). Groceries come up in the "kitchen lift," not in a DUMBWAITER. For dinner, you have a "sweet"—the MASQUERADE for dessert; the "biscuits" served at tea time are neither hot nor are they biscuits in our sense; they are what we call cookies. You get a "cut from the joint" rather than a slice off the roast.

To realize how far American slang differs from British, you need only imagine a Britisher (of the type of Wodehouse's silly-clever heroes) describing the American scene:

American night clubs are extraordinary places. I dropped into one where they had a tall girl as "chucker-out." The place was full of bagmen, who brought with them creatures "dressed up to the nines," presumably models. When someone at the next table began a bit of badinage, I could think of no "retorts," and I fear they thought me a bit of a "duffer." I certainly felt a perfect "mug," since I'm not used to cutting "capers." One of the girls held out a little WHIRLIGIG device, and said, "Pop, don't monkey with the buzz-saw!" My American escort told me that meant, "Mind you don't cut your fingers, sir!" Odd, what?

His American escort should also have told him that a "chucker-out" is a "bouncer"; "bagmen" are "drummers" or "butter-and-egg men"; "dressed up to the nines" is "all dolled up"; "retorts" are "comebacks"; a "duffer" is a "dub"; a "mug" is a "sap" or "dope"; "capers" are "didoes." As for translating "pop" as "sir," that was just American tact.

On a more UTILITARIAN level, there are also terms for common objects that differ in British and American. A British bride, recently landed to

75

join her soldier husband in the United States, starts out on a shopping tour. She has on her list: a dust-bin; a scent-spray; a tin-opener; a washing-up bowl; a spanner; and minerals. She first draws a blank when she asks for these items from a clerk in a chainstore (she thinks of it as a "multiple shop"). After explaining her needs, she finally piles into the baby-carriage ("PERAMBULATOR" to her) a garbage can, an ATO-MIZER, a can-opener, a dishpan, a monkey-wrench, and some ginger-ale and bottled soda—these last-named items are the "minerals."

When later she wants to get a "keyless" watch, she finds it's called a "stem-winder." If she goes into a garage, she learns that "PETROL" is "gas" in American; a "gear-lever" is a "gearshift"; "first speed" is "low gear"; an "ACCUMULATOR" is a "storage battery," or just a "battery"; an "anti-bounce clip" is a "shock-absorber."

Instead of asking to have something bought on credit "put down," she learns to say "Charge it, please." On the telephone, she finds she has to ask for "long distance," not a "trunk line." "Porridge" is "oatmeal," "tart" is a "pie"; a "BARROW" is a "push-cart." If she wants "gum" she must ask for MUCILAGE; otherwise she gets the chewing compound. And when she wants the "GEYSER" (the British pronounce it "geezer") re-paired, she finds that the plumber calls it a "hot water heater."

Probably the present-day literary form which is most nearly common currency in the United States and England is the detective story. Traffic goes both ways. Americans now stand in greater need of a GLOSSARY. Take this passage from an (imaginary) British detective yarn, with the necessary translations supplied:

As we came out of the booking-hall (ticket office), we saw a breakdown lorry (wrecker, or tow-car) in a towering hurry. We thought of hailing it, but Tommy said "That cat won't jump" (that idea's no good). However, we chased it, and as the driver changed down (shifted into low gear) at the hill, we hopped it. The driver saw us in his rear-view mirror, as he swung around a sharp turn, and he called out, "Who yer tryin' to do down, mates? I don't want no dust-up (row), but hoppin' rides is disallowed (forbidden) by the company. And it aren't fair on me (to me) for you to stick it (hang on)." "How about being a bit matey (friendly), chum," Tommy asked him, "and letting us ride to the edge of Brighton?" "Yes, and 'ave you lead me up the garden path (deceive me), and get me into trouble with the lorry (truck) inspector," the driver answered. "The inspector in Brighton is a fair nosey-parker (snoop), 'e is, and death against pickin' up PEDESTRIANS (hitch-hikers) or yobos (street-corner loafers)."

76

Since British slang has INFILTRATED into the United States much more slowly, Americans are still UNVERSED in British English. At first try we find it difficult to follow broadcasts on the BBC. A reference to an "accident-tout" is puzzling; we need it translated as an "ambulance-chaser." Going to the "chemist's" the SCRIPT-writer must change to going to the "drugstore." The "pictures" are the "movies," the "gangway" in a theater is the "aisle," the "wireless" is our "radio," and a "GRAMOPHONE" is a "phonograph." The British say "hire-purchase system" for our instalment plan buying. In London you take the "underground" or the "tube" instead of the subway as in New York. In London, a "subway" is an underground pass from one side of a railway track to another. On the British railways, there are "sleepers" instead of ties; a freight car is a "goods wagon"; a switchman is a "pointsman," the conductor is a "guard"; and the ticket agent a "booking-clerk."

Note that the differences are nearly all in the realm of everyday life. Slang and COLLOQUIAL usage also differ. But it's not much of a trick picking up these BRITICISMS. It is amusing, like learning a dialect. And the DIVERGENT words are all concrete.

It is always relatively easy to acquire a new set of concrete terms needed in a trade or craft—even if it's writing detective stories with a British setting. AIRCRAFT mechanics in the army picked up the names of engine parts as they learned how to tinker the engines. Hardware clerks gradually master the several thousand terms found in a hardware catalogue, and link them up with the gadgets which the words identify. The names of flowers, animals, chemicals, and ordinary objects simply call for a politician's memory. They have to be learned gradually, by main strength and awkwardness. But nobody needs to know all these terms. It's a matter of picking and choosing those that fit in with individual interests and activities.

The case is different when it comes to the more general, abstract terms that figure so large in Thorndike's second ten thousand. These come closer to being words-of-all-work. They turn up in widely diverse connections. Anyone who wants to read great fiction, poetry, or drama, or who intends to keep abreast of cultural and scientific developments, or who is keen on following political and social controversy, needs a firm grasp on this part of the vocabulary. And he should tackle these words in the second ten thousand with a full appreciation of their importance.

22. Page 70. Words in *Time*, October 9, 1944, beyond the commonest 10,000. *Words not included here are standard American.*

Miscellany:
[slang] comeuppance   [coin.] cinemagnate   [over 20] mantises

U.S. at War:
[slang] sideswipe	[over 20] kaleidoscopic	[over 20] beret
[slang] conking	[over 20] mezzanine	[over 20] columnists
[coin.] zeroed	[over 20] punitive	[over 20] docket
[slang] totting up	[over 20] coercion	[over 20] ideologically
[slang] play footie	[Latin] Quis custodiet	[over 20] legalistic
[over 20] haberdasher	ipsos custodes?	
[over 20] dastardly		

World Battlefronts:
[over 20] stalemate	[over 20] trek	[over 20] debouching
[over 20] hodgepodge	[tech. slang] bugs	[over 20] ideology
[slang, Ger.] strafing	[over 20] red-beret	[over 20] sampans
[slang, Br.] nipped	[Fr.] "C'est la guerre"	[over 20] harassment
[over 20] semaphoring	[new word] paratroops	[coin.] quisling
[over 20] riposted	[over 20] guerrilla	[over 20] grenade
[over 20] lunge	[over 20, inf.] jibe	

Foreign News:
[over 20] highlighted	[over 20] raucous	[not in T] gullied
[Ital.] bordello	[over 20] appeasement	[over 20] Marxism
[Fr.?] Boche	[over 20] stalemate	[over 20] circa
[over 20] chits	[Latin] sine die	[Sp.] guerrilleros
[over 20] inevitability	[over 20] trulls	[over 20] fascism
[over 20] invalidism	[over 20] warpish	[over 20] Naziism
[over 20] nationalized	[Fr.] coups par jour	[Fr.] coup d'etat
[over 20, coin.] collabora-	[Fr.] gourmandes	[Ger.] Schmeisser
tionist	[over 20] cryptic	[over 20] federated
	[over 20] inviolability	

Latin America:
[over 20] haggling	[over 20] queued	[over 20] jettisoned
[? over 20] swatch	[over 20] queues	

People:
[slang] trap ("Keep my	[over 20] exposé	[slang] phony
trap shut")	[coin.] cinemarmful	[Br. slang] full of beans
[coin.] cinemactress	[over 20] fascists	[Fr.] agents provocateurs
[over 20] nostalgia	[? over 20] hobo	[over 20] racketeer
[not in T] Isolationist	[slang] bust	[not in T] faker
[coin.] musicomedienne	[Inf.] rabble-rouser	[Inf.] fake

78

Art:
[over 20] decadent   [over 20] cubism

Music:
[over 20] fiasco   [over 20] repertory   [coin] batoneers   [over 20] anticlimax
[over 20] beige   [slang] eight ball   [over 20] economics   [slang] prepped

Science:
[over 20] Radiological   [over 20] cathode

Religion:
[over 20] agnosticism   [over 20] Evangelism   [over 20] autopsy

Education:
[Gr.] barbaros   [Lat.] Punica fides

The Press:
[over 20] furor   [coin.] argentinity   [slang] newshens

Army & Navy:
[over 20] minutemen   [over 20] federalization   [over 20] poncho
[over 20] outmoded   [over 20] pacifists   [over 20, Inf.] frazzled
[over 20] mobilization   [over 20] setup   [over 20] mascot
                           [slang] leathernecks

Milestones:
[coin.] cinemadolescent   [over 20] expatriate

Radio:
[slang] short snort   [over 20] farcical   [over 20, not in T] en-
[over 20] microphone   [over 20!] television   visioning

Business & Finance:
[over 20, Inf.] bigwigs   [over 20] lathery   [over 20] a-glimmering
[slang] butted   [over 20] automotive   [over 20] enamored
[over 20, not in T] re-   [over 20] attrition   [over 20] blueprinted
  conversion   [slang] hangovers   [over 20] devaluation
[over 20] joker   [over 20, Inf.] hijacking [over 20] burgeoned
[over 20] riffled   [over 20] format   [over 20] autopsy
[over 20] bloc   [over 20] socialization

Medicine:
[over 20] pathologist   [not in T] arcane   [over 20] endemic   [over 20] peritonitis

Cinema:
[coin.] cinemadaptation   [over 20] titillated   [Ger.] ersatz
[over 20] tarpon   [Fr.] noblesse   [coin.] multimillion-
[coin.] cinemaddicts   [over 20] domesticity   heiress
[slang] sexy   [coin.] glollog   [over 20] clichés
[coin.] oofs   [over 20] flibbertigibbet [coin.] musicomic
                           [coin.] musicomedienne

Books:

[over 20] clichés
[over 20] liquidate
[slang] goons
[over 20] ideological
[over 20] unobjectivity

[not in T] polemic
[over 20] polemicists
[over 20] adjectival writing styles
[Rus.] Agitka

[over 20] indirection
[over 20] pomposity
[over 20] inferentially
[over 20] bestiality
[over 20] saboteurs

Vice-versa Quiz for Chapter IV

1. Mixing in cheaper and oftentimes injurious substance in a food or chemical is called _____.
2. What is a polite word for *graft*? _____
3. The curve traversed by a projectile in flight is called its _____.
4. How does the technical diplomatic term for *one-sided* eliminate a possible misunderstanding?
5. The methods of reasoning and arguing used by Marxists are called _____ (and a good many other meaner names).
6. The _____ of the Pope among the bishops is called into question by the Orthodox Communion.
7. A recompense just barely sufficient to keep a worker alive is called a _____ wage.
8. The medical books usually call "clotting" of the blood _____.
9. A very loud and powerful voice is labelled, after the greatest "loud-speaker" in the Greek army before Troy, _____; or in the American, such a "loud mouth" is said to have a voice like a hog-caller.
10. A soldier, sailor, or marine who has been wounded, killed, or lost is listed as a _____.
11. The adjective meaning "having to do with public finance or Treasury matters" is _____.
12. The solution of the plot of a play is the _____.
13. A plane which can take off from either land or water is called _____. An invasion by land, sea, and air Churchill described as _____ (a coined word).
14. Among the Pennsylvania Dutch, putting a spell on someone is called _____.
15. The inculcation of certain views or attitudes in newcomers to a church, political party or an army is called _____.
16. Someone who is fond of words may or may not be a _____ in collecting them.
17. When *Time* wanted to say "Remember there's a war on" or "It's the war," it used a foreign phrase _____. Was that necessary?
18. A diplomatic messenger who makes long trips is called a _____.
19. If a disease that has caused epidemics shows a few cases always around and may break out into an epidemic any time, it is said to be _____.
20. In British English, a "sit-down strike" is called a "_____ strike."

21. What we call a *billboard* is a —————— in England.
22. The British word for a "bouncer" is a ——————.
23. An *atomizer* is a —————— in Britain.
24. If you want gas for your car while driving in England, you ask for
——————.
25. What would the spoken phrase "an explosive old geezer" mean in England?
26. A military boot, named from the winner of the Peninsular Campaign, is
a ——————.
27. A "king-maker," even on a small scale, is called a ——————, from the
English earl of the name who made and unmade monarchs at the time
of the Wars of the Roses.
28. A carriage named from the last reigning queen of England is a
——————.
29. If you catch hold of a touch customer, you're said to have caught a
——————.
30. Tyrants usually have a palace guard, and such a guard is often called,
from the famous headquarters troop that guarded (and sometimes unseated) Roman emperors, a —————— Guard.
31. The opposite to *static,* in discussions of motion in physics, is
——————.
32. A word which literally means "two-valued" is specialized to describe
atoms that are "double-hooked," that is they may join up either by one
hook or by both with other elements. The word is —————— (and it is
not in the OED, nor in the Concise Oxford, nor in Thorndike, nor in the
New Word List in the Webster's Collegiate, 4th edition!)
33. A malingerer in the army is said to —————— illness.
34. A politician who will take money over or under the counter for his services as a "fixer," is said to be ——————.
35. If we say "Polybius the historian looked back on the year 146 B.C., which
he had just lived through, and thought of the destruction which he had
witnessed of two great empires, one Oriental, one Western [sounds quite
like our own 1946 A.D., doesn't it?]," the use of the date 146 B.C. is an
——————, since Polybius could not have foreseen the birth of Christ
146 (?) years later; he would have dated the year as in a certain Olympiad.
36. In your desk dictionary, how far do the editors subdivide technical
words? Do they distinguish different sciences: do they label words *geol.,
math.,* etc., or do they just lump them as *technical?* Do any of them mark
the old-fashioned rhetorical 'lingo' for figures of speech and the like
"technical"? They should, if such words are given, since they are now
unknown country to most readers. Can you define a *metonymy?* a
litotes? a *synechdoche?* an *anacoluthon?*
37. Tell what *correlation* means in words a seventh-grader could understand.
38. A stenographer once told an editor who was dictating business copy to

her that a lot of the subscribers would not know the word *mollify*. Was she right, or was it simply that she didn't happen to know it? (It is in the 14th commonest thousand.)

39. What is meant by "consulting the Vergilian lots"?

40. Do you take any stock in a method of —————— called water-witching, employed for locating a good well? Do you believe in any methods of locating hidden minerals or oil?

[V]

THE CASE FOR LONG, HARD WORDS

There is a case for long, hard words. You will not often hear it argued. The contrary doctrine is more fashionable: Keep to short, simple, Saxon. Ever since Herbert Spencer set this half-truth going, it has snowballed in the way that half-truths usually do. It is sound advice as far as it goes. You cannot help using a PREPONDERANCE of Saxon, since the small change of the language and most of its connective tissue come from that source. But there are at least four COGENT reasons why some of the long, difficult words are needed, though they should be used sparingly.

First, one such word can sometimes do the work of ten. It just looks long. The rate of increase of speed of a moving or falling object is ACCELERATION. The capacity to adjust to changes in environment by altering responses or habits is ADAPTABILITY. Mixing in a cheaper and less EFFICACIOUS substance in some food or chemical is ADULTERATION. An index or small number written above and to the right of an ALGEBRAIC symbol or quantity to show how many times the symbol or quantity is to be used as a factor is an EXPONENT. Think what a nuisance it would be always to go around Robin Hood's barn by using the long phrase when we wanted to express the meaning in such words as these. The long word is really verbal shorthand.

Such words may also be needed as SYNONYMS, for variety as well as for COMPACTNESS. If two DISPUTANTS are so far apart that they can't patch up their quarrel, it helps a reporter if he can say—at the second mention of the fact—that they're IRRECONCILABLE or UNCOMPROMISING. If "graft" is involved, it is handy to know about "squeeze" and "pickings," but sometimes the polite term is also useful: PERQUISITES. If you have to call somebody *stingy* three times, PARSIMONIOUS and *tight-fisted* suggest themselves.

Again, the long or unusual word may be needed to express an exact shade of meaning. There is only one possible word for a time scheme covering a series of events or a succession of DYNASTIES: CHRONOLOGY. And the curve traversed by a PROJECTILE is its TRAJECTORY. The case is still stronger if descriptive words are involved. Shaw somewhere talks

83

of *"breath-bereaving* insolence." Just try expressing that any other way.

John Hersey, in his memorable *New Yorker* story on Hiroshima, has occasion to indicate the mounting hostility toward all foreigners as the war drew nearer to Japan. He uses the one right word to convey this with full force: ". . . Father Kleinsorge, of the Society of Jesus . . . felt the strain of living in an increasingly XENOPHOBIC Japan . . ." The word means "stranger-fearing" in Greek, and the association we have with PHOBIA makes it all the more expressive. It suggests a touch of maddened suspicion.

When the Russians, after a war in which they were BELLIGERENTS for only one week, rammed ahead and *without consulting their allies* yanked half a billion worth of machinery out of Manchuria, we could not call this a *one-sided* move without making the misunderstanding worse. For *one-sided* might mean merely that it benefited them, not China or the other allies—which is true, but not what is meant. The word needed is UNILATERAL, the exact way to describe an action taken by one side without consulting the other. Frank Sullivan can make all the fun he likes of the word, as he does when he has his mouthpiece Aunt Sarah say:

"I REDEPLOYED myself. . . . Came down on the train unilaterally."

"Unilaterally?"

"On one side of the Hudson. I like those fancy new DIPLOMATIC words that nobody quite knows what they mean. Give a statesman enough words like unilateral and he can wiggle out of any fix."

Mr. Dooley would have ticked Sullivan off on that one. The fact is that diplomatic negotiators need words like *unilateral*—if they are to button up agreements more tightly. It might also help if the negotiators dealing with the Kremlin studied a little MARXIAN DIALECTIC—even if only in the way the atheist studies Scripture: to confound it. Otherwise East-West diplomacy is likely to continue in a semantic fog.

It is this need for precise terms that can be taken in only one sense that accounts for extensive borrowing directly from Greek and Latin, when new words are required for scientific or technical gadgets, substances, or processes. And this type of term needed to convey a specific technical sense cannot well be replaced by any simple Saxonism. That is a fourth reason justifying long, hard words.

And the older words from classical sources, long used in discussing politics, ECONOMICS, literature, religion, philosophy and other fundamental subjects, have often been in the language unchanged (except as to spelling) since the sixteenth century—and every LITERATE person needs to know them.

23. WHAT'S THE ONE LONG WORD FOR IT?

What single word conveys the meaning for each of the following?

1. Familiar with many languages.
2. Adhering to a political party which advocates wider distribution of land, AGRARIAN reform, cheap money, etc. Such a party was formed in the U.S. in 1891.
3. Possible latent power or capacity, as opposed to already ACTUALIZED achievement.
4. Being first in rank, order, or importance.
5. Custom or law that devolves inheritance or title on the eldest son.
6. Act or process of spreading out from a center.
7. Greedy grabbiness.
8. Mutual exchange, especially of trade privileges and concessions between two countries.
9. Sufficient to keep alive.
10. To EVADE immediate action, in order to gain time or avoid trouble.

24. WHAT'S ANOTHER WORD FOR IT?

What's an alternative word, to give variety, for each of the following?

1. peppery (of somebody's disposition)
2. roundabout
3. mercy
4. clotting (of the blood)
5. smugness
6. QUALM
7. accompanying
8. dictionary
9. double-talk
10. blot out

25. WHAT'S THE EXACT WORD FOR IT?

How many times somebody says, "I have the idea, but I can't think of the word for it." For each of the following ideas or definitions, four possibilities are offered. Only one is right. Pick the right one in each case:

1. To destroy completely:
(a) ANNOTATE   (b) INCARCERATE   (c) annihilate   (d) PETRIFY

2. Government in which a privileged upper class rules; that class is a:
(a) TIMOCRACY   (b) MOBOCRACY   (c) aristocracy   (d) tyranny

85

3. Hired murderer:

(a) BLACKGUARD (b) assassin   (c) THUG   (d) bandit

4. Making up for a wrong, loss, sin, or injury:

(a) SCAPEGOAT   (b) agony   (c) atonement   (d) redemption

5. To declare frankly and openly:

(a) ASSEVERATE (b) AVOW   (c) protest   (d) ACCLIMATE

6. Officer of court who has charge of prisoners in the courtroom:

(a) CHANCELLOR (b) prosecutor (c) BAILIFF   (d) COUNCILLOR

7. Having to do with public finances or treasury matters:

(a) FIDUCIARY   (b) trusting   (c) FISCAL   (d) MONOPOLISTIC

8. Tool for boring holes in wood, or in the earth:

(a) TERMITE   (b) gear   (c) AUGER   (d) plane

9. Soldier or sailor who has been wounded, killed, or lost:

(a) CASTAWAY   (b) CASUALTY   (c) STOWAWAY   (d) CATALYST

10. Stand or rack for seasoning bottles:

(a) slot   (b) CASTOR   (c) ANTIMACASSAR (d) DOILY

11. Condition of having an evil and unwholesome character:

(a) DELIQUESCENCE (b) MALTREATMENT (c) DEVIATION (d) DEGENERACY

12. To bend or turn aside:

(a) slip   (b) DEFLECT   (c) REGRESS   (d) encircle

13. To trace the outline of:

(a) CIRCUMNAVIGATE (b) traverse (c) survey   (d) DELINEATE

14. Condition of having become worse; or the process of worsening:

(a) DETERIORATION(b) ENCOMIUM   (c) PROFANATION (d) DETONATION

15. To disregard the sacredness of:

(a) DISINTEGRATE (b) DESECRATE (c) disfigure   (d) ICONOCLASM

16. Having many shapes:

(a) POLYGONAL   (b) MULTIFORM   (c) MORPHOLOGY (d) ELUSIVE

17. All-devouring:

(a) ESURIENT   (b) OMNIVOROUS (c) CARNIVOROUS (d) RUMINANT

18. Act or process of swinging back and forth:

(a) DEVIATION   (b) dependency (c) OSCILLATION (d) OSCULATION

86

19. Established by long usage or custom:
(a) insured   (b) TABOOED   (c) PRESCRIPTIVE (d) MANDATORY

20. Circular tower, building, or pit in which green food for farm animals is stored:
(a) bin   (b) SILO   (c) elevator   (d) CHUTE

21. Sudden outrush of troops from a besieged fort or town, to attack the besiegers:
(a) ONSLAUGHT   (b) SORTIE   (c) breach   (d) CATAPULT

22. Very loud or powerful in sound:
(a) RAUCOUS   (b) explosive   (c) STENTORIAN   (d) MNEMONIC

23. Harsh-sounding, creaking, or grating:
(a) RACHITIC   (b) STRIDENT   (c) DETONATING   (d) BANSHEE

24. To come as something additional or interrupting:
(a) AGGRANDIZE   (b) SUPERSEDE   (c) DEVIATE   (d) SUPERVENE

25. Solution of plot in play or story—the outcome:
(a) suspense   (b) climax   (c) DENOUEMENT (d) disaster

DOUBLING YOUR WORD-SCORE

What the NUMEROLOGY of words keeps turning up is just this fact: *standard words in Thorndike's second ten thousand are, in the main, of classical origin.* A Chinese MANDARIN has to know thirty thousand separate picture-characters to read his classics. Luckily most books, magazines, and newspapers in English can be read easily by anybody who has a vocabulary of twenty thousand words. And while some of our learned phrase patterns and allusions are as complex as Chinese picture-writing, ours still are made up of combinations of twenty-six letters. So it's not so hard to double a vocabulary in English.

The master key to the problem of acquiring these long, abstract words, indeed, is the fact that they are most of them derived from Greek and Latin—five thousand of them from seventy Latin and thirty Greek roots, with special twists of meaning given by prefixes or SUFFIXES *from the same source.* It may seem odd to bring two dead languages into the picture to speed up learning new words in English. But once you know these few key roots, prefixes and SUFFIXES, you can take a lot of long words apart without any trouble, when you meet them, and make a good guess at their primary or literal meaning.

Actually you already know a lot of these roots, whether you're consciously aware of it or not. And learning the rest is no great trick. A beginner in a foreign language does well to master a thousand new words in a year, learning them all three ways: for reading, writing, and speaking. It should not be such a heavy chore to acquire a hundred basic Greek and Latin stems, *for recognition purposes only*. It's a prize short cut that will pay big dividends in extending the command of words. And it will help make the other short cuts shorter.

Quiz Keys for Chapter V

23. Page 85.

1. polyglot	6. radiation
2. populist	7. rapacity
3. potentiality	8. reciprocity
4. primacy	9. subsistence
5. primogeniture	10. temporize

24. Page 85.

1. choleric	6. compunction
2. circuitous	7. concomitant
3. clemency	8. lexicon
4. coagulation	9. equivocation
5. complacency	10. expunge

25. Page 85.

1. (c)	6. (c)	11. (d)	16. (b)	21. (b)
2. (c)	7. (c)	12. (b)	17. (b)	22. (c)
3. (b)	8. (c)	13. (d)	18. (c)	23. (b)
4. (c)	9. (b)	14. (a)	19. (c)	24. (d)
5. (b)	10. (b)	15. (b)	20. (b)	25. (c)

100 WILL GET YOU 5000

Before World War I we got along with only one PHOBIA. That was HYDROPHOBIA, the fear of water, the most startling symptom of rabies. It was acquired by the bite of a mad dog, and was a relatively simple, though SPECTACULAR, affliction. Now, since Freud and Jung, we have a whole flock of phobias, mysterious HOBGOBLINS of the mind which may be lurking in anyone's SUB-CONSCIOUS, ready to pop out any time. Here's a partial list from the PSYCHOANALYST'S REPERTORY, all manufactured out of Greek stems grafted onto phobia:

ACROPHOBIA	acro-, high place	fear of heights
AGORAPHOBIA	agora-, market-place	fear of open spaces
ALGOPHOBIA	algo-, pain	fear of pain
ASTROPHOBIA	astro-, star	fear of thunder and lightning
CLAUSTROPHOBIA	claustro-, closed	fear of closed places
COPROPHOBIA	copro-, filth	fear of filth
HEMATOPHOBIA	hemato-, blood	fear of blood
GLOSSOPHOBIA	glossa-, tongue	fear of speaking
MYSOPHOBIA	myso-, dirt	fear of contamination
NECROPHOBIA	necro-, dead	fear of dead bodies
NYCTOPHOBIA	nycto-, night	fear of darkness
PATHOPHOBIA	patho-, suffering	fear of suffering
PHONOPHOBIA	phono-, sound	fear of speaking aloud
PHOTOPHOBIA	photo-, light	fear of light
SITOPHOBIA	sito-, food	fear of eating
TAPHOPHOBIA	tapho-, burial	fear of being buried alive
THANATOPHOBIA	thanato-, death	fear of death
TOXOPHOBIA	toxo-, poison	fear of being poisoned
XENOPHOBIA	xeno-, stranger	fear of strangers
ZOOPHOBIA	zoo-, animal	fear of animals

Is there anybody in the house who didn't already know phobia? And of the Greek stems combining with it to describe these PATHOLOGICAL forms of fear, it's an even bet that you also knew *claustro-, phono-, photo-, thanato-, patho-,* and *xeno-* for 'foreigner'—if the account of John Hersey's use of it in his Hiroshima article clicked (see p. 84).

Such compounds as ANGLOPHOBE and RUSSOPHOBE are also familiar. Here the fear gets mixed up with hate. You can make up similar compounds, if you're annoyed with anyone. Just hitch -*phobe* onto the name —FRANCOPHOBE, for instance. Already this adds up to twenty-five words from one, *phobos*, fear. And it's still open for return engagements.

So far nobody has coined a single word for "fear of ATOMIC bombs." But this unnamed and most rational of all fears has brought into the news the SPELEOLOGICAL Society of America. Its members, nicknamed "Spelunkers," have begun intensively cruising the lower levels of the Mammoth Cave, the Carlsbad Caverns, and other great caves into which our key industrial plants and workers may have to be moved if some other power also develops atomic bombs.

"Spelunkers" comes from the Latin *spelunca*, a cave, which in turn is first cousin to the Greek word, *spelunke*. SPELEOLOGY means the "science of caves." Coiners of the term took the combining form *speleo-*, from *speleum*, Latinized spelling of Greek *spelaion*, cave, and added -*logy*, from *logos*, word. Because words play such a large part in reasoning, *logos* came also to mean in Greek "reasoning," and finally "study" or "science."

Undoubtedly you've long known about "-ologies," and heard irreverent persons joke about them, sometimes with reason. But the jokers might have more respect for *logos* if they knew that it enters into at least 156 words in English. Here's a partial collection. Remember that the stem can mean either "word," "reasoning," "study (of)," or "science (of)."

26. How Many -Ologies Do You Know by Name?

1. ANALOGY	16. DECALOGUE	31. LOGARITHMS	46. PHILOLOGY
2. ANGELOLOGY	17. DEMONOLOGY	32. logic	47. PHRASEOLOGY
3. ANTHOLOGY	18. DIALOGUE	33. LOGISTICS	48. PHRENOLOGY
4. ANTHROPOLOGY	19. DOXOLOGY	34. LOGOGRAM	49. PHYSIOLOGY
5. APOLOGUE	20. ECLOGUE	35. LOGOTYPE	50. PSYCHOLOGY
6. APOLOGY	21. ENTOMOLOGY	36. LOGOGRAPH	51. PROLOGUE
7. ARCHEOLOGY	22. EPILOGUE	37. METEOROLOGY	52. TAUTOLOGY
8. ASTROLOGY	23. ESCHATOLOGY	38. MINERALOGY	53. TECHNOLOGY
9. BACTERIOLOGY	24. ETHNOLOGY	39. MONOLOGUE	54. TERMINOLOGY
10. biology	25. ETYMOLOGY	40. MORPHOLOGY	55. TETRALOGY
11. CATALOGUE	26. EULOGY	41. MYTHOLOGY	56. theology
12. CHRONOLOGY	27. GENEALOGY	42. NEOLOGISM	57. TRAVELOGUE
13. CONCHOLOGY	28. geology	43. ORNITHOLOGY	58. TRILOGY
14. COSMOLOGY	29. HISTOLOGY	44. OSTEOLOGY	59. ZOOLOGY
15. CRIMINOLOGY	30. ILLOGICAL	45. PATHOLOGY	60. DENDROLOGY

How Many of These Are Greek to You?

Similarly, if we take the stem GRAPH- from the Greek *grapho,* to write, we find that a great many English words derive from it. How many of these can you define?

1. AUTOGRAPH	8. COSMOGRAPHY	15. LEXICOGRAPHER	22. PHOTOGRAPHER
2. BIBLIOGRAPHY	9. DICTOGRAPH	16. LITHOGRAPH	23. PYROGRAPHY
3. BIOGRAPHER	10. DIGRAPH	17. LOGOGRAPH	24. SEISMOGRAPH
4. CALLIGRAPHY	11. geography	18. MONOGRAPH	25. STENOGRAPHER
5. CEROGRAPH	12. GRAPHIC	19. MULTIGRAPH	26. STYLOGRAPH
6. CHIROGRAPHY	13. GRAPHITE	20. ORTHOGRAPHY	27. TELEGRAPH
7. CINEMATOGRAPH	14. HOLOGRAPH	21. paragraph	28. TYPOGRAPHY

This is just a small sample of the Greek you've been using, even if you didn't know it for Greek. Much of this Greek element came into English through the Latin. The Romans were the great TRANSMITTERS of HELLENIC culture to Western Europe and England.

What we call the *Romance* element in English comes either direct from Greek and Latin, or through the French. It makes up three fifths of the words in the total English vocabulary, so it deserves a close look. Since it is so MASSIVE and RAMIFYING a collection, we need to pick out the key exhibits so we'll know our way around the museum.

Latin in the Headlines

Luckily most readers know a lot of Latin even if they aren't aware of it. Check through the 20,000 commonest words in English and you'll find 261 have come over absolutely unchanged from Latin, spelling and all, as against only 89 from the Greek—a third as many. Of the 261 Latin imports, nearly all are in the higher brackets. They are learned words to us, even those that were household words to the Romans. Besides these Latin words that have been thoroughly DOMESTICATED in English, there are many others that can on occasion be used in everyday writing.

A headline in *Time* for September 9, 1946, runs: *Jus, Imperium, Pax.* The story is about the 2000th anniversary of Julius Caesar's landing in Britain. It's pegged on an editorial in the London *Times,* which admits it may be fanciful to imagine. . . .

that by any MYSTICAL communion a spark of the VIRGILIAN light of empire was tended through the centuries in Merlin's cave. Yet somehow the grand ideals of Roman dominion have not been lost in the modern world: *jus,* the conception of a law that should TRANSCEND the limitations of the small people who first conceived it, and become at last the GUARANTOR of justice to all sorts and conditions of men; *imperium,* the principle of a dominion that can enable all manner of races, languages and faiths to live together within the bounds of a single system of ordered rule, and of a citizenship that, though it may begin as the privilege of a governing race, will gradually be extended until it is enjoyed by all; and *pax,* the product of the other two, the belief in the mission of imperial government, based evenly upon the foundations of justice and national authority, to bring in the golden age when war shall cease from the earth.

Jus Romanum, Imperium Romanum, Pax Romana—by changing the adjective Britain has given to each of them a changed flavor and CONNOTATION. But that is only because the tradition at the heart of them is a living thing, and grows continually. After two thousand years an imperial people can with a clear title claim its spiritual ANCESTRY.

Jus Britannicum, Imperium Britannicum, and *Pax Britannica* might not waken the same editorial admiration in Ireland, The Dutch Indies, or Palestine, but just as language these historic Latin expressions have an organ tone that *British law, British Empire,* and *British peace* could not equal.

As if it were open season for Latin, the *New Yorker* for the same week has a four column footnote, "Antepenultimatum," by its wittiest and most learned WORDSMITH, A. J. Liebling, giving the newspaper headline writers a going over for calling the U.S. note to Tito an ULTIMATUM. As you'll remember, we didn't threaten to go to war unless Tito returned our fliers who had been shot down, but only to take him before the United Nations Security Council. So, says Liebling, this was not an ULTIMATUM, and he continues:

After reading newspapers about the "ULTIMATUM" all day, I began to wonder whether I *did* know what the word meant. It was as if I were in one of those dreams in which familiar words become *dissociated* from their usual meanings, or as if I were listening to Whitey Bimstein talk double-talk. So I got down a ninety-five-cent dictionary which I bought one time in a cigar store and which gives only one meaning for each word, and that the commonest one; it is an excellent guide to everyday usage. It says, "Final conditions offered as the basis of an agreement, prior to the declaration of hostilities"—which is how I have always used "ULTIMATUM." Only in part reassured, I carried my research to *Webster's* UNABRIDGED, which says, "A final proposition or condition; esp., the final propositions, or terms, offered by either of the parties in a DIPLOMATIC negotiation; the best terms that a NEGOTIATOR will offer, the rejection of which usually ends negotiations." It was evident in the note to Yugoslavia, though, that the United States contemplated further negotiations, via the United Nations, in the event of a rejection. To make surer than sure, I went to the thirteen-volume Oxford Dictionary. It defines "ultimatum" as "In DIPLOMACY, the final terms presented by one power (or group of powers) to another, the rejection of which may lead to the severing of DIPLOMATIC relations, and eventually to a declaration of war." The rejection of the note to Tito could have led immediately only to a complaint to an international diplomatic TRIBUNAL, and while that might have eventually led to a break, and that to war, the note could at worst have been described as no more than a kind of antepenultimatum.

Liebling's punch line, which explains his title, is all the more apt because it's based on one of the first rules taught in Latin grammar, that Latin words are accented on the next to last syllable—or PENULT—if the vowel is long; otherwise on the ANTEPENULT, the syllable third from the end. So an *antepenultimatum* is three stages short of war!

27. WHEN WE TALK ROMAN

A good many of the Latin words that have come over into English unchanged, are, like *ultimatum,* concerned with diplomacy, politics, or law. How many of the following forty can you define?

ALIAS	LICTOR	QUAESTOR	SPONSOR
ARBITER	MEDIATOR	QUORUM	STATUS
BONUS	MODERATOR	QUOTA	superior
CAUCUS	orator	REFERENDUM	TESTATOR
COADJUTOR	PERPETRATOR	REGIMEN	TOGA
DICTATOR	PERSECUTOR	ROSTRUM	TRANSGRESSOR
DICTUM	PLEBS	rumor (cf. "rumor	TRIUMVIR
ELECTOR	PRAETOR	factory" and	
FIAT	PROCONSUL	"whispering	
GENS	PROCTOR	campaign")	
INTERREGNUM	PROCURATOR	sanctum	
LEX	PROPAGANDA	solicitor	

28. MEDICAL LATIN THAT'S ALSO COMMON ENGLISH

Most of our everyday words for parts of the body, common complaints, and remedies, come from Anglo-Saxon. Since these terms are not precise enough for medical use, doctors have continued to employ the Latin (and Greek) terms which they once used exclusively when all physicians wrote and lectured in Latin (as they still for the most part write prescriptions in abbreviated PHARMACIST's Latin). Of these medical Latin terms, 46 have SHUTTLED into the 20,000 commonest words in the language. How many of them do you know well enough to convince a doctor?

ANEMIA	INSOMNIA	REFLUX	STERNUM
AORTA	IRIS	REGIMEN	STUPOR
CANCER (liter-	LAUDANUM	REJUVENATOR	TETANUS
ally, a crab)	MANIA	RETINA	THALLUS
CEREBRUM	MATRIX	SALIVA	THYMUS
CEREBELLUM	MEDULLA	SANITARIUM	TIBIA
CORNEA	NAUSEA	SERUM (news to the	TUMOR
CORTEX	NITER	Romans, in the	TYMPANUM
CRANIUM	OPIUM	modern medical	TYPHUS
DELIRIUM	OVUM	sense; in Latin it	ULCER
FEMUR	PALLOR	means "whey" or	
FUNGI	PELVIS	"watery fluid")	
GENUS	PLEXUS	SINUS	
INCISOR	RECTUM	SPUTUM	

Besides these forty words from politics and forty-six from medicine, the remaining 180-odd that have come over from Latin unchanged are mostly words that express a single specific meaning (see p. 125). They are single-shot terms.

THE ROMANS WERE LONG ON ACTION

To locate the Latin words that have fathered a flock of DERIVATIVES in English, we have to look elsewhere. Among those that have been most PROLIFIC are certain words expressing action, which was the thing the Romans were best at. And each of these Latin verbs may figure in English in any one of several forms, so you have to know not only the stem form, but its main changes. But you soon learn to detect these mild disguises.

One Latin stem, *fac-*, from the verb *facio*, means both "do" and "make." This one stem yields sixty-five English words, without exhausting its possibilities. The last eighteen are beyond the commonest 10,000.

29. USING WORDS THAT COME FROM FAC

In the words which follow, *fac* enters in one of its various forms: *fac, fic, fact, fect, fict, factur,* etc.

fact	feature	affection	feat
perfect	manufacture	defeat	forfeit
difficult	sacrifice	difficulty	imperfect
effect	affect	perfection	certificate
fashion	factory	artificial	edifice
affair	official	defect	faction
benefit	sufficient	faculty	fashionable

deficiency	beneficial	affectation	facilitate
defective	counterfeit	artifice	forfeiture
effective	efficacy	benefactor	surfeit
facility	efficient	efficiency	unaffected
factor	infection	facile	

IMPERFECTION	CONFECTION	BENEFICIARY	EXEMPLIFICATION
PROFICIENT	AFFECTED	PONTIFICAL	COMFIT
FEASIBLE	DISAFFECTION	PUTREFACTION	FACSIMILE
INEFFICIENCY	MANUFACTORY	REFECTION	
SUFFICIENCY	UNIFICATION	VERSIFICATION	

Taking the group from IMPERFECTION down to the end, which is the right word to fill in the blank in each of the following sentences:

1. The meat was far gone in —————.
2. A poet needs to know the rules of ————— and when to break them.
3. The troops were in a state of —————.
4. It was an admirable ————— of democratic methods.
5. He gave Araminta a ————— box for her birthday, and acquired great merit in her eyes, since she loved sweet things.
6. He was the chief ————— under the will.
7. She had a MINCING and ————— manner.
8. He wrote in a TOPLOFTY and ————— style.
9. The POLITBURO fired the top officials in the COSMETICS industry, because of their —————.
10. The process of ————— is not yet complete in Jugoslavia.

Taking the stem *pon-*, from *ponere,* to put or place, we find that it also gives a big yield: 35 DERIVATIVES. Omitting those in the commonest 10,000, as already familiar in meaning, we find a sizable number remaining in the higher brackets.

30. SPOTTING WORDS DERIVED FROM PON

The combining forms for *pon* include also *pos, posit.* Choosing among its derivatives, can you put the right word in each sentence blank?

DEPOSITION	DEPOSITORY	IMPOST	POSITIVIST
COMPOSITE	INTERPOSITION	APPOSITE	TRANSPOSITION
DECOMPOSITION	COMPOST	EXPOSITOR	
EXPONENT	JUXTAPOSITION	PROPOUND	

1. The picture was a ————— photograph.
2. ————— duties are never popular, but are any taxes?
3. It was an ————— quotation.

4. The judge ordered that a _____ be taken, since the witness was BEDRIDDEN and could not come to court.
5. Dean Inge is a notable _____ of ANGLICAN views.
6. A long spell of hot sun following the rain speeded up the _____ of the _____ heap.
7. The pianist had mastered the difficult tricks of _____.
8. The _____ of the two diagrams caused the confusion in interpretation.
9. A Swiss bank was picked as a _____ for the funds.
10. Byrnes left Dunn to _____ the American view.

Leadership was a Roman specialty and the stem DUC, from *ducere,* to lead, has gone on playing a strong role in English. In fact, via the Italian, it has recently given us a new loan word of unhappy memory, *Il Duce,* closely tied in with FASCISM, from the *fasces,* or bundle of rods carried by the LICTORS who guarded Roman CONSULS.

31. FORTY WORDS FROM ONE

Here are forty derivatives from *duc, duct:*

produce	introduction	DEDUCT	EDUCE
conduct	seduce	AQUEDUCT	TRADUCE
education	duchess	CONDUCIVE	DUCHY
introduce	reproduce	DEDUCTION	ABDUCT
reduce	reproduction	VIADUCT	INDUCTION
duke	productive	DUCAL	ABDUCTION
induce	conduit	SEDUCTIVE	CONDUCIBLE
conductor	dukedom	DUCAT	DEDUCIBLE
production	CONDUCE	ADDUCE	INDUCT
educate	DEDUCE	DUCTIBLE	SEDUCTION

Fill in the blank with the right word, drawing on the derivatives of DUC from CONDUCE to the end:

1. His record did not _____ to confidence.
2. He was able to _____ very good reasons for the move.
3. An _____ from the SERAGLIO was not easy to contrive.
4. The conclusion was _____ from the premises.
5. The lawyer tried to _____ his opponent.
6. He had not taken all the _____s which the income tax law permitted.
7. Reasoning by _____ cannot give the certainty possible in _____ logic, since it is not possible to exhaust the instances.
8. Da Vinci did not find the _____ service wholly to his taste in Milan.

9. Molotov's tone was not —————— to the best feeling.

10. —————— is under some circumstances punishable as a crime.

The Romans had a handy system for building up a flock of verbs from a single basic stem. The Latin word for "write" is *scribere*. Its combining forms are SCRIB, SCRIPT. Take a close look at the string of derivatives we have from it:

ASCRIBE	SUPERSCRIBE	inscription	subscriber
CIRCUMSCRIBE	TRANSCRIBE	manuscript	SUPERSCRIPTION
INSCRIBE	(all of above	indescribable	scribe
prescribe	are verbs)	NONDESCRIPT	scribble
PROSCRIBE	CONSCRIPT	prescription	script
subscribe	description	RESCRIPT	scripture

The first eight describe certain special types of writing, by putting a prefix on the basic stem *scrib*. In Saxon English we say "write him down as one to be killed in the purge." The Romans used the one word, *proscribere*, which meant to "write forth" or "publish" a name on the condemned list. We have borrowed this word practically unchanged, to express the same meaning. *Prescribere* was "to give advance directions, to write beforehand (*prae*)." *Where we tend to hitch* DIRECTIVE *words loosely to the far end of a verb, the Romans put theirs in front, and glued them to the main stem.* Instead of saying "sail around" they said *circumnavigare*, from which we get "CIRCUMNAVIGATE." Rather than asking a man to "write his name under" a petition, they said *subscribere*, from which we get *subscriber* and *subscription*.

ROMAN SMALL CHANGE STILL CIRCULATING

Many of these classical prefixes—and SUFFIXES, too, such as the *-able* in *indescribable*, are still in active use in English. Using *ante*, the Latin prefix meaning "before," "in front of," we make new words quite freely, writing ANTEDILUVIAN, or ANTEDATE, or ANTECHAMBER, without any worry over the fact that such words did not exist in classical Latin. Similarly we use *post*, "after," when we speak of *postwar* legislation, just as we use the opposite prefix, *pr(a)e*, "before," in PRENATAL or pre-war. *Co-*, and *con*, combining forms of *cum*, "with," provides us with *corespondent*, "one jointly answerable with another," now specialized to mean the "other man" or "other woman" in a divorce suit. We have *coed*, a COLLOQUIAL abbreviation of *coeducational student* (feminine gender).

The prefix *re*, meaning "back" or "again" we use almost recklessly.

97

We even add it to a Latin word which arrived in our language already equipped with it, and *re-refer* something to a committee.

Of the SUFFIXES hitched on at the end of words, *-able* or *-ible*, from the Latin *-abilis, -ibilis*, meaning "able to be" or "causing," is found in INNUMERABLE English words. So with *-il, ile*, from Latin *ilis, ile*, "belonging to," as in SERVILE "belonging to a slave" and hence "submissive" or "CRINGING." A very common one is *-ive*, from Latin *-ivus, -ivum*, "relating to" or "involving," as in the instances *fugitive*, "relating to flight," CURSIVE, "involving running," as a cursive hand, referring to the difference between a running and a printed script. *-Ion*, meaning "act of," or "state of," is also in widespread use.

GREEK IS AN EXACT LANGUAGE

Greek prefixes and suffixes, fewer in number, are mostly used in exact, fixed, and unvarying senses. *Anti*, meaning "against," is one of the most common. In fact we use it colloquially to mean just a plain "anti"—an "againster." A man may be *anti*-PROHIBITIONIST, *anti-New Deal*, *anti-Russian*, or, like the cartoon character in the DEFUNCT humorous magazine *Life*, *Old Anti-Everything*. The Greek prefixes

a, an,	not		*hyper,*	over
apo,	from		*hypo,*	under
cata, kata,	down		*meta,*	beyond, after
dia,	through		*peri,*	around
ec, ek,	out of		*syn,*	with

are still employed in compounding words the Greeks never heard of. DIATHERMY, "a heating through," by deep heat which warms the tissues beneath the skin, without heating the surface, is drawn from a word coined out of Greek in 1833 by a French PHYSICIST, Melloni. *Diathermy* itself first appeared in print around 1910.

When it comes to Greek suffixes, there are only a few in common use in English, but they are hard-worked. *-Ism* is hitched on to all sorts of words, to a degree that leads us to speak of "isms" when we mean doctrines that are much discussed, such as COMMUNISM, Fascism, Buchmanism, New Humanism, and Existentialism. By changing the ending a little to *-ist*, we get the suffix which distinguishes an ADHERENT of any of these "isms." As Harold Laski said to a lot of heckling American Communists when he was lecturing in New York, "Come, come, we're all Marxists here, you in your way, and I in Marx's."

The Greek suffix -ize, meaning "make," or "make like" is very active. It forms such compounds as SYSTEMATIZE, "to make systematic"; AUTOMATIZE, "to make automatic," often used to refer to the reduction of a person to an AUTOMATON through HYPNOTISM, or to the process of converting a complicated learning-pattern into a habit requiring little conscious attention. We also attach this SUFFIX freely to proper names; *Russianize, Hitlerize, Babbittize.*

Besides these authentic Greek suffixes, parts of Greek words are sometimes split off, and used as if they were suffixes. *Walkathon,* made by analogy with MARATHON, is one instance, *talkathon* another. *Walk* and *talk* are good Anglo-Saxon words, and to hang on them the tail-end of a Greek word, *-athon,* which is in no sense a suffix, is a triumph of language manufacture by the Greekless.

Actually these HYBRIDS are no funnier than the popular newspaper term, *atom-splitting.* Literally, this means "splitting the UNSPLITTABLE." (Remember the gag about unscrewing the INSCRUTABLE?) Democritus deliberately labeled what he surmised to be the smallest particle of matter *atomos,* from *a,* not, and *tomein,* to cut: that which cannot be cut, split, or divided is an atom. But anybody who wants to talk about "atom-splitting" can be sure of being understood—although the PHYSICISTS who turned the trick prefer to speak of "NUCLEAR FISSION."

OPEN SESAMES

What all this Greek and Latin small change still in circulation amounts to is this: once you have it in hand, it multiplies amazingly the number of words you master every time you fix in your mind a new Latin or Greek root. Once you know the common prefixes and suffixes, you can break hard words down into their component parts much more readily, and make a good stab at the literal meaning. You can sight-read

male	*DICT*	*-ion*
"evil"	"spoken"	"that which"

which RESHUFFLES into "that evil which is spoken"—or a curse.

The basic Greek and Latin stems thus indicate clearly *the main families of classical words* in English, while the prefixes and suffixes mark relationships of meaning within each clan group of DERIVATIVES. Old-fashioned work in word-analysis used to include so many roots, and throw so many prefixes at the reader all at once, that he got bogged down. Often the method proved to be like one of those memory-systems which doubled the work of memorizing.

To avoid such a hazard, a Word-Analyzer has been placed toward the end of this chapter, presenting in a compact table the prefixes and suffixes needed, and a summary list of the 100 main Greek and Latin stems, plus some additional Latin and Greek words that have yielded a good many derivatives. While you're making analyses a few at a time, with the Word-Analyzer, it's a good idea to try a much easier approach by seeing how readily you can slip words already identified as coming from a given stem into the right slots in a short fable. That's why for each of the groups of derivatives that follow, an anecdote or fable is supplied, with blanks for the key words which have to be sorted out from the list just above. You don't have to worry about the ETYMOLOGY: that's VOUCHED for by the grouping. Just concentrate on meanings. As to these, you can proceed by trial and error to decipher the literal meaning, then make your best guess as to which word will make sense in the context.

32. Put the Whole Family to Work

The list which follows comprises those Latin stems, in their various combining forms, which, with those already treated, have contributed most largely to the vocabulary of English. The Frenchified form of the Latin stem is often given, too. Each stem is followed by a list of derivatives. How does the meaning of the Latin stem afford a clue to the present meaning or meanings of the English word? The fables under each group contain blanks to be filled in with the appropriate word.

Study the stems, and the words derived from them, at the rate of five stems a day; or, at the outside, not more than ten. Take plenty of time to look up in the dictionary all the words of which you have the least doubt, after you've made your best guess. Spread out the work over several weeks, while you are continuing with the rest of the book and the accompanying shorter word-quizzes.

Note carefully: There are in each list more words than there are blanks to be filled in the sentences. The numbers in the blanks refer to the answers in the key at the end of the chapter, p. 135.

AG, ACT (ig, g, actu), from *agere, actus:* to do, move, urge on, put in motion, drive.

act	agent	prodigal	PEDAGOGUE [1]	COGENT	MANAGEABLE
exact	management	transaction	AMBIGUOUS	EXIGENCY	AGENDA
manage	manager	mitigate	AMBIGUITY	LITIGATION	
agency	agitation	navigate	VARIEGATED	CASTIGATE	
actor	enact	synagogue [1]	ACTUATE	COGITATE	

WAR ON THE LANDLORD

What the renting ——1—— called an ——2—— in the lease, I called downright SKULLDUGGERY. They had a lot of fancy and ——3—— legal VERBIAGE which just invited ——4——. Add to that the fact that the building ——5—— was a thoroughly bad ——6——, and you'll readily see why I ——7—— the ——8—— for the landlord when he called for the rent. The ——9—— was not exactly ——10—— with heat, either. I wrote them a few ——11—— reasons why I might have to appeal to OPA. They said they didn't want any of that kind of ——12—— starting and that so far as they were concerned, I could move into the ——13—— next door, or buy a houseboat, trailer, or Quonset hut. This didn't ——14—— my wrath, and ——15——d by the strongest public spirit, I wrote back a letter full of massive insults for all landlords.

APT (att, ept), from *aptus:* fit or fitted, the p.p. of obsolete verb *apere,* to fasten, join together.

apt	adapt	APTITUDE	ADAPTABLE	INAPT	INEPT
attitude	adaptation	ADAPTABILITY			

REPORTER'S ARCH-ENEMY

The cluck on the copy desk was so ——1—— that he'd murder any ——2—— phrase that survived the rewrite man. Every time he uttered PLATITUDES in stained glass ——3——s, he broke the glass. His ——4—— was NIL, and his ——5—— to the work was minus zero.

CERN, CRET (cre), from *cernere, cretus:* to see, to sift, to distinguish, to separate.

certain	secretary	certainly	discretion	certify	DISCERNMENT
secret	decree	certificate	secrecy	EXCRETION	INDISCRETION
concern	discern	discreet	secretion	INDISCREET	DISCERNIBLE
		SECRETIVE			

BUTCH

The Mayor, while a man of ——1——, was famous for his calculated ——2——s. Though ——3—— by habit, he could on occasion be glaringly ——4——. His motives for exploding were not always immediately ——5——, but his secretary usually could make a pretty good guess as to what was in the wind. Sometimes the blast backfired, and the Mayor was accustomed to say, "When I make a mistake, it's a beaut."

[1] Strictly, from the Greek through the Latin.

ART (artis, ert), from *ars, artis:* skill, art, method.

art	artistic	inert	ARTLESS	INERTIA	INERTLY
artist	artillery	artifice	ARTIFICER	ARTISTRY	ARTIFACT
artificial	artful	artisan			

You Can't Hurt an Elephant with Buckshot

It was always hard to say when Claire was just being ——1——, when ——2——, and when ——3——, so skilfully were her personal and political ——4——s INTERWOVEN. When she moved up the lighter ——5—— of her wit to shoot buckshot at the ——6—— and CHUCKLE-HEADED leaders of her party, she showed rare ——7—— in placing her shots. Not that she really jolted the massive ——8—— of the elephant, or reached its MAHOUTS with their still thicker hides; but for the moment the beast and its riders gave the illusion of moving less ——9——. But even Claire could not dislodge the PETRIFIED FOSSIL planks in the platform; these will last until they are dug up as ——10—— by the ARCHAEOLOGISTS of 4946, and pronounced the work of clumsy ——11——s.

AUD, AUDIT (audi, edi, ey, eis), from *audire, auditus:* to hear.

obey	obedient	auditor	OBEISANCE	AUDITORIUM	AUDIT
audience	disobey	disobedience	AUDITORY	INAUDIBLE	AUDITION
obedience	audible				

Too Bad It Can't Happen

The Radio Listeners Guild, not content with writing nasty letters about soap opera, spot announcements, middle commercials and other abominations, decided to organize flying SQUADRONS to salt studio ——1——, and make their disapproval ——2——. When the cheerleader called for applause, they hissed or jeered, and kept it up until the succeeding lines were ——3——. Refusing to make ——4—— to the HUCKSTERS of the air, they were denied tickets to programs; but other members of the Guild took their places. Pretty soon ——5—— for the advertising agencies and the sponsors reported that the jeering caused a drop in sales of the product advertised; and, even more deadly, the Hooper ratings were falling fast. Soon these ——6——s had their effect. Programs improved, and there were a lot of ——7——s for new talent.

CAN, CANT (cent, chant), from *canere, cantus:* to sing.

| accent | enchant | CANT | CANTO | RECANT | CANTATA |
| chant | enchantment | ACCENTUATE | RECANTATION | CANTICLE | |

Collegiate Conductor

The CHORAL conductor had a slangy ——1——, wore a sweater and unpressed slacks, but he could cast a kind of ——2—— over his singers. Whether he was conducting a ——3——, a ——4——, or a stately ——5——, he got results. He was criticized for swearing, but far from being willing to ——6——, he violently ——7——d the negative. And he never talked musical ——8——.

CAP, CAPT, CAPTUS (cip, ceiv, cept, ceipt, ceit), from *capere, captus:* to take, seize, hold.

except	capable	exception	exceptional	susceptible	RECIPIENT
accept	conceive	reception	precept	acceptable	PARTICIPLE
occupy	capture	captivity	participate	deception	INCIPIENT
deceive	occupation	conceit	anticipation	emancipation	PARTICIPANT
principal	capacity	deceit	incapable	municipal	
perceive	captive	capacious	principality	CAPABILITY	

THE POLITICO

Politics is an odd trade, but make no mistake about it, it's a full-time ——1——. A politician must have a good ——2—— of himself, must be able on occasion to ——3—— without getting a reputation for ——4——. He has sold himself into ——5—— to his backers, and he is usually ——6—— to pressure. WILLY-NILLY he must be a ——7—— in community activities, must attend ——8——s and other ceremonial functions, and on occasion demonstrate his ——9—— to carry liquor. While in office, he cannot hope for ——10—— from these social duties, even if ——11—— affairs suffer. He must mouth conventional ——12——s at church gatherings, and have a fund of ——13—— jokes for service club luncheons. Yet he will be criticized if he gets tangled up in a dangling ——14—— when he orates, and accused of ——15—— SENILITY if he muffs his words in a radio talk.

COR, CORD, CORDI (cour), from *cor, cordis:* the heart.

according	encourage	accord	discord	core	RECORDER
record	accordingly	discourage	concord	encouragement	CONCORDANCE
courage	cordial	courageous			

SON OF A LEXICOGRAPHER GOES ASTRAY

A Shakespeare ——1—— shows that he used just 17,677 different words in his works. It is hard to reconcile this figure with the recent findings by a son of a LEXICOGRAPHER that a good American vocabulary runs to 150,000 words—8½ times as many as Shakespeare used. There's a ——2—— here somewhere.

CRED, CREDIT (cre), from *credere, creditus:* to believe, trust to.

credit	creed	discredit	CREDENTIAL	CREDIBLE	CREDENCE
creditor	credulous	CREDITABLE	MISCREANT	ACCREDIT	INCREDIBLE
credulity	incredulous	INCREDULITY			

THE MYSTERY OF FAITH

Tertullian said that he believed the Christian ——1—— because it's ——2——. Cynics say that such ——3—— ——4—— is to the Church Father's ——5——. Themselves giving no ——6—— to faith, they do not ——7—— it with the efficacy which believers find in it.

103

CED, CESS (ceed, ceas), from *cedere, cessus:* to go, yield, give up.

proceed	exceed	ancestor	precede	procedure	ANTECEDENT
success	process	procession	predecessor	accessory	CESSATION
succeed	successful	access	concede	cede: recede	PRECEDENT
proceed	recess	decease	intercession	ACCESSIBLE	ACCESSION
			ABSCESS		

A LEGAL PUZZLE

The ——1—— server finally ——2——ed in catching up with him, and he was hauled into court for failure to pay the third month's rent. He ——3——d it was due, but said he couldn't pay because he hadn't recovered his government check for the hogs he had agreed not to raise under the AAA program. His lawyer said that the young man's immediate paternal ——4—— of the same name had collected the check. The lawyer thought the court could well take a long ——5—— on the case while action was PENDING in an upstate court to recover the check. He did not ask for a ——6—— of the action, he said. Nor did usual ——7—— call for any ——8—— by the local court. However, he wished to say for the record that he felt the upstate judge would be hard put to it to find ——9——s on which to decide which of the two, father or son, had not raised the hogs.

CURR, CURS (curri, corri, cur, cor, couri, cours) from *currire, cursus:* to run, more quickly.

course	incur	occurrence	COURIER	CONCUR	DISCURSIVE
current	excursion	succor	COURSER	CURSORY	PRECURSOR
occur	corridor	recur			

AN OPPENHEIM OPENING

The State Department ——1—— was traveling in a plane which just out of Denver ran into heavy weather that proved to be the ——2—— of a terrible storm. DOWNDRAFTS ——3—— again and again. The pilot told everybody to get ready to bail out, remarking this wasn't exactly an ——4—— trip. The State Department man, with more than a ——5—— glance at the pouch he was carrying, said he ——6——ed in the pilot's view, and added he was under instructions to destroy the pouch rather than risk having it picked up from the wreck. "What is it, the atom bomb formula?" the pilot asked.

CLAUS (clos), (clud, clus, in compounds), from *claudere, clausus:* to shut.

close	closet	clause	cloister	SECLUSION	CLOSURE
include	exclusive	conclusion	exclusion	PRECLUDE	INCLUSION
conclude	inclose	exclude	RECLUSE	SECLUDE	

NO MORE LONELY HEARTS

The modern ——1—— need not lead a hermit life, even though his retreat is ——2——d. In his ——3——ed retreat, he is not ——4—— from enjoying the radio, and he may ——5—— in his REGIMEN luxuries delivered by PARACHUTE from an air express.

CLAM, CLAMAT (claim), from *clamare, clamatus:* to call, to cry out.

claim   clamor   reclaim   ACCLAIM   CLAIMANT   DECLAIM
exclaim   exclamation clamorous   RECLAMATION DECLAMATION EXCLAMATORY
proclaim   proclamation

CHANGE THE NAME OF DEAR OLD ARKANSAS?

Senator Foghorn had won the ——1—— prize at his high school com-
mencement, and never forgot it. His style was ——2—— and ——3——.
In fact the ——4—— mark was his favorite form of PUNCTUATION. He
would ——5—— at the drop of a hat, even at dinner parties. On the floor
of the Senate, he set up an equally loud ——6—— over a pension
——7—— or a ——8—— bill affecting three Western states. Burt Wheeler
once remarked sourly that if they could only ——9—— and condense the
verbal fog which Foghorn engendered, they could irrigate all Montana with
it.

DIGN (digni, deign, daint, dain), from *dignus:* worthy.

dignity   disdain   dignify   disdainful   DIGNITARY   CONDIGN
dainty   indignation indignant   indignity   DAINTINESS

REFUGEE DE LUXE

This pompous and ——1—— old POUTER pigeon felt he was being subjected
to ——2——s if he had to walk two blocks or carry a small parcel home.
He had been some kind of minor ——3—— at a Ruritanian court, and his
——4—— knew no bounds if the doorman forgot his title. He stood on
his ——5——, which was about all he had left to stand on, his legs having
shrunk to mere PIPESTEMS. Not so the rest of him, for he loved pastry and all
sorts of ——6——s.

CAPIT (cipit, cipic, capt, chatt, catt), from *caput, capitis:* the head.

captain   chapter   precipitous PRECIPITATION RECAPITULATION OCCIPITAL
cattle   precipitate CHATTEL   CAPITULATION   PRECIPITANT   CAPITALISM
capital   capitalist

WALL STREET MYSTERY

Why the stock market should take such a ——1—— drop when production
is rising, savings are huge, pent-up demand for goods immense, and dividends high, is a mystery. Is ——2—— under COMPULSION to ——3—— a
crisis? Is it close to its last ——4—— as the Marxists claim? Certainly the
chief factors in the downward turn of the market are psychological. But if
these violent swings continue, we'll be going back to barter, and be using
——5—— for money once more—which, at the present price of steaks, is
not so hard to imagine. ——6——s of finance should not even think of
——7—— to such PESSIMISM. It's up to——8—— to save the system, in
their role as managers. And this calls for a ——9—— of fundamental principles, as well as a REVAMPING of labor and FISCAL policies.

DAT, from *dare, datus:* to give, do, plan, yield, put.

add	surrender	editorial	EDIT	ANTEDATE	ABSCOND
date	tradition	perdition	DATUM	EXTRADITION	EDITORSHIP
addition	edition	RENDEZVOUS	DATA	DATIVE	EXTRADITE
render	editor	TRADITIONAL			

UNDERGROUND NEWS

The ——1—— of the underground sheet wrote as he fought, toughly. A ——2—— soon grew up around him. Give him a few scraps of ——3——, and he'd RECONSTRUCT a story. If a whole ——4—— of the paper was captured and burned, he'd rewrite the ——5—— a VERBATIM, ——6—— the news from a few scrappy notes, and have a complete run on the streets by nightfall. When a traitor ——7——ed with the paper's funds, he wrote a double-talk story suggesting methods for "——8——ing" the offender from Nazi headquarters; and it wasn't long before the spy had a forced ——9—— with an underground TRIBUNAL. His epitaph appeared in the paper surrounded by a black border of SWASTIKAS.

DIC, DICT, from *dicere, dictus:* to speak say.

INTERDICT	ABDICATION	MALEDICTION	DITTO	DICTAPHONE	VALEDICTORY
DICTION	ADDICT	DICTUM	ADJUDICATE	DICTOGRAPH	VALEDICTION
PREDICATE	CONTRADICT	DICTATORIAL			

WHAT D'YOU MEAN, DEMOCRACY!

Democracy is virtually under an ——1—— in a country which keeps over 10,000,000 persons at slave labor, and permits no free speech, free press or assembly, while one party numbering 2% of the population ——2—— the fate of all the rest. This is ——3—— rule with a vengeance. For democracy is ——4——d on government by consent, majority rule, and the civil liberties of the individual. The ——5—— of Lord Acton, that power corrupts, and absolute power corrupts absolutely, is clearly proven in this instance. There has been no ——6—— of democracy, for this country has never known it. It has been well acquainted with ANARCHY, but in paying a ——7—— tribute to anarchy it shifted at one jump to tyranny.

CUR, CURAT, from *curare, curatus:* to take care of, care for, heal.

sure	procure	security	accuracy	CURATE	INACCURATE
secure	assurance	accurate	reassure	CURATOR	INSECURITY
cure	insurance	surety			

SPENDING MONEY TO KEEP IT

The ——1—— of the museum to his horror found the accounts inaccurate; but he was relieved to discover that the error was in bookkeeping, not in the actual state of the funds, which were ——2——. He decided to hire a more expensive ACCOUNTANT, in the interest of ——3——; and he put him under ——4—— bond.

FORM, from *forma:* figure, shape, appearance.

form	transform	formula	formality	CONFORMATION	FORMULARY
inform	conform	informal	formulate	FORMULATION	REFORMATORY
information	deform	reformation	REFORMER	INFORMER	FORMALISM
uniform	formal	transformation	UNIFORMITY	CONFORMABLE	INFORMALITY
reform	formation	deformity			

Is Your Etiquette Showing?

ETIQUETTE is always in danger of becoming ——1—— without content. Too much ——2—— and too close ——3—— to rigid rules is indeed apt to freeze social life into the mold of ——4——. There is no sovereign ——5—— for good manners, and anyone who tries to ——6—— such a code runs the hazards which even Chesterfield did not wholly CIRCUMVENE. Mere ——7—— out of Emily Post is sufficient for arranging the forks, but not for effecting the subtle ——8—— of outward gestures into inward feeling required for putting a company into high good humor. Here that measured ——9—— which is the desirable end result of all social ——10——s is the requisite.

FER, LAT (lay) from *ferre, latus:* to bear, carry.

difference	refer	translate	defer	REFERENDUM	TRANSFERENCE
different	relate	ferry	fertility	SUPERLATIVE	ABLATIVE
offer	relation	reference	infer	CONIFEROUS	FLORIFEROUS
suffer	relative	fertilize	proffer	REFEREE	FRUCTIFEROUS
delay	confer	preference	translation	VOCIFEROUS	ILLATIVE
elate	conference	prelate	inference	CORRELATION	OBLATE
prefer	fertile	sufferance	DEFERENCE	PESTIFEROUS	PROLATE
differ	transfer	circumference			

The Dialecticians

The conference was exasperated at these newcomers to the international scene, who took nothing on ——1——, but in the most ——2—— and ——3—— manner worried every proposal to death with their DIALECTIC. They made interminable ——4——s, insisting on constant ——5——s to earlier documents, and showed endless ——6—— of resource in HAGGLING over minor points of procedure. They orated for three hours at a time, and it then took six hours to translate their HARANGUES. They would not cut across a circle if there was a chance to go around its ——7——, and they showed a positive ——8—— for going off at TANGENTS. ——9—— them a concession or a compromise, and they were suspicious of it. They had no ——10—— toward tradition, in fact despised it on principle; but they were facile and ready at erecting their own prejudices into eternal principles, from which they would not abate one jot. In fact, they reminded the French and British delegates of American NEGOTIATORS in the days when the Republic was young—brash, TENDENCIOUS, their dignity easily offended, and great STICKLERS for the letter of the law.

EQU (equi), from *aequus:* equal, just.

equal	unequal	adequate	equatorial	EQUITABLE	EQUINOCTIAL
equality	equator	equation	INEQUALITY	EQUIVOCAL	EQUANIMITY
equity	equivalent	inadequate	EQUABLE	EQUINOX	COEQUAL
		EQUIVALENCE			

Double-Talker

He was ADEPT at making ——1—— statements, and if confronted later with a DISCREPANCY between his words and his actions, he was quite ——2—— to twisting his own earlier remarks. In fact, his ——3—— when thus caught out was astonishing to colleagues who had more precise notions of ——4——. Had he been a GEOGRAPHER he would have had a globe with a shifting ——5——, and the ——6—— storms would have come at whatever time of year suited his convenience. As it was, his COWORKERS came to feel that there was not much ——7—— in any verbal ——8—— he devised, and they expected in dealings with him to come out on the ——8—— —and losing—side of the deal.

FRANG, FRACT, FRACTUR, from *frangere, fractus:* to break.

frail	frailty	fracture	FRACTIONAL	FRANGIBLE	IRREFRAGABLE
fraction	suffrage	infringe	INFRACTION	INREFRANGIBLE	REFRANGIBLE
fragment	fragile	REFRACTORY	REFRACTION	INFRINGEMENT	

Reductio ad absurdum

This ——1—— group had purged and expelled its ——2—— members for various minor ——3—— of the supposedly ——4—— truths of party doctrine. As a result, many ——5——s appeared in the ——6—— structure of the party. Finally this small remaining ——7—— was so split that they had to divide their journalistic organ into three sections: Right, Left, and Center. Their annual report of party membership, required of all groups operating newspapers, showed three members, all sovereign British electors ready to exercise their ——8——. Thus radicalism in England returned to the tradition of the famous three TINKERS, who began their proclamation, "We, the People of England."

HAB, HABIT (ab, habitu, hibit), from *habere, habitus:* to have, hold.

able	enable	prohibit	prohibition	INHIBIT	HABILIMENT
debt	exhibit	exhibition	habitual	HABITAT	REHABILITATION
habit	inhabit	habitation	disable	INHIBITION	PROHIBITIVE
ability	inhabitant	debtor	habitable	DEBILITY	

Paul's Parodies

The characters in Elliott Paul's amusing detective story PARODIES have few ——1——s. They constantly behave as if they were at a Beaux Arts ball, and the ——2—— of culture and wardrobe alike rest lightly on them. Their ——3—— liquor INTAKE is fantastic, yet drink seems to have no ——4—— effect on them. They ——5—— great RESOURCEFULNESS in fighting, and Miss Montana in particular shoots French THUGS with an ——6—— of *sang froid* that does credit to her training in the Great Open Spaces.

GER, GEST, GESTUR (gist, gistr, jest), from *genere, gestus:* to bear, or carry on, perform.

register	gesture	digestion	indigestion	BELLIGERENT	GESTICULATION
suggest	suggestion	digestive	registration	CONGEST	GERUND
jest	digest	indigestible	congestion	JESTER	CONGERIES
		VICEGERENT			

THE JOKER

Medieval banquets were spared the stale stories of a toastmaster, lifted out of Bennett Cerf's borrowings (without quotes) from Winchell and Lyons. Instead, a professional ——1—— produced a ——2—— of ——3——s designed to aid ——4——, not impede it. His ——5——s and antics were exaggerated in STYLIZED fashion, with ——6——s of both HARLEQUIN and clown. And he LAMPOONED his betters, acting always as a licensed ——7—— of the devil, talking BAWDY so that everybody could join in who wished, as the mead and ale flowed more freely.

GRAT (gratu, grati, grai, gre), from *gratus:* pleasing, deserving thanks, thankful; *gratis,* by favor, without reward.

grace	disgrace	gratitude	gratify	GRACELESS	GRATUITY
agree	gracious	disagreeable	disagree	DISAGREEMENT	INGRATITUDE
agreeable	grateful	congratulation	gratification	INGRATE	

DIVISION OF THE POWERS

Cleveland remarked that every appointment he made yielded him ten enemies and one ——1——. Indeed, most seasoned politicians in the top office are ——2—— when they encounter ——3—— for favors done. But if they're wise, they never ——4—— themselves until their course is run; for toward the end of a second term, the ——5—— and RANCOROUS hostility of Congress toward a President is PROVERBIAL. ——6—— between the two arms of government is the expected thing; and anything a President gets from Congress in that period is in the nature of a ——7——, flung to him with a snarl.

MAN (manu, main), from *manus:* the hand.

manner	manifest	manual	MANEUVER	MANACLE	AMANUENSIS
maintain	manure	emancipation	MANIPULATE	MANICURE	MANUMISSION
manage	manuscript	manifestation	MANUFACTORY	MANIFESTO	BIMANOUS
		QUADRUMANOI			

THE BEST PEOPLE DIDN'T LIKE HIM

Jefferson tired of acting as his own ——1——, copying all the foreign correspondence of the State Department into a letter book. He finally ——2——ed to have Congress grant him one clerk, but the FEDERALISTS in the Senate tried to block his appointment of Freneau, the poet, as too violently JACOBITE. Always Jefferson's efforts to strike off the shackles and ——3—— from the mind aroused opposition. Even his ——4—— of his slaves in his will was objected to, after his death. But to Jefferson the Declaration was no mere ——5——; it was also a way of life and action.

JECT (jet, jut), from *jacere, jactus:* to lay, throw, cast.

object	project	conjecture	DEJECTION	EJACULATION	CONJECTURAL
subject	jut	inject	INJECTION	INTERJECTION	EJECTION
reject	abject	projection	REJECTION	JETTY	JETSAM
jet	adjacent	subjection	OBJECTIVE	TRAJECTORY	
objection	adjective	eject	PROJECTILE	SUBJECTIVE	

BACK TO THE CAVE, BOYS

There is cold comfort in the ——1——s into the future made by the atom-bomb experts. They plan a rocket ——2—— with an atomic WARHEAD which will have a ——3—— over the North Pole, and can thence be radio-steered to land anywhere on earth. They leave to ——4—— only the time factor. It's scant comfort to realize that there is some slight uncertainty only about the date when they will be able to reduce any given ——5—— to FLOTSAM and ——6—— by merely pushing a button. Most of us hope that the next Hiroshima will not be too closely ——7—— to the cave we've staked out to live in.

MITT, MISS (mit, mis), from *mittere, missu:* to send, cast, throw, let go.

promise	commit	remit	remittance	INTERMIT	COMMISSARY
admit	committee	compromise	submissive	MISSILE	MANUMIT
permit	submit	surmise	transmit	MISSIVE	TRANSMIT
dismiss	omit	emit	admittance	REMISS	
commission	mission	intermittent	EMISSARY	DEMISE	

THE WORMS TURN

The faculty sent him to the CHANCELLOR as their ——1—— on behalf of the two instructors who had been ——2——ed, OSTENSIBLY for reasons of economy. The Chancellor's sense of humor, at best ——3——, was not working when he told his secretary "to ——4—— the faculty's walking delegate to come in." He didn't actually heave any ——5——s at the professor's head, but he looked as if he were about to explode. "I've already looked at this impertinent ——6—— your committee sent in," he roared, "what else do they want to say?" "My ——7—— from them is simply to tell you orally what they thought it more tactful not to put in writing: that they think you're dead wrong, even from the point of view of your own interest," the professor said coolly. "What, they think I've been ——8—— in my duty—," the Chancellor almost gasped. "It's simply that you'd do better to save the money on supplies, buildings and grounds OUTLAYS, and the like, rather than taking it out of the hides of your staff." "You seem to think I can take more grub out of the ——9—— than there is in it," said the Chancellor, thus reminding the professor none too gently that he was one of the 1500 retired generals of World War II. But he SIMMERED down, no longer ——10——ing blue rays, and after meeting with the faculty's executive ——11——, he ——12——d the case by granting the two professors involved nominal SABBATICALS at half pay—and they both landed jobs at twice their current salaries.

JUNG, JUNCT, JUNCTUR (join, joint, jointur), from *jungere, junctur:* to bind, connect, unite.

join	conjunction	adjunct	CONJUGAL	DISJOIN	DISJUNCTION
joint	injunction	conjugate	JOINER	CONJOIN	JOINTER
adjoin	conjugation	REJOIN	JUNCTURE	CONJUNCTIVE	CONJUNCTURE
enjoin	junction	SUBJUNCTIVE	SUBJUGATE	JOINTLY	DISJOINTED

TRIPPING OVER THE TERMS

One reason grammar's hard is that there are so many technical terms to master. The ——1—— is laid upon the student to study the ——2—— of verbs. Words that serve as CONNECTIVES are ——3——s; certain other relationships are ——4——, a very subtle distinction in logic. A verb expressing a condition contrary to fact must be in the ——5—— mode, now gradually vanishing. Once the student is properly ——6—— by these stern necessities of TERMINOLOGY, he has little energy left to form the language habits and patterns which would make grammar come alive for him. He gets at best a ——7—— view of the whole process by which language functions.

LEG, LECT, LECTUR (lig, less), from *legere, lectus:* to read, gather, choose.

lesson	collection	coil	recollect	legacy	ELIGIBLE
collect	election	legend	colleague	collector	LEGIBLE
elect	lecture	selection	cull	INTELLIGIBLE	PREDILECTION
neglect	legion	dialect	intellect	ELEGANCE	DIALECTICS
	LEGIBILITY		ILLEGIBLE		INTELLIGIBILITY

BIBLIOMANIAC

This BIBLIOMANIAC had an odd ——1—— for picking books on the basis of their ——2——. He liked big type and wide margins. He cared little about ——3—— or ——4—— of style. He would as readily read a ——5—— as a ——6——, if the former appeared in more ——7—— type. As a result his ——8—— was a strange one, containing among other items a DE LUXE edition of Lenin's ——9—— printed on rag instead of on the usual butcher paper; and the DOMINICAN translation of AQUINAS, on VELLUM, apparently stolen from a monastery library.

PAR,[2] PARAT (ver, pair), from *parare, paratus:* to see, to get ready, or make ready.

prepare	repair	separation	apparatus	REPARATION	IRREPARABLE
several	preparation	sever	preparatory	DISSEVER	SEPARABLE

HERO IN THE LABORATORY

Only the courageous PHYSICIST's quick action in ——1—— more widely the two small masses of PLUTONIUM prevented irreparable damage. Some slip had occurred in the ——2—— arrangements, and the blue EMANATION showed that they were too close, and that it was imperative to ——3—— them. Once an inch closer, they would have been ——4——ed, but by FISSION.

[2] Do not confuse with *par,* equal.

MOV, MOT (mo), from *movere, motus:* to move.

moment	remove	remote	movable	immovable	MOVIE
move	motive	emotion	promotion	MOMENTOUS	MOBILIZE
automobile	movement	locomotive	commotion	MOMENTUM	
motion	motor	mob	removal	MOTIF	

RABBLEROUSER

His speech gathered more and more ——1——. He was ——2——ing the ——3——s of the audience and for no good. I began to wish the chairs were not ——4——, and as the crowd began restless and aimless ——5——, I decided we'd have to start a counter ——6——. The RABBLEROUSER kept recurring to his main ——7——, that there was a lot of money in California, and every man Jack there should get his share, and fast. He was steamed up like a ——8——, and it looked as if there'd be no stopping him. But luckily some loggers blew into the back of the hall who spotted him as a onetime fink in the woods. They rushed the platform and broke up the meeting without any waste ——9——.

NOT, from *noscere, notus,* or *gnoscere, gnotus:* to know.

note	notion	ignoble	notary	INCOGNITO	DENOTATION
notice	ignorance	denote	NOTATION	ANNOTATION	
noble	notable	notorious	COGNIZANCE	CONNOTE	
ignorant	notify	recognition	COGNITION	CONNOTATION	

WORD-PICTURES

Chinese picture-writing is a ——1—— SCRIPT, though ——2——ly hard to learn. It is perhaps better at expressing poetic ——3——s than at rendering the exact ——4——s of words which are so necessary in Western science. But in Chinese, the character not only ——5——s the idea, but illustrates it GRAPHICALLY at the same time—which Blake could do in English only by INTERWEAVING his copper engravings and paintings with his text. No great Chinese CHIROGRAPHER could remain ——6——. His brush strokes identified him. What would we not give for a HOLOGRAPH copy of Li Po's poems, permitting ——7—— of his very AUTOGRAPH style!

PET, PETIT (petu, peat), from *petere, petitus:* to ask, to seek, to rush at, to fly to.

repeat	competition	competitor	competent	INCOMPETENT	CENTRIPETAL
appetite	repetition	impetuous	IMPETUS	PETULANT	REPETITIVE
petition	compete				

COLLECTIVE OPEN SHOP

The spirit of ——1—— gave an immense ——2—— to work in the plant. A new type of ——3—— pump was needed, and it was invented. Many processes were so broken down that they could be performed by the ——4—— techniques of the assembly line. ——5—— craftsmen and ——6—— grumblers were quickly weeded out and shipped to Siberia or the Arctic North.

PAND, PANS, PASS (pac); from *pandere, pansus* or *passus:* to spread, step.

pass	compass	passenger	expand	expansion	EXPANSE
pace	passage	surpass	trespass	encompass	EXPANSIVE
		PASSABLE			

Universal Man

What the mind of man could ——1——, da Vinci's embraced. He ——2——ed the frontiers of TECHNOLOGY and of art. He had ——3——ing skill as a DRAUGHTSMAN, and used it alike in preparing the CARTOONS for his painting, in ANATOMICAL drawing, and in engineering design.

MOD (modi), from *modus:* measure, manner, fashion.

model	modest	commodity	modification	MODISH	MODAL
modern	moderate	modify	moderator	COMMODE	
mode	accommodation	commodious	modulation	MODICUM	

Selling to Music

She decided to open her first branch in Dallas, next to New York the best outlet for ——1—— furniture and DÉCOR. She found ——2——s for a ——3—— SALON, which she decorated in the same ——4—— as her New York shop, using, however, Southern pine instead of Philippine mahogany, a ——5—— which seemed an appropriate concession to Texan sensibilities. She installed a chamber orchestra in a musicians' gallery, but she had them play Southern ballads, using John Powell's and Annabel Buchanan's ——6—— arrangements. Her shop became the ——7—— thing with all the social BELLWETHERS of Dallas. Her rivals, who at first thought she had acted without a ——8—— of sense, began to follow suit. Only they had cowboy singers, who drew their numbers from John Lomax's collection.

PORT, PORTAT, from *portare, portatus:* to carry, convey, bear long.

important	sport	transport	export	purport	DEPORTATION
report	support	porter	deportment	importation	DISPORT
port	import	transportation	portable	EXPORTATION	COMPORT
		DEPORT			

Filibusterer—New Style

He sailed into ——1—— on an old rusty tramp Liberty ship, one of two he owned. He rented an office and set up what was OSTENSIBLY an ——2—— - ——3—— business, but the officials of the banana republic, who got their cut, knew it was really smuggling. He had a big launch, supposedly for personal ——4—— around the harbor and up-river. Its compartments held an armory of easily ——5—— artillery, Tommy-guns mostly. When he got too handy with these while landing a drug CONSIGNMENT, and shot about half the republic's REVENUERS, and, by accident, four of his own ——6——s, the officials had had enough of this FILIBUSTERER. They didn't issue a ——7—— order, they just ran him out of the country, on the grounds that he was upsetting the good-neighbor policy.

PLAC, PLACIT (pleas, plais, plead, plea), from *placere, placitus:* to please.

please	pleasure	plea	pleasing	implacable	COMPLAISANCE
pleasant	plead	placid	complacent	PLEASANTRY	PLACATE

THE OFFICE EGOTIST

His facility and ADROITNESS perhaps justified a certain ——1—— in his manner, but this EGOTIST had a kind of ——2—— ruthlessness and arrogance when his slightest opinion was challenged, that made him decidedly an unpleasant person. His ——3——es were heavy-handed and humorless, and all in all he was unbeloved, but far too ——4—— ever to guess it.

PLIC, PLICAT, PLICIT (ple, pil, ply, ploy, play, plex), from *plicare, plicatus:* to fold, bend, turn.

reply	multiply	complex	supple	MULTIPLICITY	COMPLICITY
simple	employee	employer	complication	PLIABLE	MISAPPLY
apply	simplicity	imply	PLIANT	DUPLICITY	DEPLOY
employ	comply	supplication	IMPLICATION	DUPLEX	
application	ply	plait	IMPLICIT	REPLICA	
display	multiplication	simplify	EXPLICIT	PLEXUS	

RATIONALIZATION

He started out as a parlor SOCIALIST, wobbled into weak-kneed LIBERALISM, and wound up in advertising. He had a——1—— and ——2—— mind, which lent itself easily to the necessary ——3——es of the HUCKSTERING trade. He understood the ——4——s of his activities, but never let them become too ——5—— in his thinking about himself. He tried to avoid developing ——6——es about his sell-out by CORRALING the accounts calling for INFORMATIONAL advertising. It seemed to lessen his ——7—— in the business if he kept away from ads based on fear motive, or on social stigma—bad-breath accounts, they were called around the agency. The ——8—— of his outside interests helped to keep him from feeling like a three-——9—— scoundrel. At night, in his DUPLEX, he used to ——10—— his thoughts about going into public service, in his RATIONALIZATION following the example of Benton and Bowles.

SENT, SENS (senti, sensu), from *sentire, sensus:* to feel, think, perceive.

assent	nonsense	resent	sense	SENSIBILITY	sentence
consent	nonsensical	RESENTFUL	senseless	sensual	SENTENTIOUS
dissent	PRESENTIMENT	scent	sensible	sensuous	sentiment

UNSENTIMENTAL

SERMONS AND SODA WATER THE DAY AFTER

The ——1—— advice of ASCETICS and saints counseling against ——2—— delights has had little effect on the average ——3—— man. He does not ——4—— in theory, only in practice. Ignoring finer ——5——es he goes on his ——6—— way, savoring the ——7——s, joys, and diversions of the primrose path. He may have a ——8—— of sorrow and regret, but it seems ——9—— to yield to such gloomy worries, until he gets a hangover.

PART (port, parti, par, pars), from *pars, partis:* a piece, portion, share.

part	particular	partner	departure	partition	PARSE
party	portion	proportion	partial	compartment	PARTITIVE
apart	department	impart	particle	COUNTERPART	
depart	parcel	apartment	impartial	APPORTION	

THE SOUL OF WIT

The Dean read out a fancy new piece of legislation. "It won't ——1——,"
the old math professor called out, and there was a roar of laughter. Nobody
had noticed the dangling "whether" until he spoke. He had been educated
before knowledge was walled off in ——2——s. He had no ——3——
in the faculty, and was much beloved, perhaps because he distributed his
JIBES quite ——4——ly, and without a ——5—— of RANCOR. Also he had
a fine sense of ——6——, and his wit ——7——ed flavor to his one-
sentence speeches.

PREHEND, PREHENS (prign, prent, pris, priz), from *prehendere, prehensus:*
to seize, lay hold of.

apprehend	APPRISAL	enterprise	prize	REPRISAL
apprehension	comprehend	IMPREGNABLE	REPREHEND	surprise
apprentice	COMPREHENSION	PREHENSILE	REPREHENSIBLE	SURPRISAL
APPRISE	comprise	prison	REPREHENSION	

TAX DODGER EXTRAORDINARY

The proprietor of this restaurant chain not only had a ——1—— grasp.
He also lived up to Mark Twain's definition of a MARSUPIAL: an animal with
a large pouch. And what went in to the pouch, the owner didn't like to let
out—even for income tax. How people could pay taxes so blithely, was beyond his ——2——. When the Treasury was ——3——d of his original
views on this subject, it naturally felt them slightly ——4——, and decided
on ——5——s. Although he had shown rare ——6—— in cooking up two
sets of books, with the aid of an ——7—— who didn't get much of a pay-
off, his position proved far from ——8——. In fact he was ——9——ed,
forced to DISGORGE, fined heavy penalties, and sent to ——10—— for several
years.

RAP, RAPT, RAPTUR (rav, rept), from *rapere, raptus:* to seize, snatch, hurry
away.

rapid	rapine	rapt	ravage	ravenous	RAVISHING
rapids	RAPACIOUS	rapturous	raven	RAVINE	SURREPTITIOUS

SHARKS

The big five in the combine were as ——1—— as hungry COYOTES. Their
appetite for money was ——2——, and what they could not ——3—— by
direct means, they got by ——4—— methods. They short-changed the
foreign outfits, with which they had RECIPROCAL arrangements. If any of
their victims were reported as hungry, they said, "Let the ——5—— feed
'em."

QUER, QUISIT (quir, quest), from *quaerere, quaesitus:* to seek, search for, ask, inquire.

acquire	conqueror	INQUEST	PERQUISITE	require	INQUISITORIAL
acquisition	conquest	inquire	question	requirement	
ACQUISITIVE	DISQUISITION	inquisitive	request	REQUISITION	
conquer	exquisite	inquisition	quest	requisite	

THERE'S A CATCH SOMEWHERE

Judging by the RECURRENT meat famines under the revived OPA, an ——1—— society doesn't respond very well unless maximum profits can be made. Even the stiffest ——2—— methods by the black market investigators have little effect. About all the OPA can do is hold an ——3——. But the cattle men and packers, deprived of their usual ——4——s, simply go on strike. It won't do for laymen to be too ——5——, but the ——6—— is often raised by angry housewives, why doesn't the government ——7—— the cattle and COERCE the packers? That smacks too much of the Russian method, ladies. Besides, it's a law that got us into this jam. There are too many laws, already. Read Mr. Hazlitt's *Economics in One Lesson,* and eat free enterprise, if you can't get meat.

RUPT, RUPTUR (rout, rut), from *rumpere, ruptus:* to break, destroy, burst.

abrupt	corruption	INCORRUPTIBLE	IRRUPTION	route	RUPTURE
bankrupt	DISRUPT	interrupt	rout	routine	RUT
corrupt	eruption				

EIGHTH WONDER OF THE WORLD

The sudden ——1—— of the new Mexican volcano, Paracutín, which started as a mere anthill, and grew to a 1500-foot cone in a year, ——2——ed life in nearby villages. The black ash and lava put to ——3—— all plant life for twenty miles around. Numerous ——4—— occurred in the side of the main cone, and eventually these smaller mouths threw up cones of their own.

SAL, SALT (sali, sili, sail, sult, sault), from *salire, saltus:* to leap, rush, issue suddenly forth.

assail	exult	RESILIENCE	result	SALACIOUS	salmon
assault	EXULTANT	RESILIENT	RESULTANT	SALIENT	SALTATION
DESULTORY	exultation				

THE JOYOUS CRUSADER

La Guardia made a FRONTAL ——1—— on evil in the metropolis. He banned ——2—— magazines, drove out the madams, and scotched gambling. There was nothing ——4—— about his methods. He showed positive ——5—— in battling sin, and explained his ——6—— moves on the air. Any ——7—— backfire merely roused his scorn, and he showed remarkable ——8—— whenever he had a setback, as he did when he ordered raids on bingo games in church parlors.

REG, RECT (roy, rig, regi, ress, recti), from *regere, rectus:* to rule, direct, arrange.

address	direct	INCORRIGIBLE	REALIST	regal	resource
correct	direction	INSURGENT	reality	REGIMEN	resurrection
CORRECTIVE	director	insurrection	rectify	regiment	ruler
dress	DIRECTORY	irregular	RECTITUDE	REGNANT	source
dressing	erect	real	rector	reign	REGIME
dressy	erection	realty	redress	regular	IRREGULARITY

FORCED EXIT

What started as an ——1—— turned into a ——2—— revolution. Its ——3—— were crafty ——4——. They knew that Machado was ——5——, and that he would be merciless to ——6——. So they had to win, and end his ——7—— once and for all. There could be no compromise. They imposed a severe ——8—— on their forces, and showed a degree of ——9—— about property and women unusual in revolutions in that part of the world. They tried to avoid ——10—— that would set sections of the populace against them. So they finally ended the tyrant's ——11—— beyond any possibility of its ——12——.

SED, SESS (see, sidu, siz, sid) from *sedere, sessus:* to sit.

ASSESS	ASSIZE	possess	preside	reside	resident
assiduous	INSIDIOUS	PREPOSSESS	president	residue	RESIDUARY
		SEDENTARY			

EXERTION IS FOR SERVANTS

There was a certain ——1—— charm about the ——2—— way of life of the old style Chinese MANDARINS. They were ——3—— LEGATEES of a long poetic tradition celebrating the quiet life without exertion. They were ——4—— in cultivating the art of doing nothing gracefully. The last of the great mandarins, Wu Ting Fang, while presiding at a Chinese-American banquet in Peiping, the first one at which dancing went on between courses, asked the American Ambassador, "Why do you go to all this exertion? Why not have the servants do it for you?"

SIGN, from *signum:* a sign.

assign	COUNTERSIGN	DESIGNATION	resignation	signature	UNDESIGNED
assignment	CONSIGNMENT	INSIGNIFICANCE	sign	signify	UNDERSIGNED
ASSIGNATION	design	resign	signal	significance	
consign	designer	resigned	signet	SIGNIFICATION	

V-SIGN

The opening bars of Beethoven's Fifth Symphony, starting out as the theme ——1—— on BBC programs broadcast to the undergrounds in occupied countries, became a kind of musical ——2—— for the resistance movements. The Roman numeral for five is V, so this music came to ——3—— Victory, and was EQUATED with the V-——4——. It acquired increasing ——5—— as the war went on.

STA, STAT, SIST (st, stet), from *stare, status:* to stand; intensive, *sisto, sistere,* to (cause to) stand.

arrest	contrast	instance	rest	statuary
ARMISTICE	desist	instant	RESTITUTION	statue
assist	destitute	INSTATE	SOLSTICE	statute
assistance	distance	INSTITUTION	RESTIVE	subsist
consist	distant	irresistible	stable	substance
circumstance	EQUIDISTANT	OBSTETRICS	STANCHION	substantial
CIRCUMSTANTIAL	establish	obstacle	stanza	SUBSTANTIVE
consistency	estate	persist	state	SUBSTITUTION
constable	exist	PROSTITUTION	stately	superstition
constant	existence	REINSTATE	statement	TRANSUBSTAN-
constitute	extant	resist	station	TIATION
constituent	INCONSISTENCY	resistance	stationary	
constitution	insist	RESTATE	stationery	

NATURE OF THE COMIC

It's hard to say just what comedy ——1——s of. Certainly it is no ——2—— thing, but varies from place to place, and from one period to another. Shakespeare, who should know, said that the prosperity of a jest lies in the ear of him that hears it. The evidence is more than ——3——, indeed, that comedy thus depends a lot upon prepared ground in the mind of the listener. A story about footballers dancing a "BALLET moose" in a varsity show isn't funny to children who never heard of a ballet, let alone the Ballet Russe, and who don't know what a moose is. The ——4—— is often made that the COMIC depends on sudden INCONGRUITY or ——5——. But not all incongruities are funny, only those that show a particular kind of crack in the smooth wall of normal, ——6—— reality. We feel amused when an ——7—— wolf's hide turns up as a lady's fur coat. Jokes at the expense of an ——8—— —the church, for instance,—are laughable if we don't like it; but make us very ——9—— if we admire it. We develop a high ——10—— to contrived gags and worn out wheezes. Yet Rabelais or Mark Twain could re-work these old ones into witcracks that would make an Indian ——11—— laugh. In their hands, some very dull dross underwent a ——12—— into high though still profane wit.

STRING, STRICT, STRICTURE (strain, straint, strait, stren), from *stringere.* *strictus:* to bind, draw tight, filter.

ASTRINGENT	CONSTRICTOR	district	restrict	strait	STRICTNESS
constrain	DISTRAIN	restrain	strain	STRAITEN	STRICTURE
CONSTRAINT	distress	restraint	STRAINER	strict	restriction
CONSTRICT	distressing				

TRAGIC WIT

Swift's wit was ——1——. His ——2—— on British landlords' INHUMANITY to the poor of Ireland were ——3——ing to many of his friends, who felt ——4——ed to urge him to put some ——5——s on his wit, lest more forcible ——6——s be imposed on his person.

SEQU, SECUT (sec, sequi, su, sect, suit), from *sequi, seculus:* to follow.

CONSECUTION	execution	persecute	pursue	sect	suitable
consecutive	executive	persecution	PURSUANCE	SECTARY	suite
consequence	executor	prosecute	pursuit	SECTARIAN	suitor
consequently	OBSEQUIES	prosecution	second	sue	
ensue	obsequious	PROSECUTOR	secondary	suit	

SHADES OF RED

The bitterest disputes in politics are the ——1—— wrangles of the left. Factions ——2—— each other, or if one is in power, it ——3——s DISSENTERS if it can catch them, and ——4——s them even into foreign countries. No matter how ——5——ly heretics make their submission, they are LIQUIDATED. Nor does the ——6—— end with their ——7—— and ——8——. They are still EXCORIATED in the histories prepared by official order, and held up as an awful example to other ——9—— who have so far escaped purging.

SERV,[3] SERVAT, from *servare, servatus:* to save, protect, give heed to.

conserve	CONSERVATORY	observance	preserve	reservation	reservoir
conservation	observe	observation	preserver	reserve	unobserved
conservative	observer	preservation	PRESERVATIVE	reservedness	UNRESERVED

JOE MILLER'S NEMESIS

This publisher was devoted to the cause of ——1——. He ——2——ed all the jokes he heard his friends tell, and made enemies of the columnists by EXPROPRIATING their best *bons mots* without acknowledgment. None of their hunting ——3——s were safe from his hawk-eyed ——4——. To be sure, he applied the ——5—— of his wit to their often ——6—— and straggling phrases. But they tired of having him drain off their ——7—— of humor without paying any water-right. They abused him without ——8——, keeping score on his borrowings, and finally proved his NEMESIS by POPULARIZING his name as a new synonym for PLAGIARISM. Had they known enough, they would have called him a *Gehirnfresser.*

TEN, TENT (tin, tinu, tain), from *tenere, tentus:* to hold.

ABSTAIN	continual	detain	lieutenant	retinue	tenant
ABSTINENCE	continue	discontent	maintain	sustain	tenement
appertain	continent	entertain	obtain	sustenance	TENURE
content	countenance	impertinent	pertain	TENABLE	UNTENABLE
contentment		incontinent	retain	TENACIOUS	CONTINENCE

SCOTCHING A COMMON ERROR

The Puritans, says Grierson, were not remarkable for either ——1—— or ——2——. The only ——3—— view as to the origin of the term Puritanism is that it arose from their doctrine of the need for purifying church worship of Romish customs. Any other ETYMOLOGY is ——4——; yet the erroneous view as to its meaning has been held with great ——5——.

[3] Do not confuse with "to serve" from *servio, servire.*

TANG, TACT (ting, tag, tigu, tain, teg, tegr, tactus, tast), from *tangere, tactus:* to touch, to reach, to handle.

attain	contain	CONTINGENT	INTEGER	TACTFUL	TANGIBLE
ATTAINMENT	contagion	disintegrate	INTEGRAL	TACTILE	taste
contact	contagious	INTACT	INTEGRATION	TACTUAL	TASTELESS
CONTACTUAL	CONTIGUOUS	integrity	tact	TANGENT	TANGENTIAL

WAY OF THE DIGRESSOR

His mind was always going off at ——1——s. Yet so persuasive was his voice, and his enthusiasm was so ——2—— that he carried his listeners with him into these BYPATHS which were not even ——3—— to the subject in hand. His personal ——4—— was so great that his hearers were scarcely aware of his ——5——ing effect on their reasoning. His ——6—— was never affected, and he kept his GENIALITY no matter how far afield his ——7—— habits of discourse might lead him.

TEND, TENS, TENT, from *tendere, tensus,* or *tentus:* to stretch, strive, try.

attend	DISTENSION	INTENDANT	portend	superintend	TENSION
attendant	extend	INTENSIVE	PORTENT	superintendent	TENSILE
attention	extension	intent	pretend	tend	tent
contend	extensive	intention	PRETENDER	tendency	
contention	extent	OSTENSIBLE	pretense	tendon	
DISTEND	intend	OSTENTATION	SUBTEND	TENSE	

THE SHABBY DUKE

The late Duke of Rutland not only avoided ——1—— and ——2—— in his way of life; he was often positively shabby when he pursued his researches in the Reading Room of the British Museum. But his learning was as ——3—— as his wardrobe was meagre. Yet he showed no ——4—— toward pride of ERUDITION. If the rest of the House of Lords should suddenly become equally learned, it might ——5—— a counter-revolution in the British social scheme, with the aristocracy regaining by its brains what it lost through its INFLEXIBILITY.

VOC (voice, vou), from *vox, vocis:* voice.

advocate	CONVOKE	IRREVOCABLE	revoke	VOCABLE	voice
AVOCATION	invoke	provocation	UNIVOCAL	vocation	vouch
convocation	EQUIVOCATION	provoke	vocal	VOCIFEROUS	vowel

STORMY PETREL

War was at once his ——1—— and his ——2——. He ——3——d the Deity on all occasions. There was never any ——4—— in his talk, and his command of profane ——5——s was unequalled in the Army, even by the top sergeants to whom the general was closely akin in temper. ——6—— as he was, he realized that his tongue was a worse danger to him than the Germans; but he could not curb it. Off the battlefield he was like Nelson away from his QUARTERDECK: a liability to peace and order, but a great addition to the gaiety of nations.

TRAH, TRACT (trac, trail, train, tray, trait), from *trahere, tractus:* to draw.

abstract	CONTRACTILE	extract	RETRACT	TRACTILE	TRAINER
abstraction	DISTRAUGHT	portray	RETRACTION	TRACTION	TRAIT
attract	DETRACT	portrait	subtract	trace	
contract	distract	PROTRACT	SUBTRAHEND	trail	
contractor	entreat	protractor	tract	train	

CHINAMAN'S LAST CHANCE

General Marshall was increasingly ——1—— over the TORTUOUS EVASIONS and downright bad faith of both Chinese factions. The ——2——ed dispute had dragged on for two decades, and basic differences over property rights and control of STRATEGIC areas ran so deep, that he felt completely STYMIED. He would make a three-way agreement, which both Chinese groups would break without bothering to make a ——3——. Both sides mouthed freely ——4——s about democracy and peace, but these big words meant nothing.

UT, US, USUR (usu), from *uti, usus:* to use.

abuse	disuse	usage	useless	usury	utility
ABUSIVE	misuse	use	usual	utensil	UTILITARIAN
PERUSAL	peruse	useful			

TAKING INTEREST NO SIN AFTER A.D. 1550

The EXACTION of any interest whatever was regarded as ——1—— by the MEDIEVAL Church. It was a sin against nature, because gold and silver did not grow by natural increase. The Fathers and Doctors leveled ——2—— language at anyone who exacted interest. A ——3—— of the canon law as it then stood is instructive. However, by GLOSSARIAL re-interpretation the canon lawyers, following the rise of CAPITALISM, brought the law into harmony with actual ——4——. They made taking interest a sin only if the rate was over 10 per cent.

VEN, VENT, VENTU (veni, venu, ventu), from *venire, ventus:* to come.

CONTRAVENE	covenant	convent	EVENTUALLY	INVENTORY	venture
adventure	advent	convention	intervene	prevent	VENUE
avenue	convene	CONVENTUAL	invent	revenue	
CIRCUMVENT	convenient	event	INVENTIVE	SUPERVENE	

VOLPONE; OR HOW TO OUT-FOX A WHITE-COLLAR UNION

The problem was to ——1—— the union without ——2——ing the Wagner Act. He showed a good deal of ——3——ness in the ——4——. He ——5——ed some doubtful Thomases from joining, by sending his loyal stooges to work on them. It was noised around that there would be a drop in ——6——, and next in size of staff. "Loyal" employees got out circulars to this effect. Luck ——7——d on his behalf: several union members took jobs elsewhere; others left to get married. When the union came to take ——8—— of its chances in an election, it found it no longer had a majority. So the ——9—— of UNIONISM in this office was put off, perhaps forever.

VID, VIS (vey, vic, view), from *videre; visus:* to see.

advice	PREVISION	prudent	REVISIT	survey	visit
evidence	providence	PURVEY	SUPERVISE	SURVEYING	VISITANT
advise	PROVIDENT	review	supervision	view	
evident	provision	revise	SURVEILLANCE	visage	

INQUISITION

All members of the Embassy staff were kept under close ——1——. Any who had ——2——s of the wrong political complexion found his life more closely ——3——d, and it required no SUPERHUMAN ——4—— for him to realize that he would soon be shipped back to the United States. The Ambassador soon turned on him a ——5—— as forbidding as the Escorial walls, and made careful ——6—— to neutralize his actions. The more ——7—— followed the course so well described by Blake in the line, "Sneaking submission can always live."

SPEC, SPIC, SPECT (spici, speci, spy, spi), from *specere (spicere), spictus:* to look at.

aspect	ESPIONAGE	perspective	RETROSPECT	spectacles
AUSPICES	expect	PERSPICACITY	RETROSPECTION	spectator
AUSPICIOUS	expectant	PERSPICUITY	special	speculation
CIRCUMSPECT	expectation	prospect	SPECIFICATION	spice
CIRCUMSPECTION	INAUSPICIOUS	prospective	SPECIFY	spy
DESPICABLE	inspect	respect	specimen	suspicion
especial	inspection	respectable	SPECIOUS	
ESPIAL	introspective	respective	spectacle	

OFFICE OF SOCIAL SWANK

The OSS made ——1—— more than respectable, it gave it glamor. Under high-toned social ——2—— from the very start, it showed rare ——3—— in setting ——4——s for its feminine CONTINGENT. Family background and money were ——5——ly desirable attributes. Many an elegant ——6—— of the GENUS DEBUTANTE fought the war in the old red brick building in Washington. The agency did not engage in much ——7—— activity; it was all for action. It liked ——8—— in its AIDES, and did not encourage too much ——9—— habit of mind. The ——10—— of so much youth and beauty saving the Army and Navy Intelligence Services from mistakes they might otherwise have made, was indeed edifying. Yet in ——11—— there may be a few doubts; if so, these have not penetrated to Hollywood, which has put its most fetching glamor girls right into the OSS films, where they will pass ——12—— as well up to the wartime standard of PULCHRITUDE in the actual agency.

GREEK WORDS WITH MANY DERIVATIVES

DERIVATIVES from the following Greek words are mostly technical, so it is not feasible to weave them into fables such as were supplied for the

Latin derivatives preceding. Many of these words will turn up again in the section on technical vocabularies (Chapter XI). Notice that most of them have highly specific, DELIMITED meanings. You either know them or you don't.

ARCHE, beginning, rule, chief—ARCHANGEL, ANARCHY, ARCHIVES, ARCHETYPE, ARCHDUKE, architect, ARCHIPELAGO, ARCHITRAVE, HIERARCHY, monarchy, OLIGARCHY, PATRIARCH.

AGON, a contest—PROTAGONIST, agonizing, agony, ANTAGONIST.

ALLOS, another—ALLOTROPE, ALLOMORPH, ALLOPATHY, ALLOPHANE, ALLEGORY.

ASTER or ASTRON, a star—ASTER, ASTERISK, ASTRAL, ASTROLABE, disaster, ASTEROID, ASTROLOGY, ASTRONOMY.

BIBLOS or BIBLION, a book—BIBLIOPHILE, BIBLIOGRAPHY, BIBLICAL, BIBLIOMANCY, Bible, BIBLIOMANIA.

DEMOS, the people—democracy, epidemic, DEMOS, DEMOTIC, democrat, demagogue.

DRAO, I do, act—DRAMATURGY, dramatics, MELODRAMATIC, dramatize, drama.

DUNAMIS, power—DYNAMICS, dynamite, HYDRODYNAMICS, AERODYNAMICS, DYNAMOMETER, DYNAMO, DYNE.

EIDOS, form—KALEIDOSCOPE, SPHEROID, GEODE, CYCLOID, ANTHROPOID.

ELECTRON, amber—electricity, ELECTRON, ELECTRONICS, ELECTROLYSIS, DIALECTRIC.

ERGON, work—energy, METALLURGY, ALLERGY, ERG, ERGOMETER.

GE, the earth—geography, geology, geometry, GEOMORPHOLOGY, GEODESY, GEODETIC, GEOID, GEODE, GEOCENTRIC.

HUDOR (hydro-), water—hydraulic, hydrogen, HYDROPHOBIA, HYDRO, HYDROSTATIC, HYDRANT, DEHYDRATE.

HOMOS, the same—HOMOGRAPH, HOMOLOGUE, HOMONYM, HOMOMORPHY, HOMOLOGOUS, HOMOGENEOUS.

IDIOS, one's own, peculiar—IDIOM, IDIOSYNCRASY, idiot, IDIOCY, IDIOMORPHIC, IDIOCRACY, IDIOMATIC.

ISOS, equal—ISOCHRONOUS, ISOSCELES, ISOTHERM, ISOSTASY, ISOGONAL, ISOCLINE, ISOBAR, ISOTOPE.

K(C)LINEIN, to bend, slant, lean—CLINIC, DECLINATION, recline.

K(C)RYPTOS, hidden—CRYPTOGRAM, CRYPTIC, CRYPTOGRAPHY.

METRON, a measure—ANEMOMETER, BAROMETER, diameter, "FOOLOMETER" (Sydney Smith), GASOMETER, geometry, HEXAMETER, HYDROMETER, meter, PENTAMETER, PERIMETER, SYMMETRY, thermometer, TRIGONOMETRY.

MONOS, alone—monarch, monastery, MONOSYLLABLE, MONOGAMY, MONOLITH, MONOMANIA, MONOGRAPH, MONOGRAM, MONOCLE, monotonv.

NEOS, new—NEOLOGY, NEOPHYTE, Neocene, NEON, NEOLITHIC, NEOLOGISM, NEOPLASM.

PHOS, light—PHOSPHORUS, photograph, PHOTOMETER, PHOSPHATE, PHOTOSYN-THESIS, PHOTOSTAT.

PHILOS, loving, fond of—PHILOLOGY, philosophy, PHILANTHROPY, PHILHAR-MONIC.

PHONE, a sound—ANTIPHON, EUPHONY, EUPHONIOUS, PHONETICS, PHONIC, phono-graph, POLYPHONIC, PHONOLOGY, symphony.

PHUSIS, nature—PHYSIOGNOMY, PHYSIOGRAPHY, physic, PHYSICIST, METAPHYSICS, physician, physiology.

PROTOS, first—PROTONOTARY, PROTOCOL, PROTOMARTYR, protoplasm, PROTON, PROTOTYPE.

PSYCHE, soul, mind—PSYCHIATRY, PSYCHOANALYSIS, METEMPSYCHOSIS, PSYCHOSIS, PSYCHOTHERAPY.

SKOPEO, I see—bishop, episcopal, KALEIDOSCOPE, microscope, SCEPTIC, telescope, STEREOSCOPE, STETHOSCOPE.

TOPOS, a place—topic, TOPOGRAPHY, TOPONYM, TOPICAL, TOPARCHY.

ZOON, an animal—zoology, ZOOPHYTE, ZODIAC, EPIZOOTIC, PROTOZOAN, AZOIC, AZOTE, ZOON, ZOOTOMY (and at least 200 others in the OED).

WHAT ENGLISH WORDS COULD PLINY SIGHT-READ?

Among these words of classical origin that make up three fifths of our total stock, there are a surprising number that have come into English unchanged, even in spelling. The Greeks and Romans would not in some cases get the same meaning from one of these words as we do, if they could come back to life and see it in print. Caesar would know that *tractor* means something that draws something else along, a "puller"; but he could hardly be expected to identify it as a caterpillar tractor, powered with a gasoline engine. The Roman scientist Pliny, however, who knew his Greek as well, would spot a good many of the Greek words in something close to our sense, because he was the first to use them in that way: *naphtha* for crude oil, for example, and *pyrites* in our sense. ASBESTOS he knew was unburnable but he thought it a plant fiber. CINEMA (Gk. *kinema*) would stump him completely. He would know it meant "motion," but he couldn't realize that our word is short-ened from CINEMATOGRAPH, which is literally motion-picture.

If you want to check on your knowledge of CULTURAL history, you might amuse yourself by guessing which of the following 260 Latin words resurrected Romans would understand in the same sense we do; and how many of the subsequent 85 Greek words Pliny the Elder (A.D. 23-79) could sight-read. We'd have to print them in capitals for him, since he wouldn't know our lower-case type.

Where Greek words have come to us through the Latin, and where it's the Roman spelling that persists in English, I have for the most part included these immigrants in the Latin list, marking the clue word (Gk.) to distinguish them. I have also included many Late Latin and MEDIEVAL Latin words; but not those which since 1700 have been formed on ANALOGY with ancient rules from Greek or Latin stems by scientists or trade name inventors.

33. LATIN WORDS TAKEN INTO ENGLISH UNCHANGED

Some of these you have already met, on p. 93 *et seq.* As you will note from the fact that they're printed in SMALL CAPITALS, and have high frequency numbers, most of these words belong to the range between 11 and 20 thousand. You should know them if you want to have a thorough command of English. Since they come about midway in the book, it seems like a good idea to use them also as a comprehensive check on your vocabulary range. For each group of ten, match the key word with its right meaning in the second column. For 17 ( ) cancer, below, the right meaning in the second column is (j) malign tumor, so you put "j" in space in PARENTHESES after 17.

1. [ ] ALIAS (16)	[a]	Roman living room
2. [ ] ALMA MATER (20+)	[b]	halo; visible emanation
3. [ ] ALUMNI (13)	[c]	MEDIATOR plus; also ARBITER
4. [ ] ANTIPODES (16)	[d]	sharpest-pointed tip
5. [ ] AORTA (14)	[e]	graduates
6. [ ] APEX (12)	[f]	fake name
7. [ ] ARBITRATOR (11)	[g]	the great artery (Gk.)
8. [ ] ATRIUM (20)	[h]	foster mother
9. [ ] AURA (17)	[i]	extra pay
10. [ ] BONUS (14)	[j]	exactly opposite points on earth (Gk.)

11. [ ] CAESURA (19)	[a]	husk; SEPALS of flower (Gk.)
12. [ ] CALCULUS (17)	[b]	just under the bark
13. [ ] CALIBER (16)	[c]	top brain
14. [ ] calyx (10)	[d]	taker
15. [ ] CAMBIUM (12)	[e]	fluxions
16. [ ] camera (8)	[f]	diameter; quality
17. [ ] cancer (7)	[g]	pause
18. [ ] CAPTOR (17)	[h]	vote-fixing powwow
19. [ ] CAUCUS (13)	[i]	picture-taking device
20. [ ] CEREBRUM (14)	[j]	malign tumor

21. [   ] CEREBELLUM (17)
22. [   ] circus (5)
23. [   ] COADJUTOR (15)
24. [   ] COLOSSUS (17)
25. [   ] COMPENDIUM (20+)
26. [   ] CORNEA (20)
27. [   ] CORPUS (15)
28. [   ] CORTEX (12)
29. [   ] CRANIUM (14)
30. [   ] CORONÁ (19)

[a] digest
[b] outer coat of eye
[c] body
[d] brain case
[e] muscle-control center
[f] big tent show
[g] sun's AURA
[h] first aide (esp. to bishop)
[i] giant statue
[j] gray matter (lit., bark)

31. [   ] CRUX (19)
32. [   ] CUMULUS (20+)
33. [   ] CURATOR (16)
34. [   ] CURRICULUM (14)
35. [   ] CYCLOPEDIA (17)
36. [   ] DECORUM (11)
37. [   ] DELIRIUM (12)
38. [   ] DESIDERATUM (17)
39. [   ] DETRITUS (19)
40. [   ] DICTATOR (11)

[a] keeper
[b] raving frenzy
[c] propriety
[d] something sought after
[e] worn-off particles
[f] course of study
[g] all (?) about everything (Gk.)
[h] aut Caesar aut Stalin
[i] main point (lit., cross)
[j] rounded cloud

41. [   ] DICTUM (17)
42. [   ] DOLOR (15)
43. [   ] elector (8)
44. [   ] EQUILIBRIUM (13)
45. [   ] EQUINOX (14)
46. [   ] error (2)
47. [   ] EXPOSITOR (19)
48. [   ] EXTEMPORE (16)
49. [   ] FACTOTUM (20)
50. [   ] FEMUR (20)

[a] balance
[b] expounder
[c] on the spur of the moment
[d] do-it-all
[e] voter
[f] thigh-bone
[g] pronouncement
[h] night equals day
[i] grief
[j] mistake

51. [   ] FIAT (15)
52. [   ] FLAMEN (19)
53. [   ] focus (7)
54. [   ] FULCRUM (13)
55. [   ] FUNGI (14)
56. [   ] GALENA (20)
57. [   ] GENERATOR (15)
58. [   ] GENII (16)
59. [   ] genius (4)
60. [   ] GENS (20)

[a] molds
[b] clan; tribe
[c] dynamo; begetter
[d] where rays meet at a point
[e] spirits
[f] priest serving one god
[g] let there be; ukase
[h] supreme natural endowment
[i] lever rests on it
[j] lead SULPHIDE ore

61. [　] GENUS (11)
62. [　] GLADIATOR (11)
63. [　] GLADIOLUS (18)
64. [　] GYPSUM (20)
65. [　] HIATUS (20)
66. [　] HUMUS (14)
67. [　] IMPEDIMENTA (20+)
68. [　] IMPETUS (11)
69. [　] INCISOR (14)
70. [　] INCUNABULA (20+)

[a] gap
[b] (army) baggage (including baggages)
[c] earth
[d] CATEGORY between species and family
[e] Roman arena fighter
[f] species of iris
[g] front tooth
[h] books printed before 1500 A.D.
[i] HYDRATED CALCIUM
[j] forward drive

71. [　] index (6)
72. [　] INCUBATOR (11)
73. [　] INCUBUS (16)
74. [　] INERTIA (15)
75. [　] INFLUX (14)
76. [　] INSIGNIA (13)
77. [　] INSOMNIA (13)
78. [　] instructor (8)
79. [　] INTERIM (12)
80. [　] INTERIOR (12)

[a] inflowing
[b] sleeplessness
[c] teacher
[d] meanwhile
[e] non-hen egg-hatcher
[f] emblems
[g] key to contents
[h] inside
[i] tendency to stay put or keep moving
[j] burden

81. [　] INTERREGNUM (16)
82. [　] inventor (10)
83. [　] INVESTIGATOR (11)
84. [　] INVESTOR (14)
85. [　] isthmus (3)
86. [　] janitor (9)
87. [　] junior (5)
88. [　] LABOR (16)
89. [　] LABURNUM (18)
90. [　] LACUNA (20+)

[a] work
[b] younger
[c] gap (esp. in MS.)
[d] yellow-flowered shrub
[e] first maker of something new
[f] a breather between kings
[g] one who digs up the facts
[h] one who puts up money
[i] narrow land-bridge (Gk.)
[j] caretaker who also cleans

91. [　] LANGUOR (11)
92. [　] LAUDANUM (16)
93. [　] LEX (16)
94. [　] LICTOR (16)
95. [　] liquor (4)
96. [　] LUBRICATOR (14)
97. [　] major (4)
98. [　] MANIA (16)
99. [　] MANIPULATOR (20)
100. [　] MATRIX (17)

[a] slick handler
[b] greasing device; grease monkey
[c] more important (than a captain)
[d] madness
[e] law
[f] he carried the fasces
[g] mold for casting
[h] any liquid (esp. over 30% C_2H_5OH)
[i] opium in alcohol
[j] weariness

101. [ ] mediator (10)	[a] one who hoards and gloats
102. [ ] medium (4)	[b] brain switchboard
103. [ ] MEDULLA (18)	[c] go-between
104. [ ] MILLENNIUM (18)	[d] spiritual guide
105. [ ] minimum (8)	[e] trifling details
106. [ ] minister (2)	[f] midway between extremes
107. [ ] minus (10)	[g] presiding officer
108. [ ] MINUTIAE (20)	[h] less
109. [ ] miser (5)	[i] 1000 years (esp. after second coming)
110. [ ] MODERATOR (16)	[j] least

111. [ ] MODICUM (19)	[a] that seasick feeling (Gk.)
112. [ ] MOMENTUM (15)	[b] he plots the ship's course
113. [ ] museum (4)	[c] many in the Milky Way
114. [ ] NAUSEA (15)	[d] saltpetre
115. [ ] nautilus (10)	[e] pearly-shelled cephalopod
116. [ ] navigator (8)	[f] treasure-house of art, etc.
117. [ ] NEBULA (16)	[g] nothing
118. [ ] NIL (20+)	[h] what keeps it rolling
119. [ ] NEUTER (12)	[i] pinch; small amount
120. [ ] NITER (14)	[j] neither masculine nor feminine

121. [ ] NOSTRUM (15)	[a] pain-easing poppy extract
122. [ ] nucleus (7)	[b] HARBINGER
123. [ ] OCTOPUS (15)	[c] smell
124. [ ] ODIUM (20)	[d] quack remedy
125. [ ] odor (3)	[e] Carmen is one
126. [ ] omen (8)	[f] hatred
127. [ ] opera (4)	[g] one who bears down hard
128. [ ] operator (8)	[h] eight-armed sea mollusk (Gk.)
129. [ ] opium (7)	[i] one who runs the works
130. [ ] oppressor (8)	[j] central core

131. [ ] OPPROBRIUM (20)	[a] egg
132. [ ] orator (6)	[b] one of the conic section curves (Gk.)
133. [ ] OVUM (15)	[c] paleness
134. [ ] PALLADIUM (17)	[d] cure-all
135. [ ] PALLOR (16)	[e] tiny nipple-like projection
136. [ ] PANACEA (17)	[f] equal
137. [ ] PAPILLA (14)	[g] severe reproach
138. [ ] PAR (17)	[h] Cicero was one; so's Churchill
139. [ ] PARABOLA (15)	[i] one who takes a share
140. [ ] PARTICIPATOR (20+)	[j] safeguard (Gk.

141. [　] pastor (5)
142. [　] PAX (19)
143. [　] PELVIS (17)
144. [　] peninsula (5)
145. [　] per (2)
146. [　] PER CAPITA (17)
147. [　] PERPETRATOR (17)
148. [　] PERSECUTOR (13)
149. [　] petroleum (6)
150. [　] PLEBS (19)

[a] the HOI POLLOI; the common folks
[b] where hipbones and spine meet
[c] oil
[d] peace
[e] clergyman
[f] each
[g] relentless annoyer
[h] so much apiece
[i] the man whodunit
[j] next thing to an island

151. [　] PLEXUS (20)
152. [　] plus (8)
153. [　] PRAETOR (16)
154. [　] PRECEPTOR (15)
155. [　] PRECURSOR (17)
156. [　] premium (7)
157. [　] prior (7)
158. [　] PROBOSCIS (12)
159. [　] PROCONSUL (15)
160. [　] PROCTOR (19)

[a] extra inducement
[b] teacher
[c] forerunner
[d] MacArthur is one
[e] Roman judge
[f] long snout; trunk (Gk.)
[g] more; and; added to
[h] balled-up mass of nerves, etc.
[i] before; one which takes precedence
[j] university moral policeman

161. [　] PROCURATOR (16)
162. [　] progenitor (9)
163. [　] projector (10)
164. [　] PROLIX (16)
165. [　] PROPAGANDA (11)
166. [　] PROSPECTOR (15)
167. [　] pupa (8)
168. [　] QUAESTOR (17)
169. [　] QUASI (16)
170. [　] QUIETUS (17)

[a] Roman public treasurer
[b] usually found in cocoon
[c] ore-hunter; now after uranium
[d] spreading opinions
[e] tax-extractor for a Roman province
[f] we run film through it; a schemer
[g] wordy
[h] half-way; seeming; as if
[i] COMEUPPANCE; finishing stroke
[j] forefather

171. [　] QUONDAM (16)
172. [　] QUORUM (17)
173. [　] QUOTA (14)
174. [　] radius (8)
175. [　] RANCOR (15)
176. [　] ratio (7)
177. [　] rector (9)
178. [　] RECTUM (17)
179. [　] REFERENDUM (11)
180. [　] REFLUX (15)

[a] relative magnitude
[b] extreme hatred
[c] referring legislature's act to people
[d] onetime
[e] Episcopal parish clergyman
[f] backflow
[g] end of large intestine
[h] distance from center to rim
[i] number needed to do business
[j] share of total

181. [ ] REGIMEN (13)   [a] holy place for refuge
182. [ ] register (3)   [b] speaker's platform
183. [ ] REJUVENATOR (18)   [c] eye's sensitive image-receiver
184. [ ] REPLICA (19)   [d] week of whoopee late in December
185. [ ] RETINA (11)   [e] spit
186. [ ] ROSTRUM (13)   [f] airborne gossip
187. [ ] rumor (4)   [g] exact reproduction
188. [ ] saliva (8)   [h] youth-restorer
189. [ ] SANCTUM (17)   [i] list for record
190. [ ] SATURNALIA (20)   [j] the doctor lays it down

191. [ ] SECTOR (16)   [a] expressed comparison
192. [ ] SEMI (20)   [b] fancy word for a menial
193. [ ] SEPULCHER (7)   [c] sequence
194. [ ] series (4)   [d] part of military area
195. [ ] SERUM (11)   [e] bone cavity
196. [ ] SERVITOR (13)   [f] sun
197. [ ] SILVA (18)   [g] half
198. [ ] simile (8)   [h] forest
199. [ ] SINUS (15)   [i] tomb
200. [ ] SOL (14)   [j] ANTITOXIN is one

201. [ ] solicitor (8)   [a] endurance; staying power
202. [ ] spectator (7)   [b] stock-gambler: bull or bear
203. [ ] SPECULATOR (17)   [c] magnificent show
204. [ ] splendor (4)   [d] he drums up business
205. [ ] SPONSOR (18)   [e] he looks on
206. [ ] SPUTUM (20)   [f] to blame for soap opera; godparent
207. [ ] STADIUM (16)   [g] coughed-up spit
208. [ ] stamen (9)   [h] pollen-carrying ANTHER
209. [ ] STAMINA (15)   [i] condition
210. [ ] STATUS (11)   [j] AMPHITHEATRE for games

211. [ ] STERNUM (20)   [a] overseer (of slaves or teachers)
212. [ ] stimulus (8)   [b] one who outlives others
213. [ ] STRATA (13)   [c] above
214. [ ] STUPOR (13)   [d] Greek drink-and-talkfest (Gk.)
215. [ ] SUBSTRATUM (12)   [e] daze
216. [ ] SUPER (20)   [f] above the average; man over you
217. [ ] superior (2)   [g] underlayer
218. [ ] supervisor (9)   [h] breast bone
219. [ ] survivor (7)   [i] layers
220. [ ] SYMPOSIUM (18)   [j] it stirs or excites action

221. [   ] TANTALUS (17)
222. [   ] TAURUS (19)
223. [   ] TEDIUM (18)
224. [   ] TESTATOR (16)
225. [   ] TETANUS (13)
226. [   ] THALLUS (19)
227. [   ] THYMUS (19)
228. [   ] TIARA (13)
229. [   ] TIBIA (16)
230. [   ] TOGA (19)

[a] thicker lower leg bone
[b] muscular spasm (Gk.)
[c] jeweled headdress or crown
[d] he couldn't reach the grapes (Gk.)
[e] sign of the bull; a constellation
[f] maker of a will
[g] boredom
[h] Roman gentleman's outer robe
[i] gland in neck (Gk.)
[j] a mushroom is one (Gk.)

231. [   ] TORPOR (18)
232. [   ] tractor (9)
233. [   ] TRANSGRESSOR (12)
234. [   ] TRANSLATOR (16)
235. [   ] TRIUMVIR (16)
236. [   ] tuber (10)
237. [   ] TUMOR (11)
238. [   ] tutor (5)
239. [   ] TYMPANUM (14)
240. [   ] TYPHUS

[a] a potato is one
[b] necessary since BABEL
[c] pestilential fever
[d] one of three men ruling
[e] sluggish state
[f] heavy puller
[g] sinner; he steps over
[h] drum
[i] teaches one student at a time
[j] swelling growth

241. [   ] ulcer (10)
242. [   ] ULTERIOR (18)
243. [   ] ULTRA (18)
244. [   ] UTERUS (18)
245. [   ] vapor (3)
246. [   ] VELLUM (14)
247. [   ] VERSUS (20)
248. [   ] VERTEBRA (14)
249. [   ] VERTEX (17)
250. [   ] vesper (9)

[a] highest point
[b] against
[c] evening song or service
[d] backbone
[e] finest parchment
[f] womb
[g] steam; fog
[h] pus-discharging sore
[i] hidden
[j] beyond

251. [   ] veto (10)
252. [   ] via (10)
253. [   ] vice- (3)
254. [   ] victor (10)
255. [   ] vigor (3)
256. [   ] villa (9)
257. [   ] VIRUS (17)
258. [   ] VISCERA (17)
259. [   ] VORTEX (15)
260. [   ] vox (20+)

[a] whirlpool; WHORL
[b] the "innards"
[c] strength
[d] voice
[e] to "nix" a bill or act (lit. *"I forbid."*)
[f] winner
[g] suburban mansion
[h] by way of
[i] in place of: No. 2 man
[j] FILTERABLE infectious substance

Find out how you've scored by consulting the key at the end of the chapter and checking off your errors. Subtract your error score from 200. Multiply the resulting figure by 50 and add 10,000. This should be a conservative estimate of your vocabulary within the 20,000-word range. Of the 260 words above, 54 are in the first 10,000 for FREQUENCY and range—hence, by our assumption, you should undoubtedly know them; 13 are in the range 20 to 30,000, so half of them are arbitrarily discounted. Many of the 260 are semi-technical, hence they are probably harder nuts to crack than many of the words that belong in the same frequency groups with them. However, you have an advantage here that you would not have if you came on the words in your reading. Clues are given, in scrambled lists to be sure, but these afford something of the same advantage that the clues do in a crossword puzzle. You can arrive at some meanings by guesswork and the method of RESIDUES; and in other cases the clue synonym, definition, or catch phrase CRYSTALLIZES a connection that was very vague indeed until you ran down the column of ten possible meanings and finally hit on one that clicked in your mind. Balancing off the PROS and CONS, this is therefore probably a relatively fair measure of what proportion you know of the "highbrow" words in the 20,000 commonest.—Just as a teaser, can you spot the one word in the right-hand clue column which should be included among the actual Latin words that have come in unchanged?

34. GREEK WORDS TAKEN INTO ENGLISH UNCHANGED

Follow the same procedure as you used for the Latin words above.

1. [ ] ACME (13)	[a] food of the gods
2. [ ] AETHER (17)	[b] first letter of Greek alphabet
3. [ ] ALPHA (20)	[c] color-changing lizard
4. [ ] AMBROSIA (14)	[d] slender tube for body orifices
5. [ ] analysis (8)	[e] upper air
6. [ ] ANTITHESIS (16)	[f] high point (of a quality)
7. [ ] APOTHEOSIS (18)	[g] breaking it up; in statistics, a breakdown
8. [ ] ASBESTOS (11)	[h] unburnable
9. [ ] CATHETER (19)	[i] glorification
10. [ ] CHAMELEON (13)	[j] direct opposite
11. [ ] chaos (6)	[a] basis for judging
12. [ ] character (2)	[b] disease due to liver DYSFUNCTION
13. [ ] CHIMERA (16)	[c] wild fancy
14. [ ] CHOLER (17)	[d] movie
15. [ ] CINEMA (18)	[e] anger
16. [ ] COSMOS (13)	[f] world order; universe
17. [ ] CRATER (13)	[g] nature; make-up
18. [ ] CRITERION (15)	[h] bowl-shaped hole in volcano
19. [ ] delta (6)	[i] ultimate in disorder
20. [ ] DIABETES (13)	[j] area around river mouth, silt-built

21. [ ] DIAGNOSIS (15)   [a] puzzle
22. [ ] DIAPASON (15)   [b] gullet
23. [ ] DILEMMA (13)   [c] I have found it
24. [ ] DOGMA (11)   [d] unit minus electrical charge
25. [ ] drama (5)   [e] swelling musical sound
26. [ ] ENIGMA (12)   [f] naming the disease from the symptoms
27. [ ] EPITOME (14)   [g] brief version
28. [ ] ESOPHAGUS (18)   [h] a play
29. [ ] EUREKA (20+)   [i] AUTHORITARIAN doctrine
30. [ ] ELECTRON (20)   [j] either way, you're stuck

31. [ ] EXODUS (13)   [a] dictionary
32. [ ] GANGLION (13)   [b] EXAGGERATION for effect
33. [ ] HALCYON (16)   [c] laughing or crying fit
34. [ ] HYPERBOLE (15)   [d] nerve cluster
35. [ ] HYSTERIA (19)   [e] a going out
36. [ ] ICHNEUMON (18)   [f] jot; "i" was smallest letter
37. [ ] idea (2)   [g] MONGOOSE-like animal
38. [ ] IOTA (20)   [h] happy and peaceful
39. [ ] ISOSCELES (20)   [i] something conceived in the mind
40. [ ] LEXICON (16)   [j] with two sides equal

41. [ ] metamorphosis (8!) [a] goddess of RETRIBUTION
42. [ ] metropolis (7)   [b] musicians or where they sit
43. [ ] MYRMIDON (16)   [c] henchman
44. [ ] NAPHTHA (14)   [d] chief city
45. [ ] Nemesis (15)   [e] change of form
46. [ ] oasis (7)   [f] inflammable volatile liquid
47. [ ] OMEGA (17)   [g] fertile spot in desert
48. [ ] ONYX (16)   [h] ornamental stone
49. [ ] OPHTHALMIA (18)   [i] last letter of Gk. alphabet; it is long "o"
50. [ ] orchestra (5)   [j] eye-infection

51. [ ] osmosis (10)   [a] curved lines used to set off insert
52. [ ] PAPYRUS (17)   [b] light carriage
53. [ ] PARALLAX (17)   [c] observable things
54. [ ] PARALYSIS (11)   [d] sadness
55. [ ] PATHOS (12)   [e] two-way SEEPAGE through porous membrane
56. [ ] PHAETON (19)   [f] paper from pith
57. [ ] PHALANX (11)   [g] angle change in direction as eye shifts
58. [ ] PHARYNX (12)   [h] back of mouth
59. [ ] PARENTHESIS (20)   [i] wedge-shaped fighting group with locked
                                shields
60. [ ] PHENOMENA (16)   [j] palsy

133

61. [ ] phenomenon (7)	[a] Cupid's girl friend; the soul
62. [ ] PHOENIX (13)	[b] iron SULFIDES
63. [ ] plasma (10)	[c] plural marriage; POLYGYNY or POLYANDRY
64. [ ] POLYGAMY (15)	[d] elder
65. [ ] POLYGON (19)	[e] a glass that breaks up white light
66. [ ] PRESBYTER (15)	[f] Book of Psalms
67. [ ] prism (7)	[g] liquid part of blood
68. [ ] PSALTER (16)	[h] plane figure with more than four sides
69. [ ] PSYCHE (11)	[i] it's unusual
70. [ ] PYRITES (19)	[j] it rose from its own ashes

71. [ ] PYTHON (19)	[a] goat-footed nymph-chasing god
72. [ ] PYX (19)	[b] stone coffin
73. [ ] SARCOPHAGUS (17)	[c] male reproductive cell
74. [ ] satyr (8)	[d] big snake; a constrictor
75. [ ] SPERMATOZOON (20+)	[e] mark of disgrace
76. [ ] STIGMA (17)	[f] bird's eye view; summary
77. [ ] STOMA (17)	[g] combining parts into whole
78. [ ] STROPHE (17)	[h] stanza
79. [ ] SYNOPSIS (18)	[i] mouth
80. [ ] SYNTHESIS (11)	[j] container for Host

81. [ ] THERMOS (17)	[a] figure of speech
82. [ ] THESIS (12)	[b] beginner; raw recruit
83. [ ] THORAX (11)	[c] chest
84. [ ] TROPE (14)	[d] essay submitted for degree
85. [ ] TYRO (18)	[e] heat-conserver

Check by the key as you did for the Latin words. Subtract your error score from 85. Multiply the resulting figure by 117 and add 10,000 to it, to get another estimate of your vocabulary within the 20,000-word limit. How does your vocabulary score on the Greek refugees compare with the luck you had with the Roman fugitives?

QUIZ KEYS FOR CHAPTER VI

29. Page 94.	30. Page 95.	31. Page 96.
1. putrefaction	1. composite	1. conduce
2. versification	2. Impost	2. adduce
3. disaffection	3. apposite	3. abduction
4. exemplification	4. deposition	4. deducible
5. comfit	5. exponent	5. traduce
6. beneficiary	6. decomposition, compost	6. deduction
7. affected	7. transposition	7. induction, deductive
8. pontifical	8. juxtaposition	8. ducal
9. inefficiency	9. depository	9. conducive
10. unification	10. propound	10. seduction

32. Page 100.

AG:
1. agency   2. ambiguity   3. variegated   4. litigation   5. manager
6. actor   7. castigated   8. agent   9. management   10. prodigal
11. cogent   12. agitation   13. synagogue   14. mitigate   15. actuated

APT:
1. inept   2. apt   3. attitudes   4. aptitude   5. adaptability

CERN:
1. discernment 2. indiscretions 3. secretive 4. indiscreet   5. discernible

ART:
1. artistic   2. artless   3. artful   4. artistries   5. artillery
6. inert   7. artistry   8. inertia   9. inertly   10. artifacts
11. artisans

AUD:
1. audiences 2. audible   3. inaudible   4. obeisance   5. auditors
6. audits   7. auditions

CAN:
1. accent   2. enchantment 3. cantata   4. chant   5. canticle
6. recant   7. accentuated 8. cant

CAP:
1. occupation 2. conceit   3. deceive   4. deception   5. captivity
6. susceptible 7. participant 8. receptions   9. capacity   10. emancipation
11. municipal 12. precepts   13. acceptable 14. participle   15. incipient

COR:
1. concordance 2. discord

CRED:
1. creed   2. incredible   3. incredulous 4. credulity   5. discredit
6. credence   7. credit

CED:
1. process   2. succeeded   3. conceded   4. ancestor   5. recess
6. cessation 7. procedure

CURR:
1. courier   2. precursor   3. recurred   4. excursion   5. cursory
6. concurred

CLAUS:
1. recluse   2. secluded   3. cloistered   4. precluded   5. include

CLAM:
1. declamation 2. clamorous   3. exclamatory 4. exclamation   5. declaim
6. clamor   7. claim   8. reclamation 9. reclaim

DIGN:
1. disdainful   2. indignities   3. dignitary   4. indignation 5. dignity
6. dainties

CAPIT:
1. precipitate   2. capitalism   3. precipitate   4. chapter   5. cattle
6. captains   7. capitulation 8. capitalists   9. recapitulation

DAT:
1. editor   2. tradition   3. data   4. edition   5. editorials
6. edit   7. absconded   8. "extraditing" 9. rendezvous

DIC:
1. interdict   2. adjudicating 3. dictatorial   4. predicated   5. dictum
6. abdication   7. valedictory

CUR:
1. curator   2. secure   3. security   4. surety

FORM:
1. form   2. uniformity   3. conformity   4. formalism   5. formula
6. formulate   7. information 8. transformation 9. informality 10. forms

FER, LAT:
1. sufferance   2. pestiferous   3. vociferous   4. delays   5. references
6. fertility   7. circumference 8. preference   9. proffer   10. deference

EQU:
1. equivocal   2. equal   3. equanimity   4. equity   5. equator
6. equinoctial   7. equivalence 8. equation   9. unequal

FRANG:
1. fractional   2. refractory   3. infractions   4. irrefragable 5. fractures
6. fragile   7. fragment   8. suffrage

HAB:
1. inhibitions   2. habiliments 3. habitual   4. debilitating 5. exhibit
6. exhibition

GER:
1. jester   2. congeries   3. jests   4. digestion   5. gesticulations
6. suggestions 7. vicegerent

GRAT:
1. ingrate   2. grateful   3. gratitude   4. congratulate 5. graceless
6. disagreement 7. gratuity

MAN:
1. amanuensis 2. maneuvered 3. manacles   5. manifesto   4. manumission

136

JECT:
1. projections   2. trajectory   3. conjecture   4. objective   5. jetsam
6. adjacent

MITT:
1. emissary   2. dismissed   3. intermittent 4. permit   5. missiles
6. missive   7. commission 8. remiss   9. commissary 10. emitting
11. committee   12. compromised

JUNG:
1. injunction   2. conjugation 3. conjunctions 4. disjunctive   5. subjunctive
6. subjugated   7. disjointed

LEG:
1. predilection 2. legibility   3. intelligibility 4. elegance   5. lecture
6. legend   7. legible   8. collection   9. dialectics

PAR:
1. separating   2. preparatory 3. sever   4. dissevered

MOV:
1. momentum   2. mobilizing   3. emotions   4. movable   **5. movements**
6. commotion   7. motif   8. locomotive   9. motion

NOT:
1. noble   2. notoriously 3. connotations 4. denotations 5. denotes
6. incognito   7. recognition

PET:
1. competition 2. impetus   3. centripetal   4. repetitive   5. incompetent
6. petulant

PAND:
1. encompass   2. expanded   3. surpassing

MOD:
1. modern   2. accommodations   3. commodious 4. mode   5. modification
6. modal   7. modish   8. modicum

PORT:
1. port   2. export   3. import   4. transportation   5. portable
6. porters   7. deportation

PLAC:
1. complacency 2. implacable   3. pleasantries   4. complacent

PLIC:
1. pliant   2. supple   3. duplicities   4. implications 5. explicit
6. complexes   7. complicity   8. multiplicity 9. ply   10. deploy

SENT:
1. sententious 2. sensuous   3. sensual   4. dissent   5. sensibilities
6. unsentimental   7. scents   8. presentiment   9. senseless

PART:
1. parse   2. compartments   3. counterpart   4. impartially   5. particle
6. proportion   7. imparted

PREHEND:
1. prehensile   2. comprehension   3. apprised   4. reprehensible   5. reprisals
6. enterprise   7. apprentice   8. impregnable   9. apprehended   10. prison

RAP:
1. rapacious   2. ravenous   3. ravage   4. surreptitious   5. ravens

QUER:
1. acquisitive   2. inquisitorial   3. inquest   4. perquisites   5. inquisitive
6. question   7. requisition

RUPT:
1. eruption   2. disrupted   3. rout   4. ruptures

SAL:
1. onslaught   2. salacious   3. desultory   4. exultation   5. salient
6. resultant   7. resilience

REG:
1. insurrection   2. real   3. directors   4. realists   5. incorrigible
6. insurgents   7. regime   8. regimen   9. rectitude   10. irregularities
11. reign   12. resurrection

SED:
1. insidious   2. sedentary   3. residuary   4. assiduous

SIGN:
1. signature   2. countersign   3. signify   4. sign   5. significance

STA:
1. consists   2. stationary   3. circumstantial   4. statement   5. contrast
6. stable   7. irresistible   8. institution   9. restive   10. resistance
11. statue   12. transubstantiation

STRING:
1. astringent   2. strictures   3. distressing   4. constrained   5. constriction
6. constraints

SEQU:
1. sectarian   2. persecute   3. prosecutes   4. pursues   5. obsequiously
6. persecution   7. execution   8. obsequies   9. sectaries

SERV:
1. conservation   2. conserved   3. preserves   4. observation   5. preservative
6. unreserved   7. reservoir   8. reservation

TEN:
1. abstinence   2. continence   3. tenable   4. untenable   5. tenacity

138

TANG:
1. tangents 2. contagious 3. contiguous 4. integrity 5. disintegrating
6. taste 7. tangential

TEND:
1. ostentation 2. pretence 3. extensive 4. tendency 5. portend

VOC:
1. vocation 2. avocation 3. invoked 4. equivocation 5. vocables
6. vociferous

TRAH:
1. distraught 2. protracted 3. retraction 4. abstractions

UT:
1. usury 2. abusive 3. perusal 4. usage

VEN:
1. circumvent 2. contravening 3. inventiveness 4. venture 5. prevented
6. revenue 7. intervened 8. inventory 9. advent

VID:
1. surveillance 2. visitants 3. supervised 4. prevision 5. visage
6. provision 7. prudent

SPEC:
1. espionage 2. auspices 3. perspicacity 4. specifications 5. especially
6. specimen 7. introspective 8. circumspection 9. speculative 10. spectacle
11. retrospect 12. inspection

33. Page 125.

1. [f]	11. [g]	21. [e]	31. [i]	41. [g]	51. [g]	61. [d]
2. [h]	12. [e]	22. [f]	32. [j]	42. [i]	52. [f]	62. [e]
3. [e]	13. [f]	23. [h]	33. [a]	43. [e]	53. [d]	63. [f]
4. [j]	14. [a]	24. [i]	34. [f]	44. [a]	54. [i]	64. [i]
5. [g]	15. [b]	25. [a]	35. [g]	45. [h]	55. [a]	65. [a]
6. [d]	16. [i]	26. [b]	36. [c]	46. [j]	56. [j]	66. [c]
7. [c]	17. [j]	27. [c]	37. [b]	47. [b]	57. [c]	67. [b]
8. [a]	18. [d]	28. [j]	38. [d]	48. [c]	58. [e]	68. [j]
9. [b]	19. [h]	29. [d]	39. [e]	49. [d]	59. [h]	69. [g]
10. [i]	20. [c]	30. [g]	40. [h]	50. [f]	60. [b]	70. [h]

71. [g]	81. [f]	91. [j]	101. [c]	111. [i]	121. [d]	131. [g]
72. [e]	82. [e]	92. [i]	102. [f]	112. [h]	122. [j[	132.]h]
73. [j]	83. [g]	93. [e]	103. [b]	113. [f]	123. [h]	133. [a]
74. [i]	84. [h]	94. [f]	104. [i]	114. [a]	124. [f]	134. [j]
75. [a]	85. [i]	95. [h]	105. [j]	115. [e]	125. [c]	135. [c]
76. [f]	86. [j]	96. [b]	106. [d]	116. [b]	126. [b]	136. [d]
77. [b]	87. [b]	97. [c]	107. [h]	117. [c]	127. [e]	137. [e]
78. [c]	88. [a]	98. [d]	108. [e]	118. [g]	128. [i]	138. [f]
79. [d]	89. [d]	99. [a]	109. [a]	119. [j]	129. [a]	139. [b]
80. [h]	90. [c]	100. [g]	110. [g]	120. [d]	130. [g]	140. [i]

141. [e]	151. [h]	161. [e]	171. [d]	181. [j]	191. [d]	201. [d]
142. [d]	152. [g]	162. [j]	172. [i]	182. [i]	192. [g]	202. [e]
143. [b]	153. [e]	163. [f]	173. [j]	183. [h]	193. [i]	203. [b]
144. [j]	154. [b]	164. [g]	174. [h]	184. [g]	194. [c]	204. [c]
145. [f]	155. [c]	165. [d]	175. [b]	185. [c]	195. [j]	205. [f]
146. [h]	156. [a]	166. [c]	176. [a]	186. [b]	196. [b]	206. [g]
147. [i]	157. [i]	167. [b]	177. [e]	187. [f]	197. [h]	207. [j]
148. [g]	158. [f]	168. [a]	178. [g]	188. [e]	198. [a]	208. [h]
149. [c]	159. [d]	169. [h]	179. [c]	189. [a]	199. [e]	209. [a]
150. [a]	160. [j]	170. [i]	180. [f]	190. [d]	200. [f]	210. [i]

211. [h]	221. [d]	231. [e]	241. [h]	251. [e]
212. [j]	222. [e]	232. [f]	242. [i]	252. [h]
213. [i]	223. [g]	233. [g]	243. [j]	253. [i]
214. [e]	224. [f]	234. [b]	244. [f]	254. [f]
215. [g]	225. [b]	235. [d]	245. [g]	255. [c]
216. [c]	226. [j]	236. [a]	246. [e]	256. [g]
217. [f]	227. [i]	237. [j]	247. [b]	257. [j]
218. [a]	228. [c]	238. [i]	248. [d]	258. [b]
219. [b]	229. [a]	239. [h]	249. [a]	259. [a]
220. [d]	230. [h]	240. [c]	250. [c]	260. [d]

34. Page 132.

1. [f]	11. [i]	21. [f]	31. [e]	41. [e]	51. [e]	61. [i]
2. [e]	12. [g]	22. [e]	32. [d]	42. [d]	52. [f]	62. [j]
3. [b]	13. [c]	23. [j]	33. [h]	43. [c]	53. [g]	63. [g]
4. [a]	14. [e]	24. [i]	34. [b]	44. [f]	54. [j]	64. [c]
5. [g]	15. [d]	25. [h]	35. [c]	45. [a]	55. [d]	65. [h]
6. [j]	16. [f]	26. [a]	36. [g]	46. [g]	56. [b]	66. [d]
7. [i]	17. [h]	27. [g]	37. [i]	47. [i]	57. [i]	67. [e]
8. [h]	18. [a]	28. [b]	38. [f]	48. [h]	58. [h]	68. [f]
9. [d]	19. [j]	29. [c]	39. [j]	49. [j]	59. [a]	69. [a]
10. [c]	20. [b]	30. [d]	40. [a]	50. [b]	60. [c]	70. [b]

71. [d]	81. [e]
72. [j]	82. [d]
73. [b]	83. [c]
74. [a]	84. [a]
75. [c]	85. [b]
76. [e]	
77. [i]	
78. [h]	
79. [f]	
80. [g]	

1. What are the terms for
   (a) fear of closed places
   (b) fear of high places
   (c) fear of open spaces
   (d) fear of animals?
2. What is the learned term for the "study" or "science of devils"?
3. What is the term used in histories of art in discussing the "beautiful penmanship" or "writing" of the Chinese literati?
4. What was Pontius Pilate's official title?
5. The Latin word for "whey" or "watery fluid," —————, is now used to apply to certain liquid vaccines which our doctors use to fight virulent diseases.
6. An all-round handy man is called a —————, shortened from the old nickname for such a man, Johannes —————. The word really means a "do-it-all."
7. Reasoning which proceeds by syllogism from the general to the particular is called —————. Its opposite is ————— reasoning.
8. One of the famous rules of Latin grammar is that verbs compounded with *ad, ante, circum, con, in, inter, ob, post, prae,* and sometimes *super* take the dative. What does each of these prefixes mean?
9. What are some of the current "Isms" that figure large in the world today?
10. What is the technical term for "the process of heating through or deep, without warming the surface"?
11. What is the antonym of *centrifugal?*
12. A pause in poetry, corresponding to a rest in music, is called a
—————.
13. A famous political society in England, of which Wells, Shaw, the Webbs, and Sydney Olivier were members, is called the ————— Society, from the name of a Roman general and consul who used delaying tactics in fighting Hannibal.
14. A large tomb-edifice is called a —————, from King —————, who built a famous one.
15. A parting shot is often called a ————— shot, from the Persian tribesman who used to, while they were riding away at a fast pace, let fly their arrows at the Romans.
16. The catch-all for all the classical deities was called the —————.
17. What is the legal Latin for "basic facts of a crime"? —————
—————.
18. A blow-up of a photograph, transferred to a wall, is called, according to the New Word List in Webster's, a —————.
19. In advertising cant, ads which are meant merely to keep a firm name or brand name before the public, rather than to sell goods, are known as ————— ads.

20. Glare-preventing glass is labeled —————.
21. A form of union agreement with an employer which leaves him free to hire whomever he will, with the understanding that after a certain period of employment the new employee will join the union, is called the ————— shop.
22. Distinguish between the terms *wit* and *humor*.
23. A synonym for *dictionary* is —————.
24. *Lousy* is labeled by the dictionaries —————.
25. What is the literal meaning of the word *context?* What is its present day meaning in linguistics?

VII

WORD-ANALYZER

This Word-Analyzer is meant as a working tool, to be used when you feel the need of it. Regard it as a stand-by service, and consult it at leisure. It will not make you an ETYMOLOGIST overnight (see p. 146). But it should be useful in showing you how to break down classical words in English into their component parts. You can thus get at their literal meaning, which is a good start.

The Word-Analyzer includes

1. The 70 commonest Latin stems. Memorize them.
2. The 30 commonest Greek stems. Memorize them.
3. Latin prefixes and SUFFIXES.
4. Greek prefixes and suffixes.

Suppose you want to analyze the word SUPERSCRIPTION: First break it down into its parts, then look them up in the tables,—main stem first, then the suffix, finally, the prefix:

super	*SCRIPT*	*-ion*
"above"	"written"	"state of being," or "that which"

Of the two meanings of the suffix, "that which" makes more sense. Superscription is "that which (is) written above,"—such as a heading.

Here's the recipe in general terms:

First, break off the prefix and/or suffix. The main stem (or stems) should then be apparent.

Second, look up the meaning of the stem in the checklists. Put it under the stem in the breakdown.

Third, try to identify the prefix and/or suffix in the appropriate lists. Because their combining forms are tricky, and the Latin and English suffixes of identical spelling have different meanings, this may take a bit of trial-and-error procedure before you get a combination that seems to make sense.

Fourth, rearrange in English order the equivalents you have set down under the elements of the word. This should give the literal meaning.

Word-Analyzer

The 100 commonest Latin and Greek stems figure in more than 5000 English derivatives in the range just beyond the average American's vocabulary of 10,000 words. Learn to use the 100 classical stems to sight-read these five thousand words and you have a short cut that will put you a long way on the road toward doubling your vocabulary. Many of the 5000 are terms used in business, medicine, chemistry, technology. If you know the 100 stems, and the most used Latin and Greek affixes (prefixes and suffixes), you can analyze many words new to you, when you run into them in your reading. A break-down of the word will

inter-	POSIT	-ion	
between	placing	act of	'act of placing between'

LATIN STEM	MEANING	DERIVATIVES
AG, ACT	to do, to drive	transaction, exigency
AM, AMAT	to love	amative, amicability
APT	fit or fitted	adaptability, readaptation
ART	art, skill, method	artifact, artificer
AUD, AUDIT	to hear	inaudible, audition
CAD, CAS	to fall	casualty, decasualize
CAN, CANT	to sing	recantation, incantation
CAP, CAPT	to take, to seize	capacity, exceptionable
CAPIT	head	decapitation, precipitate
CED, CESS	to yield, to go	intercession, antecedent
CERN, CRET	to distinguish	discernible, indiscretion
CLAM, CLAMAT	to cry out	exclamatory, reclamation
CLUD, CLUS	to close	exclusivity, occlusion
COR, CORD	heart	discordant, concordance
CRED, CREDIT	to believe	incredibility, accredited
CUR, CURAT	to care for	insecurity, procurator
CURR, CURS	to run	precursor, recurrent
DAT	to give	extradition, antedate
DIC, DICT	to speak, to say	abdication, noncontradictory
DIGN	worthy	indignity, condign
DUC, DUCT	to lead	deduction, noninductive
EQU	equal	inequitable, inequivalent
FAC, FACT	to make, to do	benefactor, unification
FER, LAT	to bear, to carry	correlation, nontransferable
FORM	form	conformation, conformity
FRANG, FRACT	to break	irrefrangible, refraction
GER, GEST	to bear, perform	congestion, vicegerent
GRAT	pleasing	ingratitude gratuity
HAB, HABIT	to have	rehabilitation, inhibition
JAC, JECT	to throw	trajectory, interjection
JUNG, JUNCT	to join, bind	disjunctive, conjuncture
LEG, LECT	to read, choose	predilection, lectern, dialectic
MAN	hand	manumission, manuscript
MITT, MISS	to send	intermittent, emissary
MOD	measure, manner	immoderate, accommodation
MOV, MOT	to move	motivation, demobilize
NOT	to know	connotation, denotation
PAND, PASS	to spread	expansive, surpassable
PAR, PARAT	to prepare	reparation, irreparable
PART	part	departmentalize, partisan
PET, PETIT	to seek	centripetal, repetitive
PLAC, PLACIT	to please	implacability, complacency
PLIC, PLICAT	to fold, bend	complicity, implication
PON, POSIT	to place	deposition, transposition
PORT, PORTAT	to carry	deportation, exportation
PREHEND	to seize	reprehensible, apprehension
QUER, QUISIT	to seek	inquisitorial, perquisite
RAP, RAPT	to seize, hurry away	surreptitious, rapturous
REG, RECT	to rule, direct	insurrection, rectitude
RUPT	to break, destroy	incorruptible, irruption

Latin Prefixes

ab- away from
ad- to
ambi-, an-, around
ante- before
bene- well
circum- around
con-, cum- with
contra- against
de- away, down
dis- apart not
ex- out of
inter- between
in- not
in- into, in
male- evil, badly
non- not
ob- against
per- through
post- after
pre- before
pro- for
re- again
retro- back
se- away from
sub- under
super- over
trans- across

Greek Prefixes

a(an)- not	*amphi-* on both sides	*ana-* up	*anti-* against	*apo-* from	*cata-* down	*di(a)-* through	*ex(ec)-* from
hyper- over	*hypo-* under	*meta-* beyond	*para-* beside	*peri-* around	*pro-* before	*pseudo-* false	*syn-* with

show you first the stem, and by the method of remainders, the prefix and suffix that make it up. You can thus get at its literal meaning. Since you have seen it also in context, you can guess at its present meaning, once you know the literal sense. Below is the technique for sight-reading meanings: Pick out the stem involved, and locate it in the table. The prefix and/or suffix will stand out as separate. Locate them in the lists. Place the English equivalents under the prefix, stem, and suffix. Reshuffle the English equivalents to make sense. A word from the Latin is analyzed on the left hand page; a Greek word just below.

anti- against	PATH feeling	-y state of	means 'state of feeling against'

SAL, SALT	to leap	salient, exultation
SCRIB, SCRIPT	to write	indescribable, scriptorium
SED, SESS	to sit	nonsedentary, residuary
SENT, SENS	to feel, perceive	insensibility, presentiment
SEQU, SECUT	to follow	obsequious, prosecutor
SERV, SERVAT	to save, protect	conservatory, preservative
SIGN	sign	assignation, designation
SPIC SPECT	to look at	inauspicious, perspicuity
STA, STAT	to stand	transubstantiation, circumstantiality
SIST	to cause to stand	inconsistency, irresistible
STRING, STRICT	to bind	astringent, constriction
TANG, TACT	to touch	tangential, contingent
TEN, TENT	to hold	untenable, sustenance
TEND, TENS	to stretch	tensile, distension
TRAH, TRACT	to draw	retraction, contractile
UT, US	to use	usury, peruse
VEN, VENT	to come	provenience, contravene
VERT, VERS	to turn	irreversible, transverse
VID, VIS	to see	provisional, improvident
VOC	voice	provocation, vociferous

GREEK STEM	MEANING	DERIVATIVES
AGON	contest	protagonist, antagonize
ALLO	other	allotropic, allomorph
ARCH	chief, first, rule	anarchical, monarchical
BIBLIO, BIBLO	book	bibliography, bibliophile
DEMO	the people	antidemocratic, demotic
DRA	to do, act	dramaturgy, dramatize
DYNAMI	power	hydrodynamics, aerodynamic
ELECTRO	amber (electric)	electronics, dielectric
ERGO	work	allergy, ergometer
GEO	earth	geological, geometrical
GRAPH	to write	epigraphy, graphology
HOMO	the same	homonym, homophone
HYDRO	water	hydrostatic, dehydrate
ISO	equal	isometric, isotope
K(C)LINO	to bend, slant	declination, isoclinal
K(C)RYPTO	hidden	cryptography, cryptic
LOGO	word, reason, study	neologism, physiological
METRO	measure	geometrical, photometer
NEO	new	neophyte, neologist
PATHO	feeling	psychopathology, empathy
PHILO	loving, fond of	philology, zoöphile
PHOB	fear	zoöphobia, photophobia
PHONO	sound	phonology, gramophone
PHOTO	light	photoelectric, photometric
PHYS	nature	monophysite, physiography
PROTO	first	protozoa, prototype
PSYCHE	mind, soul	psychometric, parapsychology
TECH	art, craft	technological, electro-technology
THEO	god	theological, theocentric
ZOO	animal	zoöphyte, zoögraphy

Latin Suffixes

-able, -ible, able to be
-acy, state or quality of being
al, pertaining to, act of
-an, -ant, -ent, one who or -ing
-ary, belonging to
-ate, having
-ency, state of being
-er, -or, one who
-ern, belonging to
-ic, pertaining to
-ice, state or quality of being
-ive, one who, that which is
-oon, -ion, one who
-ory, relating to, thing which, place where
-ose, -ous, full of
-tion, state of that which
-tude, state of being
-ure, state or act of
-y, state of being

-ac, pertaining to (adj.) -et, one who (noun) -ic, -ical, pertaining to, made of, one who

Greek Suffixes

-ic, -ice, science of (noun) -ise, -ize, to make, to give (verb) -ist, one who (n) -y, state of being

145

Word-analysis by these methods is a challenge to anyone who likes to gamble on his own skill. An element of chance enters, but as your skill increases, you come to know which combinations offer the best odds. In the Word-Analyzer, you will find the materials for the game.

Drive with Care: Curves Ahead

Learning to distinguish the main types of building material in the classical lumberyard takes a little time; and to find out how the Greeks and Romans put the joints together, takes still more. Also, many word-carpenters have worked over the old antiques, in France, Italy, Spain, England, and the United States. Some of them were good craftsmen, who knew the rules and period styles. Others were quite clumsy artisans, and they achieved some weird combinations, putting Greek prefixes on Latin stems—*amoral,* for example. At worst, such verbal MONSTROSITIES as *walkathon* have been manufactured, by BOBTAILING off the last half of MARATHON and hanging it on an Old English word *walk.*

The most recent KIDNAPPING of this kind has occurred in the case of ELECTRON. It's been split, too. An even half of it, *-tron,* has been treated as if it were a suffix, and hitched on to form the tail end of trade names for various types of electronic tubes: CYCLOTRON, KENOTRON, THYRATRON, KLYSTRON—all of which are at least Greek stems to start with; but one huge tube has been labelled IGNITRON, thus adorning the Latin word for "fire" with a Greek suffix that is strictly homemade.

Luckily in the standard vocabulary there are not too many of these hybrids, and in any case it's amusing to crack them apart. But it is also possible to get off the track, even if the word started as an authentic Latin word which one has never encountered.

For thirty years (including nine years' study of Latin) I had been under the delusion that ANFRACTUOSITIES meant "rough edges," which would hurt anybody who ran into them. I had never looked it up, but had analyzed it thus:

an	FRACTU	os	-ity
"against"	"break"	"full of"	"state"

or "state of being full of breaks against." I thought of *fracture* and FRACTIOUS. I knew the word only in the phrase pattern "anfractuosities of the mind." I learned in consulting Webster's new *Dictionary of Syno-*

146

nyms (1942) that the word really means "SINUOSITIES—windings or QUIRKS." I had made just one mistake in my breakdown. Here's how I should have made it:

an	*FRACTU*	*os*	*-ity*
"around"	"break"	"full of"	"state"

or "state of being full of breaks around." The prefix *an-* is here a combining form of *ambo-,* around. A "break around" something implies a "curve,"—a bend, not a break. Actually, therefore the word means "state of being full of curves"—"tortuous crevices, channels or passages," says the OED, hence, figuratively, "OBLIQUITY" or "INTRICACY." The OED gives the classical passage from Johnson which I had been misinterpreting for thirty years:

Sir, among the anfractuosities of the human mind, I know not if it may not be one, that there is a reluctance to sit for a portrait.—*Boswell* (1831) IV, 336.

What I had thought a rough break was really a curve.

Not many DERIVATIVES are as tricky as *anfractuosity*. And in spite of the hazards, it's worth a gamble to try your luck at sight-reading meanings on the basis of a knowledge of the main Greek and Latin combining forms, plus the affixes that go with them.

As a memory device for tying many new words to one, this Word-Analyzer should serve you in good stead. And it will usually enable you to arrive at the literal sense of the word. But that is not enough.

To arrive at its present significance in actual use, you need to know how words change meaning.

VIII

HOW WORDS CHANGE MEANING

The "juke" in *juke-box* comes from an OBSOLETE Middle English word, *jouk,* which was kept alive in the Appalachian hills by the descendants of the Scotch and English settlers who went West in the early 1800's. The word was applied to a tavern as a "juke-joint," but this was a dialect LOCALISM until the juke-box came along. Whether the spelling of *jouk* was modified to bring it in line with the Jukes family, nobody knows. In fact, there seems to be some doubt which *jouk* is involved.

Version I, by the Staff Etymologist of the New York *Times:*

The *jouk* in question, says the New York Sunday *Times,* means "rest" or "roost." It occurs in Chaucer, but did not make the grade further for literary use. However, it crossed the ocean and was COLONIZED, as noted. Roadside taverns in the Southern uplands were called "juke-houses," meaning "resting places," and when coin-operated phonographs were installed, the patrons naturally enough labelled these devices "juke-boxes" and the nickname came into national use in spite of opposition from the manufacturers of the canned-music device.

Version II, by a Professional Etymologist:

". . . *jouk,* to dodge, to move quickly, was applied to the places where liquor was sold, in prohibition times; hence, any cheap drinking place . . ." says Professor Joseph Shipley, under the entry *juke* in his *Dictionary of Word Origins.*

SIFTING THE EVIDENCE

Which authority is right? Is it *jouk,*—"rest" or *jouk,*—"dodge," that has lent its name to the musical "dodge" which is far from restful?

For *jouk,*—"rest," the OED dates the Chaucer entry 1374, and gives no instances later than 1400. This doesn't look promising for the *Times* PUNDIT. That word had remarkable staying power, if it survived in COLLOQUIAL use for five and a half centuries without creeping into print at all. It does not appear at all in the *American Dialect Dictionary* (Thomas Y. Crowell Company, 1944).

Jouk,—"dodge" rates several entries in that work, dating from 1890 to 1896, none of them south of Pennsylvania, plus a HEARSAY report that the word was still current in 1918, the year prohibition began.

On the evidence, Professor Shipley has the better of it. It is remotely possible that both authorities are right. A "rest house" (juke-joint) might be referred to also as a "dodge-house" when the owner began a fly-by-night career, moving his liquor out fast as the revenuers appeared. Where there are two HOMONYMS with quite different meanings, one sometimes reinforces another, or provides an extension of meaning in a new sense, by folk etymology. (See p. 293.)

But a judge, in summing up, would still have to incline the balance in Shipley's favor. The professional wins out over the amateur, even an amateur with the weight of the Sunday *Times* behind him.

Version III, a Third Side of the Fence:

It is also possible that neither of the pundits has read his OED carefully enough. There is an entry under *jouk* or *jook*—"dodge," which fits as well as Shipley's etymology:

III. A place into which one may dart for shelter; a shelter from a blow, a storm etc. Mod[ern] Sc[ottish] 1808–18 in Jamieson [Scottish Dictionary].

Maybe a jook-joint was a "shelter-joint," a place you dodged into before its owner and patrons started "dodging out" of it during prohibition days. In any case, the evidence favors *jouk*—"dodge" as the ancestor.

This instance shows that you can't always depend on etymology—certainly not on amateur etymologists even in our most learned newspaper—to give the true history of a word. In its travels, a word may change its meaning several times, and wind up with a far different sense.

Luckily not many words undergo such a complete shift as *jouk,* nor do many have homonyms that fit in PLAUSIBLY to account for the meaning when the word is suddenly revived. *Jouk* is such a tricky example that it virtually provides a pit for JOURNALESE ETYMOLOGY to fall into.

As a rule, once words make their way into the standard language, they may add additional meanings, but they usually do so in accordance with processes which are pretty well defined. Once you know how the shifts happen it's usually easy to sight-read a new sense.

SHUTTLE SERVICE

Two main processes by which meaning-changes occur are so closely allied that they have to be considered together. One is *stretching,* the other *shrinking* of meaning. Experts use the terms of Latin origin: GENERALIZATION for stretching, and SPECIALIZATION for shrinking. These twin processes work back and forth, like a SHUTTLE which now pulls the threads taut and thin, and now FLARES them out wide and loose on the spindle. When the threads are CONSTRICTED in a TAUT line, the meaning is specific; when they are spread out spindle-wise, the word covers a large area of meaning, so becoming generalized.

If you're reading an old Icelandic SAGA, and come on the line

Gunnar's case was brought before the September meeting of the *Thing,* with old Njal sitting in the judgment seat . . .

you're encountering the word *thing* used in its narrow, original sense: "a political or JUDICIAL assembly." Any case, matter, or cause brought before the *Thing* came to be referred to also as a *thing;* and eventually this meaning of "matter" was extended to cover any "affair" or "business," whether before a court or not. Next the meaning was still further widened to cover "anything done," or "whatever is to be done." From that it was generalized to mean "anything that exists or can be thought about." We now use *thing* as a highly generalized word-of-all-work to apply to whatever we cannot label with a more specific term. Or it may even be used, compounded with an indefinite pronoun, as a term of contempt, to describe something CHARACTERLESS—as Blake called the eighteenth century parsons' God "Old Anything." Thus the word *thing* has been stretched until it covers an immense area of meaning. This is generalization with a vengeance.

The word *gear* has undergone the opposite treatment: SHRINKAGE. Around 1200 it meant "habits" or "manners." Then it shifted to mean "equipment": apparel, armor, harness or any kind of tool or apparatus. From "apparatus" it was narrowed to mean "an arrangement of fixed and moving parts in a machine for any special purpose"; and finally still further specialized to signify "a wheel having teeth that fit into another wheel of the same kind, usually of a different size, to make the second wheel turn at a different speed from the first." While we still occasionally speak of "household *gear*," the word alone would now call up one of the last two meanings given, and we'd think first of automobile *gears,* or steering *gear*. The specialized, restricted meaning has won out, although the second more general sense has also remained for occasional use.

The shuttle is always at work in our language, now constricting, now flaring out the threads of meaning. *Angle, line,* and *proposition* are now far gone toward generalization, following in the wake of *thing, business, concern, regard, account, circumstance, fact, matter, condition,* and *state.* These words have become the counters and markers in the game of speech; they are often called *counter* words, because they have lost specific meaning, and have no more individual character than POKER chips or billiard markers.

Contact is now going the same route. The dictionaries give it as a verb which applies only to the establishment of a JUNCTURE between two poles of an electrical circuit. But it is in wide informal use to mean "get in touch with." Education professors "contact" their colleagues; salesmen "contact" prospects, and speak of their "contacts," meaning their "connections," turning the verb also into a noun. These instances sound barbarous to literary ears, but that doesn't prevent the spread of the LOCUTION. *Contact* is one word, while "get in touch with" is four, and the shorter form will probably have its way.

Tending in the other direction are such words as FISSION, which if standing alone, would now probably be taken by most readers to refer not to any kind of "splitting," but to NUCLEAR fission. *Nucleus* would similarly be taken as the nucleus of an atom, though before Hiroshima it was specialized for most readers as a "cell nucleus." RADIATION is now likely to make us think not of the "general process of spreading out of light or heat rays, wheel-like, from a center," but of "the diffusion of RADIOACTIVE particles or EMANATIONS following an ATOMIC bomb explosion."

In like manner, *mutation* since De Vries has become specialized to mean a "sudden change in biological characteristics that becomes TRANSMISSIBLE." *Briefing* no longer suggests to most of us "preparing a written summary of legal arguments," nor its British sense of "the hiring of a BARRISTER to take into court a case a solicitor has prepared." Rather, since 1941, *briefing* in its most familiar use is what happens in the huddle before an air or COMMANDO raid, or a convoy's sailing, when the commander gives detailed instruction on route, objectives, timing, etc.

So, too, DIALECTICS is becoming specialized to mean not any kind of ARGUMENTATIVE reasoning by question and answer, but the Marxist variety used by Messrs. Gromyko, Molotov, Vishinsky, and their SATELLITES.

151

SPECIALIZATION is thus constantly taking place. Sometimes it has happened within our lifetimes. So the "blues" (from which we get also the "blue" notes in a certain type of Negro song) have reinforced the meaning of "melancholy" which Irving wrote about in 1807: "a fit of the blues,"—short for "blue devils." And from the Red Flag, the Red Square, and the red ties of ANARCHISTS, we get the adjective and noun *Red* as the newspaper headline word for radicals, PARTICULARIZED now to COMMUNISTS of the STALINITE persuasion, the opposite pole to the ANARCHISTS earlier labeled *Reds*.

When the process of specialization has happened centuries—or even decades—before our time, we are not conscious of it. So MYTH, which at first in English meant any kind of story, now usually refers to one dealing with a god or semi-divine being in one of the mythologies of the world. There is also a further special sense of the word, used by students of comparative religion, to mean the "story" which is the central feature of a particular CULT, as the "myth" of Buddha or the "myth" of Quetzal. When the word is so used, the primary emphasis is not on the truth or FALSITY of the story, but on its role in the religion involved. Sometimes in this sense the full Greek spelling is used, MYTHOS, and MODERNIST THEOLOGIANS speak of the central "mythos" of the Christian religion.

The word *fable* used to mean any "tale." Dryden used it to cover what we call "fiction," sometimes also in the narrower sense of "plot." But the word, while it still has its general sense of "fiction" in phrase combinations such as "fact and fable," is now more likely to suggest to us its specialized sense, of "a story made up to teach a lesson, especially one in which animals speak and act like human beings"—George Orwell's *Animal Farm,* for example. *Aesop's Fables* no doubt helped to give the word this special sense.

Another word which has been specialized is *run*. If we speak of "a run," Americans will think of baseball and Englishmen of cricket. A sheepman would mean a "sheep run," a salmon fisherman a "run" of fish upstream. When a horse-racer says "he gave him a run for it" he means that the runner-up pressed the winner in a race. To a ROULETTE player, a "run" would mean a continuing RECURRENCE of the red or the black, or of some one number. It is thus that every man is his own SPECIALIZER, when it comes to ringing the changes on the meaning of common words.

35. Something Special

How have the following words become specialized in meaning, during the last few years? Which of them can still be used in their earlier senses as well, without causing misunderstanding?

1. RECONVERSION
2. RECONNAISSANCE
3. operations (man)
4. ACTIVATE
5. cross talk

6. sustaining
7. hook-up
8. fading
9. chisel
10. EXPEDITER

Radiation

Besides the shuttle-like RECIPROCAL action of generalization and specialization, there is a third important process by which words extend their meaning. This is the method of radiation. Take the word *action,* for example. Its primary or central meaning is "doing." It may refer (1) to actual and simple doing ("a prompt action"); (2) to a state of activity ("Patton's Army in action"); (3) to INITIATING court procedure ("starting an action to recover"); (4) to enterprise ("a man of action"); (5) to the succession of events in a play ("there must be unity of action"); (7) to attitude or position expressing a certain passion ("the action denoting extreme agony in Laokoön"); (8) to a military or naval battle ("the action at Midway"); to the natural or intended motion of anything ("the action of the CARDIAC muscle"); and finally (9) to a mechanism acting ("the valve action in an engine"). In all these many and varied senses of *action,* the primary notion of "doing" remains in all of them. By the necessities of printing, the different meanings are given in sequence. Actually the meanings really radiate out from the central sense of "doing," like the spokes of a wheel; and if the conventions of lexicography permitted, they should be so arranged. Only so would it be GRAPHICALLY clear how words of this type acquire extensions of meaning, at the same time retaining the primary meaning. That is what is meant by radiation.

36. Wheels of Meaning

Order, power, force, head, foot, class, rank, range, and *turn* have had their meaning extended by radiation. Jot down all the meanings you can think of for each, and arrange them like the spokes of a wheel. *Order,* for example, will require a large wheel showing its five main meanings: rank in general; rank in specific departments; sequence or arrangement; the act of giving an order; and the PHRASAL combinations (*in order, out of order,* etc.). Then small wheels will be needed at the end of each of these five main spokes, where the particular sense has radiated again, developing a satellite wheel TANGENT to the main one. The OED gives 24 meanings for *order* standing alone, plus 6 more in phrase combinations. *Turn* will also require several TANGENTIAL wheels. Make each wheel large enough so that you have room for a phrase or short sentence illustrating the use of the word in each radiated sense. After you have finished, check your work by reference to an unabridged dictionary; preferably, if you have access to it in a library, consult the OED.

TRANSFERENCE

There is a fourth way in which words shift meaning: TRANSFERENCE. Ruskin complained about it, in the well-known passage on the *pathetic* FALLACY. Quoting from Kingsley's *Alton Locke,*

> They rowed her in across the rolling foam—
> The cruel, crawling foam . . .

he continues

The foam is not cruel, neither does it crawl. The state of mind which attributes to it these characters of a living creature is one in which the reason is UNHINGED by grief. They produce in us a falseness in all our impressions of external things, which I would generally characterize as the "pathetic fallacy."—*Modern Painters,* Vol. 3, chap. 12.

Yet this projection of feeling upon inanimate objects or forces is as common as the illusion by which, when we touch the table with a pencil, we feel the contact at the far end of the pencil, though a moment's reflection will tell us that there can be no SENTIENCE in the pencil. But the pathetic fallacy and the projection of feeling to the end of the pencil are ANALOGOUS to a general method of changing word-meanings, which comes about through transference. At its lowest level, this transfer occurs in "a cold day." It is we who are cold, not the day.

What is true of words describing sensations, holds with the whole range of terms which deal with mental conceptions. Such words face either toward the person who entertains the notion, or toward the person or thing affected by it; or they may—and here arises the transference —shift back and forth from one to the other.

The word *character* is an ideal illustration, particularly since you have already (p. 48) sorted out its meanings. Here you can trace further how these meaning-changes have occurred. In the good old days when servants received "characters" when they were leaving someone's employ, these were in effect certificates of good "reputation." The term *character* was long employed in this objective sense. In the 17th century, it meant a GENERIC portrait of a certain type: the miser, the CHOLERIC man, the social climber, and the like. On the other hand, when we speak of the development of Hamlet's *character,* as revealed in his successive SOLILOQUIES and actions, we now think of something happening within him. The character of a man, as he himself conceives and reveals it, is SUBJECTIVE. The term really faces both ways, and by transference shifts from the OBJECTIVE to the subjective sense very easily.

In fact, the JANUS-FACED nature of the word accounts for a good deal of confusion in the discussion of problems of character. It is not always clear how far the LOCUS of character is in the person, and how far in the mind of the BEHOLDER. The moral aspect of character, in particular, has often been disputed bitterly, because of uncertainty as to whether the moral qualities and standards are in the man himself, or in the minds of his judges.

The Greeks, of course, did not bother about this difference between the subjective and objective. They used the word ETHOS to mean both the inward and outward aspects of character. We prefer the word *personality* for the impression which a man makes on other persons, but the Greeks, since they did not make the distinction, had no word for it. Nor did the Romans, for they used MORES ("manners," "habits," hence "character") to include both phases of character. What a man appeared to be, he was, and that was the end of it. (The word *persona* to them meant a mask assumed by an actor, so everybody in the huge AMPHITHEATER could tell what character in the play he was representing.) But we distinguish between the inward and outward aspects of experience, without always being too sure which is which. Hence the numerous terms in English which face both ways, and can be transferred from subject to object, and vice versa.

Still a fifth method by which words shift meaning is degradation. A word with respectable associations slides down in the world, acquiring a DEROGATORY sense. *Lady* is now becoming suspect, because of its misuse as a GENTEELISM in such combinations as *saleslady* and *washlady*. The word *genteel* itself, according to H. W. Fowler, is "now used, except by the ignorant, only in mockery." Old and respectable words are sometimes brought still lower in the world, becoming VULGARISMS. *Swell, hot, lousy, tight,* and *lit* have lately been overtaken by this fate.

A quotation from one of our older authors may sound odd, almost slangy, because of this process of degradation. When Robert Burton in 1626 wrote "I would not grow hot in a cold cause," he could not take out insurance against what would happen to the word *hot* at the hands of jazz ADDICTS.

Still more striking instances of the process of degradation may be noted in the case of certain words used by our older poets. In modern usage these words have acquired humorous or UNDIGNIFIED associations. So Raleigh, in the verses he wrote the night before he was beheaded, thinks how he will meet in Paradise with other pilgrims, and take them

> To slack their thirst
> And then to taste of nectar suckets
> At those clear wells
> Where sweetness dwells
> Drawn up by saints in heavenly buckets.
> And when our bottle and all we
> Are filled with immortality
> Then those holy paths we'll travel
> Strew'd with rubies thick as gravel. . . .
> [spelling modernized]

"Suckets" and "buckets" are no longer poetic words, while to fill up yourself and your bottle with immortality seems somehow faintly wrong. The words with us are familiar and homely, not suggesting proper furnishing for Heaven.

Degradation of meaning leads to one amusing consequence: verbal soft-pedaling, commonly called EUPHEMISM. An *undertaker* becomes a "mortician," a *barber-shop* a "tonsorial parlor." Canned goods are graded *Extra Fancy, Fancy,* and *Standard,* and in the process the word *standard* is down-graded to mean, in trade language, the minimum quality that meets government or trade association requirements. It's a euphemism for the "lowest grade that will pass muster."

At the opposite pole from euphemism is another process by which words decay in force: HYPERBOLE. Instead of the timid cough of the soft-pedaler, we have, in this type of exaggeration, the loud trumpet-bray of the press agent. He looks for heroically strong expressions that will convey the extremes of approval. *Delightful, magnificent, splendid, superb, wonderful, overpowering, enchanting, tremendous,* and COLOSSAL are used as EXCLAMATORY SUPERLATIVES. Hollywood has even coined *super-colossal,* which bobby-soxers have shortened to "super."

There is a fast diminishing return from the use of these steam-heated adjectives. Each hyperbole of this kind soon loses, like discharged lightning, all its real potential; then another and still stronger expression is devised, which in turn degenerates. This holds also for over-strong words used to express DISAPPROBATION. If some petty annoyance is labeled *outrageous,* BESTIAL, ATROCIOUS, *horrible,* or NAUSEATING, the strong language often defeats its purpose. We feel that the words have little more meaning than STEREOTYPED PROFANITY.

Decay brought about by hyperbole is pretty good evidence that the Greeks were right in holding that IRONY of under-statement is a better way of securing emphasis. The deadly quiet style wears better and carries more weight than loud-mouthed BRAGGADOCIO.

FIGURATIVE EXTENSION

Anyone of these five processes, generalization, specialization, radiation, transference, or degradation, may be involved in a FIGURATIVE *extension* of meaning. *Micawber* becomes a general term for all PROCRASTINATORS who "wait for something to turn up." *Servant* is specialized into one of the proudest titles of the Pope: "the Servant of the Servants of God." A business writer will speak of "the *line* he proposes to take on the financial *angle* of a *proposition,*" thus generalizing two terms from mathematics and one from logic. He is using wooden IMAGERY that would have made Mark Twain want to fry him in deep fat. Psychology, once "the science of the soul—or mind," is transferred to designate the study of how rats behave in a maze, or to measurement of nerve-muscle responses. At the same time the word retains, for old-fashioned persons, its original sense, thus illustrating also radiation. *Idea* is degraded for a philosopher when it is attached to an "idea man" in an advertising agency. To call a man a *politician* is pretty close to an insult in this country, though in British English it is a term which a member of Parliament is proud to apply to himself. POLITICO is a derogatory term in Britain, but it's coming into increasing use in American as a neutral label for anybody in public life who is not yet a statesman but who has ceased to be "a low-down politician." With all these processes of change at work, the meanings of words are indeed more fluid than we realize.

ADULTERATION

Besides these orthodox, traditional ways in which words change meaning, there is also a black market technique that is coming into increasing vogue. It consists in hi-jacking legitimate words, and pouring new meanings into them. It's easy to do in the case of OMNIBUS words, those that already carry such a heavy load of meanings that you can never be sure which one will get off when the bus stops. Such terms as *Americanism, patriotism, loyalty, peace,* and *democracy* are OMNIBUS words often appropriated by political bootleggers.

Democracy, now a word to CONJURE with, even if American army manuals quit defining it as "mob rule" only in 1941, has been waylaid in the last four years by two sets of hi-jackers, working opposite sides of the road. Communists have tried to make it mean "a government for (though not of and by) the people, in which supposedly the title to *all* means of production is in the people's name." They slide over entirely the fact that RÉGIMES which have gone in suddenly and whole hog for this system are without exception police states, dictatorships which use fear, espionage, and forced labor. The individual citizen has no rights VIS-À-VIS the government. Elections are FARCICAL because of the self-perpetuating government by a top committee acting for a party that is often less than 3 per cent of the population. These régimes do not have majority rule, nor freedom of the press, assembly and religion, and they LIQUIDATE their opposition without jury trials. Whatever the supposedly greater degree of economic equality, this adds up to the direct ANTITHESIS of *democracy.* Yet Communists bandy the term freely, and claim a monopoly on it.

On the other hand, conservative columnists have lately shown a tendency to EQUATE democracy with CAPITALISM and *complete* private ownership of the means of production. They stretch it to cover the maintenance of individual liberty for owners and employers to the nth degree.

They imply that to have democracy, you must also have the "open shop," which Mr. Dooley so neatly defined: "The big employer is willin' to shed the last drop of his wife's relatives' blood to protect the INALIENABLE right of the American workin' man to take for 90¢ a day the job his buddy was holdin' down for a dollar." This same "open shop" or "free enterprise" democracy is also called the "American plan" or the "right to work." This is actually black anarchism, which wrenches the term *democracy* as far out of its proper sense as the Communist corkscrew twists it.

Admittedly the freedoms which democracy holds to are likely to have a better chance if there is also freedom of economic opportunity; but "freedom" for monopoly and giant enterprise is not apt to help safeguard the other freedoms. No freedom can exist except within an ordered framework. Black anarchism will not promote it any more than the Red variety.

When the word *democracy* is used, it seems sensible to stick to the meaning which Juarez and Lincoln, Carl Schurz, Mazzini, and Roosevelt would have recognized: government of, *by,* and for the people, elected by a majority of them in free elections; operating with their consent and in accord with public opinion; conducting their affairs according to laws and a constitution, written or unwritten, that includes a bill of rights which safeguards the liberties of the citizen against arbitrary action by officials. The property system can be whatever the people decide; collectivized, as in Czechoslovakia; a mixture of public and private ownership, with the first emphasized, as in Mexico and in England under the Labor Party; or private ownership may predominate, as in the United States. But anybody who tries to hi-jack this potent term *democracy,* and pour his own private meaning into it, should be scotched.

Such word-wrenchers are following the practice of Humpty-Dumpty in *Alice in Wonderland:* "When I use a word, it means just what I choose it to mean." Only their purposes are not so innocent. They steal the word for its SLOGAN value, and use it to prettify the label on ADULTERATED political NOSTRUMS.

Obviously the highly charged words that figure in political, economic, religious, and social controversy are the most likely to suffer from this trick. The moral: Be sure you know what you mean when you use these "OMNIBUS words." That often means re-examining with care words that have long seemed commonplace and familiar.

What emerges from this inquiry into meaning-changes is the fact that you can greatly enlarge vocabulary by going deeper into the meanings of words you only half know. It's not only that you can trace the steps by which a word acquires a FIGURATIVE extension of meaning. If you have gone intensively into the full meaning of a complicated word such as *democracy,* you won't be fooled by SLOGANEERS; nor will you be impressed by groups that cry "peace" when what they want is to have one power get out of border areas and let another power move in its troops and PROPAGANDISTS. Whatever this is, it is not "peace," except perhaps in the sense that Tacitus used it IRONICALLY, in his famous EPIGRAM describing Roman IMPERIALISM: "They create a wilderness and call it 'peace.'"

Equipped with a real awareness—and WARINESS—about meanings, you will not easily be fooled by words. Long before the modern experts on meaning labeled their science "SEMANTICS," Bishop South wrote

Words are the Signs and Symbols of Things; and, as in accounts, CYPHERS and Figures pass for real Sums, so . . . Words and Names pass for Things themselves.—*Sermons,* Isa. V. 20 (1727) II. 333.

And da Vinci said of the disputing Schoolmen, "They mistake words for things." The close study of meaning-shifts will guard you against falling into the error against which the Bishop and the great RENAISSANCE painter-scientist issued their warnings. You will take words at their proper measure. But no quick-change artist can slip anything over on you, if you know how shifts in meaning occur.

And in the very process of sharpening and deepening your word sense, through the study of meaning-changes, you will find that you have extended your vocabulary faster than if you had done a hasty job of widening without digging down. The jibe at the youthful Bryan, as Boy Orator of the Platte, was probably unjust, when some Republican jeered that the River Platte was a mile wide, an inch deep—and very muddy! Nobody would like to have his vocabulary so characterized. Focusing on meaning-shifts may seem a TANGENTIAL approach, but often it will pay out better than a FRONTAL attack.

37. PINNING DOWN THE MEANING

1. What meaning have the Ku Klux Klan and similar vigilante groups run into the term "Americanism"?

2. What did Dr. Johnson mean when he said "Patriotism is the last refuge of a scoundrel"?

3. What meaning did the Dies Committee run into the word SUB-VERSIVE?

4. What is the literal meaning of *Propaganda* in the Catholic term PROPAGANDA *De Fide?* What has happened to the meaning of the term propaganda in recent years?

5. How did the NAZIS ADULTERATE the meaning of the term "race"?

6. In what specialized sense do Christian Scientists use the word "error"? What do COMMUNISTS mean by a "DEVIATION"?

7. What did Yeats mean by *evil*, when he said "A poet is great in the measure of his imaginative vision of evil"?

8. What did Blake mean by *Christian*, in the lines telling how Christ could have gained his freedom when he appeared before the High Priest Caiaphas:

> He had only to say that God was the devil,
> And the devil was God, like a Christian civil.

And what did Blake mean by his coinage, *Old Nobodaddy?*

9. PANDEMONIUM is the name Milton coined for the capital of hell (*Paradise Lost,* I, 756). What is its literal meaning? What does it now mean, and by what process did its meaning shift?

10. A *fossil* is literally something "dug up." Trace the steps by which it has acquired its various present meanings.

11. Trace the steps by which the words VILLAIN, BOOR, and CHURL have come to have their present degraded meanings. (See p. 170.)

12. If somebody called you *rustic*, how would you like it?

13. What do the words *quean*, TROLLOP, HUZZY, and TRULL mean? Did each always have its present meaning? What word is now in common use for each?

14. Not quite all euphemisms are soft-pedaling. When a critic remarked that the only resemblance he could see between Marquand's *Wickford Point* and Thackeray's *Vanity Fair* was that both had heroines (Bella and Becky) whose names had five letters and began with "B," what was he conveying without coming right out with it? (See p. 184.)

15. How do "blends" come to be labeled "telescoped" or "PORTMANTEAU" words?

16. Sometimes words are used in a PEJORATIVE sense (Latin, *peior*,

worse). Eric Partridge in his massive Dictionary of Slang defines a certain term which is supposed to be an insult unless you smile when you say it, as "pejorative, of a man." What is it? (See p. 184 for the parent term.)

17. How did the word BROMIDE come to have the slang sense of "a TRITE remark" or "a commonplace"? Which process of meaning-change brought this about?

18. Why have Americans and Bernard Shaw (in agreement for once) felt the need of a word AMORAL, when the terms IMMORAL, NONMORAL, and UNMORAL already existed? (Look at the four prefixes in the Word-Analyzer: a- under Greek, im- and non- under Latin, and un- under Anglo-Saxon.)

19. How did *Time* change the meaning of the word TYCOON? What process was employed?

20. The word MORON was voted into the language by the American Association for the Study of the Feeble-Minded in 1910. Exactly what does it mean? (It does not mean "feeble-minded.") Does the same stem, in SOPHOMORE, have an identical meaning? What is the force of the suffix in Dr. Eleanor Rowland Wembridge's coined word from moron, in her book title *The People of Moronia?*

QUIZ KEYS FOR CHAPTER VIII

35. Page 153.
1. See p. 243 for new specialized meaning. It would baffle most readers if used in the sense the dictionaries give: process of being converted again to the faith, after backsliding.
2. Usually now implies reconnoitering by air; an extension of its older military use for "scouting ahead."
3. "Operations man" is in effect a new compound noun. It means an official who can get things done by remote control, as contrasted to a good planner or policy man who cannot execute so well. For instance, Editor-Publisher Palmer Hoyt was the first topflight "operations man" to be recruited for a top spot in OWI.
4. See p. 253. Still good in the military sense.
5. Without the hyphen, this would mean "scolding." Here it refers to unlooked-for radio interference, where by some freak of induction one program cuts in on another.
6. A "sustaining" program is one for which the station or network pays, as distinct from a sponsored one. Outside of radio circles, the word could still be used to refer to anything that gave an underpinning or helped hold something up.

7. Specialized as radio cant.
8. Also specialized as radio cant; but the word would still be applicable to "fading" colors, etc.
9. "Chisel," meaning "to cheat," or "take undue advantage" is slang popularized by the late President Roosevelt and the late Hugh Johnson. But it still can mean "a tool for gouging away wood."
10. See p. 263. Still in good use also as a standard word.

37. Page 160.
 1. Anti-foreigner and anti-liberal attitudes were equated with Americanism by the Dies Committee. This adulteration of the term tends to make the Ku-Klux attitude resemble Nazism.
 2. Dr. Johnson meant that scoundrels hide behind a cloak of patriotism. See 1 above.
 3. The Dies Committee used the term "subversive" to attack anybody's politics they did not like—Frank Murphy's, Elmer Benson's, etc. They did not trouble the Bundists or police red squads who violated civil liberties.
 4. "Spreading." *Propaganda* has come to have a somewhat derogatory sense.
 5. The Nazis equated "race" with religious affiliation and nationality as shown by the language group. Neither criterion has anything to do with "race," as anthropologists use the term.
 6. "Error" is to Christian Scientists a wrong form of thinking. "Deviation," to Communists, is a departure from the "party line" prevailing that particular week.
 7. *Evil,* as Yeats uses it, is the deliberate eschewal of good, and a setting up of opposition to the force of righteousness. When Iago says, "Evil, be thou my good," he is using the word as Yeats intends it here. It is *evil* as the Manichaeans imagined it, as a tremendously powerful, dark force at work in the universe.
 8. He meant that the insincere eighteenth century adherents of Christianity had so reversed Jesus' values that, like the Pharisees, they had made respectable conformity and smugness their ideal, instead of the charity and pity which Jesus taught and practiced.
 9. "Abode of all demons," in Milton's sense. Now, like *bedlam,* it means a terrific din, as if all the demons of hell were let loose.
10. A *fossil* is something "dug up out of the earth." It came to be applied to petrified bones, and be figurative extension to opinions "dug up" out of the remote past. Then by transference it came to mean a person holding such antiquated opinions—"an old fossil."
11. See p. 170.
12. A matter of personal opinion; but it is hard to think how the adjective could be applied in a flattering sense to a person.
13. A woman no better than she should be. At one time *quean* and *huzzy* had innocuous meanings. *Trollop* and *trull* have always had a derogatory sense. The common synonym for all four now is "harlot."
14. Look at p. 184 again.

15. A telescope is in sections which slide together; a portmanteau is a kind of valise the two halves of which fold together: hence both apply to words which are blended to make one.
16. Continue to look at p. 184.
17. Bromo Seltzer became a popular sedative early in this century. In 1906 the magazine *Smart Set* suggested the word *bromide* for persons and sayings that tended to put one to sleep. (Shipley—*Dictionary of Word Origins*, page 58.)
18. The alpha privative (*a-*, in Greek) means "apart from," "unconcerned with."
19. *Time* took the title of the Japanese *shogun*, and by extension made it serve as a general term for "a big business man."
20. *Moron:* A person who never develops better than a normal 12-year old's intelligence. In *sophomore*, the stem *-more*, means a "fool." The *-ia* suffix could be translated "place of," or "country of."

Vice-versa Quiz for Chapter VIII

1. Experts in the science of word-meanings call their craft mystery _____.
2. The common processes by which words change meaning are: _____, _____, _____, _____, _____, and _____.
3. Verbal soft-pedaling is called _____.
4. An exaggerated mode of expression is _____. What is its usual fate, as indicated by the example of fulsome radio commercials which discharge a cascade of adjectives in praising the product?
5. What was Humpty-Dumpty's system for deciding on word-meanings?
6. How did the name of a minor nature-god come to be applied to a common flower that often grows near lakes and streams?
7. How did the term for a New Yorker come to be applied to knee britches?
8. How did the family name of a dynasty of French kings come to be applied to a favorite type of whiskey?
9. What slave-group in an ancient city-state have provided a generic name for any group held in subjection by a master-race (so in its own opinion)?
10. How did a certain type of old-fashioned sulphur-tipped match acquire one of the devil's names?
11. What is the difference between *autarchy* and *autarky*?
12. Distinguish between *homonyms*, *homophones*, and *homographs*. What hazards does each present to a stenographer?
13. How is it that *sector*, *bisector*, and *dissector* have such divergent meanings? What is the literal meaning of *anti-vivisectionist*?
14. Are *razz* and *raze* related? Is either synonymous with "mow down" in Charlie McCarthy's "I'll mow you down"?
15. What is the present day American term for pompous, intricate official

language? Does the term have any etymology, or is it a straight coinage? What other common American colloquial word is simply the family name of the coiner of the term for "chancellery style"?

16. What is the technical term for a reading-stand on which a heavy book rests?

17. If you have tried several of the commonly used desk dictionaries, which one do you find enables you to take in the meaning of words faster?

18. Explain the development of the present slang sense of *character,* found in such expressions as "I wish you'd quit inviting those 'characters' to hang around here."

19. Discuss the various sub-standard senses of the word *proposition.*

20. Pick at random twenty words from Quiz 33 (p. 125), and trace the processes by which each of these words has changed its meaning from the literal translation to its present sense.

21. Is it equally apt to label somebody who knows several languages "multilingual," as to call him "polyglot"? Or is there a shade of difference?

22. Do you prefer the diction of *Time* to that of *Newsweek*? In any case, pick ten tricky words from each of the Quizzes 21 and 22, and show how these words have changed meaning.

23. What is the learned term for "diplomatic double-talk"?

24. What is the literal meaning of *prestidigitated*?

25. What is the etymology of the word *assassin*? By what processes of meaning change did the term acquire its present sense?

IX

THE FINE SHADES OF MEANING:
SYNONYMS

Suppose you had three guesses to account for this letter:

I got on horseback within ten minutes after I got your letter. When I got to Canterbury, I got a chaise for town; but I got wet through, and have got such a cold that I shall not get rid of it in a hurry. I got to the Treasury about noon, but first of all got shaved and dressed. I soon got into the secret of getting a memorial before the Board, but I could not get an answer then; however I got intelligence from a messenger that I should get one next morning. As soon as I got back to my inn, I got my supper, and breakfast, and, having got dressed, I got out in time to get an answer to my memorial. As soon as I got it, I got into a chaise, and got back to Canterbury by three, and got home for tea. I have got nothing for you, and so adieu.

You might think Rose Macaulay made it up, as a "spoof" on Basic English. Perhaps Gertrude Stein decided to give the verb *get* a workout. Or the writer was a MONOTONE. Actually, this is a patch out of Brewer's *Dictionary of Phrase and Fable*. Logan Pearsall Smith quotes it in his tract on English IDIOMS, while exhibiting the IDIOMATIC uses of *get*, in the same breath that he cautions against thus employing it as a verb-of-all-work. If you'll just start re-phrasing the story, from the point where the record "got" stuck, you'll realize how many other verbs *get* can pinch-hit for. It is a prize specimen of a word with multiple meanings, and at the same time, in this case, a warning, heightened to absurdity, of the need for a ready command of SYNONYMS to avoid monotony, REPETITIOUSNESS, and WOOLLINESS of expression.

There is all the less excuse for thus working a word to death, because English is as rich in synonyms as in words with plural meanings. In fact, it has a greater wealth of synonyms than any other known language, ancient or modern.

Because of the COMPOSITE nature of English, there are for many of the commonest meanings in the language two words, one of Anglo-Saxon, the other of Latin origin. Sometimes the Anglo-Saxon (more precisely, *Old English*) word is the commoner, and for ordinary purposes it is to be preferred. No one but a PEDANT—or Earl Wilson, if he happened to learn the word—would speak of a LUPINE appetite, when he meant *wolf-ish;* or describe a wrestler as having a TAURINE instead of a *bull-like* neck. A politician is *foxy,* not VULPINE; and *horse-faced* conveys the idea better than EQUINE-VISAGED,—unless you're afraid the children will overhear you.

But in many cases the word of Latin origin has become more familiar than the Saxon. *Doctor* or *physician* is usual, not LEECH, which is now OBSOLETE. *Deny* and *contradict* have displaced GAINSAY except in Biblical English. *Pity* has won out over RUTH, though *harmful* has stayed on a par with *injurious.*

38. MATCH GAME

Give a synonym of classical origin for each of the following Saxon words (e.g., clothing—raiment):

1. chew	6. feed	11. BURDENSOME	16. lore
2. drink	7. give	12. healing	17. lighten
3. dwindle	8. mad	13. loathsome	18. shorten
4. draft	9. mislead	14. manly	19. healthful
5. earnest	10. outside	15. glee	20. balk

There are usually wide differences in overtones—CONNOTATION is the proper technical term—between the Saxon word and its classical ANALOGUE. It is hard to lay down any general rule, since the only Academy that determines the right usage for an English word is the accumulated practice of the best authors. We speak naturally of an *ardent* interest, but of *hot* soup; of *navigating* an ocean liner, but of *sailing* a small boat; of the INCULCATION of doctrine, but of *teaching* arithmetic. The cashier of a bank EMBEZZLES, but a common yegg *steals.* We talk of the ABATEMENT of a nuisance, but of the *lessening* of TENSION on a cable; of the *intelligence* of a great scholar, but of the animal *cunning* of an athlete in a tight spot. We dignify a BENEFACTION to a cathedral, but hand out a *dole* to the unemployed. Some of these pairs are not synonyms; others once were; and a few are still synonyms, though rarely interchangeable in all contexts.

Accumulate several thousand contrasts on this order, and it would be possible at least to gamble on the company the classical words usually keep. They seem to be used in formal and dignified circumstances. They are often employed if a FIGURATIVE rather than a plain blunt meaning is to be conveyed. If the occasion is a full dress speech from the rostrum, or a prepared lecture read from the LECTERN, expect a heavy intermixture of LATINITY. If it is just a plain talking match, where everybody can join in, the Saxon words are far more likely to fit.

Shakespeare, who wrote more memorable dialogue and more quotable tags than anybody else who has used the language, ran to about 21 per cent classical words; even if he had small Latin and less Greek, he had a superb ear for the Romance additions to our tongue. And he was writing, remember, for a popular audience, and his lines were meant to be spoken. It is of interest to the student of vocabulary-range to know that he used 17,677 different words, exclusive of proper and place names, in his plays; 14,652 of these are given as main word entries in the OED, and of this number around 1460 were first used by Shakespeare; while three-fifths of the 3025 compounds he put into circulation were of his own invention. And more than half of his word-novelties came from the Romance element in English. (A. Hart, *Review of English Studies,* 19: 128–140.)

Do not be taken in by the common nonsense which Herbert Spencer helped spread, always to prefer the Saxon word. You can't help using a PREPONDERANCE of them, for the bones, muscles, and sinews of the language come from Old English. But many who make a FETISH of SAXONISM are talking MUMBO-JUMBO. Try this puzzler on them.

39. TRAP FOR THE UNWARY SAXONIZER

Which of the following are "good old Anglo-Saxon words"?

age, art, case, cost, fact, form, ink, line, mile, pain, pair, part, pen, piece, price, rule, sound, ton, tone, and vail; apt, clear, cross, crude, firm, grand, large, mere, nice, pale, plain, poor, pure, rare, real, rich, round, safe, scarce, sure, vain, and BAST; add, aid, boil, close, cook, cure, fail, fix, fry, mix, move, pay, save, serve, try, turn and use; bull, JILT, inch, pin, pit, date

Even in popular narrative there are occasions calling for a high percentage of classical words. The most skillful rewrite artist could not Saxonize the following passage from a 1943 detective story, without ruining its effectiveness and tone.

Hyer went on, *inventing* an *elaborate* and *pointless anecdote,* interlarding it with *parentheses,* drifting off now in this bypath now that, taking up and dropping *random biographies,* MEANDERING, GARRULOUS, *genial.* It was a *magnificent* FILIBUSTER.—Kurt Steel, *Ambush House,* p. 66.

(The words of classical origin are in italics or SMALL CAPITALS.)

168

A lot of near-synonyms in the language turn up in the form of doublets, words that have come in from the same classical stem, but which entered at different stages in the development of the language. The usual pair of doublets comprises one word from the Latin direct, and another from the Latin through the French. Sometimes they have diverged widely in meaning; but in other cases the general significance is the same, only the words are used for different occasions.

We *abbreviate* a word, and we *abridge* a book. A *canal* is an artificial *channel*. An employer can be in a *devilish* bad humor without having DIABOLICAL intentions. A *crevice* in a rock is not usually dangerous; a CREVASSE in a glacier is. A university may be *endowed* with money without being *endued* with the virtues of learning. An *example* may—or may not—be a fair *sample* of a mass of data. A mushroom may be of an *edible* variety but not *eatable* after a bad cook has ruined it. The WARDEN of a PENITENTIARY may also be, as Thomas Mott Osborne was, an admirable *guardian* of the interests of society. Secretary Wallace *hurls* a BOOMERANG, but after it is launched, it HURTLES through the air. *Palsy* now suggests the quivering that follows partial PARALYSIS.

All these doublets had originally much the same area of meaning, and even yet, in the instances chosen, there is a similarity of meaning, but not an IDENTITY. Many are no longer synonyms. Perhaps *eatable* and *edible* are most nearly INTERCHANGEABLE. But try translating Wilde's EPIGRAMMATIC description of the English country squire chasing the fox, "the unspeakable in full pursuit of the uneatable." Using the classical words, it becomes "the INEFFABLE in full pursuit of the inedible." Even Dr. Johnson at his most SESQUIPEDALIAN would not have said this.

40. A PRECARIOUS TEST FOR SYNONYMITY

Of the following doublets, which are interchangeable throughout all their uses and shades of meaning?

1. zero, CIPHER
2. pry, peer
3. REPRIEVE, reprove
4. mode, mood
5. naked, NUDE
6. guarantee, WARRANTY
7. entire, INTEGRAL
8. ENWRAP, envelope
9. evil, ill
10. plum, prune
11. shuffle, scuffle
12. SNIVEL, SNUFFLE
13. tight, TAUT
14. squall, SQUEAL
15. NAIVE, native
16. fiddle, VIOL
17. complacent, COMPLAISANT
18. church, KIRK
19. guile, vile
20. fancy, PHANTASY

There are also closely allied words from the same root, which, while not doublets, are particularly tricky. An URBAN person may or may not be URBANE, though the original IMPLICATIONS of the latter adjective held that a city man was AUTOMATICALLY polished in his manner; while a *rural* dweller was supposed to have a certain RUSTICITY. The adjective *rustic* is now applied mostly to pastoral scenery, or furniture which looks as if it was not long out of the woods. The noun *rustic* has that flavor, at once DEROGATORY and condescending, that all words associated with farm life seem finally to acquire in literary language determined by the CITYFIED. The word *villain,* originally a serf (*villanus*) attached to a country estate (*villa*), came to mean, in the Middle Ages, anyone not of noble birth, hence unacquainted with courtesy and CHIVALRIC manners; so *villain* was applied to a BASEBORN or low person, and finally *villainy* came to mean any low conduct. Eventually it took on its present meaning of SCOUNDRELISM. The words *churl* and *boor* have come down in the world in much the same way.

The word *farmer* showed some signs of a similar descent, but its decay was arrested in this country as farmers began to get more political power, and as the Ford car and mail order houses increased their MOBILITY and access to urban styles. However, as late as 1938 a retired major-general turned governor in a northwestern state was defeated for RENOMINATION largely because he used the word in a contemptuous sense. He told a DELEGATION of GRANGERS, "You farmers should go home and tend to your spring plowing, listen to the birdies sing, and leave politics to your betters." Westerners, it may be added, have shown surprising INVENTIVENESS in devising a rich RETALIATORY slang SYNONYMY for "dudes" and "city-slickers."

WATCH FOR THE HAZARDS

Interesting as the approach to synonyms through etymology may be, it is not a direct FRONTAL mode of attack for a writer who is worried over the right word. As we noted, the headline writer or rewrite man CUDGELS his wits for a synonym, when he has to refer several times, in the same sentence, or in successive sentences, to a term or an idea. Pronouns of reference will go only so far to meet this need. Here is where plenty of practice is needed in conjuring up, on short notice, synonyms for the commonest words and ideas.

Notice, however, the difficulties encountered. The original word may have a number of meanings. *Balance* may mean either a *scales,* or EQUILIBRIUM, but equilibrium will not serve as a synonym for *scales. Business* may mean (1) *occupation,* as "She was in the business of baby-farming." Or it may mean (2) *affair* or *matter,* as "What was the business before the meeting?" Again, in its commonest sense in our *business* culture, it means (3) *trade* or *commerce,* including all the activities connected with purchase, barter, sale and exchange of commodities, plus financial transactions involved in these, as distinct from the production of goods in agriculture and industry; though *business* is also used loosely to include industry, but not farming. The word may also mean (4) a "going concern," as "He sold his business." And it has a minor, specialized sense of (5) stage tricks,—gestures and actions put into a play while it is in production, as "George Kaufman put in a lot of smart business when he directed *The Front Page."* The obsolete literal sense of (6) mere activity, or "keeping busy," has been replaced by a modern coinage, BUSYNESS, as "the bright, brisk busyness of the squirrel," still observed in such forms of *business* as radio, advertising, public relations, and other EMPORIA peddling METAPHYSICAL goods. Clearly, the various synonyms for *business* are not INTERCHANGEABLE, and it takes some careful analysis to spot the particular meaning for which an equivalent is wanted.

Another difficulty often arises. *There may be no exact* synonym *for a given word,* not even one close enough to serve without doing violence to the sense intended. Gertrude Stein had the right answer for this DILEMMA. She told Ernest Hemingway to use the same word over, and he did, and see what it did for him. It almost did for her, too, when she overdid it. But she was not out of her mind, just outside of everybody else's. However, she was very lucid about refusing to strain for a synonym when none exists. Repeat the word, and while EUPHONY may suffer, what is lost in variety is gained in precision and emphasis. Not many of us can worry an idea as long as Miss Stein could, nor does it come home to us with the poetic vividness that forced her to an ECHOIC use of one word. But the fact that some words have no synonyms does not free those of us who are non-Steins from the obligation to search for syno-

171

nyms, or the duty to find the best one to express a given shade of meaning. There is no excuse for impoverished language.

41. Is There a Real Synonym for It?

For any of the following words that have only one meaning, supply a synonym if there is a real one. For those that have multiple meanings, furnish a synonym, if possible, for each of these meanings, as was done for *business*.

1. account	26. degree	51. move	76. sense
2. act	27. earth	52. music	77. sex
3. adjustment	28. edge	53. nation	78. shade
4. amount	29. effect	54. need	79. shock
5. amusement	30. error	55. offer	80. side
6. approval	31. exchange	56. opinion	81. size
7. argument	32. feeling	57. order	82. sleep
8. attention	33. fiction	58. pain	83. slope
9. attraction	34. government	59. pleasure	84. sort
10. balance	35. harmony	60. point	85. statement
11. base	36. hate	61. power	86. stretch
12. birth	37. history	62. price	87. suggestion
13. breath	38. humor	63. produce	88. support
14. burn	39. increase	64. profit	89. surprise
15. burst	40. insurance	65. protest	90. system
16. cause	41. interest	66. punishment	91. thing
17. chance	42. join	67. push	92. time
18. change	43. learn(ing)	68. question	93. trade
19. comfort	44. level	69. range	94. trouble
20. company	45. limit	70. rate	95. twist
21. control	46. liquid	71. reaction	96. way
22. cover	47. loss	72. reward	97. writ(ing)
23. current	48. mass	73. rule	98. word
24. damage	49. measure	74. scale	99. work
25. death	50. middle	75. self	100. wound

The 100 words above are all from the Basic English list of 400 names of "general things" which C. K. Ogden, the inventor of Basic, regards as the most essential ideas for which terms must be maintained in the severely restricted vocabulary of Basic, numbering only 850 words in all. These ideas will recur often in ordinary discourse, and since most of us will not be writing Basic, it is particularly necessary to build up a stock of synonyms for these terms.

What is Basic English?

This is not meant as a reflection on Basic English. That admirable invention is not a plot to impoverish vocabulary. It is a practical form of English for international use, simplified so that an intelligent Russian or Chinese who knows his own language well can learn to read Basic in a month, and to talk and write it after six months' work. It reads like ordinary English, except that there are a good many roundabout phrases. Also, it's likely to seem rather bare, abstract and colorless. But it serves very well for ordinary purposes of business, social and scientific communication, for which it was devised.

For a number of reasons Basic is of interest to any INQUIRER into vocabulary. Ogden, who has made a very careful philosophical analysis of our language, is of the opinion that a 20,000-word vocabulary is adequate for reading most ordinary English and American material. Note that his view sustains the premise on which this book is based. Ogden maintains that nearly all the necessary 20,000 words can be provided with equivalents and definitions in the 850 words of Basic. *The Dictionary of Basic English* makes this claim good. In this connection, an independent study shows that the Basic English words yield a total of 12,425 meanings (if limited to the senses accepted in Basic), an average of 14.6 meanings per word; or 18,418 meanings if the additional senses given for them in the OED are included—an average of 21 meanings per word (Fries—*Word Lists,* p. 81). Evidently the bright Russian or Chinese does well to master that many meanings in a short time.

Basic Throws Light on Synonyms

One of the neat tricks that makes Basic possible is of especial interest in the study of synonyms. Because of a peculiarity of our language which permits the formation of PHRASAL verbs by adding to a simple verb a preposition indicating direction, Ogden in this SUPPLEMENTAL form of English replaces 4000 common verbs by 18 simple verbs plus tagged-on prepositions. Instead of saying CIRCUMNAVIGATE, *circle,* DETOUR, or *skirt,* you say in Basic "go round," or "go around." To be sure, there is a little legitimate FUDGING. Two hundred of the Basic names of "general things" are terms denoting action, but you do not use them as verbs. Instead of *walking,* you "take a walk." So you don't have to learn to conjugate these verbs, or master their principal parts. But the point is that about 4000 verbs can be reduced to *come, get, give, go, keep, let, make, put, seem, take, do, have, say, see, send, may, will, can,* plus the directive prepositions such as *about, round, around, down, in, with, from, to, through, for, against, out, over, of, up,* etc. These verbs and prepositions alike are called "operators" in Basic, because they all indicate action, direction, motion—something doing, so to speak.

The Basic method of providing phrasal equivalents for a flock of specific verbs throws a good deal of light on the requirements for a true synonym. "Go round" gives a fairly precise substitute for *circle,* and you can put it in the place of CIRCUMNAVIGATE, in "Magellan's expedition was the first to circumnavigate the world." But "go round" doesn't convey all the meaning in circumnavigate, which is to "sail round." "Go round" is more general. You can also "go round" the world by flying, though there is no verb *circumfly.* And you'd be more likely to say that the plane *circled* the field than that it "went round" it. Evidently a word acquires a certain "feel" as well as OVERTONES of meaning, which call for the use of a particular word in a given CONTEXT. *Such* CONNOTATIONS *call for careful* DISCRIMINATION *between* synonyms. But Basic is particularly stimulating in forcing us to focus on the exact *denotation,* which DELIMITS essential meaning.

Starting with one of the Basic verbs, we can also build up a whole collection of related and ANALOGOUS words, some of which are synonyms for each other, and some not, though they overlap in some respects, and all of them share the essential, broad, general sense of the original Basic "operator." Take *go,* for instance. When Shakespeare wrote, "Stand not on the order of your going" (*Macbeth,* III iv), a polite way of saying "Scram," the advice was good for his character, but not apt for anybody who is choosy about synonyms.

For the order of going is important. The various ways of going are: *to walk, to run, to ride, to fly, to crawl, to swim, to jump.* Each of these expands to describe the various manners and modes of walking, running, etc.:

Walk, plod, trudge, HOBBLE, limp, stalk, strut, tramp, march, shuffle, toddle, WADDLE, mince, stroll, SAUNTER, ramble, amble, CAREEN, slouch along, lumber, promenade, pace, tread, prowl, MEANDER, loiter, linger, lag, stride. (Cf. the slang, "mosey along.") (Cf. "barge," as "barge into a room.")
Run, scamper, scurry, scuttle, SCUD, scour, pace, gallop, trot, lope, sprint, sweep.

Ride, gallop, trot, LOPE, canter, jog, amble, motor, cycle.
Fly, flit, hover, wing, glide, soar, dart, float.
Crawl, creep, "inch along," GROVEL, drag.
Swim, dive.
Jump, dive, hop, leap, skip, vault, HURDLE.

In addition, there are many slang inventions and phrases to express the sense of "go" as "get out." One of Shakespeare's contemporaries, Richard Carew, obligingly collected in 1595 the Elizabethan LOCUTIONS for conveying this *denigratory* sense:

> . . . neither can any tongue . . . deliver a matter with more variety than ours, both plainly and by proverbs and metaphors; for example, when we would be rid of one, we use to say *be going, trudge, pack, be faring, hence, away, shift,* and by CIRCUMLOCUTION, *rather your room than your company, let's see your back, come again when I bid you, when you are called for, sent for,* INTREATED, *willed, desired, invited, spare us your place, another in your stead, a ship of salt for you, save your credit, you are next the door, the door is open for you, there's nobody holding you, nobody tears your sleeve, etc.* (spelling MODERNIZED)

Joyce adds the Dublin insult: "Who's keeping you?" In American slang, to meet this need, we have had successively (according to the date of first appearance in print), ABSQUATULATE (1833), *vamoose* (1848), *skedaddle* (1861), *scat* (1880), *cheese it* (1900), *git* (?), *skiddoo* (1907), *fade away* (1911), *take a sneak* (1911), *Rous* (1919), *scram* (1920), *beat it* (1926). (Only *skedaddle* is marked colloquial by the dictionaries; the rest are still slang.)

By taking a few afternoons off you could probably work out a similar ELABORATION of the modes of *saying, making, keeping,* etc. Luckily it has all been done, not only for verbs, but for the whole range of language. Only since mid-1946 has it been possible, however, to get hold of a word-treasury which also includes the most significant slang under the right headings. The Thomas Y. Crowell Company's latest revision of *Roget's International* THESAURUS has this feature, so vital for short story, magazine, and radio script writers, and others who want a record of the spoken language as well as of literary idiom. Slang, colloquial, and JOCULAR words are clearly marked as such. They represent the cream of the immense collection of substandard American LOCUTIONS brought together by Lester V. Barrey and Melvin Van den Bark in *The American* THESAURUS *of Slang,* also published by the Crowell Company.

The new Roget has a further refinement on the TRADITIONAL method of grouping words by idea or subject. It makes a BREAK-DOWN, where a word has multiple meanings, and puts together the synonyms of each sense. A 500-page index guide lists all entries in alphabetical order, enabling the user to turn to the right section to find the group that he wants. If he is looking for an ELUSIVE SYNONYM to express the exact idea or shade of meaning he has in mind, he can turn to some nearly related word in the index, and through its subject entry, quickly find a whole battery of synonyms to choose from. This makes the work invaluable as a word-finder. For anyone already well versed in synonyms, it is the quickest and most efficient tool. Since, however, it runs to over 200,000 word-entries and 1194 pages, the Roget cannot allow space for detailed discriminations between synonyms. These the reader must furnish for himself—which is a provocative challenge to his problem-solving ability. Here again, however, most of us are well-advised to check on our best surmises by consulting in the nearest library, if necessary, an authority with ninety years of accumulated experience in discriminating synonyms.

WHAT IS A SYNONYM?

Anyone using Roget who looks at a whole page of words relating to some subject will quickly realize that a HAZY-minded person may easily go wrong on synonyms. A word is not synonymous with another because of:

1. onetime identical meaning,
2. a mere likeness in meaning, or
3. some OVERLAP in the two areas of meaning.

A definition which rules out all BORDERLINE cases is found in *Webster's Dictionary of Synonyms:* [1]

A synonym in this Dictionary will always mean one of two or more words in the English language which have the same or very nearly the same *essential* meaning.

This definition, exemplified fully in the 900 pages of SYNONYMIES which follow, should stop all arguments on what a synonym is—and isn't. The same Dictionary's definition of ANTONYM, while equally satisfactory, calls for a little preliminary warming-up exercise, to prepare for the ORDEAL.

[1] By permission. From *Webster's Dictionary of Synonyms,* copyright, 1942, by G. & C. Merriam Co.

What an Antonym Is Not

The French claim you prove that you know the meaning of a word if you can supply its precise antonym. The catch is in the word *precise*. If the French are right, whoever wrote the following CREDO for a new Monterey commercial art gallery had quite hazy notions:

> When given to choose we shall prefer the incessant to the temporal, the magic to the MUNDANE, the DYNAMIC to both the STATIC and the nervous, the FULGENT to the SEDATE, and the organic to the contrived.

In these pairs, in only one case, *static* and *dynamic,* does one word come within miles of being an antonym of the other, and that ANTITHESIS is blurred because the writer apparently thinks *nervous* is a kind of middle term between them, which it is not. By mind-reading, you can make out that he means the gallery would follow a middle-of-the-road policy, but what kind of art lies on either side of the road, nobody could guess. If the painters supplying the gallery are as hazy-minded as the writer who "plugs" their wares, the exhibit must be something to behold. The *New Yorker,* which picked up this specimen of word-torture in its issue of September 21, 1946, p. 120, added the comment: "Any of these pictures for sale, by the way?"

With this awful example in mind, try your hand at the craft of antonymy.

42. Can You Hit on the Exact Antonym?

Give an ANTONYM for each of the following:

1. PESSIMISM	7. ALLEVIATE	13. ANODYNE	19. CHAOTIC
2. ORNATE	8. AMELIORATE	14. BENIGNANT	20. CIRCUMSTANTIAL
3. HETERODOXY	9. AMITY	15. INTOLERANT	21. CLANDESTINE
4. ideal	10. AMORPHOUS	16. carnal	22. PLIABLE
5. ACCELERATE	11. ANALYTIC	17. URBANE	23. VERBOSE
6. zenith	12. ASCETIC	18. anterior	24. rigid

25. PROVISIONAL

What an Antonym Is

You're probably now ready to take Webster's definition of antonym on trust. It sounds a little as if the editors had sent up a V-2 rocket with instruments attached, to take a reading of the HEAVISIDE layer: [2]

[2] By permission. From *Webster's Dictionary of Synonyms,* copyright, 1942, by G. & C. Merriam Co.

An antonym is a word so opposed in meaning to another word, its equal in breadth and range of application, that it NEGATES or NULLIFIES every single one of its IMPLICATIONS.

As Damon Runyon might have translated this: "It's a word says nix to another word all along the line, Mac."

RUNNERS-UP

While the editors do not recognize Mr. Runyon's gifted recordings of spoken American, they do make a few concessions to human frailty. Under each synonym entry, they add, after the synonym and the antonym, groups of analogous and contrasted words. The analogous words are those closely related in meaning, but not having the same or nearly the same *essential* meaning as the key word; sometimes, say the editors, they merit the name of "near-synonyms." The contrasted words are those which are sometimes very near synonyms of the antonym; others are opposed to the key word in only part of its meaning. The editors recognize that these analogous and contrasted words will be useful to anyone who wants to use the *Dictionary of Synonyms* as a word-finder or vocabulary-builder.

MEMORY PEGS FOR NEW WORDS

For this last purpose the work is an admirable tool. Here are whole clusters of words, grouped according to essential likeness of meaning. *Nearly always one word in each group will be familiar. It will serve as a memory peg for the others.* If a word has more than one sense, the editors make the break-down, and place the synonyms for each sense together. For each group, the essential meaning which they have in common is stated in the first sentence. Then come the discriminations: the true glory of the work. *Through these, the reader can deepen his word-sense at the same time he extends his word-range.*

An example is the best way to prove it. The entry on *dialect* bears directly on vocabulary-building. The G. & C. Merriam Company, publishers of Webster's *Dictionary of Synonyms,* have kindly permitted it to be reproduced here (see pp. 180–181).

Throughout, as in this instance, distinctions are drawn with a sure hand. They start from the central circle of essential meaning (DENOTATION) common to the key word and its synonyms. For each synonym, the circle may have bulged out differently, so that the areas of meaning for the various words in the group no longer COINCIDE. Each has, besides the common central core of EXPLICIT meaning, its additional area of COVERAGE. Around each bulged-out circle, an AURA also may have developed, DIVERGENT in color and pattern for each SYNONYM represented, so that the words in the group no longer match in their fine *shades* of meaning. Each SYNONYM has thus acquired its own CONNOTATIONS, as great writers have more or less fixed its AURA, determining what company the word shall keep, and in what phrase patterns it can appropriately figure.

The resulting differences are stated by the editors in precise logical fashion. But they also try to give the true "feel" of each word. Often they do it by supplying APPOSITE quotations, chosen from the more than 1000 British and American writers who in the last six centuries have by CUMULATIVE use really DIFFERENTIATED synonyms. The quotations are perhaps a bit on the solemn side. Also, the editors have passed up many a chance that the Fowlers would have taken, to contrive some of that ironic higher mischief which only the discerning would detect. But perhaps the editors, feeling this might be distracting, preferred to leave it to readers to make their own humorous COLLOCATIONS.

REFINEMENTS OF RANCOR

One of the first things that strikes a systematic explorer in this treasure-house of synonyms is the extraordinary richness of our vocabulary in terms of abuse. Joseph Conrad always thought it possible to convey in English the effect of PROFANITY without using it. This is a speculation worth testing.

If a writer wants to describe a man venting his spleen on an enemy, he can have his character *abuse, accuse, criticize, curse,* BULLDOZE, CASTIGATE, DISPARAGE, *frighten, malign, scoff at, scold* or *threaten,* without ever re-peating himself. For no one of these words is a synonym for any other in the list. They are just the main simple, direct, UNREFINED ways of going after somebody. All permit of refinement, however, to express the exact degree of rancor felt. Many of the synonyms are longer than the parent word, and more satisfying, like POLYSYLLABIC profanity with a long roll-ing cadence. As a choice among the forms of simple abuse there are:

VITUPERATION, INVECTIVE, OBLOQUY, SCURRILITY, BILLINGSGATE,

which can be delivered with ACRIMONY, or one of its two finer shadings,

ACERBITY or ASPERITY;

179

dialect, *n.* **1** Dialect, vernacular, patois, lingo, jargon, cant, argot, patter, slang are here compared as denoting a form of language or a style of speech which varies from that accepted as the literary standard. **Dialect,** as here compared (see also LANGUAGE, 1), is applied ordinarily to a form of a language that is confined to a locality or to a group, that differs from the standard form of the same language in peculiarities of vocabulary, pronunciation, usage, morphology, and the like, and that persists for generations or even centuries. It may represent an independent development from the same origin as the standard form (as, the Sussex *dialect*) or a survival (as, the *dialect* of the Kentucky mountaineers). The term is often, in spite of some philological opposition, applied to a corruption of the standard language (as, the Gullah *dialect*, a corrupted English used by descendants of African Negroes living chiefly along the coast of South Carolina and Georgia). "A Babylonish *dialect* Which learned pedants much affect" (*Butler*). **Vernacular** (usually *the vernacular*) has several applications, though it always denotes the form of language spoken by the people in contrast with that employed by learned or literary men. In the Middle Ages, when the language of the church, of the universities, and of learned writings was Latin, the vernacular was the native language of the people, whatever it might be in the locality in question; as, to translate the Bible into the *vernacular*. "Freeman ...laments...that the first Christian missionaries from Rome did not teach their converts to pray and give praise in the *vernacular*" (*Quiller-Couch*). When a contrast with the literary language rather than with Latin is implied, *the vernacular* is an underogatory designation for the spoken language, that is, for the language that represents the speech of the people as a whole, that is colloquial but not necessarily vulgar, and is marked chiefly by the spontaneous choice of familiar, often native (as opposed to exotic), words and phrases. "Pope... is absolute master of the raciest, most familiar, most cogent and telling elements of the *vernacular*" (*Lowes*). In current use, *vernacular* often implies a contrast with scientific nomenclature; as, the botanical and the *vernacular* names for flowers. **Patois,** a French word adopted in English, is often used as if it were the equivalent of *dialect*. It tends, however, to be restricted, especially in North America, to designating a form of speech used by the uneducated people in a bilingual section or country; the word often specifically refers to the hybrid language (English, and French Canadian) spoken in some parts of Canada. **Lingo** is a term of contempt applied to any language that is not easily or readily understood. It is applicable to a strange foreign language, a dialect, a patois, or to the peculiar speech of any class, cult, or the like. "I have often warned you not to talk the court gibberish to me. I tell you, I don't understand the *lingo*" (*Fielding*). **Jargon,** which originally meant the twittering

By permission. From Webster's Dictionary of Synonyms, copyright, 1942, by G. & C. Merriam Co.

or chattering of birds, and later was applied to any unintelligible or meaningless speech (as in a foreign tongue or a patois) suggestive of such chattering, is now used chiefly in reference to the technical or esoteric language of a subject, a class, a profession, or a cult, often, but not always, from the point of view of one unfamiliar with it and confused or baffled by it. "Cockets, and dockets, and drawbacks, and other *jargon* words of the customhouse" (*Swift*). "Whitman...has a somewhat vulgar inclination for technical talk and the *jargon* of philosophy" (*Stevenson*). **Cant,** which is etymologically related to *chant*, seems to have been applied first to the whining speech of beggars; in later times, it has been applied variously, as to the secret language of gypsies and thieves, to the technical language of a rade or profession, and to the peculiar phraseology of a religious sect or of its preachers. From the last of these applications, not only has a new sense been developed (see HYPOCRISY), but a new connotation has been derived for the word in the sense here considered. For *cant*, when referred to the peculiar language of a subject or profession usually suggests the hackneyed use of set words or phrases, often in a specialized or "off" sense; *cant*, therefore, does not usually imply unintelligibility; thus, the language of sports writers is a *cant* (not a *jargon*); the scientific nomenclature used by physicians in official reports may be called medical *jargon* (not *cant*) by those who do not understand it; a person who repeatedly calls an investigation a "probe," a large book a "tome," a preacher a "parson," his wife "my better half," and the like, may be said to be given to *cant*. **Argot** is applicable chiefly to the cant of the underworld, originally to that of Paris; it is now sometimes used of any form of peculiar language adopted by a clique, a set, or other closely knit group. **Patter** always implies rapid voluble speech, such as is characteristic of a circus barker or of a faker selling wares, or is found half-recited, half-sung as a farcical act on the stage or in a musical comedy. In extended use it usually also implies a cant; as, the *patter* of an auctioneer; the *patter* of a clown. **Slang** does not as often denote a form of language or a type of speech as it does a class of recently coined words or phrases or the type of word which belongs to that class; as, in the *slang* of college students a drudge is a "greasy grind"; the difference between American *slang* and British *slang*. *Slang* implies comparatively recent invention, the appeal of the words or phrases to popular fancy because of their aptness, picturesqueness, grotesqueness, or humorousness, and either an ephemeral character or, if the words or phrases persist in use, their nonacceptance by the authorities as a permanent addition to the language; thus, "to escape with the skin of one's teeth" sounds like *slang*, but it is not so designated because it is derived from the Authorized Version of the Bible (*Job* xix. 20).

2 *Language, tongue, speech, idiom.

while if mere DETRACTION is not enough, it amplifies into

BACKBITING, CALUMNY, *scandal* or *slander*.

If the aim is to achieve that "measured MALIGNITY of slander" with which Lecky credited the later Junius, the offender will soon realize that *malign* may be refined by a VERSATILE opponent to—

TRADUCE, ASPERSE, VILIFY, CALUMNIATE, DEFAME, *slander* or *libel* him.

And the *libel* (as a noun) may be in the form of a

SKIT, SQUIB, LAMPOON, or PASQUINADE.

This last sounds like a formidable insult, and it can be. It was originally an ANONYMOUS lampoon, usually in verse, posted up on a mutilated statue of Pasquino, in Rome, as GRATUITOUS publicity for the writer's enemy. This happened before there were newspapers and magazines. Nowadays pasquinades are usually printed in EPITHET form in *Time,* or posted on a bulletin board. Some anonymous wag writing in the old *Bookman* provided George Moore with a pasquinade for his tombstone in the form of a premature epitaph:

> Women he loved, and after women art;
> Good friends he had, and used them all for copy.
> Had but his head been matchéd by his heart,
> Time had not mixed his laurels with the poppy.

When it comes to more serious and sustained attack, however, the language still has many UNEXHAUSTED resources. When the object is to *curse* someone out roundly, you can choose whether to

EXECRATE, OBJURGATE, *damn,* or ANATHEMATIZE

him, though the last implies ECCLESIASTICAL language, and in view of the blasphemy laws, should perhaps be done with discretion. If long words seem inadequate to explode compressed rancor, consider the merits of *scoff.* Trailing it as synonyms are

jeer, GIBE, LEER, GIRD, *sneer* and FLOUT,

expressive MONOSYLLABLES all.

If the occasion is a battle of the books between rival scholars where unduly strong language is barred, one can *disparage* the other or, with delicate DISCRIMINATIONS in the form of DISPARAGEMENT, can the other's reputation. In a faculty exchange of this kind, the DEROGATOR can be sure of an appreciative audience, with a nice feeling for the GRADATIONS of meaning involved. As for the professor on the receiving end, he will understand all too well. No danger of his being in the predicament of one of Earl Wilson's friends:

Izzy Grove, the amazingly successful dance promoter, was at a meeting of the Anti-DEFAMATION League when somebody used some long words.
"Wait a minute," said Grove. "What do them words mean? Ya know, once I was nominated for oblivion, and I accepted, with thanks, and it wasn't till two years later I found out what it meant."

To do the learned faculties justice, however, their wrangles conducted in public print are seldom as mild as mere depreciation. Take that battle over the 100 Great Books, between President Stringfellow Barr and Sidney Hook, apostle of PRAGMATISM and "progressive" education. Hook has turned it into a slanging match and battle of EPITHETS. He has rung all the changes on *scold;* in turn we have heard him

upbraid, rate, BERATE, *tonguelash, jaw, bait, bawl out, wig, rail, revile,* and *vituperate*

the St. Johns College plan. President Barr, UNRUFFLED, has usually replied with dead-pan but joyous parables ridiculing the FARRAGO of intellectual PEMMICAN mixed with sawdust now dished out to students in many college courses—especially in those outlines of everything called surveys, in which the student learns less and less about more and more until he becomes intellectually unbuttoned. Perhaps St. Johns goes in for too much DIALECTIC per cubic inch of content, but its faculty and students do have good CONTROVERSIAL manners.

For disputation on Hook's level, however, there is a rich synonymy, especially if the scolding is shifted over to the distaff side. One woman need not stop at labeling her BÊTE NOIR a VIRAGO: this expands into

AMAZON, TERMAGANT, *scold, shrew,* VIXEN, or *barge,*

all words which call for utterance in a

CAUSTIC, MORDANT, SCATHING, or MORDACIOUS

tone. Suppose, however, that the target, rather than being a BULLDOZING virago, is somewhat clinging, and neither toils nor spins, she can be put in her place as a *parasite,* or

SYCOPHANT, *favorite*, LICKSPITTLE, *bootlicker, hanger-on, leech,* or *sponge.*

Or if her "cat-chat" resembles that of the characters in Claire Booth Luce's *The Women*, it can be characterized not merely as *poisonous*, but as

venomous, VIRULENT, TOXIC, MEPHITIC, PESTILENTIAL or MIASMIC,

depending on the particular kind of poison EXUDED. But all these methods are probably too crude. To express a really telling insult in elegant and IMPECCABLE English, reflection on the other woman's taste in clothes is probably indicated. Here the INTIMATION that her taste runs to the

gaudy, TAWDRY, GARISH or FLASHY

is too blunt. The one remaining synonym in the list is the one wanted for the very ACME of polite insult: "Isn't her taste in clothes a little MERETRICIOUS?" Admittedly, this is not the term now in use in the world of fashion, but it should be. It's really an ideal solution to the problem of PROPRIETY which *PM* skirts around so delicately in the following:

. . . its first scheduled production is one called *Scarlet Street*, a DE-CANINED AMERICANIZATION of its original French title, *La Chienne,* a term which one doesn't sling around in free translation for family audiences. *PM*, April 9, 1945.

Beaumont and Fletcher would have solved that instantly, retaining even the CANINE CONNOTATIONS: they'd have rendered the title *Merrytricks.* (Latin *meretrix,* "harlot.")

Surely this exhibit shows Conrad was right. PROFANITY is a crude expedient in comparison with the far richer resources of DENIGRATORY and PEJORATIVE terms available in English. Conrad demonstrates his point pretty well when one of his NARRATORS tells how he was cursed out:

. . . began by calling me Pig, and from that went CRESCENDO into UNMEN-TIONABLE adjectives.

Runyon, Lardner, Cain, and O'Hara have also shown great RESOUCEFUL-NESS in conveying the effects of profanity and RIBALDRY through the use of slang equivalents—and in this department the PENCHANT of our language for developing synonyms is very much in evidence (see p. 221).

On the sober and serious side, there is infinite variety in synonyms, too. And it is one of the great pleasures of reading to be able to appreciate the fine shades of meaning which a master of synonyms can convey. The best of all tests for vocabulary depth—as well as width—is an ability to distinguish between synonyms, by supplying from a list the *one* which is most apt, and most in accord with the tone and color of the thought expressed.

43. PICK THE RIGHT SYNONYM

The synonym lists which follow are picked from Webster, to allow for the addition of the maximum numbers of words to vocabulary. Most of the key words and equivalents belong to the learned part of the language. The ILLUSTRATIVE sentences, in which you are to fill in each blank with the best synonym, are not from Webster's examples, which are almost without exception on the sober side. Unless a source is cited, the sentences are by the author of this book; but they are devised to keep as close as possible to the DISCRIMINATIONS in Webster. To get the best results, do only one or two entries at a time, and try to fix each group of new words in your memory, at the same time mastering the NUANCES of meaning for each.

ABJURE: renounce, FORSWEAR, RECANT, RETRACT
1. He was unwilling to take the pledge, because he knew he would soon —————— himself.
2. Galileo was forced publicly to —————— his belief that the earth revolved around the sun.
3. Gandhi requires his followers to —————— force.
4. Drew Pearson threatened to sue Mr. Wallace for libel, unless he would —————— his statement that Pearson had obtained the Wallace letter to the President about foreign policy by backstairs methods.
5. George II of Greece was unwilling to —————— his claim to the throne.
Ant.: pledge, elect

ABRIDGEMENT: abstract, brief, SYNOPSIS, CONSPECTUS, EPITOME
1. The secretary asked him for an —————— of his paper to include in the published program.
2. When Eutropius called his short history of Rome an ——————, he stretched the meaning of the word.
3. The professor asked each RESEARCHER to submit a —————— of his thesis.
4. In his presentation to the publisher, he featured a —————— of the whole book in a form that could be taken in at a glance.
5. They sold an —————— of the book in a quarter edition.
Ant.: expansion

ACTIVATE: ENERGIZE, VITALIZE
1. Pure proteins are found to have the maximum ——————— effect in aiding CONVALESCENCE from MALNUTRITION.
2. An artist in residence at a university is found to ——————— the creative work of students.
3. All National Guard units were ——————— early in 1942.
Ant.: arrest

ADJACENT: adjoining, CONTIGUOUS, ABUTTING, TANGENT, COTERMINOUS, JUXTA-POSED
1. The airline route to Moscow was ——————— to the great circle course followed by ships, only at ——————— (a naval secret!).
2. Their estates were ——————— for three miles back from the point where they joined on the Potomac to the old mill which lay half on one property, half on the other; beyond that, they diverged.
3. The nearest ranch house ——————— to the headquarters of the great King Ranch is distant a long day's ride.
4. The Hay and Adams mansions in Washington were ———————, and doors opened between them.
5. He bought land ——————— on the river.
6. The City of Seattle and King County in which it lies are ———————.
7. A passage from North's translation of Plutarch ——————— to Shakespeare's lines covering the same ground, shows what a fast and slick REWRITE job he could do.
Ant.: NONADJACENT

ACCIDENTAL: casual, FORTUITOUS, CONTINGENT, incidental, ADVENTITIOUS (all are synonyms of *accidental,* but not always of one another)
1. To the British Foreign Office, the question of Palestine is merely ——————— to Arab-British relations and the protection of the Mosul and Haifa oil pipelines.
2. Lucretius spoke of the ——————— CONCOURSE of the atoms, but NUCLEAR PHYSICISTS would not agree with him.
3. Rhine claims that the results obtained in his SUPRASENSORY experiments cannot be merely ———————, since the hits exceed the misses to a degree not to be accounted for by the laws of PROBABILITY. Other STATISTICIANS dispute his claim.
4. His research methods were seemingly ———————, but he got living offspring from a cross between a sea-urchin and a sand-dollar, which was as if, said the Director of the laboratory, he had successfully cross-bred a lion with a jackass.
5. The very high CORRELATION (.98) between the rate of melting of a certain Greenland glacier and the birth rate of the Bantus in equatorial Africa is purely ———————.
6. Pay raises in this concern were ——————— on the state of the business as shown in the balance sheet at the close of the fiscal year.
Ant.: planned, essential

Cumulative: accumulative, additive, summative
1. The education attained by the study of the 100 great seminal books is in the truest sense —————, since the influence of each earlier writer upon his successors is noted, until a closely reticulated and integrated whole is attained.
2. The ————— effect of repeated dosages finally weakened his heart, though curing his glandular deficiency.
3. Integration is a short-cut to replace the cumbersome ————— methods which yield in any case only an approximation.
4. The ————— whole which results from the efforts of the mound-building ants is very impressive.

Addict: votary, devotee, habitué, fiend, fan (I add *aficionado,* because you often need a synonym for "fan")
1. He came to the club, he said, expecting to see some of the old —————s, but it was such a stormy night that all he saw at the table were the sons of —————s.
2. Had Casanova been born in ancient Rome, he would have been a ————— in the temple of Venus.
3. Coleridge was a laudanum —————, but in no sense a drug —————.
4. Anybody living in Brooklyn who is not a Dodger ————— is anathema to the rest of the baseball —————.
5. Moore is a ————— of pure science, and considers that Edison was not a scientist in any real sense, since he added nothing to theory.

Allegory: (I) symbolism
1. Proust's ————— often depends on memory-encrusted sensations of taste or smell.
2. Diego Rivera's great mural pageant of Mexican history above the grand staircase of the National Palace is a superb ————— of his country's long struggle against oppression.
(II) parable, myth, fable, apologue
1. It is no disparagement to speak of the Christian religion as having the most moving and effective ————— of any world faith; and the fact that Paul and St. Augustine turned it into an ————— for their own doctrines in no sense weakens the overwhelming impression made by the words of Christ, taken by themselves. The notion that Jesus is an invented character argues the existence of an epic-poet-dramatist greater than Homer, Shakespeare, and Cervantes rolled into one. Who was he? History is even more silent on this score and the silence argues that it was Jesus who existed, not some unknown literary creator.
2. Christ often taught by —————s.
3. *Animal Farm* is a true ————— though there are those who think that George Orwell draws an immoral moral.

APPARITION: PHANTASM, phantom, WRAITH, fetch, ghost, spirit, specter, shade, REVENANT, spook, haunt, hant (to which I add *zombie* and *Poltergeist*)

1. Hamlet, I am thy father's —————.
2. Saul asked the Witch of Endor to summon up the ————— of Samuel.
3. The ————— of buried Denmark.—*Hamlet.*
4. The figure of the old Earl, appearing suddenly by the PARAPET in the twilight, looked too substantial to be an —————; yet the record showed that he had gone down at sea last year.
5. Looking on the ruins of Nurnberg, where he had spent so many happy days during his *Lehrjahren,* he knew how that illustrious Prince of India must have felt in revisiting Tyre, where three thousand years earlier he had known King Hiram when the city was in its high glory.
6. As he came out of the COMA, his fever was still high, and persistent ————— kept recurring—one, a group of Dutch travelers, carrying tulip bulbs and leading horses. Five months later he saw these people in life, getting on a river steamer—an authentic instance of PREVISION.
7. A ————— is a lively —————, but the records show that the only one seen of man was the one which John Wesley saw at the Epworth Rectory.
8. The —————s which worried Hawthorne were really —————s from the Puritan past.
9. "It's no common —————," old Silas said; "for it comes in different shapes, but always whispers at him the same way. Maybe it's Old Nick himself, trying to collect on a bet for Jabez' soul, but Jabez' idear of gettin' Daniel Webster to defend him is a crazy notion. Daniel would uphold the contract, even if it was made with the devil himself."
10. Ichabod Crane saw the grisly ————— of the headless horseman.
11. The last time he saw Hopkins, Harry was a mere —————.
12. It's hard to tell if a ————— is dead or alive; the resurrected OPA was a perfect instance.
13. Judging by his story "The Horla," Guy de Maupassant must have been one of the few persons to see his own —————. Soon after he went mad and died.
14. Half way between sleeping and waking, as he napped one drowsy afternoon, he thought he saw through the French window his old collie LOPING through the garden; and it proved to be no —————; the old dog had found his way across three states to rejoin his master.

AESTHETE: DILETTANTE, VIRTUOSO, CONNOISSEUR

1. Horace Walpole was a mere ————— of the Gothic, but has to be taken seriously as a letter-writer.
2. Iris Barry of the Museum of Modern Art is not only a great collector of films, but one of the best ————— of CINEMATIC art alive.
3. Most —————s are —————s of several arts.

AMATEUR: dilettante, dabbler, TYRO (or TIRO) (Note that DILETTANTE also overlaps in meaning with AESTHETE.)
1. MacArthur is no _____ in the field of Oriental government.
2. A _____ usually tries to arrive at results as did George Eliot's Mr. Tulliver, by his own unaided intellect.
3. An _____ in all the arts may still become master of one.
4. Margaret Webster may seem to scholars a mere _____ of Shakespeare, but that is not how she strikes old stage hands—of whom Shakespeare was one.
Ant.: professional, expert

AMBIGUITY: EQUIVOCATION, TERGIVERSATION, AMPHIBOLOGY, AMPHIBOLOGISM. DOUBLE ENTENDRE (or DOUBLE ENTENTE) (I add *double-talk*)
1. Danny Kaye's famous songs in _____ are written by his wife, Sylvia Fine.
2. No one has ever found an _____ or _____ in Bertrand Russell's writing, for he always uses words to DELIMIT meaning—nor does he go in for _____s in his writings on love and marriage.
3. What he called an _____ in the wording of the contract seemed to me an INTENTIONAL _____, so I called the deal off.
4. There has been downright _____ in the Russian use of the terms democracy and freedom, though it is evident that they use *peace* in the same sense we do—to mean the temporary absence of war.
Ant.: LUCIDITY, EXPLICITNESS

APPENDAGE: APPURTENANCE, adjunct, accessory
1. In *Oklahoma* the ballet is no longer a mere _____ to musical comedy, but an INTEGRAL part of the plot action.
2. They worked out a scheme for beating the OPA ceiling price on new cars by providing virtually built-in _____s.
3. St. Paul had no intention of becoming a mere _____ to Minneapolis.
4. He sold the manor and all its _____, except the gatehouse which he gave as a FREEHOLD to the old porter.

CHANGEABLE: changeful, variable, MUTABLE, PROTEAN
1. It is hard to devise tests that really measure vocabulary range, because the difficulty of words, even in groups of like frequency and range of occurrence is _____ within wide limits for different persons, depending on their experience and reading choices.
2. Bette Davis has a _____ genius for assuming many different characters.
3. The _____ temper of the skies.—Dryden.
4. They put the CHAMELEON on _____ silk, but it did not burst.
5. The INFINITESIMAL universe within the atom is revealed as infinitely _____.
Ant.: stable, UNCHANGEABLE

189

CELERITY: ALACRITY, LEGERITY
1. The motto of the University Restaurant in Greenwich Village is "Service with ——————," not "Service with a sneer," as at some places.
2. Voltaire's style always kept that certain —————, even when he was eighty; and Shaw's style keeps it, too.
3. She reached for her gun with the ————— of a crocodile snapping at a stick.

CHANGE, n.: (I) alteration, variation, MODIFICATION
1. Shops dealing in men's suits usually undertake ————— free.
2. Taft suggested a slight ————— in the wording, which effectively EVISCERATED the bill.
3. Human nature may be always the same; but there are tremendous ————— in the methods of reading it; from humors to COMPLEXES is a long jump.
4. There were a good many —————s between the books he presented to the Internal Revenue and the set of accounts which he kept for use in negotiations with the union.
(II) MUTATION, PERMUTATION, VICISSITUDE, ALTERNATION
1. The total of possible moves in a game of chess is a number so great that a hundred billion years would not suffice to try out all the —————s.
2. There proved to be very rapid —————s of phase in the CIRCUIT.
3. The —————s of the twenty-one civilizations that have so far existed are interpreted by Toynbee in his *Study of History*.
4. General PHYSIOLOGISTS are now trying to find the PHYSICOCHEMICAL processes which account for the sudden —————s which DeVries discovered.

CLEAR, adj.: (I) Transparent, translucent, lucid, PELLUCID, DIAPHANOUS, LIMPID
1. Glass bricks are ————— but not —————.
2. Her spoken words had a ————— quality, and her "voice delicately divided the silence" (Elinor Wylie).
3. In British drapery shops, *muslin* means a ————— fabric, not suitable for men's pajamas.
4. It is a myth that all French styles have in common the quality of being —————. Proust often is not; and the SYMBOLISTS were often obscure, as were the TROUBADOUR poets who favored the *trobar clus*.
5. Ellis's style was both ————— and —————.
(II) PERSPICUOUS, lucid
1. Veblen did not have, nor does Dewey have, a ————— style in the lecture room, yet they have been two of the most influential teachers America has produced.
2. Bertrand Russell commands a style as ————— as his thought.
Ant.: (I) TURBID (of air, days, water), confused (as to minds, thoughts, etc.);
(II) UNINTELLIGIBLE, ABSTRUSE

INCONSONANT: inconsistent, INCOMPATIBLE, INCONGRUOUS, UNCONGENIAL, UN-
SYMPATHETIC, DISCORDANT, DISCREPANT

1. Welles gave the Argentine diplomat a decidedly ——————— hearing.
2. Salisbury found Disraeli a rather ——————— colleague; and the feeling was reciprocal.
3. Santa Ana's and Zack Taylor's accounts of the battle were not merely ———————; they were ——————— in details beyond the point where the DISPARITY could be explained as due to different standpoints for observation. Actually, Santa Ana and Taylor both lied.
4. Elizabeth's court orchestra was called The Queen's Noise, but not because there was anything ——————— about their playing.
5. That they were mentally and morally ——————— was apparent.
6. There was nothing ——————— between Jefferson's taste and his powers of assimilation, even on the level of food and wine. As he put it, "I am blessed with a digestion that can accept and CONCOCT whatever my palate chooses to consign to it."
7. The toastmaster's humor was decidedly ——————— with the occasion.

Ant.: consonant

APPETIZER: HORS D'OEUVRE, ANTIPASTO, SMÖRGÅSBORD, APÉRITIF

1. The Grand Ticino in Sullivan Street has very good ———————.
2. If you offer most Americans an ——————— in solid form instead of liquid, they won't come to your parties again.
3. During the war, the quality of ——————— even at Charles Aux Pommes Frites fell off.
4. Maxwell Bodenheim used to be famous for his capacity to eat up practically all the ——————— provided for a Greenwich Village studio tea.
5. We had ——————— at the Stockholm Restaurant.

DICTATORIAL: MAGISTERIAL, MAGISTRAL, authoritative, AUTHORITARIAN, DOG-
MATIC, DOCTRINAIRE, ORACULAR (Webster, at the entry for
authoritarian, gives TOTALITARIAN)

1. The ——————— tone of the Pope's ENCYCLICALS is to be expected, since he is the chief lawgiver of the Church when he speaks *ex cathedra*.
2. To judge by Stalin's pictures, he does not have a ——————— manner; but his utterance in answering questions is ———————.
3. So long as it leaves to Caesar the things that are Caesar's, the Church is not a ——————— REGIME, though it may be called ———————.
4. Mr. Justice Holmes did not indulge in ——————— language, preferring a dry, ironic style; and while he spoke with finality he was never ———————, being a disciple of Hume's skepticism.
5. The dogma that human nature is always the same has ——————— finality with generals and cheapjack politicians.
6. A petty classroom tyrant usually assumes a ——————— manner; whereas a great teacher, as a rule, keeps to a simple natural style.

ENORMOUS: immense, huge, vast, giant, gigantic, colossal, mammoth, ELE-
PHANTINE, TITANIC, HERCULEAN, CYCLOPEAN, ANTEAN, GAR-
GANTUAN, BROBDINGNAGIAN

1. The road-building machine, moving slowly down the island at night, with its single searchlight high on the forty foot mast from which the boom swung, seemed like some ——————— monster.
2. Hamsun's novel, *Growth of the Soil,* has an ——————— power to re-mind us how closeness to elemental things is a source of strength.
3. He had ——————— strength and no sense of how to use it.
4. The famous GOURMAND of Monterey had a ——————— appetite, which required five pounds of steak and eleven chickens at a meal.
5. The HULLABALOO over Hughes' movie, *The Outlaw,* can be described by Hollywood's favorite adjective, ———————, with IDIOCY APPENDED.
6. The CYCLOTRONS involve ever more ——————— VOLTAGES.
7. Beyond the cliff lay only the ——————— reaches of the ocean.
8. Many of the HIDALGOS' HACIENDAS covered an ——————— expanse.
9. Recent discoveries in the Peking area indicate that PREHISTORIC man may have attained ——————— proportions.
10. Ringling's circus is no longer a ——————— spectacle.
11. Dr. Johnson had an ——————— gait.
12. Hitler cast a ——————— and horrifying shadow upon world history, quite in contrast to his actual insignificance of body and soul. He was the worst of the half-witted geniuses who have scourged mankind.
13. The ORCHID attained ——————— size.
14. e. e. cummings' ——————— room was the best novel of prison life to come out of World War I.
15. Even among the prehistoric animals, the DINOSAUR loomed up as ———————.

IMPOSTOR: FAKER, EMPIRIC, quack, MOUNTEBANK, CHARLATAN

1. Was Nostradamus a ——————— and a ———————, or was he an in-spired prophet?
2. Huey Long had a good deal of the ——————— about him, perhaps a carryover from his peddling days; but he also had great though misused powers, as Robert Penn Warren shows in his *roman à clef* about the first American *Führer,* and, one hopes, the last.
3. Most of Huey Long's followers who have tried to assume his mantle are nothing but cheap political ———————s.
4. NATUROPATHS and CHIROPRACTORS are considered ——————— by or-ganized medicine, and are labeled ———————s who have not taken advantage of the experimental discoveries and of the PHARMACOPEIA on which orthodox doctors rely.
5. The Indian RAJAH who escaped from his own funeral PYRE was con-sidered an ——————— by all his relatives for twenty-five years, until a week before his death he was VINDICATED by the Privy Council.

COMPENDIUM: SYLLABUS, digest, PANDECT, survey, sketch, PRÉCIS, APERÇU
1. A ——————— course often involves little first hand contact with the SALIENT works of the periods covered; at its worst, it is a comic ———————.
2. Protagoras' summer course was a ——————— of his winter lectures.
3. Peale's Popular Educator was an old-fashioned ——————— of knowledge on all subjects, much of it inaccurate and none of it the result of original research.
4. Jefferson asked Freneau to put a ——————— on the back of each document filed.
5. The ——————— for the course gave its mere bare bones.
6. Coleridge excelled at giving ———————s which provided for his listeners sudden flashes of insight.
7. The ———————s of Justinian as transmitted to Western Europe had curious results on local law.

DISCERNMENT: DISCRIMINATION, perception, PENETRATION, insight, ACUMEN, DIVINATION, CLAIRVOYANCE
1. Very few American news interpreters have Elmer Davis' blend of logical ——————— and INTUITIVE ———————. And he brings to bear also natural ——————— in deciding on a course of action.
2. Madame Perkins ran the Labor Department by intellect, not by ———————.
3. In the main, Roosevelt seemed to have what amounted to positive ——————— during the War. Perhaps his ability to make things happen accounted in part for the correspondence between his PREVISION and the ultimate outcome.
4. Caesar had particular ——————— in picking men.
5. ——————— between *mystical* and *mysterious* is no problem for any one with acute ——————— as to the basic distinction in meaning. The two words come close to being antonyms.

INCONSTANT: fickle, capricious, MERCURIAL, UNSTABLE
1. An ——————— policy in government REGULATORY activity is less easily endured by business than CALCULABLE severity. Under the latter, business at least feels that the government knows its own mind and will stay put.
2. For anyone who likes variety, a ——————— temper in a spouse is more endurable than a stolid one.
3. An ——————— woman used to be more of a shock to society than a man of the same breed.
4. A ——————— woman may or may not be ——————— as well. She may take out all her VAGARIES on one man.
Ant.: constant

193

CONTROVERSIAL: POLEMIC, POLEMICAL, ERISTIC, APOLOGETIC
1. Adler's —————— methods are as bad as Hook's, and he adds to Hook's shin-kicking technique a great flair for organizing BOREDOM; nor does Adler have Hook's skill in the —————— art.
2. Dean Inge's series of sermons in St. Mary's Church at Oxford on "What is Christianity" were rather —————— than ——————. He chiefly indulged in —————— blasts against the schools of religion which he disliked: MODERNISM, the social gospel, etc.

INSUBORDINATE: rebellious, mutinous, SEDITIOUS, FACTIOUS, CONTUMACIOUS
1. The Copperheads during the Civil War engaged in activities that were downright ——————.
2. The —————— spirit in the Democratic Party is always LATENT, and loud squabbling in its ranks is no sure HARBINGER of a pending split of the type which led to the formation of the Republican Party in 1854.
3. Savonarola persisted in his —————— conduct, and finally got himself burned at the stake.
4. The —————— sailors at Kronstadt became heroes in the annals of the Russian Revolution.
5. An —————— attitude in the staff usually argues a failure to lead in a way that gains consent.
6. The openly —————— MANEUVERS of the colored troops in an Arizona camp were not allowed to get into the news.

INTEGRATION: ARTICULATION, CONCATENATION
1. The —————— of events that lead up to World War I can be given a variety of explanations.
2. The St. Johns CURRICULUM of the 100 Great Books at least makes possible a complete —————— of the materials, with none of that SPECIOUS and forced —————— between subjects which so-called progressive educators are fond of boasting about, when all they have done is to find TENUOUS and IMPERMANENT cross-connections between DISPARATE subjects.
Ant.: DISINTEGRATE

NEUROLOGIST: PSYCHIATRIST, ALIENIST, PSYCHOPATHOLOGIST, PSYCHOTHERA-
PIST, PSYCHOANALYST
1. Although he has no M.D. degree, he is one of the best ——————s now in the country, with rare skill in DIAGNOSING personality disorders.
2. William A. White, although he edited the *Psychoanalytic Review*, was recognized as one of the best all-around —————— in the country, since he used ordinary medical THERAPY and HYDROTHERAPY to supplement the techniques of the ——————.
3. The —————— whom George Gershwin was consulting had no suspicion that the real difficulty was a brain tumor, which decidedly called for the services of a —————— skilled also in brain surgery.
4. The —————— declared that Rudolf Hess was sane.

ORNATE: ROCOCO, BAROQUE, FLAMBOYANT, FLORID (I add *flossy* [slang])
1. There is more that's ——————— about most opera than the style of decoration of the opera houses where it is given; but Wagner suggests rather a relapse into ———————, with German-PSEUDO-Gothic trimmings.
2. The FOYER of the typical movie palace is worse than ———————. It's ——————— statues of over-ripe cupids and nymphs, and occasional fountains surrounded by the best bathing-beauty art of the ——————— period, prepare the discerning patron for the tasteless MONSTROSITIES of De Mille and his rivals.
3. There is nothing ——————— about the New York University buildings downtown. They are in the best warehouse tradition: strictly UTILITARIAN and ATROCIOUSLY ugly.
Ant.: chaste, austere

PACIFY: appease, PLACATE, MOLLIFY, PROPITIATE, CONCILIATE
1. The Aztecs believed that human sacrifices would ——————— the wrath of Huitzilopocholi.
2. The Democrats have found it hard to ——————— the hostility of business after fourteen years under the New Deal.
3. Even Aaron could not ——————— Moses' wrath at the Jews for setting up the Golden Calf.
4. The Americans and Russians accuse each other of ———————ing the Germans.
5. Camacho has done a good job in ———————ing the conservatives in Mexico, and gaining their acceptance for the more radical policies which Cardenas INITIATED, or rather revived from the programs of Hidalgo, Morelos, and Juarez.
6. MacArthur seems to be doing a better job of ———————ing Japan than the Four Powers are succeeding in doing in Germany.

PSEUDONYM: ALIAS, NOM DE GUERRE, pen-name, NOM DE PLUME, INCOGNITO, ALLONYM
1. Some authors have come to be known almost exclusively by their ———————s, Mark Twain, George Sand, and George Eliot, for instance.
2. We should like to know what ——————— Haroun Al Raschid used when he went slumming in Bagdad.
3. That second-story man had a curious sense of humor: he used as his ——————— the name Jay Gould. Strictly, this was an ———————.
4. Henry Adams chose to write his SATIRIC novel *Democracy* under a ———————; after all he was a historian by trade.
5. Stalin is the ———————, so to speak, of Josef Djugashvili; but when he was sticking up silver-trains in the hills above Tiflis to fill the Party Treasury, he had another ———————.

Realize: (I) actualize, embody, incarnate, materialize, externalize, objectify, substantiate, substantialize, hypostatize, reify

1. Da Vinci spent fifteen years trying to —————— in the face of Christ, in the Last Supper, all the complex and many-sided character which he felt lay behind Jesus' seeming simplicity.
2. James was able to —————— his own thoughts to analyze them.
3. Laymen, accustomed to —————— time and space, find Einstein's theories very hard going.
4. Some spiritualists hold that soul-stuff is —————— in ectoplasm.
5. A great actor is adept at ——————ing the emotion which the character is supposed to feel; but the actor cannot without grave risk to his acting, indulge in the luxury of feeling the emotion he is projecting.
6. The Athanasians held that in Christ was ——————d the actual substance and essence of God; that Jesus was not merely of like nature, but of the same nature as the Father.
7. He was able to —————— his project of starting a modest publishing business when one of his friends made him a character loan.
8. The energy latent within the nucleus of the plutonium atom was —————— as explosive power at Los Alamos.
9. Some theologians —————— the factors involved in the sacraments, in order to symbolize for the layman the doctrine conveyed.
10. The communicant is supposed to accept the bread and wine as ——————, or strictly, transubstantiated into the body and blood of the Savior.
11. To make the inward workings of the atom clear to laymen, popular expositors of science often —————— the energy-bundles concerned, to a degree that does violence to strict scientific views.

(II) Think, conceive, imagine, fancy, envisage, envision

1. It is hard for the non-mathematician to —————— infinity, though he —————— he understands zero, because he can readily —————— its symbol: O. If he knew the symbol for infinity, a figure eight on its side, would that help him —————— what infinity is? It would not.
2. I ——————, therefore I am.—Descartes.
3. Southey's poetry, said Coleridge, was based on ——————, not imagination.

Vociferous: clamorous, blatant, strident, boisterous, obstreperous (to which I add stentorian)

1. Sarah was a decidedly —————— girl, and her play for attention was quite ——————, but her methods worked.
2. A hog caller needs a —————— voice.
3. He was so —————— in protesting his innocence, that I concluded he was guilty.
4. Russia's demands are even more —————— than those of her opponents, and her spokesmen speak in more —————— tones, as Americans did in 1846, when they were preparing to slice off half of Mexico.

JEST: joke, JAPE, QUIP, WITTICISM, wisecrack, crack, gag (to which I add *wit-crack* [Shakespeare, *Much Ado About Nothing,* V, iv, 102])
1. He was as full of merry ——————s as Bob Hope.
2. True ——————s are as rare as ——————s are plentiful.
3. Deems Taylor got off a good —————— when somebody asked him, during the musical price fight between ASCAP and the radio industry, if radio did not have its Achilles' heel. "Yes," said Taylor, "and a lot of heels not named Achilles."
4. Many a —————— contrived by Benny's —————— men deserves the ARCHAIC term ——————, already OBSOLETE in Shakespeare's time.
5. "You take that —————— back, or I'll get your mother to paddle you," the director told the pert child actor.
6. The Devil's —————— Book is truly a DIABOLICALLY funny work.
7. The best —————— of the evening, as you might expect, was an ad lib from Fred Allen, who reinforced it with an action ——————, grabbing his neck with his hand, elbow extended,—the trick of the old comedian who was apparently being held in the wings by somebody, but who, when he appeared, was just holding his own neck.

SAYING: saw, maxim, ADAGE, proverb, motto, EPIGRAM, APHORISM, APOTHEGM
1. "There's no arguing over questions of taste" is an —————— more honored in the breach than in the observance.
2. A prospector must always bear in mind the old ——————, "All is not gold that glitters."
3. Our ——————, "Penny-wise and pound foolish" is put more concretely by the Chinese: "What profiteth it a man if he retire early to bed to save candlelight, and beget twins?"
4. Erasmus liked to collect ——————s from the Greek and Roman MORALISTS, and he invented some of his own, such as "It's no fun discussing prohibition when your GULLET's dry."
5. Motley adopted as a firm ——————, "Clothes make the woman."
6. Polonius was full of wise ——————s.
7. "You can't get blood from a turnip" is a popular American ——————.
8. "Those who marry for money always earn it" comes pretty close to being an ——————.

SUAVE: URBANE, diplomatic, bland, smooth, politic
1. LaGuardia could not be called ——————, but he was actually —————— in his bluntness, and he DISCOMFITED —————— and oily hypocrites to good purpose.
2. Chesterfield's manners were both —————— and polished, but they had at core the essence of good breeding: consideration for others.
3. Byrnes' last speech shows that he has developed an even ——————r manner, in the best —————— tradition; yet he has not lost his plainness and LUCIDITY of expression.
Ant.: bluff

Sensuous: sensual, luxurious, voluptuous, sybaritic, epicurean

1. The *Gourmet* caters to —————— tastes in food, but is no friend of gluttons.
2. Milton's imagery in English is often strongly ——————; but he confined strongly —————— moments to his Latin verse.
3. Before 1700 the word —————— meant either lascivious or passionately desirous after something.
4. That Tiberius retired to Capri to indulge in —————— pleasures was widely believed; but the notion that the only Puritan among the Roman emperors would take to venery at the age of 66, and still maintain his vigor and powers until he was 78, is fantastic, according to Beasley.
5. Beaumont and Fletcher wrote plays full of —————— interludes.

Substitute, n.: (I) surrogate, resource, resort, expedient, shift, makeshift, stopgap

1. Often his —————— appointments proved to be permanent, for he was notoriously reluctant to fire anybody.
2. When he could not get Congress to accept a long-range solution, Roosevelt was a master hand at devising ——————s and —————— measures.
3. The OED is the court of last —————— on English usage.
4. Queen Elizabeth liked ——————s and stratagems; particularly she delighted in fooling her Council.
5. Bridge is a welcome —————— when the guests have little gift for conversation.
6. In logic, there is no easy —————— for rigorous thinking.
7. Instead of adopting the learned word, ——————, in connection with foodstuffs, we have imported *Ersatz* from the German.

(II) supply, locum tenens, alternate, understudy, double, stand-in, pinch hitter

1. A —————— in Hollywood leads a dog's life.
2. As a —————— for Roosevelt, Truman's batting average is not too high.
3. It is very hard to find an adequate —————— for Tallulah Bankhead.
4. In his prime, Shaw came close to being a perfect —————— for Pope Innocent X, not only in looks, but in pontifical tone and manner.
5. Each member country sends an —————— as well as a regular representative to the Security Council.
6. Well-to-do draftees could hire ——————s during the Civil War.
7. The doctor got a —————— to come down from London to handle his practice while he went on vacation.
8. The Huguenot clergyman who came over to London as a —————— during the summer was supposed to have adequate English. His first text he gave as "Cahn de layopar shanzh his spoe, or the Aytiope hees skã? ("Can the leopard change his spots, or the Ethiope his skin?")

TRANSIENT: TRANSITORY, passing, EPHEMERAL, momentary, fugitive, fleeting, EVANESCENT, short-lived

1. The AMETHYSTINE glow in the West was ——————, and quickly gave way to heavy purple as the storm clouds closed in.
2. Virgilia's PREVISIONS were hardly more than —————— and —————— glimpses into the future, but —————— as they were, they shook her to the core of her being, for she soon learned that they would be borne out by the event.
3. Heyst knew that his joy would be ——————, but it was nevertheless a fulfillment of his deepest hopes.
4. What started as a —————— fancy, developed into a permanent LIAISON.
5. Pleasures of the senses are ——————; study, says Gibbon, is the only passion that is not destroyed by its satisfaction.
6. The only French hotel in New York, the Lafayette, now rarely takes in —————— guests; it has no rooms for them; but its famous restaurant is as crowded as ever.
7. A dragon-fly enjoys only an —————— life.

Ant.: perpetual

UNIVERSAL: (I) ECUMENICAL (or OECUMENICAL), catholic, cosmopolitan, COSMIC

1. Caesar became a true —————— without ceasing to be a Roman.
2. The —————— order is now more extensive than it was in Newton's time; yet we are informed by Kasner that it is still FINITE, and that the universe will hold PROTONS and ELECTRONS to the number of 10^{110}, assuming no blank spaces.
3. The Patriarch of Moscow has now become the —————— head of all the Orthodox communion.
4. The —————— truths affirmed by Medieval science have been knocked, if not into a cocked hat, at least into cocked-hat curves by modern mathematics.
5. PENICILLIN and the SULFA drugs are quite —————— remedies.

(II) general, GENERIC, common

1. These traits were clearly ——————, not specific.
2. The English language is —————— to the United States, Great Britain and the Dominions, but slang used in these different areas is by no means —————— to all.
3. The —————— reading of human nature which a novelist accepts or invents in part determines his chances of being —————— in his appeal, while his skill in INTERLACING the —————— with the particular is the measure of his power as a thinker—as witness Tolstoi, Stendhal, and Proust.

Ant.: (II) particular

199

PRESUPPOSE: presume, assume, POSTULATE, PREMISE, POSIT
1. If we _____ for the sake of argument that TELEPATHY occurs, many PARAPSYCHOLOGICAL PHENOMENA can then be explained in QUASI-scientific terms.
2. In urging that we are not forced to choose between two such polar opposites as FASCISM and COMMUNISM, Korzybski _____s that Aristotle's principle of the excluded middle is wrong and that the logic of classes is of limited application.
3. No writer can succeed as a POPULARIZER who _____s on the possession by his reading audience of too wide a vocabulary.
4. The French wit _____ed his syllogism thus: "All general propositions are more than half wrong (including this one)."
5. He next _____, as his minor PREMISE, "That human nature is always the same is INCONTESTABLY a general proposition"; therefore, he concluded, it is more than half wrong.
6. According to Paley, just as the existence of a watch argued that there must have been a watchmaker, so the creation _____s a creator.

SECRET: COVERT, stealthy, FURTIVE, CLANDESTINE, SURREPTITIOUS, UNDERHAND, underhanded, privy, backstairs (or backstair)
1. The OSS necessarily had to employ some _____ scheming.
2. The Cardinal's *Eminence grise* was available for his _____ intrigues, political and AMOROUS.
3. The President has at his disposal some _____ funds, but nobody could think of it as his _____ purse.
4. A _____ visit to his bride was the only kind permitted to a young Sparton husband. Such a _____ approach was thought to develop greater ardor.
5. A _____ RENDEZVOUS is usually carried out in _____ fashion, and invariably has about it a suggestion of _____ intrigue.
6. Richelieu preferred to use _____ methods, even to achieve good purposes.

UNRULY: UNGOVERNABLE, INTRACTABLE, REFRACTORY, RECALCITRANT, willful (or wilful), headstrong
1. The Old Bolsheviks were _____ and _____ men, and since they threatened the ruling dynasty, they were LIQUIDATED.
2. _____ peasants, especially the Kulaks, were finally shipped off to Siberia, or to the work camps in the Arctic area.
3. The General had an _____ tongue and an _____ temper, but in battle he was cool and LACONIC.
4. Shaw has always been quite _____ to all efforts to form his mind by bullying; but he was never _____ merely out of WAYWARDNESS, rather from conviction.
Ant.: TRACTABLE, DOCILE

VAGABOND: vagrant, truant, tramp, tramper, hobo, bum, stiff, swagman (or
    swagsman), sundowner (I add bindle stiff or bundle stiff)
1. The —————— News has quite swank offices in New York City.
2. ——————s are so called because they usually try to arrive at a station
    in the bush in time for dinner.
3. A —————— in Australia corresponds quite closely to a ——————
    in the Northwestern U. S., only the former carries food as well as blanket-
    roll; the latter usually carries only his bedding.
4. A boy who starts out as a —————— may turn into a ——————.
5. The yard police rounded up all ——————s and ——————s they
    caught riding the rods, and took them into police court, where they were
    entered in the record as ——————.
6. George Borrow loved a —————— life, but he was not himself a
    ——————.
7. HALLELUJAH, I'm a ——————.

WINDING: SINUOUS, SERPENTINE, TORTUOUS, FLEXUOUS, ANFRACTUOUS (I add
    MEANDERING)
1. We followed the —————— paths through the Carlsbad Caverns.
2. The channels of the middle ear are very ——————.
3. A HAREM dancer needs a more —————— body than a tap dancer.
4. At one point Route 101 is so —————— that it doubles back under
    itself.
5. The Meander had a —————— course.
6. If there was any place else to carry —————— curves, that baby star
    would have brought art to the aid of nature; but she didn't need to.

It may have struck you that in this list of synonyms, very few technical
or scientific words are found. Even in the complete Webster collection
of synonyms, technical jargon has very little place. The reason is a simple
one: most technical and scientific terms are names of specific objects or
processes, for which there are no synonyms, nor are any desired. What
the writer wants is to have the meaning DELIMITED. He wants a word that
will mean a particular thing or process and nothing else.

Yet these technical words are often such convenient verbal shorthand
that many of them make their way into common use in a figurative sense
derived from their narrower technical DENOTATION. There is a kind of
shuttle service which carries these words across the gap that separates
technical and scientific jargon from the common stock of usable words.
(See diagram on page 57.) So we speak of learning by *osmosis:* letting
facts seep into the mind; not, it must be admitted, the most fully alert
type of learning.

PSYCHOLOGICAL terms have in the last three decades been the most numerous MIGRANTS, invading the standard language as the Goths and the Vandals over-ran the Roman Empire. PURISTS usually think these terms barbarous, but the barbarians seem to have settled down to stay.

In any case, this shuttle service for technical terms is of commanding interest to the explorer of the English vocabulary,—all the more because the methods by which these jargon terms become NATURALIZED in the common stock have been too little examined by the literary persons who in the main COMPILE our dictionaries. This technical element is treated fully in Chapter XI.

SHORTHAND SYNONYMS

There remains one very important CATEGORY of synonyms which are not synonyms in the strict Websterian sense; yet they are of great use in the economy of language. Suppose you want a word to express the following:

The theory and practice of power politics: how to seize and hold power by guile, fraud, force, or frightfulness (used in that order). How to combine the traits of the lion and the fox in ruling a city or a country. The UTILIZATION of common enemies as political cement to tighten an alliance; and the techniques of deceiving and discarding such allies when the common enemy is defeated. How to trick your enemies into a trap where you can massacre them with impunity. Using SCAPEGOATS to escape the consequences of harsh actions by a ruler: in situations requiring frightfulness, dirty under-cover espionage, and the killing of some victims to scare the rest, the ruler should use as his tools and EXECUTORS persons whom he can put an end to, when their dirty work is done. By these means he can avoid the stigma of public crime, and put the blame on his subordinates. Reasons of state justify any degree of departure from private morality; a ruler cannot take account of Christian or any other ETHICS except the rule of expediency and the aim of preserving and extending his power; to those ends everything must give way. The ruler needs to control and manipulate all propaganda media. He should never forget that in politics it is not the facts that are decisive, but men's opinions and feelings about them; therefore propaganda should address itself to spreading whatever version of the facts will suit the convenience of the government. Particularly the ruler should remember the Roman maxim for empire: divide and conquer.

The word for all that is MACHIAVELLIANISM. Once when he was out of a job, and needed one badly, Machiavelli wrote *The Prince,* telling how the CONDOTTIERI or bandit-rulers of Italian city-states turned the trick of acquiring and holding power. Machiavelli was himself no believer in the

INIQUITOUS doctrines that go by his name. He was a stout republican (as you'll find by looking into his *Florentine Histories* and *Discourses on Livy*) and he was socially democratic to a degree that made his womenfolk complain when he sat around with the local woodcutters and charcoalmen in the local pub near his small farm. But like any politician who wanted to make a comeback, Machiavelli was willing to do a bit of pamphleteering (campaign-speaking was not yet in vogue) to attract attention to himself—and it happened that his pamphlet was just what the princes and tyrants were looking for. So from Catherine de' Medici to Hitler and Mussolini, Machiavelli's pamphlet trying to promote himself a job has been an invaluable handbook on how to fool the people and keep a throne.

The "ism" from Machiavelli's name is therefore a SHORTHAND synonym for a very big package of meaning. It saves a half page or so of writing every time we want to refer to the concept. In view of the evil implications of the power-politics doctrine, it is not surprising that the name of the hardworking Florentine secretary of state was twisted into Make-evil, and Match-a-villain; but these left-handed compliments should not distract us from seeing that he gave the classic description of SKULL-DUGGERY in high places. And when we want a single word to express all this complex of theories and activities that make up Big-Power MANEU-VERING, even today, Machiavellianism is the word. And there are many more such words, which are ALLUSIVE (they should not be ELUSIVE) and difficult going at first encounter; but they open up a PANORAMA of persons, places, and ideas, once you get acquainted with them. They are in very truth EPITOMES, or condensed versions, of cultural history.

44. PROPER ADJECTIVES PACKED WITH MEANING

Match each adjective from a famous name with the right clue.

1. [ ]	HEGELIAN	[a] Music-drama at Bayreuth
2. [ ]	MARXIAN	[b] *Decline of the West*
3. [ ]	NIETZSCHEAN	[c] Syllogistic logic
4. [ ]	WAGNERIAN	[d] Relativity
5. [ ]	SPENGLERIAN	[e] *Creative Evolution*
6. [ ]	ARISTOTELIAN	[f] *Beyond Good and Evil*
7. [ ]	NEWTONIAN	[g] Dictatorship of the proletariat
8. [ ]	EINSTEINIAN	[h] Pragmatism
9. [ ]	BERGSONIAN	[i] The Absolute
10. [ ]	JAMESIAN	[j] Laws of gravitation and of motion

11. [ ] CARTESIAN   [a] Conflict between production engineers and financiers bent on profit through scarcity

12. [ ] BACONIAN   [b] Pressure of population on food supply

13. [ ] VEBLENITE   [c] Christian non-resistance

14. [ ] MALTHUSIAN   [d] Believer in continuous world revolution

15. [ ] TOLSTOYAN   [e] New Dealer

16. [ ] KROPOTKINITE   [f] Empiricist, believer in applied science and induction

17. [ ] LENINIST   [g] Socialism first in one country

18. [ ] TROTSKYITE   [h] Socialize through hydroelectric development and collectivizing agriculture

19. [ ] STALINIST   [i] "I think, therefore I am."

20. [ ] ROOSEVELTIAN   [j] Substitution of voluntary cooperation and mutual aid for coercive power of the state

QUIZ KEYS FOR CHAPTER IX

38. Page 167.

1. masticate	6. nourish	11. onerous	16. erudition
2. imbibe	7. donate	12. curing	17. alleviate
3. diminish	8. insane	13. offensive	18. abbreviate
4. delineation	9. deceive	14. virile	19. salubrious
5. serious	10. external	15. hilarity	20. circumvent

39. Not one of these words is of Old English origin: all are part of the classical layer in our language.

40. None.

41. Page 172.

1. report	19. ease	37. chronicle	55. tender
2. deed	20. party	38. wit	56. sentiment
3. adaptation	21. authority, check	39. augment	57. systematize, command
4. aggregate	22. shelter	40. assurance	
5. entertainment	23. stream, prevalent	41. no synonym	58. ache
6. approbation	24. injury	42. unite	59. delight
7. reason, reasoning	25. decease	43. erudition	60. direct, aim
8. concentration	26. no synonym	44. even, flat	61. force, authority
9. affinity	27. world	45. confine	62. charge
10. equilibrium	28. border, margin	46. fluid	63. yield
11. low	29. consequence	47. no synonym	64. avail, benefit
12. no synonym	30. mistake	48. bulk, volume	65. object
13. no synonym	31. swap	49. no synonym	66. discipline
14. char	32. sensibility	50. center	67. shove
15. no synonym	33. fabrication, fable	51. impel	68. inquiry
16. reason	34. administration	52. no synonym	69. scope
17. hazard	35. consonance	53. race, people	70. upbraid, value
18. alter	36. loathing	54. want	71. function

72. bonus
73. law, govern
74. ascend
75. no synonym
76. sensibility
77. gender
78. shadow
79. concussion
80. angle, aspect
81. extent, volume
82. slumber
83. slant
84. kind
85. account, bill
86. expanse
87. intimation
88. advocate, maintenance
89. astonish
90. method, plan
91. object
92. occasion
93. profession
94. distress
95. turn, curve
96. manner
97. no synonym
98. term
99. toil, labor
100. no synonym

42. Page 177.

1. optimism
2. austere
3. orthodoxy
4. actual
5. retard; decelerate
6. nadir
7. aggravate
8. worsen; deteriorate
9. enmity
10. morphous
11. synthetic
12. voluptuary (Webster gives bon vivant!)
13. stimulant; irritant
14. malignant
15. tolerant
16. spiritual
17. rude; clownish; bucolic
18. posterior
19. orderly
20. direct, abridged; summary
21. open
22. obstinate
23. laconic
24. elastic
25. definitive

43. Page 185.

Abjure:
1. forswear
2. recant
3. abjure
4. retract
5. renounce

Abridgement:
1. abstract
2. epitome
3. synopsis
4. conspectus
5. abridgement

Activate:
1. energizing
2. vitalize
3. activated

Adjacent:
1. tangent
2. contiguous
3. adjacent
4. adjoining
5. abutting
6. coterminous
7. juxtaposed

Accidental:
1. incidental
2. fortuitous
3. accidental
4. casual
5. adventitious
6. contingent

Cumulative:
1. accumulative
2. cumulative
3. summative
4. additive

Addict:
1. habitué, habitués
2. votary
3. addict, fiend
4. fan, aficionados
5. devotee

Allegory:
(I)
1. symbolism   2. allegory
(II)
1. myth, apologue   2. parables   3. fable

Apparition:

1. spirit	5. revenant	9. hant	13. fetch
2. shade	6. phantasm	10. specter	14. phantom
3. ghost	7. *Poltergeist,* spook	11. wraith	
4. apparition	8. haunts, revenants	12. zombie	

Aesthete:
1. virtuoso   2. connoisseur   3. aesthetes, dilettantes

Amateur:
1. tyro   2. dabbler   3. amateur   4. dilettante

Ambiguity:
1. double-talk   2. amphibology,   3. ambiguity, equivo-
                      amphibologism,   cation
                      double entendre   4. tergiversation

Appendage:
1. adjunct ——— 2. accessories   3. appendage   4. appurtenances

Changeable:
1. variable   2. protean   3. changeful   4. changeable
                                5. mutable

Celerity:
1. alacrity   2. legerity   3. celerity

Change:
(I)
1. alteration   2. modification   3. changes   4. variations
(II)
1. permutations   2. alternations   3. vicissitudes   4. mutations

Clear:
(I)
1. translucent, transparent   2. pellucid   3. diaphanous   4. clear
                               5. lucid, limpid
(II)
1. lucid   2. perspicuous

Inconsonant:
1. unsympathetic   3. inconsistent, discrepant   5. incompatible   7. incongruous
2. uncongenial   4. discordant   6. inconsonant

Appetizer:
1. antipasto   2. apéritif   3. hors d'oeuvre   4. appetizers
                                        5. smörgasbord

Dictatorial:
1. authoritative   3. totalitarian, authori-   4. dogmatic, doctrinaire
2. dictatorial, oracular   tarian   5. magisterial
                                6. magistral

Enormous:
1. Cyclopean   5. colossal   9. Brobdingnagian   13. giant
2. Antaean   6. titanic   10. mammoth   14. enormous
3. herculean   7. vast   11. elephantine   15. huge
4. Gargantuan   8. immense   12. gigantic

Impostor:
1. quack, charlatan   2. mountebank   3. fakers   4. quacks, empirics
                                    5. impostor

Compendium:
1. survey, sketch   3. compendium   5. syllabus   7. pandects
2. digest   4. précis   6. aperçu

Discernment:
1. penetration, insight,   2. divination   4. discernment   5. discrimination,
    acumen   3. clairvoyance   perception

Inconstant:
1. unstable   2. mercurial   3. inconstant   4. capricious, fickle

Controversial:
1. controversial, eristic   2. polemical, apologetic, polemic

Insubordinate:
1. seditious   3. contumacious   5. insubordinate   6. rebellious
2. factious   4. mutinous

Integration:
1. concatenation   2. articulation, integration

Neurologist:
1. psychotherapist   2. psychiatrists,   3. psychoanalyst,   4. alienist
                             psychoanalysts   neurologist

Ornate:
1. flamboyant, baroque   2. flossy, florid, rococo   3. ornate

Pacify:
1. propitiate   3. placate   5. conciliating   6. pacify
2. mollify   4. appease

Pseudonym:
1. pseudonyms   2. incognito   3. nom de guerre, alias   4. nom de plume
                        5. pen-name, allonym

Realize:
(I)
1. embody   4. substantialized   7. realize   10. substantiated
2. objectify   5. externalize   8. actualized   11. reify
3. hypostatizing   6. incarnated   9. substantialize

(II)
1. conceive, imagine, envis-   2. think   3. fancy
   age, envision

Vociferous:
1. boisterous, vociferous   2. stentorian   3. blatant   4. clamorous, strident

Jest:
1. quips   3. witcrack   5. crack   7. gag
2. witticism, wisecracks 4. joke, gag, jape 6. jest

Saying:
1. aphorism   3. proverb   5. motto   7. saying
2. adage   4. apothegm, maxim   6. saws   8. epigram

Suave:
1. smooth, politic, bland   2. urbane   3. suaver, diplomatic

Sensuous:
1. epicurean   2. sensuous, sensual   3. luxurious   4. sybaritic
                        5. voluptuous

Substitute:
(I)
1. makeshift   3. resort   5. resource   7. surrogate
2. expedients, stopgap 4. shifts   6. substitute

(II)
1. stand-in   3. understudy   5. alternate   7. locum tenens
2. pinch-hitter 4. double   6. substitutes   8. supply

Transient:
1. evanescent   3. short-living   5. transitory   7. ephemeral
2. fleeting, momentary, 4. passing   6. transient
   fugitive

Universal:
(I)
1. cosmopolitan   2. cosmic   3. oecumenical   4. universal
                        5. catholic
(II)
1. generic   2. common   3. general, universal

Presuppose:
1. assume 3. presumes 5. posited 6. presupposes
2. postulate 4. premissed

Secret:
1. covert 3. secret 5. clandestine, furtive 6. underhanded
2. backstairs 4. surreptitious, stealthy

Unruly:
1. headstrong, wilful 3. unruly, ungovern- 4. intractable, refrac-
2. recalcitrant able tory

Vagabond:
1. Hobo 3. swagman, bundle 4. truant, tramp 6. vagabond, tramper
2. sundowners stiff 5. bums, stiffs, 7. bum
  vagrants

Winding:
1. winding 3. flexuous 5. meandering 6. sinuous
2. anfractuous 4. serpentine

44. Page 203.

1. [i]	6. [c]	11. [i̇]	16. [j]
2. [g]	7. [j]	12. [f]	17. [h]
3. [f]	8. [d]	13. [a]	18. [d]
4. [a]	9. [e]	14. [b]	19. [g]
5. [b]	10. [h]	15. [c]	20. [e]

VICE-VERSA QUIZ FOR CHAPTER IX

1. In rewriting a long article in the business field, an editor found he needed short, lively synonyms for the following terms. Supply them:

1. juxtaposed	7. penetration	13. surreptitious	19. conspectus
2. variation	8. discrepant	14. locum tenens	20. coterminous
3. mutation	9. contumacious	15. ephemeral	21. tyro
4. cycles	10. mollify	16. refractory	22. adventitious
5. précis	11. envisage	17. sinuous	23. tergiversation
6. appurtenances	12. dictum	18. incremental	24. revenant
		25. legerity	

While you're at it, guess the profession of the author of the article.
2. What are the synonyms for *gag?* How does it differ slightly in meaning from its synonyms?
3. What is the technical term in chemistry for "drying out"?
4. Are there synonyms for *medium, median,* and *medial?*

209

5. What is a slang word which expresses a slightly different shade of meaning than any of the words *deride, heckle, bedevil,* or *insult?* How long will this slang word remain slang, in your opinion?
6. Is there any single word in our language which is exactly synonymous with *xenophobic?*

[X]

WORDS
EPITOMIZING CULTURAL HISTORY

If you could combine H. G. Wells' time machine with an Oriental magic carpet, and follow some English words back through space and time, you'd do some tall traveling. You could go with ODYSSEUS on the original ODYSSEY; find out about QUIXOTIC conduct by following Don QUIXOTE on his adventures; hear DEMOSTHENES give a PHILIPPIC against Philip of MACEDON; learn true EPICUREAN doctrine by walking with Epicurus in his garden; and acquire the SOCRATIC method by listening to the IRONIC old soldier and stonemason himself.

Words of this ALLUSIVE type are the literary COUNTERPARTS of scientific symbols. Each condenses a fund of meanings into a shorthand term. The difference lies in the greater richness of associations—or AURA—in the case of the literary and historical allusions. "Quixotic" is an EPITOME of a great book. The Romans had no name for the high, generous, and fantastic gallantry which the word describes. Nor would most Romans have been able to understand what is meant by the FAUSTIAN spirit: that heaven-storming, adventurous thirst for the infinite which led FAUST to sell his soul to the devil in return for universal knowledge and experience.

The spiritual history not merely of a decade, but of a whole epoch, is summed up in such a word. There is a certain substance in Fielding's claim that the great novelist is a better historian than most professional CHRONICLERS. Certainly the great poets and dramatists have often given a "local habitation and a name" to the spirit of an age, "in little room confining mighty men,"—as GOETHE did with Faust and Shakespeare with Hamlet. Or a poet's own name may come to express a quality and temper for which we have no other single word. So we speak of VERGILIAN pity: that sense of POIGNANT, sensitive sadness over the tragedy IMPLICIT in most human life, and the feeling of regret over vanished beauty and the doom visited on great-hearted courage in the face of a malign destiny—all rendered through the golden autumnal haze of memory. Again, "Socratic"—to expand on the reference a little—epitomizes the apparently artless and innocent technique used by Socrates to help his hearers realize what they did not know, at the same time bringing home to them the limitations on knowledge and the knowable.

It may have occurred to you by this time that we actually have an invention which comes pretty close to the time machine–magic carpet combination: the book. The allusions which great books have left in the language constitute a guide to good reading, if you want to take them that way.

Here, however, we are concerned with acquiring the meaning of these allusions in summary form. Since a literary or historical reference often telescopes an incredible wealth of meaning into one word, it is a hard task to boil it down into a short CUE phrase, and still convey anything like its full import. But if you can identify many of these allusions from significant CLUES that suggest even a part of their rich content, it is pretty good PRESUMPTIVE proof that you know your way around in CULTURAL history—which includes many characters who lived only in their creators' imaginations, and numerous incidents which never happened. Yet they are as real as, if not more real than, actual historical personages and events.

You have already tried your hand at identifying fifty of the commonest of these allusions (p. 12), all of them occurring in the 20,000 commonest words in English. Here are eighty more, of less frequent occurrence; but they present a challenge to anyone who likes to bring history up into the vivid present.

45. SHORTHAND SYMBOLS OF CULTURAL HISTORY

Match the scrambled clues with the names or terms given in the left hand column. They are grouped by tens. For example:

101. [   ] ISHMAEL

[d] he prophesied Christ's coming
[e] Jacob's new name after he wrestled with the angel
[f] outcast driven into the wilderness

Here the right clue is "outcast driven into the wilderness," so you put *f* in the parentheses following 101. Now for the list:

1. [ ] Circe
2. [ ] ADONIS
3. [ ] DON JUAN
4. [ ] MRS. GRUNDY
5. [ ] MUNCHAUSEN
6. [ ] THERSITES
7. [ ] TARTUFFE
8. [ ] BUMBLE
9. [ ] SHYLOCK
10. [ ] POLONIUS

[a] champion grumbler and SEDITIONIST in the Greek camp before TROY
[b] wanted his pound of flesh as penalty interest on loan
[c] worldly PSEUDO-pious hypocrite, supposedly SATIRIZING JESUITS
[d] long-winded self-appointed NESTOR, full of wise saws
[e] fussy, pompous, self-important small time DIGNITARY
[f] enchantress who turned Odysseus' men into swine
[g] No. 1 wolf in literature
[h] fertile, RESOURCEFUL and ingenious liar on the grand scale
[i] the beau ideal of masculine beauty (yes, beauty)
[j] self-appointed female POLICER of conventional proprieties; what Will Hays was to Hollywood

11. [ ] BOBADIL
12. [ ] RODOMONTADE
13. [ ] BRAGGADOCIO
14. [ ] BABBITT
15. [ ] FRANKENSTEIN
16. [ ] PECKSNIFF
17. [ ] NESTOR
18. [ ] SINBAD
19. [ ] ALI BABA
20. [ ] LOTHARIO

[a] the wisest old Greek COUNCILLOR at TROY; silver-tongued
[b] Doctor of that name who brought his ROBOT monster to life (not the monster)
[c] buddy of the forty thieves
[d] the most famous sailor before Popeye
[e] No. 2 wolf in literature
[f] THRASONICAL soldier, captain or better
[g] loud-mouthed RANTING, from the speech habits of an ARIOSTO character
[h] jovial ROTARIAN, apostle of business culture
[i] fancy boasting, named from a character in the Faerie Queene
[j] unctuous hypocrite, prating of benevolence; won't give more than a quarter

21. [ ] FALSTAFF

[a] alley cat who liked variety; her motto: TOUJOURS GAI

22. [ ] EUPHUISM

[b] female REVELER, given to wild abandon in liquor and love

23. [ ] PETER PAN

[c] flossy, elaborate VERBIAGE, full of FAR-FETCHED images

24. [ ] VOLPONE

[d] a witty young woman who knows the ways of the world; object: MATRIMONY

25. [ ] MEHITABEL

[e] the boy who never grew up; the ultimate in WHIMSY

26. [ ] BACCHANAL

[f] a married, adventurous MINX, looking for a SUPPLEMENTARY *sugar daddy*

27. [ ] MILLAMANT

[g] Charlemagne's PALADIN as a mad RENAISSANCE epic hero

28. [ ] BECKY SHARP

[h] foxy schemer who outfoxes himself; the biter who gets bit

29. [ ] Old NOBADADDY

[i] Blake's label for the 18th century parson's God

30. [ ] ORLANDO

[j] Shakespeare's greatest COMIC character: the fat knight who loved sack and wit

31. [ ] Job

[a] he built the hanging gardens of Babylon and ate grass in them

32. [ ] GOLIATH

[b] Queen Esther got him hanged, with his own cooperation

33. [ ] SAPPHIRA

[c] wife of King AHAB, wickeder and more IMMORAL than her husband

34. [ ] BELSHAZZAR

[d] backed up her husband's lies to help him best the church tithe on land which he had sold

35. [ ] SENNACHERIB

[e] saved her home town BETHULIA by seducing and beheading HOLOFERNES

36. [ ] NEBUCHADNEZZAR

[f] had the head of John the Baptist served on a platter for scorning her

37. [ ] HAMAN

[g] had more troubles and afflictions than anybody else in the Bible

38. [ ] JEZEBEL

[h] giant who was felled by stone from David's SLINGSHOT

39. [ ] JUDITH

[i] the Assyrian (who) came down like a wolf on the fold

40. [ ] HERODIAS

[j] saw the handwriting of doom on the wall at a banquet; "pillar of the Babylon-Jerusalem axis"—(H. Rome)

41. [ ] GOLGOTHA

42. [ ] ARIAN

43. [ ] ATHANASIAN

44. [ ] NICENE

45. [ ] LAODICEAN

46. [ ] MANICHEAN

47. [ ] GREGORIAN

48. [ ] PAULINE
49. [ ] AUGUSTINIAN

50. [ ] THOMIST

[a] LUKE-WARM ADHERENT looking for a third side of the fence

[b] believer in perpetual struggle between forces of Light and Darkness

[c] church chant style; calendar system from a later Pope of same name

[d] describing "Crosstianity" spread by the Apostle to the Gentiles

[e] describing OUTLOOK and doctrines of the African Bishop of HIPPO

[f] describing doctrine that Jesus was one of the sons of God, of like nature but not the same

[g] Creed adopted at Church Council which NIXED the above heresy

[h] same as [g]

[i] hill in Jerusalem on which the Cross was erected

[j] describing the doctrines and philosophy of the Angelic Doctor, still dominant in Catholic and ADLERIAN philosophy

51. [ ] BOWDLERIZE
52. [ ] COMSTOCKERY

53. [ ] EMILYPOSTING

54. [ ] BRISBANEFUL

55. [ ] PEGLERIZED

56. [ ] PINCHBECK
57. [ ] SYBARITE

58. [ ] THESPIAN

59. [ ] FRANKCRANING
60. [ ] HOLLYWOODEN

[a] SHODDY FAKE; phony

[b] SNOBBISH talking or writing about small points of ETIQUETTE

[c] given the works in a savage, INTEMPERATE but polished style

[d] to EXPURGATE a classic for use in a young ladies' SEMINARY

[e] SNOOPING and hounding of writers and artists for violating Puritan TABOOS

[f] ham actor; any actor

[g] EDITORIALIZING in PLATITUDES and EQUIVOCATIONS; writer knows better

[h] filling the PLATITUDINOUS seas with GRENADINE

[i] STEREOTYPED in the movie tradition

[j] elegant VOLUPTUARY and BON VIVANT

61. [   ] ARISTOPHANIC

62. [   ] EURIPIDEAN

63. [   ] HOMERIC

64. [   ] SOPHOCLEAN

65. [   ] AESCHYLEAN

66. [   ] HORATIAN

67. [   ] JUVENALIAN

68. [   ] CICERONIAN

69. [   ] LUCRETIAN

70. [   ] OVIDIAN

[a] characterized by noble restraint, supreme mastery of dramatic construction, and controlled intensity

[b] characterized by ARCHAIC grandeur, awe at the SUPERHUMAN fearlessness of great rebels, and Miltonic phrasing

[c] combining immense COMIC VIRTUOSITY, lyric grace, a mastery of SYNCOPATED verse, and COLLOQUIAL elegance

[d] moving even more to pity than to fear, intensely human, SKEPTICALLY IRONIC about political and religious traditions

[e] polished, SOPHISTICATED, and given to higher naughtiness in elegant and beautiful phrasing

[f] SATIRIC in a hard, iron-biting style; CENSORING evil and corruption with REMORSELESS wit

[g] expressing philosophical and scientific ideas in lofty and majestic verse, giving the poetry of science

[h] characterized by superb FELICITY of phrase, expressing sentiments with Pope's precision, LIN YU TANG's COMPLACENCY

[i] ORATORICAL, in the grand manner, sometimes FULSOME, sometimes ATTIC in phrasing

[j] characterized by greatness of accent, MAGNANIMITY, open-air ROBUSTNESS, superb sweep and fast action; heroic

71. [　] PETRARCHAN

[a] COMIC in the broadest and most RO-BUST style, dealing with heroic feats of eating, drinking, jesting and begetting

72. [　] BOCCACCIAN

[b] gifted in telling of AMOROUS intrigue in frank but polished narrative

73. [　] RABELAISIAN

[c] CONFESSIONAL lyric style marked by Romantic SENSITIVITY and classical feeling for form

74. [　] BALZACIAN

[d] characterized by HYPER SENSITIVITY in describing sensations as the key to memory, and immense skill in social high comedy

75. [　] PROUSTIAN

[e] revealing the human comedy throughout its range

76. [　] SWIFTIAN

[f] a crushing, pile-driver style full of POLYSYLLABIC LATINITY, but immensely convincing and memorable

77. [　] JOHNSONIAN

[g] characterized by lyrical wit, great skill in nonsense patter, a respectful treatment of the ludicrous

78. [　] GILBERTIAN

[h] characterized by genial humor, fine touch in character PORTRAYAL, and strong social sympathies

79. [　] DICKENSIAN

[i] characterized by MORDANT wit, CONCISION of phrase, and savage indignation quietly expressed

80. [　] SHAVIAN

[j] expressed with exasperating levity, and profound conviction of having ultimate truth by the tail; also with breath-bereaving insolence; but deeply concerned about human welfare

The two- or three-line clues for these richly allusive terms merely skim the surface of their meaning. It would take a wide and varied course of reading to gather the full sense of many of these terms. They are deposited in the language like valuable old coins that have acquired a rich PATINA with age.

Readers quite rightly object if a writer plasters his text thick with these ALLUSIVE words. But their occasional use is quite justifiable, to save spelling out at great length the qualities that are intended.

Once an Oxford tutor, well known as a kindly man, was irked by a student's reply upon being asked to read Bossuet's sermons:

"But, Doctor, I don't read French."

"Don't boast of your ignorance, my boy. Go to France and remedy it," the tutor answered.

Luckily, to remedy a lack of knowledge of cultural history, we need not go to France: only to the nearest library.

46. AFTERTHOUGHT

After you check your score on QUIZ 45, you may want to use it for a further workout. It is very much the type of matching test you'd get at the University of Chicago in the freshman or sophomore survey courses (not to be confused with the 100 Great Books program which President Hutchins supports and 870 of his faculty do not). On a quiz of this kind, you might encounter additional questions about the list:

1. Which groups of ten refer to imaginary characters?
2. In the group of BIBLICAL references, for which characters named do we have independent historical evidence, apart from the Bible?
3. Which group consists of theological terms, except for one?
4. Which group consists of terms derived from proper names used in a DERISIVE sense? How many of these are of American origin?
5. Which group refers to classical authors?
6. How many British authors' names are the basis for the entries in the group in which they appear? Why, do you suppose, is SHAKESPEAREAN omitted?
7. Can you suggest five other invented literary characters (e.g., Cyrano)?

Quite a different—and in some ways homelier—phase of cultural history is represented in the proper or place names which have come to be used to designate inventions, fabrics, CULINARY discoveries, and innovations in fashion. Here's a job lot of them.

47. ODDS AND ENDS

What are they, and from what person or place was each named? Can you place each one in the right century?

1. LILLIAN RUSSELL	4. DEMIJOHN	7. PRUSSIC acid
2. BAZOOKA	5. MORPHINE	8. muslin
3. bloomers	6. NICOTINE	9. CAMBRIC
	10. bovril	

Of all the proper names which have become common nouns, perhaps the richest in historical associations is the word BEDLAM, now used to mean a tumultuous confusion, or mad jumble of noises. Late in the era of the Crusades, there was a religious house in the Holy Land dedicated to St. Mary of Bethlehem, that is, the Virgin. A branch of this in London was at first a HOSTEL for visiting members of the order traveling in England. Eventually this London branch devoted itself to caring for a certain type of afflicted, namely lunatics. When Henry VIII DISESTABLISHED the monasteries, this HOSPICE was turned over to the City of London, which continued it as an insane asylum, under the name of Bethlehem Hospital, or Bedlam, as it was called for short, with that turn for telescoping proper names so marked in England,—as witness the pronunciation "Chumley" for CHOLMONDELEY, and "Marchbanks" for MARJORIBANKS. Bedlam came next to be applied to any insane asylum. From the continual din heard in bedlams, it was not long until the word became a general term for any noisy confusion.

It is interesting to observe that in the history of this word we have involved the FOUNDING of the Christian religion, the passing of the Holy Land into the control of the Saracens, the Crusades, which restored it to CHRISTIANITY, the continued relations between the Latin Orient and Western Europe, the whole theory and practice of monastic institutions and fraternities, with their labors in behalf of the poor and sick, the Reformation in general, and, in particular, the Reformation in England under Henry VIII, with its confusion of religious and secular motives. —Greenough and Kittredge, *Words and Their Ways in English Speech*, p. 389. (Used by permission of The Macmillan Company, publishers.)

The title *Chancellor* has a curious history. It comes ultimately from cancer, "a crab." This had a plural diminutive CANCELLI, which meant "a grating," from the resemblance of cross-hatched bars or lattice-work to a crab's TENTACLES. Cancelli was thus the name given to the gratings which separated from the rest of the chamber the part of a large hall used as a court. The usher of the court, who stood just inside the gratings was ad cancellos, "at the cross-bars"; he was called cancellarius, which became "chancellor" in Law French. As his office grew in dignity, the title came to be one of great honor; and it is now applied to a high legal official or the head of a great educational system. The original connection with crabs and gratings is usually quite forgotten.

CABAL, for a political intrigue or a group of conspirators, has an interesting history. It comes from the Hebrew word for a hidden or mysterious interpretation of the Scriptures: kabbala, which we have borrowed in this more proper form to refer to the mystical writings of MEDIEVAL Jewish schoolmen. But cabal was reinforced in its present sense by the accident that Charles II had a clever and intriguing cabinet council for foreign affairs whose initials spelled CABAL: Clifford, Arlington, Buckingham, Ashley, and Lauderdale. And so it goes. There are countless words whose records are INTERWOVEN with the movements and events of history.

There is no better index to the course of CULTURAL history than the changes in meaning which occur in words having to do with the feelings, the will, the instincts, or the mind—in short, all terms which relate to human nature and its interpretation, whether individual or social PSYCHOLOGY is concerned. For while the old saying of the HUMANISTS, that human nature is always the same, may be partly true, so soon as one raises the question, wherein does the sameness consist, a great variety of answers will be offered. And there is no simpler way to study the many readings of human nature than by tracing the changes of meaning in a single PSYCHOLOGICAL term. We have already noted this fact, in examining the word *character*. But there are terms which yield just as much.

The word *humor,* for example, means literally, in Latin, "liquid." It early came to be specialized in English to the four bodily *humors,* which according to ARISTOTLE and GALEN, and ancient PHYSIOLOGISTS generally, determined, by their balance, the temperament of a man. If the blood was dominant, a man had a sanguine temperament; if the CHOLER was in excess, he was CHOLERIC; if the BILE ruled over his body, he was melancholy; and if the PHLEGM was in the ASCENDANCY, he was PHLEGMATIC. These terms remain in the language, though the science from which they come is OUTMODED.

By an easy transfer, the word *humor* was also applied to the mood or EMOTIONAL set resulting from a PREDOMINANCE of one humor over the others. As Ben Jonson puts it, speaking of the use of the term to which he was to give a wide currency,

> It may, by metaphor, apply itself
> Unto the general disposition;
> As when some one peculiar quality
> Doth so possess a man, that it doth draw
> All his affects, his spirits, or his powers
> In his CONFLUCTIONS, all to run one way,
> This may be truly said to be a humor.
> —Ben Jonson, INDUCTION to *Every Man out of His Humour.*

Humor in this sense meant more than a QUIRK or queer VAGARY; it implied a single dominant passion or PREOCCUPATION; and Shadwell in the late seventeenth, and Dickens in the early nineteenth, century employed this conception of a humor as the basis for character construction, just as Ben Jonson had done. Uriah Heep is an animated *humor* walking around, a bundle of sneaking, crafty submission.

From the fact that *humors* characters were employed on the stage as COMIC creatures, the word *humor* acquired the further extension of meaning which it now has. It came finally to mean a gay, good-tempered variety of the comic. In *humor* proper in the modern sense, one is inclined to laugh both with and at the person, or in some cases, only with him. Humor still retains its association with the emotions, although they are only lightly involved; and traditionally humor has been DISTINGUISHED from *wit* on the grounds that the latter involves the intellect. *Wit* may be chiefly intellectual, but if it's at somebody's expense, it also calls into play the unkinder feelings, both in the sender and in the receiver. But that is another story, which would take as long as *humor* to unfold. Luckily, when we start prying into the DERISIVE use of language as a key to cultural history, we have at hand a rich storehouse of material.

SLANG

Take, for example, the incredible wealth of American slang—a real EPITOME of our history. This slang is a kind of wrong-way poetic IMAGERY. At its best and most inventive, it is marked by picturesque and PROVOCATIVE similes:

go *like a bat out of hell*
crazy *like a fox*
lit up *like a cathedral* (or *Christmas tree*)

Slang deriving from underworld CANT is often full of metaphors as grim as they are funny:

chill, give a permanent, take for a slay ride, scrag (all mean "kill")
crow-bait or clock-stopper (for a homely girl)
Chicago piano (for six-barreled pompoms or anti-aircraft guns, ANALOGOUS
  to the next)
Chicago mowing machine (for a machine gun or Tommy gun);

and full of other figures that are funny without the grimness:

oil eater (an old automobile)
office piano (a typewriter)

no three-alarm fire (MEDIOCRE)
I. O. U. S. A. (a hint at the size of the national debt)

A slang EUPHEMISM for unpleasant or distasteful experience does not always pretty it up. In Gangland they warn a man that he's not long for this world:

They'll be measuring you for a wooden kimono.
There'll be eight going out and seven coming back. (An allusion to the cemetery trip in *Frankie and Johnnie*.)

On the other hand, the elaborate names for comic creatures are full of innocent amusement. A donkey or a BURRO is variously a *Rocky Mountain canary*, a *Missouri hummingbird*, or an *Arcadian nightingale;* or he may be just a *barnyard* YODELER. The bedtime howling of Alaska sled dogs is *dog-opera*. And the slang terms for certain trades are apt:

baggage-smasher (for a porter)
gold-mining (plumbing)
ten-percenter (an actor's agent)

Slang often has the COMPRESSION that helps out wit:

cat-chat (malicious female gossip)
yawner (a flat or boring joke)
duck a date (to fail to keep an appointment)
shoot Niagara (take a desperate chance)
bum steer (bad advice, often given deliberately)
fakealoo (a hard luck story to get money)
on ice (all settled and arranged)

or, on occasion, the EXPANSIVENESS and EXAGGERATION that aid broad humor:

mule with a rumble seat (a camel)
beard with a haircut (a VANDYKE)
blow the kid whistle (sound the CURFEW)
sailor's blessing (a curse)
Sunday-school word (PROFANITY)
six hat and a fifty shirt (of a strong and stupid man)
hell bent for election (recklessly)
build a high line (tell an incredible story)
saw off a whopper (tell an incredible story)
be hit with a horseshoe (have good luck)

On the cultural score sheet, where else but in the Land of JAZZ and JITTERS could these be found? Such slang may rank with comic strips,

CARTOONS, and Tin Pan Alley songs. But Mark Sullivan, Frederick Allen, and other POPULARIZERS of cultural history have not looked down their noses at the song hits or cartoons; no more should slang be left out of the reckoning. For the whole ROBUST side of folk life—habits of eating, drinking, PUB-crawling, merry-making and lovemaking—slang gives the flavor. Circus, MOVIE, RADIO and theatrical cant is often side-splitting (see p. 8, on *Variety* lingo). Slang tells what people laugh at, and how they cheer themselves over the tough breaks inventing comic or EUPHE-MISTIC phrases for the main hazards of life.

In the main, slang is DERISIVE, or at least DEROGATORY. While it includes many invented or scrambled words, it also calls into service a job lot of standard words. In doing so, it gives their RESPECTABILITY the "old heave-ho." Ruling out the actual coinages, such as "fakealoo", take apart any of the slang phrases above and you'll find that the elements which compose it can be used as legitimate words. But in combination they form a decidedly "blue" jazz chord.

Slang is in fact to language what jazz is to music. Slang is off the beat. It SYNCOPATES and BLURS standard words. Just as jazz employs many regular CHORDAL combinations in UNORTHODOX style, so slang fuses words, makes PUNNING blends, and generally plays monkey tricks all along the verbal scale. Like jazz, slang is best when it's used for humor-ous effect, by a speaker or writer who knows what he's doing. As steady diet, it's a poor substitute for the standard article; but it makes a fine oc-casional sauce in the hands of a good MIXER.

In using slang as an INDICATOR of cultural history—of the social pat-terns and habits of mind which gave it birth—the first necessity is to date it. The one FEASIBLE way to do so is to find out the date when the term first appeared in print. By the time it gets into print, a slang phrase has presumably been knocking around in oral use for some time.

The regular dictionaries are not much help in dating slang, except that the OED records vintage slang. Writers who plan to use a slang phrase as supposedly current in a certain past period—as *Time* often does—have to be very careful not to get slang of different decades mixed up. That's where dating becomes a necessity. How is it to be done? If the word is American slang in vogue before 1936 which had also made its way in England, it is possible to find the date the locution first ap-peared in print, in Eric Partridge's *Dictionary of Slang and* UNCONVEN-TIONAL *English*; or if it was in vogue only in the U. S.,—in the GLOSSARY

223

of American LOCUTIONS in his *Slang Today and Yesterday*. If it is not in Partridge, the next likely work to consult is Henry L. Mencken's massive *American Language* (4th edition, 1936) or its *Supplement One* (*Two* will be out shortly). If the slang phrase or word is not in Mencken, comb the back numbers of the QUARTERLY *American Speech* (1925–), by all odds the most amusing of learned journals.

48. CAN YOU TELL RECENT FROM VINTAGE SLANG?

In the following FABRICATED passage, check slang you think of recent American VINTAGE,—say not older than ten years.

MAC LEADS WITH HIS SCHNOZZLE

I am having me a fit of the blues until I feel low enough to crawl under a snake, so I go over to Buckshot Dull's joint and get into a small crap game. When the *bones* come round to me, I feel they are *fishy*, and it is gefüllte fish, too. Second time round, I cannot stand it and I say to Buckshot, Why don't you send these back to *uncle?* I am *cuckoo* to say it out loud, for Buckshot socks me and then I am watching the *claret* run down my shirt from where he hit my nose. Also he is calling me a *lily-livered skunk* and saying no doubt I will be expecting him to *pony up hush money* on account of he is running a *chiseling* game, and how would I like to be measured for a wooden kimono that will *fit to a T*. Then he bursts out in a *horse-laugh* and says for a minute, Mac, I think you are frightened. So I laugh back and tell him it is a good *gag,* but that is not what my nose tells me. I drift out and get me a *lift* home with Peewee Jones in his truck. We stop for a big *feed* at McGinty's place. Peewee tells me I am a sap to tangle with Buckshot. I am too low to come back at him with *"You're another"* for telling me. But next week I hear Buckshot is in the *jug* and I do not feel bad.

In this patch of narrative, written in the Damon Runyon historical present (though evidently not by Runyon), none of the words in ITALICS is original American slang in the sense used here. In CHRONOLOGICAL order, here are the first known instances of the use of each word in the sense occurring above, the date it appeared in print, and the author or source:

bones (dice)	c. 1386	Chaucer
You're another	1534	Udall
claret (blood)	1604	Dekker
uncle (pawnbroker)	1607	Dekker
lily-livered	1605–6	Shakespeare
bull (a blunder)	1642	Milton
hush-money	1709	Steele

lift (a ride)	1711	Swift
horse-laugh	1738	Pope
fit to a T	1791	Boswell
blues (melancholy) (from "blue devils")	1807	Washington Irving
chisel (to cheat)	1808	Jamieson
gag (an actor's interpolation)	1823	
feed (a meal)	1830	Lytton
jug (prison)	1834	
fishy (dubious)	1858	Brooks

The fact that the best authors have used the words in the same slang sense that Mac does, does not make them any less slang today. As a matter of fact, many of them are not very apt because of the mixture of several STRATA of slang. The real Mac of 1946 would not be so "old hat" as to talk about "claret" when he meant "gore." However, a little inquiry of this kind is very revealing. To begin with, all the words concerned have also legitimate meanings, not in question here. Each has had a derogatory slang sense "wished on" it, too. This slang sense lingers anywhere from five and a half centuries to a minimum of eighty-eight years, judging by the instances given. Even the shorter interval is a long time for a word to retain its worsened meaning, in spite of all the dictionary experts can do to stop it. Notice, too, that many of the authors who get credit (or discredit) for these locutions are engaged in writing comedy or satire.

All this rather effectively confounds the schoolmarm view of slang. Actually, since it is language in the making, hot off the forge, slang is of extraordinary interest to professional—and amateur—students of LINGUISTICS. Slang, like technical words, is at the growing edge of the great coral reef which makes up the English vocabulary, and the choicer bits of it eventually turn into colorful if not elegant ornaments of the language. (This is not meant as any defense of slang VULGARISMS, or of those tiresome and REPETITIOUS slang CLICHÉS which bobby-soxers use—the modern ANALOGUES of *sweetie, all rightie,* such as *natch* (for naturally) and similar BANAL ATROCITIES.)

To measure the progress of American slang, it is only necessary to compare two short story writers, forty years apart, who have used it as a major and integral part of their work.

Around the turn of the century O. Henry was one of the first to make extensive use of slang, not only in dialogue but in the narrative proper. His collection of slang locutions is fearful and wonderful.

He sometimes uses slang as an important plot device. In one of his stories in *Cabbages and Kings,* the president of a banana republic has eloped with all the money in the treasury and the opera singer of whom he is ENAMORED. American FILIBUSTERERS helping the REVOLUTIONISTS in the capitol went to wire their U. S. assistants in the port town to warn them that the president is making for the coast, and to head him off before he embarks. They baffle the Spanish TELEGRAPHERS, who are in the president's secret service, by sending this message over the wires:

His Nibs skedaddled yesterday per *jackrabbit* line with all the coin in the *kitty* and the *bundle of muslin* he's *spoony* about. The *boodle* is six figures short. Our crowd in good shape, but we need *spondulicks*. The *main* guy and the *dry goods* are headed for the *briny*. You know what to do.

This smacks of 1904. But a lot of the contrived slang here is even older. *His Nibs* dates from around 1860; *skedaddled* (*Colloquial* since ca. 1900, *Slang* until then) is a Civil War coinage, with a probably fanciful ETYMOLOGY from the Greek *skedunamai,* to scatter; *jackrabbit* is a mule, from the long ears the two animals have in common; *bundle of muslin* (from 1823) is one of the innumerable derogatory terms for a woman; *spoony,* now almost obsolete, was current from 1836; *kitty,* for the "jackpot", dates from 1892; *spondulicks* from 1857,—it was ANGLICIZED around 1885. *Briny,* says Eric Partridge in his *Dictionary of Slang* (from which the above dates are taken) has been colloquial since 1856.

One can never be sure whether or not O. Henry's slang was really current at the time he wrote, since he depended as much on books as on his ear. He was himself a wordsmith of RABELAISIAN or JOYCEAN PROCLIVITIES, except that he had to keep within narrower limits of DECORUM. Within these limits he FABRICATED to his heart's content.

Not so Damon Runyon. There is nothing bookish about his MANIPULATION of the VERNACULAR. He collected it along Broadway and Third Avenue. He does not, like O. Henry come on the stage himself and put fancy VERBIAGE into his characters' mouths. He keeps the language always within the compass of his first person narrator, who is usually a small time hanger-on of the Broadway mob or amusement outfit which figures in the story.

Actually, Runyon's American is much more a matter of sentence pitch and rhythm than it is of slang. He does not, like O. Henry, use orthodox SYNTAX, but keeps to the historical present. His narrators run on and on, but always keep in the clear. They have an ARGOT of their own, and the words in it are slang or the wreckage of legitimate words. A man is a "guy," a nasty one a "wrong gee"; a girl is a "doll," and the "guy" telling the story does not approve of calling her a "tomato" or a "broad," though he knows the terms, and now and then quotes some "wrong gee" as using them. A killer "cools off" somebody to order, while a kidnaper is "on the snatch." ADULTERATED liquor is "cut goods." A "doll" takes a "run-out powder" on her husband. There is a code for sums of money: a "grand" is $1000; a "c" or century $100; $10 is a "sawbuck," $5 "a finnif," or "a pound note"; $2 is "a deuce" or a "two-spot"; and a dollar is a "buck" or "bob"— These are all the terms which E. F. Bentley, writing a most appreciative introduction for *The Best of Damon Runyon,* thinks the British reader needs by way of GLOSSARY. The rest he should be able to guess at from the CONTEXT. If that's true, an American should be able to sight-read them even out of context. To keep the game honest, cover up the right-hand column of equivalents in the following GLOSSARY, and check each of Runyon's *bons bouches* that you can translate.

49. Do You Know Runyonese?

1. sneezer	prison
2. mouser	mustache
3. what is eating him	what's bothering him?
4. the main drag	Main Street
5. burg	town (usually small)
6. noggin	head
7. gendarmes	police (euphemism for)
8. once in a coon's age (colloq.)	rarely
9. from A to Izzard	from alpha to omega is the Biblical equivalent
10. sored up at	enraged at
11. sucker	he who gets trimmed
12. old equalizer	a revolver
13. John Roscoe	a revolver
14. blows his topper	flies off the handle
15. off his nut	crazy
16. scrag	kill
17. loogan	insignificant person
18. corned	drunk
19. bang	excitement, "lift"
20. old do-re-mi	money
21. moola, mazuma	money
22. potatoes	money

23. a rock	a diamond
24. old warm squativoo	the electric chair
25. churned up	angered
26. to gum up	to mess up
27. to holler copper	to call in the police
28. a beef	a complaint (also a verb)
29. hoofer	a dancer (usually tap or buck and wing, etc.)
30. heave into the can	put in jail
31. deal off the arm	wait table ("sling hash" is equally common in the West)
32. pitching	making a play for, making love to
33. give a tumble	pay addresses to; or encourage such addresses
34. dodge	business or occupation, equivalent to "racket" in the innocuous sense—the same meaning it had in 1812—simply a "line of business"
35. heel	a bounder plus, e.g. Pal Joey
36. bending in an ear	listening
37. shivved	killed (literally, "knifed")
38. moxie	courage
39. ticker	courage (literally, "heart")
40. artichoke	old fashioned gold-watch, and by extension "pickpocketing"
41. had a piece of the joint	owned a share of the place—of some enterprise
42. sawed-off	clipped form of "sawed-off shotgun"
43. rodded up	armed (with one or more revolvers)
44. hotter than a stove	illicit: police are on the lookout for it— whether it's a joint or stolen goods
45. haybag	old, large, and shapeless (generally of a woman)
46. guzzled	killed
47. put the old sleeve on	arrest
48. kisser	mouth
49. half-portion	very small (usually of a person)
50. scratch	money
51. put the blast on	excoriate; kill
52. convincer	a gun
53. marker	I. O. U.
54. high grade merchandise	good though illicit liquor
55. lammister	fugitive, one on the run
56. croaker	a doctor
57. promote	persuade someone to give something—a loan —"for free" tickets—whatever it is. The verb takes a personal object.
58. duckets	tickets

59. chinee	an Annie Oakley (see p. 11) or free ticket ("chinee," from Chinese cash with a hole in the center—like complimentary tickets which are punched full of holes)
60. beezer, schnozzle	nose
61. monicker	name
62. put the lug on	"hit up for," impose on
63. boff	sock or hit, usually with a blunt weapon
64. bladders	newspapers (from German *Blatt,* newspaper)
65. scribe	a newspaper man
66. boat race	a "fixed" horse race
67. poke	(woman's) purse
68. flea bag	hotel one notch above flop house
69. cutting up old touches	recounting old exploits
70. jerry	aware of ("hep to")
71. slum	trashy (jewelry)
72. jug	bank
73. ka-zip	head
74. flogger	overcoat
75. cocoanuts	money
76. tongue	lawyer
77. mouthpiece	lawyer

Adding the slang locutions listed by Bentley, Runyon's slang ration runs to about 96 words—or perhaps 100, if BORDERLINE phrases are included—in the 200 pages of *The Best of Damon Runyon,* roughly 75,000 words. There are many repetitions, but even allowing for these, the percentage of slang to standard words is under one-half of 1 per cent. He gets his effects with a relatively slight infusion of slang, which flavors the whole mixture. Taken in CONJUNCTION with the use of the historical present, it gives the impression of an argot very remote from the standard language. Actually it is not, except in carefully chosen spots.

Dr. Louise Pound observes that a good deal of the dialogue and narrative in such work as Runyon's will before many years require a glossary, just as Chaucer does. The Runyon stories in the collection referred to, put out by Pocket Books, were written between 1928 and 1935, a period which includes the great days of bootlegging and rum-running. Judging by one reader's reaction, about 13 of the slang locutions listed above are now in LIMBO. They would no longer be intelligible to most American readers, and with the Broadway user of slang they have given way to more recent inventions. Can you pick the 13 specimens of slang already OBSOLETE, among the 95 above (including Bentley's list for Britishers)?

50. Can You Sight Read Recent Slang?

Here is a PASTICHE which uses Runyon's historical present, and in part draws on his reservoir of slang. It brings a Tin Pan Alley character in contact with the work of the leading academic authority on our sub-standard language and reports a song plugger's version of a learned lecture on slang as a key to American cultural history.

The song plugger, Mac, talks in the 1946 Broadway idiom.

Sub-stander Language

Mr. Runyon and Mr. Mencken Take Mac
to Hear Dr. Louise Pound on Slang. Mac Reports:

I now got me a good job with the work drained off. I work for this guy three days, and all he asks me to do is talk. He buys me my goulash in Mindy's, and I give out. But I think may be he is in some racket that I do not want any piece of, and I keep waiting for the gimmick. This morning he tells me a sidekick of his named Heinie is coming up from Baltimore and we are going to hear a spiel by a croaker with the monniker Doc Pound. I think now we are getting to the gimmick and I wonder if I am ganged up with some health-nutty act for grasseaters, or maybe with some coke-and-snow-shoveleers.

We meet Heinie at Penn Station around six and he is a hefty red-faced guy. We put on the feed-bag at Mindy's, and I am guessing to myself where Doc Pound has his pitch. The master-minds lead the way, and I find we are going way out in the sticks and when we get there it is near where the Columbias play football. We go in a big hall and nobody puts the sleeve on us for ducats, so I figure the boss knows the guy on the gate.

We sit down in the front of the house. I look around but I do not see anybody that looks like a croaker. Pretty soon a little thin guy wearing a beard with a haircut and superficial walks out on the platform and trailing him there is an old doll who is a tintype.

She is wearing a brown dress that is a real floor-swabber and buttoned up tight around her tonsils. The only time I see a dress like this is on another old doll who is playing the rapsichord on the Keith Circuit in Boston. I am glad Buckshot Dull and the Greenpoint Bullfrog are not along, or any other guys interested in artichokes, because this tintype is wearing a big gold watch pinned on her dress right below her left shoulder, and these characters from Brooklyn are not content to leave before they snatch this piece of inlay. But I do not think they are having easy pickings at that, for the old doll is wearing cheaters and if she hangs onto her watch as tight as she does up her hair, she has a good clutch on it. She sits down in a chair like the one a Holy Joe sits in. The half-portion shrimp steps to the front of the platform and begins to wrap it up in pink ribbons with a lot of talky-talky. After about ten minutes of this run-on spiel I am a monkey's uncle if I do not tumble that he is

230

talking about the old doll and she is Doc Pound. This guy is no three-alarm fire as a talker, and I am glad when he signs off.

Doc Pound stands up and I notice she is palming a bunch of cards which she plunks down on a slant-top stand like the one the cashier sits at in Frenchy Jeanne's joint over at 54th on Ninth Avenue. The old doll starts giving out slow and easy, and I soon see she is no lame brain but knows all her marbles. She says this talk is a kind of what-cha-ma-call-it about our sub-stander language, and from some of the words she mentions later I am thinking it is the subway standers' language after someone is stepping on their feet. She says she is taking us on a cookie's tour of squirrely lingo or American as she is spoke and I wonder if maybe she is a little weak on her grammar because this sounds like Portugoose talke to me or maybe Greek. My boss and Heinie are both grinning, and some of the young dolls in the row ahead of us, wearing knee-dusters and bobby-sox, are laughing out loud. But the old doll plays it so deadpan she would make Ned Sparks look like his face is doing a contortionist act. As near as I can figure it, she is telling us about the guys who put the hiss in history by springing cock-eyed words which pretty soon some scribe writes down and she is giving us a tip about when is the first time each word gets played on somebody's office piano. I am thinking you can run a nice numbers game with these, and if you can get a guy to make book on who can guess closest to the number. I see she is not taking us on any sleigh-ride or telling us a bedtime story when she says she will call her shots and not leave us in the dark about the words she is hanging these numbers on. She picks up one of her cards and lines them out real slow:

macaroni, wild-cat, absquatulate, skedaddle, scram, ring-tailed roarer, bear grease, guyascutis, Barnumize, roaratorio, flapper, bobby-soxer, scoop, fan, boyology, bumpologist, malarkey, magoo, and Pollyannanias.

When Heinie hears this last one, he laughs out loud. The old doll looks at him and says she is sorry she does not have time to take up hash-house Greek and the lingo of drinking and lost week-ends but it is maybe just as well she is not planning to go into that, because there is an expert in the hall tonight who knows not only the terms but the facts in this department at first hand, although he is not a professor. Everybody in the hall but me gives out with a loud horse-laugh at this, in fact it is the first time she rolls 'em in the aisles, and they all turn and look at Heinie who gets plenty red around the gills. I hear my boss asking him at dinner how he is getting on with his piano homework and I think maybe she is putting the bee on Heinie because he is once a professor playing piano in a honkytonk. Then she is saying but I must get back to my Runyons or that is what I think she says and my boss's name that he gives out to me is Runyon, but nobody else registers on this so I decide I am hearing wrong. Maybe it is onions, because she is pretty soon talking about Italian hash.

She says the *macaronis* are a bunch of dandies who start themselves a club in the big limey town about fifteen years before we are cutting loose from the old country. They do not like limey grub but get them a wop cook and so they are called *macaronis* [first in print in 1764—Ed.] which is wop for hash. Also they put on a big front and strut around. So this monniker for a dandy comes over here and the limey croaker who writes Yankee Doodle sticks it in the song about the pony:

> He puts a feather in its cap
> And calls it macaroni.

And the Yankees take it up and this shows that we do not like dudes very much. So the word for a dude in the Wide Open Spaces or in Hickville is always a snoot. I know she rings the bell on this because once when I am in an appleknocker town in Jersey, I am given the Bronx cheer by a bunch of young punks because I am wearing at the time my snazzy new check suit and a green benny and they yell hot-shot at me.

Doc Pound says a *wild-cat* is not only a man-eating bobcat in the woods but also is a bank around the time of a guy named Jackson and this bank is putting out a wad of paper moola which is about as good as a bundle of queer. Also a wild-cat is any proposition that is around ten to one you will be taken to the cleaners if you are sucker enough to fall for it.

And she says about this time also when they want to tell a guy to fade away fast they tell him to *absquatulate* [first in print in 1837—Ed.] and when the Yankees are mixing it with the Dixies they each say the other is doing a *skedaddle* when they hightail it for the tall timber. But now we do not have time to stretch it out with these sixty-four dollar words so we say *scram* [1926—Ed.]. This shows we are stepping it up all the time and jazzing up the old lingo to keep up with the big town razzle-dazzle, so we will have plenty of pepper and zing.

About this time also a bozo named Crockett is whooping it up and a guy named Bowie is making the shiv which is named after him and guys are going around wearing bear grease to duco the old thatch, instead of Wild-root. And when they get corned up they shoot off their bazoos and go zoople-zoople like something in the zoo and they say they are ring-tailed roarers. She says a ring-tailed roarer is an animal like nobody ever sees and it is a cousin of the guyascutis, a sidehill badger that has its legs longer on the south side to keep it from slipping down hill because it has to keep on moving West while it mooches its grass. And she says ever since these ring-tailed roarers the limeys are always saying we are a lot of loud-mouthed bull-horn characters who are talking ourselves up, and they are saying we Barnumize as loud as old main-most Barnum himself plugging his own circus with a roaratorio.

And I think she has something there for I know many characters around town who blow their own bazookas, especially song-pluggers. The only time they are mum is when they are making a play to be asked to Edgar Leslie's table at Mindy's. I am sitting in the next booth one night when Irving Berlin who is his own song-plugger is sitting with Edgar. Irving is telling them he is the ring-tailed roarer of Tin Pan Alley and he is also singing a roaratorio in his thin tenor until George Meyer says Irving you are fighting all our wars with a show and Irving then clams up quick. And once Stan Walker is coming in and says he is just over to Barney Josephson's joint on 58th and he is hearing Hazel Scott jazz up Bock and Edgar Leslie says: I know Bock, but who is this Hazel Scott? Oh yes, she is the colored girl who lets the white folks speak to her.

I am also thinking about the bang I get out of seeing Edgar give the old heave-ho to other ritzy characters who are flounce-butting around when I come to and hear the old doll say the ring-tailed roarer is not hitched up with the roaring girl that a guy named Dekker puts in a play, on account of a roaring girl is a doll who kicks up her heels and is loose on the town and throws a lot of hooch down the hatch and is generally such a doll as I am not caring to be in her neighborhood. And flappers in the Land of Jazz and Jitters are like the roaring girl only with a lot more soda and less hooch in the glass. And the *bobby-soxers* are just the coca-cola kids, maybe with two drops of rum.

Doc Pound says we are now having a great yen for short words like *scoop, muff, fluff,* and *fan,* which she says somebody puts the clipperoo on, the way they do on a mob. But she does not have time to put the acid on these and give us their etymology, which reminds me I am hungry and I wonder if there is a grease joint round and about.

Then she is saying we are lately having some new words like *boyology* for the way dolls put the old sleeve on guys, and *bumpologist* for the guy who gives your noggin the feeleroo to tell you what you go for in a big way but I do not need any bumpologist to tell me this.

And she says she is wanting to tell the scribes about a once-word for which they are feeling around and about inside their heads, and this is a word to hang on anybody who dishes out the old malarkey or magoo about things that cannot be worse. And she says this once-word they need is *Pollyannanias* which she says is a combo for a glad girl and a character who doesn't whack up with the church and lies about it so he gets fried. This sounds to me like a zombie mix, but she says a *Pollyannanias* is always putting on the old false-front over the state of the I. O. U. S. A., and that it is a very popular pastime around and about here and there and that there are also a lot of nifties that say nix to this type of baloney:

angel food, applesause, banana oil, salve, eyewash, hogwash, hokum, phooey, tripe, whoopla, and quit handing us the very best butter [The Doormouse apologizes to Alice for spilling hot butter on her by saying that it's the very best butter.—Ed.]

and I think she is covering it pretty well as I do not think of any other word for it except those any nice old doll is not supposed to know.

She signs off on this *Pollyannanias* and *the very best butter,* and they give

233

her a big hand. Heinie and my boss go up and shake her mitt along with a lot of others and when they come back we taxi down to Mindy's. I ask Heinie over the cheesecake why this old doll talks for free when she could get maybe three centuries a week at the Diamond Horseshoe, because even if she says a lot of these gags of hers are oldies, I am not hearing them before and I do not think many of the guys and dolls round about are hearing them either. Also Billy Rose can sell these brand-new oldies again in his column, and can save the Doc's salary by firing three of his spook writers. No, says Heinie, this is all a pipe dream, on account the Doc is a professor and they have to talk for free. But I say the Yales and Harvards like to go out and make plenty of moola for themselves at jobs with the work drained off. That is so, says Heinie, but they do not like a professor to be interested in money. But I am thinking I had better get a ten percenter to see Doc Pound and tell her how to get some real mazuma for her act. For free, it's good. For a chunk of the old do-re-mi, it's better. And I am asking the flesh peddler to hold out that Pollyannanias gag as my cut and I am selling it to Fred Allen for a C, on account of it is right up his alley.

Supply standard equivalents for the slang locutions in the preceding pastiche. Point out the folk etymologies (see p. 293). Where Mac's dates are a bit sketchy, specify the decade meant. Do you detect any sour notes, i.e., slang that would not pass muster along Tin Pan Alley?

One very significant point emerges from the observation of slang patterns. Slang phrases made up of ordinary standard words in effect furnish new and colorful synonyms (strictly, equivalents) for criminal and hobo activities; for the whole range of the amusement world—circuses, carnivals, gambling joints, movies, theaters, radio studios and Tin Pan Alley. Politics also adds to the slang lexicon. Various crafts, trades, and professions contribute, and that catchall occupation, business, has its own word lore.

At this point, slang often verges on jargon: the "trade lingo" or shop talk of a particular occupational group. Such shop-talk needs to be explained for the layman. The terms employed are often legitimate words, but the dictionaries label them *Technical* or *Scientific*. If used in speaking or writing intended for the general public, such words call for UNOBTRUSIVE translation in the text. But such words are constantly shuttling over into standard use, and they are such an important factor in adding to the growing English vocabulary that they call for special treatment. It is the *technical terms* in TRANSIT that concern us in our own vocabulary-building.

45. Page 212.

1. [f]	11. [f]	21. [j]	31. [g]	41. [i]	51. [d]	61. [c]	71. [c]
2. [i]	12. [g]	22. [c]	32. [h]	42. [f]	52. [e]	62. [d]	72. [b]
3. [g]	13. [i]	23. [e]	33. [d]	43. [g]	53. [b]	63. [j]	73. [a]
4. [j]	14. [h]	24. [h]	34. [j]	44. [h]	54. [g]	64. [a]	74. [e]
5. [h]	15. [b]	25. [a]	35. [i]	45. [a]	55. [e]	65. [b]	75. [d]
6. [a]	16. [j]	26. [b]	36. [a]	46. [b]	56. [a]	66. [h]	76. [i]
7. [c]	17. [a]	27. [d]	37. [b]	47. [c]	57. [j]	67. [f]	77. [f]
8. [e]	18. [d]	28. [f]	38. [c]	48. [d]	58. [f]	68. [i]	78. [g]
9. [b]	19. [c]	29. [i]	39. [a]	49. [e]	59. [h]	69. [g]	79. [h]
10. [d]	20. [e]	30. [g]	40. [f]	50. [j]	60. [i]	70. [e]	80. [j]

46. Page 218.

1. First, second and third groups.
2. 34, 35, 36, 40.
3. 41–50, except Golgotha.
4. 51–60.
5. 61–70.
6. Five. Try and characterize Shakespeare in three lines!

47. Page 218.

1. A bustle. So named in the late nineteenth century from the popularizing of this adjunct to fashion by the American actress whom King Edward VII so greatly admired.
2. First, a rudimentary musical instrument, named from the slang word for mouth, "bazoo," also by analogy with *kazoo*, by Bob Burns, in 1905; by figurative extension, because of a resemblance in shape, also applied to a crude rocket-gun invented by an American in World War II.
3. Ample gymnasium knickers for girls and women. First devised by the American feminist, Dr. Amelia Bloomer, about 1850.
4. Corruption of French *dame-jeanne*, "Lady Jane." OED gives instances with the French spelling as of 1769, but cites the 1828 Webster for the spelling *demijohn* and gives a quotation from Dickens' American Notes of 1842.
5. Named from the Roman god of sleep, Morpheus. First quotation in OED is dated 1828.
6. The chief drug in tobacco. Named by a Frenchman, Jean Nicot, 1560.
7. Named from Prussian blue. First in print, according to OED quotation, in 1790.
8. A diminutive Italian form of Mosul, in Mesopotamia, is *mussolina*, from which we get muslin.
9. From Cambray, in France. The more recent *chambray* is from the same source.
10. A trade name for a kind of concentrated meat extract for making beef

tea by pouring on boiling water. A manufactured word, presumably from *bos, bovis,* "a cow," plus *v(i)rilis,* "manly" or "powerful."

Vice-Versa Quiz for Chapter X

If a writer wants one word—an allusion—that will epitomize the following traits, he has to draw on the common stock of literary and historical allusions. Supply the right name in each case, from the clue given:

1. A professional trouble-maker in the ranks or the forecastle, always grumbling and always stirring up disaffection.
2. A champion liar in the grand manner.
3. Self-appointed policer of public proprieties, initially female. Will Hays fulfilled the function in Hollywood.
4. An artist whose creation proves the death of him, when he finds he has devised something monstrous.
5. Anyone with a lot of troubles and miseries, who is thoroughly unlucky.
6. Expurgation of a classic, such as Rabelais' *Gargantua,* for use in a young ladies' seminary. Rabelais became a mere pamphlet in Walter Besant's edition, which was thus ——————.
7. A pleasure-loving voluptuary who savors all the delicacies and luxuries he can lay hands on.
8. A style characterized by "curious felicity" of phrase, by polish, compression, and rightness of accent, is often called ——————.
9. Immense comic virtuosity, lyric grace, and a mastery of syncopated rhythms in verse and slang diction, can properly be said to combine into an —————— quality. W. S. Gilbert was sometimes called the British ——————, but the accent should be on the British.
10. Snobbish writing or talking on small points of etiquette, with a consequent lessening of emphasis on the real basis of good manners—consideration for others—all this can be called ——————. Yet to her justice, the authority who gives her name to this kind of wrong focusing of attention is herself rarely guilty of the literary and social sin implied in the profane use of her name.
11. To express the type of character described in Blake's line, "Sneaking submission can always live," a character in Dickens is a handy symbol. Name him.
12. A style marked by extraordinary impishness, by a turn for challenging the respectable ideas held by the best people, by the use of very long, fast-moving sentences and sparkling wit,—all this is ——————.
13. A crushing, steam-roller style, full of long, hard words, and dogmatic statements, is properly said to be ——————.
14. Humor which is robust, and full of ribald and bawdy jesting, is labeled ——————.
15. Mordant wit is often called ——————, from the Gloomy Dean of Dublin.

236

16. A Roman empress's name is given to a kind of stout, coarse fabric. What is the fabric?
17. An upswept hairdo, piled high on the head, and terminating in a peak, is called after one of Louis XV's mistresses, a ——————.
18. A watch pinned on a woman's frock about where a lapel would be if she were wearing a man's coat, is called a —————— from another king's mistress, Louise ——————.
19. Bob Burns' musical instrument gave its name also to a rudimentary rocket gun, during World War II.
20. Of the desserts named after diplomats at the Congress of Vienna, —————— pudding is one of the favorites.
21. Famous physicists whose names are imbedded in the terminology of electrical measurement are ——————, ——————, ——————, ——————, for whom the various units of measurement are named: ——————, ——————, ——————, ——————.
22. Any would-be tide-stopper—that is, anyone who tries to stop the inevitable—can be labeled a ——————.
23. Anybody who gets so foxy that he out-foxes himself can be called a ——————, after Ben Jonson's character.
24. Probably the "ism" which causes the most controversy in the world today is ——————. Can you give an ABC summary of its basic tenets, to make clear say to a seventh-grader what the row is about? And can you distinguish this "ism" from the policies followed in the great country which has adopted the name for its economic and social philosophy?
25. There has been a good deal of scoffing at the sort of ideal friendship between a man and woman which is usually called, for brevity of reference, ——————; but if the French aphorist is right in thinking that where passion begins friendship ends, it may be well to weigh up once more the advantages of friendship as set over against the grand passion which all our romancers—including those who ply for hire—would have us value as the supreme good in human relations.
26. Biblical allusions are no longer so readily understandable by everyone as they once were. At one time all literate readers could have identified by name the following Biblical characters and allusions. Try it:

a headlong, reckless driver;
a liar who was struck dead for holding out on the church when he sold a piece of land;
the longest-lived man in the Bible;
the three sons of Noah;
the friend of Solomon, a brother king;
the beloved disciple;
the man who was hanged highest;
the King of Babylon who saw the handwriting on the wall;
the words of the handwriting (the translators of the Authorized Version transliterated them from the Hebrew);

the meaning of certain other Hebrew words which the translators re-tained, merely transliterating: *selah, mizpah, Eloi, Eloi, lama sabach-thani,* and *manna.* How many of these do you know?

How far was it from Dan to Beersheba?

27. The period of wildcat banks in the United States was the ——————, about the time of ——————'s presidency.
28. Favorite frontier terms for "leaving hastily" were —————— and ——————, both coinages. One, ——————, is now colloquial American.
29. Is there an actual Tin Pan Alley?
30. What is your own notion as to the origin of the term *jazz?*

TECHNICAL TERMS IN TRANSIT

The shuttle service which carries some technical terms into standard use is no one-way train. It takes a return load of common words back to the shop, office, factory or laboratory. There, like ISOTOPES exposed to ATOMIC pile EMANATIONS, these words radiate new meanings—though they still look just the same.

Take *sport,* for example. How did it come to mean, in biology, a "freak" or "MUTATION"—a sudden departure from type, such as a white or pink elephant? The Latin phrase *lusus naturae* was translated "sport of nature," nature supposedly having its fun by creating such freaks. BIOLOGISTS found the term handy. It gradually lost its humorous CONNOTATIONS, just as we have long since quit laughing at human freaks. Now "sport" in the sense of a sudden DEVIANT from type, is a proper and sober technical term—and what a stumbling block it is to readers UNVERSED in its scientific sense.

It is these everyday words that have acquired by RADIATION a special technical meaning, that really make trouble. *Know-how* gives the translators a tough time at United Nations conferences. At the International Business Conference at Rye, the problem was solved by going the long way round. *Know-how* was spelled out in the English text in a form that would go into the other fifty languages represented:

Technical knowledge of the tricks of the trade which make it possible to put into mass production new machines, processes, or chemicals by utilizing patents and/or formulas, at the same time eliminating IMPERFECTIONS ("bugs") in the end-product.

That's the technical sense of *know-how* in thirty-nine words. It won't go into French as *savoir faire,* either, because that's pretty well specialized to "social savvy."

Not only is *know-how* a tribute to the FLEXIBILITY of English in permitting us to tack a conjunctive adverb onto a verb in this easy way. The coinage will also be significant to future historians when they write about the controversy over the RETENTION by the United States of the "know-how" in connection with the atomic bomb. The Russian PHYSICIST Peter

Kapitza, who was a star pupil of Lord Rutherford, probably knows the theory of NUCLEAR FISSION as well as the Manhattan Project group do. What the Russians could hardly be expected to arrive at by DIVINATION is the "know-how" developed by two hundred American industrial firms in conjunction with our Manhattan physicists.

The term, though first in print as a noun in 1935, really came into wide vogue only during the war. The dictionaries haven't got around to it yet. But it needs no help from them. It has already made its way, not only in the technical sense, but as a word-of-all-work. So, too, there is already a familiar ring to the other verbal shorthand which World War II produced: SNOOPERSCOPE and SNIPERSCOPE, *drone planes;* and the alphabet-soup compounds, RADAR, LORAN, SHORAN, and now TELERAN—*tele*vision *ra*dar *na*vigation. Note that in the case of the last four, a very long and complex phrase describing even more complex apparatus and processes is telescoped in each instance into a short usable word.

Time was that technical lingo ran to long and mouthfilling words, to impress the layman, and keep amateurs from muscling in. Ten-dollar words in ten-dollar books led to ten-dollar fees. Latinized terms were a part of the craft mystery. But modern American TECHNOLOGISTS prefer to use contractions if it's feasible to do so. And it's not only in technology and science that verbal shorthand develops.

Ours is a business culture, and magazines and books dealing in a professional way with business activities have developed a SPECIALIZED vocabulary. Many of the terms come from statistics, accounting, or ECONOMICS. Others are ordinary words used in a specialized sense—and these are the tricky ones for the layman.

Of the business terms needed to read *Fortune* and *Business Week* with full understanding, there are about twenty odd which are employed in non-business writing in other senses. Here are the specialized meanings they have acquired in business usage:

1. Margin. (a) Difference between cost price and selling price, at any level of production or distribution.

(b) In Wall Street, collateral security, as a percentage paid in money, deposited with a broker to protect him from loss on contracts entered into by him on behalf of his principal. Trading on margin was for a while not permitted by the Federal Reserve Board and the SEC (Securities and Exchange Commission). You had, up until mid-October 1946, to buy stocks outright, for cash. Now you can buy on 50 per cent margin— i.e., put up $500 to cover the purchase of $1000 worth of stock.

2. Edge. Advantage (slang, says Thorndike).
3. Capacity. Amount a plant can turn out if operated at maximum.
4. Merger. CONSOLIDATION of two or more enterprises.
5. Potential. Possible as distinct from actual current production; degree to which output could be stepped up.
6. Output. Production—actual amount of goods turned out.
7. Liquidation. Settling of accounts and distributing the assets of a corporation or partnership.
8. Facilities. Factories or any other plants and productive establishments that produce goods or render services.
9. Equipment. Mechanical and electrical devices in facilities that enable them to operate.
10. Tools. Short for machine tools, and for ANCILLARY devices such as electrically-powered screwdrivers or drills. (This does not mean a workman's kit of small tools, when used in the business sense.)
11. Subsidy. Payment to a manufacturer, exporter, mine or ship operator, to enable him to compete with more favored ENTERPRISERS, at home or abroad, or payment to an agricultural producer or low-end (q.v.) goods manufacturer, to enable him to keep prices down.
12. Inventory. Amount and value of goods or parts on hand: to take INVENTORY is to make an exact check on the above.
13. Index. Ratio between the level of prices, wages, output, or any other MEASURABLE factor at any time or period, and the same factor or factors at a fixed and agreed upon date or period (see PARITY, p. 243). The base is customarily taken as 100 per cent.

   None of the desk dictionaries is of much use on this. Thorndike comes nearest, but he defines it merely as "number or formula expressing some property or ratio, in science." This is true, but it is not enough. If you take, as the Bureau of Labor Statistics does, the base period 1935–39 average for the cost of living as 100 per cent, and find out how far the figure is above that on a given date, say May, 1947, that percentage increase is the reading of the BLS cost-of-living index. If it stands at 157, the cost of living is up 57 per cent above the base rate.
14. Monopoly. Loosely, a degree of control of the market either for buying or selling a given commodity or service, which enables the possessor either to raise the price above that which would exist under free competition, or to exclude others from the market, etc. Legally the degree of control that constitutes monopoly is whatever the courts say it is under the Sherman Anti-Trust Act and the Clayton Act. When Wilson Mizner used to ask, if anybody made him a business proposition, "Where's the monopoly in it?" he meant what is the inside track or exclusive feature that will give a half-Nelson on the market. The Constitution rightly grants an inventor, author, or composer a monopoly on his intellectual property for a certain number of years. Even in the case of patents which are a LEGALIZED monopoly, or pooled copyrights, the courts will not tolerate the use of these monopoly rights to a point where competition is pre-

241

cluded. The holder of these rights cannot do what is called "full-line forcing," i.e. requiring the customer to buy some things "in the line" he does not want in order to get something he must have.

15. Channeling. Orderly routing of scarce goods to users.
16. Absorption. Under OPA, the requirement that manufacturers, wholesalers, jobbers, or retailers absorb all or part of a price increase granted their suppliers. In effect, their profit margins are thus shrunk. In general, absorption occurs whenever a seller shoulders part of the charges that a buyer normally pays.
17. Discrimination. Granting an advantage or concession to one buyer that is not given to another; a violation of fair competitive practices.
18. Stabilization. Keeping price levels steady (stable), particularly during war and its aftermath.
19. Depreciation. Percentage of initial capital outlay which a business writes off (or is allowed by the Internal Revenue Commissioner to write off) in a given FISCAL year of operation.
20. Specifications. Bill of particulars fixing the standards that must be met for a given type of industrial or commercial goods; the engineering shorthand which expresses these standard requirements is usually in figures, formulas or measurements.
21. Inflation. Too little goods and too much money, so prices start ballooning upward; wages follow in a vicious price-wage spiral. Spelling this out, here's the story: When effective demand (i.e., demand with money behind it) exceeds the amount of goods available to satisfy it, the condition is present that leads to inflation, unless government intervenes by rationing and price-fixing, so that whatever there is, is shared out with fairness and justice. Otherwise prices begin to go up faster than wages, and pretty soon the lowest income group cannot afford to buy anything but the barest necessities. The purchasing power of money goes down, so you get a 90¢ dollar in terms of the base from which the inflation started; then an 80¢ dollar, and so on down to a theoretical zero.

In addition to these ordinary words used with specialized meanings, the business page has a sizable QUOTA of trade jargon (see p. 180, under definition of *dialect*)—i.e., words peculiar to business, some of them requiring unobtrusive translation when used in prose addressed to the general reader. (This shows the transit service, whereby technical terms gradually become common.)

22. End-Product. What comes off the assembly line or out of the chemical plant or any other manufacturing set-up: the raw materials, spare parts, and other components are finally put together in something ready for the buyer, and that's the end-product.
23. Set-aside. A part of the total supply earmarked for a special purpose or group, usually by government order; as 25 per cent of available meat is

set aside for the Army: this precise amount is the set-aside (verbal noun).

24. Low-end. Adjective describing goods that are below a certain fixed price point, which must be a certain percentage of the manufacturer's output, to meet the needs of purchasers with limited incomes; actually it means "low-priced," but it also means more, as noted, for it may involve government regulations making it mandatory for the manufacturer to devote a certain percentage of his materials and equipment to making these goods.

25. CARTEL. A combination of two or more business firms or trusts to limit their output, fix minimum prices (which are often MAXIMIZED), and divide the available market between or among them. Loosely, it usually means an international combine to do this kind of market-rigging and it implies a pretty large scale MANEUVER. Star examples: I. G. Farben tie-in with Dupont and Standard Oil; the international rubber cartel (synthetic played hob with it).

26. Royalties. A share of the product or profit (as of a mine, forest, etc.) paid to the owner by a user of the property; or, a compensation paid to the owner of a patent or copyright for the use of it or the right to act under it.

27. DECONTROL. ABROGATION of government regulations whereby prices, wages, etc., have been controlled during war or an emergency.

28. Cross-licensing (patents). You let me use your patents and I'll let you use mine.

29. Weighted average. A term in statistics which means that the various items are rated according to their relative importance—i.e., before you add you multiply certain items first by whatever factor is necessary to give the right weight to each, and then add up the column as thus modified, and divide by the number of items. This gives you the weighted average.

30. Bottleneck. A place or point where a log-jam or block forms in the even flow of materials or parts to the manufacturer or distributor, thus holding up production or distribution.

31. Allocation. Assignment of ALIQUOT shares to each user of materials or facilities; the enforcement of sharing according to a recognized principle of division.

32. Reconversion. Transformation back to peacetime production of plants and facilities converted for war purposes. Also used, inexactly, to denote transformation of new war facilities for peacetime use.

33. Tie-in (sales). See monopoly, where "full-line forcing" is described. The customer has to take an item he doesn't need or want, in order to get another he does want. That is a *tie-in*.

34. Parity. Parity is an ABSTRACTION about agricultural prices in terms of farmers' purchasing power that the Departmnt of Agriculture computes every month on the basis of information it gets from 20,000 reporters: (a) the current prices for every major farm crop; and (b) the costs of 174 things the farmer buys—food, clothing, furnishings, seed, feed, ma-

243

chinery, fertilizer, etc. The figures for each crop are averaged by states, then nationally, then compared with figures that show what farmers got for their produce and paid out for necessities between August 1, 1909 and July 31, 1914, a period of lush agricultural prosperity. The object of a crop price parity is to give sellers of that crop the same purchasing power now which they had in the base period. The reason: when the New Deal started in 1933 to try to get better prices for farmers, a yardstick of "fairness" was needed and LOBBYISTS and the farm BLOC in Congress picked a favorable yardstick.

35. Basing point. The geographic location on which shipping costs are determined for certain commodities, no matter what the actual point of origin, and hence on which the price quotation is based. Detroit is the basing point for most auto prices, so no matter if you buy a car assembled somewhere else the price is figured as if you had had it shipped from Detroit. The courts are now operating on this piece of business META-PHYSICS, which is in a class with the imaginary $\sqrt{-1}$, and much less useful.

36. Durable. Hard goods, i.e., stuff that will last—usually applied to such producer (i.e. manufacturers') goods as tools and machinery; and to such consumer items as autos, refrigerators and the like, which take some time to wear out; how long depends on the degree to which the manufacturer has contrived them so they won't wear too long, thus necessitating replacement orders.

37. Semi-durables. Middle term between hard and soft goods, e.g., such items as electric light bulbs. The Phillips-Eindhoven Company of Holland, which had a pre-war monopoly of the European market in light bulbs, according to *Fortune,* deliberately made them so they'd last only about a third as long as G. E. bulbs do; and the Dutch company also fixed the price at three to five times what General Electric charges us. Charles Wilson of General Electric, one of the most enlightened businessmen in the United States, believes in high standards, big output, low prices, and making capitalism work.

38. Soft goods. Consumer items that are used right away, such as food, soap, clothing, etc.

39. Write-off. Taking an item off the books or canceling it as by debiting the profit and loss account (Webster, which labels it a bookkeeping term). In other words, you kiss the amount good-by.

40. Holdbacks. Keeping any commodity off the market in the hope of a better profit; often the action itself helps to raise the price of the commodity.

41. Stockpile. Governmentally-held supply of any commodity, as a reserve against CONTINGENCIES—especially inability to get the stuff if war interferes with supply lines; also, if the economy is upset by drastic shortages of something needed to keep it functioning, it behooves a government to have some of the stuff in its kitty, so it can head off complete paralysis.

42. Marginal. Descriptive of an enterprise so near the line of UNECONOMIC

244

operation that it would be the first to fold up if times got any tougher; small farmers with poor land and meager equipment are "marginal" farmers; mines profitable to operate only with a public subsidy, below a certain world or controlled market price for their metal, are marginal mines.

43. Bullish. Optimistic; looking toward a rising stock market and a bigger take.
44. Bearish. Antonym of bullish. Bears cash in on a downward trend by selling short.
45. AMORTIZATION. Gradual reduction of capital debt aiming at extinguishing it; the annual rate of reduction is usually stated in percentage.

51. FROM BUSINESS TO ECONOMICS

For the following list of terms, which include some of those defined above, and in addition terms from economics proper, write out your own definitions, and check them with the desk dictionary you have at hand. Then see how far you can sight-read the connected passage below the list, noting down any blackouts of meaning which you experience in the case of the italicized words.

agricultural stage, amortization, bank, bimetallism, boycott, business, capital, capitalism, clearing house, commerce, communism, consumer's surplus, consumption, coöperation, corporations, cost of production, credit, currency, customs duties, direct taxation, distribution of wealth, division of labor, economics, excess-profit tax, Federal Reserve system, finance, gold standard, indemnity, interest, internal revenue, labor, land nationalization, Malthusian, margin, market, Marxism, medium of exchange, money, monopoly, paper money, par of exchange, personal property tax, private property, production, profit, profiteering, purchasing power, rationalization, *rentier*, sales tax, single tax, socialism, speculation, supply, syndicalism, tariff, taxation, tradesunions, trusts, vested interests, wealth.

Karl Marx calls his brand of *socialism* "scientific," to distinguish it from the so-called "rationalistic" socialism of Saint-Simon, Robert Owen and others. The *Utopian,* or rationalistic socialism, draws a picture of an ideal society whose members behave "reasonably," so that unhappiness and injustice are banished. This, of course, presupposes a radical change in human nature, and belongs, therefore, to the realms of fancy. *Marxism,* on the contrary, is devoid of idealistic coloring; it merely states that the *private capitalistic system* is breaking down, and that the next step in *social evolution* must inevitably be a *collective ownership* of the means of *production* by the *proletariat. Socialists* say that *labor* creates all values. As values, goods are nothing but crystallized work, and are worth the number of hours of work that has gone into their production. The cost of work is determined by the wages of labor. Under capitalistic systems, wages are minimal, hence the value of what a worker produces is in excess of what he gets for it. This is *surplus value* and constitutes the profit of the employer. The fact that part of this surplus value goes to pay *ground-rent, middleman's cost,* etc., does not bother Marx, for, he says, it makes no difference how many members of the *bourgeoisie* split the profit,—the worker is cheated of what is due him. The antagonism between the *bourgeois* and the *proletarian,* arising from the former's self-interest and injustice, Marx calls the *class struggle,* and regards it as the basis for his *economic* interpretation of history. As the gulf between the employer and the worker increases, and as the latter comes to the realization of his desperate position, a violent upheaval becomes inevitable, the proletarian revolts, dispossesses and destroys the bourgeois, and gathering all property into his hands, creates a *communistic* state. Under *communism,* the means of production are common property, and production and *distribution* of goods is in the hands of the government consisting of workers. How far has this theory been borne out in practice in Russia?

MANAGEMENT SPEAKING

Besides these general business terms, there are several areas of business activity which have in the last decade developed specialized vocabularies of their own. Management-labor relations figure large in the business picture. We find in *Business Week* for April 27, 1946, a discussion of management PREROGATIVES: zones of action which management would like to reserve from any interference by trade unions:

The industry representatives put [in the sphere of management prerogatives] such matters as *product determination, plant location, determination of layout and equipment,* processes, techniques, *financial policies,* prices, *customer relations, job content, size of work force, allocation and assignment of work, personnel selection policies, standards of workmanship, scheduling of operations, maintenance of discipline, use of plant property, selection of employees for promotion to supervisory jobs,* etc. [Italicized words are terms often used in management-labor discussions.]

This passage occurs in the *Business Week* editorial section "The Labor Angle," which is written in objective and hard-headed fashion, on the basis of a wide and thorough knowledge of trade-union policies and procedures. There is very little "slanting" one way or the other, and though the page is for business readers, there is no intent to make management feel cozy by pandering to its prejudices. The editors continue, on the subject of management prerogatives:

The point is that the very existence of a union undermines the ABSOLUTISM of private property—of management's UNIMPAIRED right to manage.

And the trade-unions, whose power is thus acknowledged by the leading business weekly, have quite naturally developed a lingo of their own. These jargon words are many of them in transit toward becoming a part of the general or standard vocabulary.

LABOR JARGON

Labor men, when they're feeling UNCEREMONIOUS, call a trade union official a "labor skate" or a "pie-card holder"—slang terms both. Such officers often maintain their power in certain American Federation of Labor locals by the use of a "goon squad" of strong-arm plug-uglies, who are sometimes ex-convicts, like the imported strikebreaking "rats," "nobles" and "finks" used by employers for union busting according to the Mohawk Valley formula.

In the Northwest, Communist members of a union who "bore from within" to gain control are often nicknamed "Elks," from their clubbable habit of holding secret CAUCUSES to plan strategy. The old-line radical workers in that area who "roll their own" economic and political dissenting doctrine, in preference to swallowing the imported Marxist variety, are usually former "Wobblies," as members of the I.W.W. were called.

Union members have plenty of DEROGATORY terms for workers who will not stick by the union. Those who work during a strike are "scabs." A "stooge" for the employer may also be called a "third ear," which is impolite language for a "spy." (Cf. the "King's Ears," for an agent of the King of Kings in Persia, according to Xenophon.) An undercover agent of the employer who FOMENTS trouble to discredit the union is a "stool-pigeon"—much like an *agent provocateur* in the service of a government. "Back-to-work" movements are derided, since they imply to labor men a clever trading by the employer upon the necessities of the weaker brethren who, along with their wives, find it hard to hold out until the union demands are won.

In addition to these cant and slang terms, there is a more respectable

247

vocabulary to describe certain features of industrial employment. In a plant that runs round the clock, the group that work from 4 P.M. till midnight make up the "swing shift"; those who are on the job from midnight till 8 A.M. are the "lobster" or "graveyard shift." If a worker has a break of several hours between stints, he's on a "split shift." If a union has negotiated a "closed shop" contract (i.e., a worker must have a union card in order to work), dues are usually collected by the "check-off": the employer deducts them from the pay-check and pays them directly into the union treasury. (See p. 159 for Mr. Dooley's definition of the "open shop.") The number of minutes allowed for tool care, attending to personal needs, and short rests to cut down fatigue, is designated as "allowed time." "Dead time" is that lost through no fault of the worker, and he is usually paid for it.

A deliberate playing of the game called in Scotland "ca' canny" is a "slowdown"—i.e., the workers, while they stay on the job and exhibit the appearance of busyness, are really "soldiering." The Fifth Avenue bus drivers in New York used this device in lieu of a strike, and slowed down a lot of people as well as their buses. These tactics gained them a great deal of public ill-will, and were altogether not as smart as the recent maneuvers of the Chinese trolley-car motormen and conductors in Shanghai, who kept the cars running on schedule but simply forgot to collect any fares for the company,—characteristic Chinese humor, by the way. The technique of the BOYCOTT originated in China.

Employers often accuse workers engaged in a slowdown of "stretching out the work" to make it last longer. As trade unionists use the term *stretch-out*, however, it has almost the exactly opposite sense. The *stretch-out* on an assembly line implies a "speed-up," to get more unit production per man without any corresponding pay increase. This is an excellent illustration of shift of meaning by transference (see page 154). It all depends on the point of view from which you look at a given piece of work, whether it's "stretching it out," or a *stretch-out*.

THE CASE OF PETRILLO'S FEATHERBED

One ironic commentary on our business culture is the existence of "featherbedding": spreading jobs by limiting the amount of work a man may do in a shift, or requiring the employer to pad the payrolls with extra job-holders. This practice has in most cases arisen because of what economists call *technological unemployment*: machines displace men.

In the music industry, for example, the addition of sound-track to film threw about 20,000 musicians in the movie theater pits out of work. Juke-boxes deprived 15,000 of employment. Radio stations have tended to use recordings and transcriptions to an increasing degree, displacing live musicians. About 800 out of the 125,000 members of the American Federation of Musicians make the master records from which millions are pressed. As President Petrillo of their union puts it, "Musicians are invited to play at their own funeral." Hence his insistence that radio stations that are financially able to do so employ a minimum number of live musicians—even if they prefer to use them only as "stand-bys."

And he further pulled his musicians off the job of recording for nearly two years, until the record companies agreed to pay the union a small royalty per record, to go into an employment and musical culture fund as some offset for the technological employment caused by mechanical music. Out of this "canned music" the radio stations make a good part of their advertising revenue.

Bungled Public Relations

James Caesar Petrillo has a case, but he has not put it in such a way as to get it to the public, nor has he briefed his serious musician members to help "sell" the program. His ban on broadcasts by the Interlachen student orchestra was an unfortunate move, whatever justification it may have had because of Professor Maddy's attempt to preëmpt eighteen half-hours of network time for his student (?) orchestra, with a consequent threat to "stand-by" musicians' services. However, Petrillo's drive for a welfare fund based on record royalties would perhaps become more respectable if the public came to envision it as a kind of insurance against further technological unemployment.

Here again, it may be noted how much social and economic history is epitomized in one word: *featherbedding*. But it takes a concrete example, fully developed, to give you the full feeling of the word—and how much heartbreak and hard fighting may lie behind this term for a "soft place to light." The term was obviously coined by the opponents of unions: it is derisive and derogatory.

Petrillo does not much like the practice of "featherbedding" either, but he has been heard to say that he didn't make the competitive economic system under which he lives. As long as that's the way the game is played by his opponents, he reasons that he has to play it that way too, until the rules are changed. While the employers limit output of goods to keep up prices, he has to limit musicians' output and share round the work, to keep up wages and increase the number of jobs.

Judging by the severe American PRAGMATIC test of success, Petrillo's system of fighting technological employment has worked: it represents the only offset payment for the displacement of men by machines that any union leader has won since the beginning of the Industrial Revolution.

In such areas of labor controversy as this, and pretty well throughout the whole range of the economy, government has intervened increasingly since 1933. As a result, a new TERMINOLOGY has developed, which is political in flavor, but economic in its main content. First, however, the regular political vocabulary calls for some notice.

THE LINGO OF POLITICS

Our old-line political vocabulary is too well known to call for much embroidery, except in a few instances. GERRYMANDERING, for example, is RE-JIGGERING the boundary lines of voting districts to give the party making the shift a majority in the newly outlined area. The process was so labeled by telescoping the surname of Governor Elbridge Gerry of Massachusetts (who in 1812 did the first job of this kind) and the last half of "SALAMANDER."

Our ordinary political cant is common knowledge. Who would miss on "ward-heeler," "graft," "lobbying," or "political fence-mending"; or, more lately, on "pressure groups," the "Gallup Poll," the "farm bloc," or "Republocrats," for the members of the conservative bloc in Congress made up of Republicans and some Southern Democrats?

Less familiar are the terms imported through Communist party politics. Numbering not more than 75,000, probably nearer 50,000, Communists have given currency to more jargon than any third party in our history except the Republican Party (which was a third party in 1854-56 before it elected Lincoln in 1860).

The Communist jargon includes a few lone words from various European languages and many American terms that are employed as near-synonyms for Russian terms.

Most of us would be stumped if we were asked to distinguish the various shades of left-wing doctrine. The late Lincoln Steffens could handle this problem with the greatest of ease. When a hopeful and admiring girl reporter on a campus newspaper asked him, as if he were an oracle,

"Mr. Steffens, could you tell us, in a word, the difference between Socialists and Communists?"

"Not in one word, my dear, but four: The Communists mean it."

Perhaps the sturdiest comment on Communism, however, was the sardonic witticism with which William Graham Sumner of Yale always wound up his final lecture of the year to his senior class:

"Gentlemen, acquire wealth; or if the country goes Communist, get on the governing committee!"

Perhaps this tells more about the American temper and values than it does about Communism. But if Graham in 1906 thought Marxist activities good for a wisecrack, forty years later most citizens who follow politics—and trade union activities allied to it—need to familiarize themselves with Communist lingo. This holds whether the motive in learning it is to confound it—as the atheist studies scripture—or the better to understand Russian DIALETIC and ways of thinking that are reflected by this jargon. Perhaps the best way to approach it is to see it in context, in an interpretive account of Communist Party structure and functioning.

52. CAN YOU SIGHT-READ COMMUNIST JARGON?

Jot down working definitions of the terms italicized in the following:[1]

The Party Apparatus

Communist Party organization shows many characteristics of the secret police pattern which developed in Europe in Napoleon's time and reached its ultimate development in the Gestapo and the *OGPU*. The Communists, as a revolutionary party frequently forced *underground,* often took on the methods and the temper of the secret police who were their chief opponents.

The basic unit of organization, whether in Paris, Belgrade or Peoria, is the "cell"—from three to ten card-holding members who know each other well and work in close harness. If the job is to penetrate a union by *"boring from within,"* either an existing cell will be assigned or the few members already in the union will constitute themselves a cell. The cells meet for advice with Party *functionaries* who are specialists in organization. The need for following a uniform *"line"* and for acting as a completely disciplined group is emphasized. This group broadens out to include *fellow-travelers* and *sympathizers,* but the initial core or cell never surrenders its identity nor genuinely merges with the broader *leftist caucus.*

The next largest unit in the Party system is a "section." Then comes a state

[1] Quoted, by permission, from a Policy Memorandum, "The Communist in Labor Relations Today," sent to its members by the Research Institute of America, 292 Madison Avenue, New York 17, N.Y.

set-up and next a regional or district body. Each in turn chooses one or more representatives to send to the next higher group. A meeting of the full membership of any level above the cell is called a "Party *plenum.*"

How They Work

The disciplined core operates on the basis of personal contacts and direct individual solicitation. Not until the group can give an impression of some numbers does it take such formal steps as issuing leaflets and making genuine appeals for support. As against the ordinary union members, often indifferent to union business, the Communist group functions as a disciplined body and is constantly exhorted to attend to every duty. Where necessary, funds are available—for instance, to provide transportation to meetings.

At a trade union meeting or convention, the Party members are well organized in advance and arrive with their policies and *strategy* thoroughly mapped out. They *caucus* during recesses and at the lunch and dinner hours to decide on *tactics* and to be assigned their roles in debate. They arrive early and stay late. They join freely in argument and parliamentary maneuvers for which they are trained. They are good at fighting *delaying actions* and often succeed in wearing out the opposition. Frequently they delay a vote on important questions until the early hours of the morning, by which time the non-left-wingers may have left the meeting. Occasionally, the Party will send in "a leading *comrade*" who specializes in the problems of a particular union or industry, to direct the strategy. . . .

Discipline in the Communist Party

The Party maintains *dossiers* on members and enemies alike. There are *star chamber trials* for *heresy,* which may result in *expulsion.* The tradition of general wariness and suspicion is deep-seated. Rarely is this visible, but the internal splits were seen on two recent occasions—Earl Browder's expulsion, and the charge by Joe Curran, head of the National Maritime Union, that his top executives were harrying him and the union with their internal *espionage.*

The need for quick and often secret action leads to highly *centralized rule* within the Party. Actual power is exerted by a small *council* headed by the Party secretary. Controlling the Party records, he tends to dominate policy and strategy. Since, according to Lenin's theory, a *dictatorship* will be necessary when the Party is seizing and consolidating power, Communist political thinking tends toward a dictatorial form of party government.

Within this dictatorship upon which even the smallest CP local is patterned, the theoretical *right of discussion* does exist among members, but only up to the point where the Party line is decided by the top policy-making body. Practically, however, important changes in Party line are not debated. They are handed down. Once promulgated, the line is not even theoretically open to debate by Party members. When it comes to applying the line in a local situation, such as a labor dispute, any unit of the Party may debate the question as to the *"correct"* tactics to be used, but once the unit is agreed all members are bound under *Party discipline* to conform. Any member who fails to do so is tried for *"deviation"* and expelled if found guilty of heresy.

CP Use of Propaganda

Coupled with the above techniques are all the devices of propaganda, including personal attacks on the anti-Communists. With Communists in strategic positions—in government, in industrial plants, among confidential clerks, foremen, even executives—there is a flow of information to the Party for such purposes. (It is interesting to note the frequency with which the Communist press publishes photostatic copies of documents or quotes from communications which are obviously of a confidential nature.)

The most effective publicity, though, is the association of the Party with the national and local issues which normally attract considerable public support. Nearly all Communist leaders are publicists, pamphleteers and debaters by trade or avocation. Opponents charge them with operating on Montaigne's principle: "In politics it is not the facts which matter, but men's opinions about them."

CHANCELLERY STYLE

Certain recent official jargon may also seem strange to some readers, though it has figured a good deal in the *Journal of Commerce,* the *Wall Street Journal, Business Week,* and *Fortune,* whose editors did not invent the lingo. It originated in Washington, D. C.

Frank Sullivan in *PM* for 22 May 1945 has some fun with this BUREAU-CRATIC jargon, which Goethe called *Kanzleistil,* "chancellery style." After paying a passing tribute to Maury Maverick, "who invented the name GOBBLEDYGOOK for that frightening, POLYSYLLABIC LABYRINTHINE form of English the Washington bureaucrats have invented to conceal the meaning of what they have to say," Sullivan gets down to cases. According to him and his spy, the ten most popular verbs in Washington are—and I venture to translate them into their colloquial equivalents:

process	put through the works
ACTIVATE	set going
DEPLOY	spread out
implement	put into effect
dispatch	send off fast
facilitate	grease the works for
execute	carry out
contact	get in touch with
EXPEDITE	hustle it along
brief	give 'em the low down

The runner-up verb to the top ten, he adds, is *to alert.*

With all due respect to Mr. Sullivan, can you suggest exact synonyms for these bureaucratic verbs? Actually, painful and relatively novel as some of these verbs are, they do the work. *Contact* came in from selling and advertising; EXPEDITE from production line usage; *deploy, activate,* and *brief,* from military jargon. *Alert,* as a verb, is just another instance of the good old English and American custom, of putting an adjective or a noun to work as a verb. The shock will wear off in time, even for such conservatives as the *PM* columnist.

53. CAN YOU TRANSLATE BUREAUCRATIC LINGO?

Sullivan continues with the ten most popular nouns among the bureaucrats. Can you give usable synonyms for these terms?

1. RECLASSIFICATION
2. JURISDICTION
3. proceedings
4. LIAISON
5. DIRECTIVE

6. ALLOCATION
7. PRIORITIES
8. assignment
9. ECHELON
10. SECRETARIAT

HOW THE UNITED NATIONS TALK TO ONE ANOTHER

When we shift from U. S. bureaucratic jargon to the U. N. variety, we find that a very few terms will go a long way in enabling us to follow proceedings. Running through one of the last issues of *Free World* (now merged with *United Nations World*) we note

diplomatic TERGIVERSATION	polite for "double-talk"
IDEOLOGICAL camps	shorthand for: 1. adherents of Communism 2. adherents of Capitalism 3. those on the third side of the fence; you name them
political ORIENTATION	facing East or West?
PRE-CONDITION	what has to happen first before any headway can be made
CHANCELLERIES	foreign offices
letters of ACCREDITATION	ambassador's credentials
PROTOCOL	right way of doing things according to diplomatic etiquette and usage
ABROGATION	annulling
BLOC	the other fellow's gang
STATUS QUO	the existing order
STATUS QUO ANTE	the way things stood before the war
JURISDICTION	sphere of authority

LEFTIST	euphemism for Communist or anybody 1 inch left of center
RIGHTIST	euphemism for reactionary
OLIGARCHIC	descriptive of the rule of the few: those who sit on what they've got; they may be well-born, they may be able, but they have to be rich, or be on the Politburo to qualify as oligarchs (see p. 252)
resistance movements	those who fought Fascism while it held their countries, and are now getting the works from their own "best people"
Great Power politics	game of political mumbledypeg between the Soviet Union, the U.S., and Great Britain, with the small powers allowed to place 10¢ side bets; but they are better advised to keep their hands off the table
colonial system	the black, yellow, and brown man's burden; EXTRACTIVE methods of the exploiting powers in Africa, Asia and the Orient: also used by the U.S.S.R. in occupied enemy countries and in Manchuria, Korea, etc., only they are better at selling a political bill of goods along with their MARSUPIAL tactics. (MARSUPIAL—an animal with a large pouch that is always hungry.—Mark Twain)
AUTONOMY	giving a subordinate or colonial group some measure of the right to conduct their own lives and affairs; if complete, it's just one step short of independence
HEGEMONY	preponderant power, as among states; leadership

These twenty special terms make up a modest enough ration. For the most part, they are standard English words used with some extra overtones of meaning.

TRADITIONAL DIPLOMATIC LANGUAGE

Earlier diplomacy used to talk a more elaborate language, though Americans were perhaps not much concerned with it, confining their verbal inventiveness in this sphere mostly to such varieties as shirt-sleeve, big-stick, black-jack, kid-glove, silk-stocking, petticoat, or dollar diplomacy. And they knew when Roosevelt I was "flying a diplomatic kite," or engineering the filibustering that split Panama off from Columbia. But the top-hat-and-spats school who succeeded the frock-coats of the Palmerston era and the knee-breeches-and-ruffles practitioners of Metternich's day had a fairly elaborate code, which still turns up now and then in the history books, or among the attention-catchers in *Time's* LEXICON.

54. Can You Define the Flossier Terms of Diplomacy?

1. CHARGÉ D'AFFAIRES	12. EXPLICATION DE TEXTE	23. ENTRE NOUS
2. PRECEDENCE	13. COUP D'ÉTAT	24. EN RAPPORT
3. ARRIÈRE PENSÉE	14. AD REM	25. EN RÈGLE
4. chancellery	15. À FOND	26. INTER ALIOS
5. PROCÈS VERBAL	16. MUTATIS MUTANDIS	27. QUID PRO QUO
6. Counsellor of Embassy	17. CETERIS PARIBUS	28. AD HOC (reasoning)
7. TELECOMMUNICATIONS	18. CHRONIQUE SCANDALEUSE	29. RAISON D'ÉTAT
8. The Kremlin	19. COMME IL FAUT	30. SUB ROSA
9. Quai d'Orsay	20. COULEUR DE ROSE	31. SUB JUDICE
10. Downing Street	21. DE NOVO	32. SUI GENERIS
11. The Vatican	22. DE TROP	33. FORCE MAJEURE

34. action paper

There is no need to give special definitions or a key for these: they are most of them in the list of foreign words and phrases in any good desk dictionary. But there are a few tags in common diplomatic use that call for a glossary. TERMINOLOGICAL INEXACTITUDE, for an EQUIVOCATION or misstatement, is

a useful parliamentary dodge coined by Churchill himself some 40 years ago. The Liberal party to which he belonged at the time had denounced the South African system of Chinese labor as "slavery." Later Churchill, as Under Secretary of State for Colonies, admitted the expression could not be used without some risk of "terminological inexactitude."—*Newsweek,* March 26, 1945.

There is the new term, GENOCIDE, "race-extermination," coined by Raphael Lemkin, onetime chief prosecuting attorney in Warsaw, in his notable book, to designate the Nazi policy of blotting out the Jewish people, and other races and peoples who were deemed inferior. And the old diplomatic Latin tag, *Quis custodiet ipsos custodes?*—Who will guard the guards themselves? (see p. 10) has given rise to several VARIANTS in English. The most notable was coined by Lord Salisbury. At a Cabinet meeting it was suggested that they call in the experts from the Colonial Office to save the situation. "Who then will save us from those saviors?" asked Salisbury.

Fortune FAVORS THE BRAVE, LEAVING TO *Time* THE STARTLING WORD

Any or all of the technical terms so far covered in the fields of business, labor, politics, and diplomacy, might turn up sooner or later in *Fortune.* There would not be too many in a single issue. *Fortune* makes a sparing but strikingly effective use of technical terms, drawing on the stock of learned language in just the right measure for emphasis. Its editors and staff writers pride themselves on interweaving economic theory with business practice. For the most part they make the theory serve OPERA- TIONAL needs: that is, it's so put that businessmen who have the wit can act on it. To achieve this result, the editors need some technical jargon, which they usually explain UNOBTRUSIVELY in the course of the story; or else they make it come alive by charts, PICTOGRAPHS, or ani- mated diagrams. If they use old words in a new sense, they provide the proper glossary. But the traditional and currently fashionable terms used in economic wrangles, they take for granted as COMPREHENSIBLE to their readers.

So in their July, 1941, issue in an article "Prelude to Total War," we find *laissez faire,* pointed up as an antonym for a *regulated* or TOTALIZED *economy.* The word *regulation* occurs often. SOCIALIZATION is perhaps a politer term than COLLECTIVIZING or CONFISCATION: in any case, anything SOCIALIZED is lost to private ownership. *Fortune* uses the toplofty word IDEOLOGICAL in its proper meaning of "pertaining to something based on systematic organization of ideas." TOTALITARIAN is a shorthand descrip- tion for a "total organization of all group activities under a CENTRALIZED police state." *Fortune* speaks of SUBVENTIONS, the special subsidies by which a government helps private enterprise of its own nationals to compete against foreign rivals. It labels our great upsurge of shipbuild- ing as a "SPATE of naval construction." Literally, "spate" is a flood. A new kind of submarine is compared to a GARGANTUAN *blowfish.*

There are some bold images drawn from cultural history. 1941 is an APOCALYPTIC year—the Day of Judgment for American industry, des- tined to see fantastic changes. That was a good guess. Henry J. Kaiser, the shipbuilder, is characterized by EBULLIENCE—he bubbles over when he's "steamed up." His six companies are PERIPATETICS—they move around a lot,—which is a far stretch from Aristotle's students who walked around while listening to the master discourse. A wild economic "hayride" is a *Walpurgisnacht* (a witches' Sabbath orgy with the devil presiding, on the eve of May 1). And Dr. Schacht is a "PRESTIDIGITATOR," a quick-fingered magician.

The *Fortune* editors now and then have a little fun with SOVIET cant. They describe the punishment of plant managers in Russia for "unpro- voked deviations from the correct technological process of production,"

—the language being translated from a Russian journal. It means "bungling," or "BOTCHING." *Deviation* and *correct* as used here are both part of Marxist-Leninist cant.

Occasionally *Fortune* runs a signed article. The contributors seem to keep to about the same proportion of specialized words. Leon Henderson, in an article (*Fortune,* July, 1941), "We Only Have Months," uses a few semi-technical terms some of which he may very well have put into currency as OPA Administrator: ATTRITION ("rubbing away"), *bottleneck,* PRIORITY, DISLOCATION (of the economic, not the SKELETAL, framework); CENTRALIZATION, EXPEDITING ("hustling it up"), and ALLOCATIONS ("Who gets what?"). Marriner Eccles, in writing "Price-Fixing is Not Enough" (*Fortune,* August, 1941) speaks of *over-expansion* and *inflation,* in contrast to *depression* and DEFLATION. He talks of *nonessentials* and of *deficit financing* ("raising by borrowing what you can't get by taxes"). But for the most part, *Fortune's* editors and contributors alike keep to plain words put together in readable style. The few technical terms and hard words they employ are essential to the meaning.

55. CAN YOU SIGHT-READ *Fortune?*

Jot down rough definitions of the following words from *Fortune* articles, indicating to what branch of science, industry, or TECHNOLOGY the term belongs:

1. COFFERDAM	9. purge	17. DIVERSIFICATION
2. rivet bucking	10. COMMISSARIAT	18. SINTERING
3. HAWSEPIPE	11. CIRCUMSTANTIAL	19. DESULFURIZING
4. ELECTRO-METALLURGY	12. ball up (slang)	20. HYDROGENATION
5. FERRO-ALLOYS	13. MEGALOMANIA	21. POLYMERIZATION
6. synthetic	14. CHANCELLERY	22. REAGENT
7. FERROCHROME	15. RAISON D'ÊTRE	23. CATALYST
8. quota	16. CONCOMITANT	24. CONSIGNEE
	25. SYMPTOMATIC	

Fortune often uses general or abstract words in a vivid and concrete way. "In shipbuilding," they say, "the impossible is a must." (August, 1941, p. 42.) They talk of the "DEMORALIZATION of inflation," of "the dismal LABYRINTHS of national FRUSTRATION," of an "AMORPHOUS HODGEPODGE"; they speak of "the PIVOTAL position of the United States." We hear of the "MANDATES of a policy board," of the "planlessness of the U. S. war effort,"—in spite, apparently of "MYRIADS of COORDINATORS."

56. *Fortune's* LONG WORDS

Give exact definitions of the following terms, in the sense in which they are generally used. Can you then add an extended or FIGURATIVE meaning appropriate in discussing the economics of industry?

1. delegated (authority)	9. INTER-RELATION	17. "pump-priming"
2. CIRCUITOUS (routing)	10. LATENT	18. FIAT
3. INCREDULITY	11. HETEROGENEOUS	19. INEPTITUDES
4. MOBILIZATION	12. DISRUPT	20. RIGIDITY
5. INADAPTABILITY	13. CARTOGRAPHERS	21. DISLOCATION
6. ENTREPRENEURS	14. TRANSCEND	22. PROLIFERATION
7. VORTEX	15. INTIMATION	23. SUBSIDIARY
8. LIQUIDATION	16. REPERCUSSIONS	24. VACUITY
	25. SUBJUGATED	

Fortune also makes a shrewd and telling use of the trickiest type of technical terminology, the kind most likely to baffle the layman, unless it is handled right: terms from technology and pure science. The editors apparently have a sixth sense which tells them just how far such terms have made progress toward acceptance as part of the common stock in English; and it is toward the acquisition of such a sense that your efforts should be directed.

Unluckily the desk dictionaries are not much help on the newer part of the technological and scientific vocabulary—even on words that have become widely current in magazines and newspapers. That is why it is necessary, in this department as in the business and labor fields, to supplement the dictionaries by providing our own lexicon for the most essential technical and scientific terms that are part of the live, growing layer of English.

SHOP TALK IN TECHNOLOGY AND SCIENCE

There are two kinds of technical and scientific words that shuttle over into general use. First: names for objects, processes, or phenomena for which there are no other terms available, so the scientists have had to invent labels. Many of these are familiar.

Nobody would be surprised by the word CAFFEINE, or by NICOTINE; THEIN and THEOBROMINE, ALKALOIDS in tea, are not so familiar. GLUCOSE has made its way into general use, in more ways than one; but FRUCTOSE and GALACTOSE, other special forms of sugar, are not so commonly known; nor do we all realize that the familiar CELLULOSE, from which

RAYON and a host of other products are made, is composed of sugar MOLECULES. We were puzzled or amused when we read that the Germans during the War were making sugar out of wood-pulp.

It's not surprising that when a technical term shuttles over into general use, most of us have only a very hazy notion of its exact scientific meaning. Hence the case for some systematic work on vocabulary in this field. We can't hope to learn all the new technical terms: what we want are those that are on their way into the common stock. These names of concrete objects, processes or phenomena we can always look up, just as we do the names of spare parts or new items of hardware, or new birds or flowers or insects.

But the second kind of scientific label that makes its way into the general vocabulary is CHARACTERISTICALLY a technical term that lends itself to FIGURATIVE use, in a PICTURESQUE extension of meaning based on its original scientific sense, but not identical with it. ALLERGIC is the most recent interloper of this kind (see p. 20). Psychoanalysis has given us such terms as PHOBIA, for an habitual fixed fear, and *complex,* for a deepset cluster of emotional associations; REPRESSION and TRANSFERENCE; PROJECTION and SUBLIMATION (though this term was already known in connection with ASCETIC self-denial and the search for ways to transform LIBIDO into art, music, poetry or mystical ECSTASY.)

When it's a problem of acquainting ourselves with the full meaning of some fundamental term of pure science, often we need to associate it with a picture, or a memory of some crucial experiment. What does the term ELECTRO-MAGNETISM mean to you? You will think straight off of motors, dynamos and other devices that depend on ELECTRO-MAGNETIC action. But it will help to recall the simple basic experiment that underlay all of Edison's and Steinmetz's inventions in this field. When Michael Faraday moved one pole of a magnet through a looped coil of wire with its ends attached to a sensitive device (a GALVANOMETER) that registered ELECTROMOTIVE force, he found that where the wire loop thus cut a magnetic field, electric current was induced in the wire. This discovery laid the way for the whole development of electro-magnetism.

ELECTRONICS

ELECTRONICS, too, is a word to conjure with. Along with ATOMIC energy, PLASTICS, SILICONES, the light metals, HELICOPTERS and jet propulsion, it is expected to usher in the post-war millennium: so the advertisements promise. Just what is electronics?

You encounter it often enough. When you have to replace a worn-out tube in your radio, you're dealing with an electronic device—in fact with one basic type of tube that utilizes electronic action. When a door in front of you opens of its own accord, just because your shadow has darkened a SELENIUM cell affecting another tube, it's again an electronic contraption at work.

Electronics is concerned with those peculiar tubes, and what happens inside them. It is the science—and industry—of regulating freely moving electrons to create devices that can "see, feel, hear, count, inspect, record, memorize, control heat, light, time and power." (*Fortune,* July, 1943).

Where Aladdin let the DJINNS out of a jar, Lee De Forest put them back into a tube. His AUDION tube which ushered in radio in the form we know it—ending the old dots and dashes in favor of reproduced sound— was the start of major electronic developments. What De Forest did was this: inside a glass tube he placed at one end a metal FILAMENT (CATHODE), at the other a metal plate (ANODE), and in between them a small metal screen or GRID. He then pumped the air out of the tube, to make it a high vacuum. He ran current into the cathode, which becoming heated, discharged a stream of negatively charged particles toward the positive anode. The grid, lying across the path of the ELECTRONS, was hooked up to a separate source of very low-VOLTAGE electricity. By varying this current ever so little to change the impulses in the grid from positive to negative, De Forest could interrupt the electron flow, then start it again, accelerating or diminishing the stream of electrons many thousands of times a second. The grid acts as a kind of shutter, or valve. Here is an instrument that can respond to the minutest variations of electric impulses set up by a sound or light source. Also, since the electrons in this case flow only one way—from the negative to the positive plate (contrary to the general rule as regards *electric* current, that the flow is from positive to negative), the electronic tube can be brought into play to turn alternating current into direct, making it a low-cost, efficient, easily managed RECTIFIER. It can also serve as a switch—as witness the electronic opening of doors. And it can measure minute changes—in time, or current.

From this beginning, 750 types of electronic tubes have been developed, to serve many different purposes. "Greek prevails among the tube names," says *Fortune* (July, 1943, p. 134, note) "largely because of the passion of one of General Electric's patent attorneys for coining Greek trade-names." *Fortune* says people in the trade call these coinages "Greco-Schenectady," but the trade says it never heard of the term and implies that *Fortune* must have manufactured this CHIMERA. Here are the main types of tube:

pliotron	radio-generator-detector-amplifier type
kenotron	rectifier type (changing alternating current to direct)
thyratron	rectifier type
ignitron	rectifier type
X-RAY	producing rays that penetrate solids and register a SHADOWGRAPH picture on photo film
phototube	responding to light changes
cathode ray	TELEVISION tubes
klystron	ultra-high frequency (heart of RADAR)
magnetron	ultra-high frequency

Radar, which depends on the last two types of tubes, is a coined word from the initial letters of "*r*adio *d*etecting *a*nd *r*anging." The klystron tube, on which it depends, puts out very short waves beamed directionally, and traveling at the speed of light. These waves bounce back when they hit airplanes or other solid objects within their 130-mile range. The returning signals give, by the elapsed time for two-way transit, the distance, location, and direction of motion of the moving object which reflects back the bunched waves.

Television depends on the band of ultra-high frequencies, just as radar does. Wartime research in radar meant parallel advances in television techniques.

57. ELECTRONICS TERMS NEEDED BY THE LAY READER

Supply definitions for the following terms (all but six of the devices are described above) used in electronics:

1. anode
2. cathode
3. ELECTRODE
4. radar
5. CYCLOTRON
6. SYNCHROTON
7. PLIOTRON
8. KENOTRON
9. THYRATON
10. ELECTRO-CHEMICAL
11. KLYSTRON
12. IGNITRON
13. MAGNATRON
14. PROTON

Plastics Glossary

A new desk dictionary published in 1946 purports to cover with especial care the newer technical terms. It does not even include the word PLASTICS. Yet plastics have been in common use ever since CELLULOID was invented. Thorndike, in the *Senior Century Dictionary* gives, as the fourth meaning of the word

any of various substances that harden and retain their shape after being molded or shaped when softened by heat, pressure, etc. Glass, celluloid, BAKELITE, rubber, etc., are plastics.

Glass and rubber are not now considered plastics by the Society of the Plastics Industry; nor by the editors of *Modern Plastics,* the leading trade journal in the field. There is another loose statement in this definition: THERMOPLASTICS, one of the two main types, soften with heat all right, and can be molded into shape; but what Thorndike omits to add is that they will not retain their shape if they are again subjected to heat. Try putting a hot iron on something made out of a *thermoplastic.* But THERMOSETTING plastics, the other main variety, set into *final* and IRREVOCABLE form on the application of *heat and pressure.*

Plastics, unlike glass, which is made from INORGANIC SILICATES, are synthetics made from organic substances such as PHENOLICS (carbolic acid family compounds); UREA; NITRATES from wood CELLULOSE or *cotton* LINTERS, ACRYLICS; VINYLS, etc.—all terms which often turn up in the *Journal of Commerce* columns. But these descriptive items still do not define the term.

Committee D-20 of the American Society for Testing Materials defines plastics as

any one of a large and varied group of materials, wholly or primarily organic in composition, which may be formed into useful shapes by the application, singly or together, of heat and pressure.

These useful shapes are molded in many different ways. One method is by EXTRUSION: forcing molten thermoplastic material through a shaping die to form continuous sheets, tubes, rods and special shapes. Another way of shaping is by LAMINATION (from Latin *lamina,* a thin plate, scale,

263

or layer of metal). Plies of material are alternated with layers of plastic RESINS, stacked between highly polished steel plates, and subjected to high heat and pressure until cured—i.e., the layers of cloth, paper, wood, or glass fibers are so tightly and permanently compacted by the plastic resin that the resulting material is immensely strong and durable.

Perhaps the best known plastic fabric is NYLON, which is actually the family name for a whole series of thermoplastics having great strength and toughness, made out of *polyamides* (Greek *poly*, "much" plus *amide*, combining form of *am* [from *ammonia*, a modern Latin word invented by Bergner in 1782 as a name for the gas obtained from SAL-AMMONIAC] and the chemical suffix, -*ide*, denoting the more electro-negative of two elements in a compound). *Ammoniac* is from the Greek *ammoniakon*, "belonging to Ammon," an Egyptian god near whose shrine in Libya were found certain AROMATIC salts and gums which were also called *ammoniaka*, after the god. *Amino*, as found in *amino-acids* that are important proteins, is another combining form of *ammonia*, the suffix -*ine* denoting an ALKALINE substance entering into a compound. The priests at Jupiter Ammon's temple would figure their god's legend has traveled a long way, and made some very powerful medicine en route!

SILICONE TERMINOLOGY

One of the oldest known families of plastics, the SILICONES (rhymes with "chilly bones"), developed in their fundamentals forty years ago, were abandoned as of little practical utility by the boys looking for an honest dollar. Under the spur of wartime necessity, they took a sudden new lease of life. Silicones are in fact outranked in importance only by atomic energy and radar among the technological advances made during the War.

When silicones get into full commercial production you'll have Dri-film on your raincoat that won't need renewing after the garment is cleaned: it will still be water-REPELLENT. It will waterproof your hats, too. You'll be able to get silicone greases and oils for your car that won't get sluggish or cake up even at 30° below zero FAHRENHEIT—though they will not LUBRICATE the car quite so well at ordinary temperatures. You'll have silicone rubber gaskets on your oven range door that will not be affected by heat up to 500° Fahrenheit. Printers will employ this type of rubber for rollers on printing presses using hot ink. This Silastic will also keep its ELASTICITY and FLEXIBILITY at temperatures of — 70°, a point where natural rubber has long since lost all its bounce.

Once a silicone oil is substituted for a petroleum type, airplane pilots flying in the STRATOSPHERE won't have to worry about their instruments going dead, when the heating system fails, because of oil caking up inside the panel. And repair men working on high-voltage lines can count on silicone INSULATION resins and varnishes retaining their effectiveness even if the wires are exposed to high heat or a lot of moisture—either of which might make ordinary insulation ineffective. Water-repellent silicone fluids are already perfected to coat paper, furnishing at last the answer to what you'll use to try out those perpetual-flow ball-bearing pens guaranteed to write under water! This would be a nice present for Mr. Peabody's MERMAID.

What, you may ask, is the trade secret of all these wonders?

Silicones are semi-organic compounds, half-brothers to the organic materials for which they can do more than pinch-hit. They are not devised by atom-splitting. Rather, some slick chemist figures out a way to CAJOLE one of the HYDRO-CARBON–ring molecules into rearranging its internal housekeeping so that it throws out one of its carbon atoms and lets a silicon atom move in. Actually, the chemist backs some organic compound into a silicon OXIDE or HALIDE, and effects the swap. The carbon atom is not left an orphan—it gets a new home, too. But once the little silicon stranger is taken into *his* new family, he sticks as tight as a leech.

The silicon atom is a tough and durable customer. And it is no such rare bird as U-235 or PLUTONIUM. In the form of SILICA (SILICON DIOXIDE, SO_2) it forms about three-quarters of the earth's crust—as quartz or sand or rock. No wonder it gives a strong backbone to the new combination into which it enters, making it more stable.

Since the basic materials from which silicones are made—brine, sand, coal, and air—are cheap and plentiful, in the long run the price should be competitive. Already several thousand silicones have been SYNTHESIZED. Since almost any organic compound may be reshuffled into a silicone form, the number that can be synthesized depends only on the number of organic compounds available for starters,—and their number is legion. Since any organic chemist can play around on paper at discovering a new silicone, and since the properties can be predicted to some degree on a THEORETICAL basis, the possibilities are almost limitless.

After this excursion into the newer technological terms not yet in the dictionaries as this is written, it seems natural to check on your command of technical and scientific terms which have been in use so long that 90 per cent of them are considered standard, even for literary use.

58. Do You Know the Commonest Technical and Scientific Terms?

Try your hand on the following quiz, devised to test the knowledge of high school and college students who have had only one year's work in general science. If you have read *Popular Science* or *Popular Mechanics*, or have had ABC work in the sciences, you should score 95 out of a hundred. Which of the key words are in current *literary* use?

Instructions: Can you supply the right word for each blank? Use the first letter and the suggestions in PARENTHESES to help you find the ONE word you need. None of the words in parentheses is the one you want. When you have thought of the right word, write it on a sheet of paper numbered to correspond to the blanks in the test.

Example: Scientists prefer to use the m————— (pertaining to a system of measurement commonly used in the natural sciences) system in physics.　　　　1. metric.

1. We felt the v————— (quick motion to and fro) of the engine.
2. The airplane has a greater v————— (speed) than the automobile.
3. The t————— (act of sending from one person or place to another) of sound without even the aid of a wire was a great discovery.
4. We have a t————— (an instrument to measure heat) in the school room to aid us in keeping the room at an even temperature.
5. Brine is a s————— (preparation made by dissolving a solid in a liquid) of salt and water.
6. The air was s————— (full of) with the perfume of flowers.
7. The violin string is r————— (able to return sound).
8. Wool and fur have a r————— (quality of not yielding to force) against wind and cold.
9. The mirror causes a r————— (change in the direction of rays of light.
10. We feel the r————— (emission of rays of light or heat from a center) of heat from the stove.
11. That is a n————— (medium) tint of blue.
12. The n————— (unfinished photographic picture) was shown to us before we ordered the pictures finished.
13. A man comes to read the m————— (an instrument to measure gas) each month.

14. The m———— (power of attraction) of the lodestone draws many things to it.
15. They used a l———— (a bar used to sustain a weight at one point of its length) to pry up the board.
16. I———— (illustrating the distribution of heat) lines connect points on the earth's surface having the same annual temperature.
17. We shall i———— (separate from other bodies by means of non-conductors) the electric wires.
18. Sand is i———— (incapable of being dissolved).
19. We did not have i———— (white or glowing with heat) lights in Benjamin Franklin's time.
20. Water is composed of h———— (a chemical element) and one other gas.
21. A h———— (pertaining to fluids in motion) pump was placed in the well.
22. Oregon has much h———— (moisture) in the air.
23. They will f———— (use a device for straining liquid) the water at the camp before drinking it.
24. The f———— (that change of organic substances by which their starch, sugar, gluten, are broken up and recombined in new compounds) of the grape juice caused it to become wine.
25. Rust causes the e———— (eating away) of iron.
26. One of the e———— (an essential ingredient) of the air is argon.
27. There is much e———— (peculiar condition of the molecules of a body or of the surrounding ether developed by friction, chemical action, heat, or magnetism) in the air tonight.
28. We saw the big d———— (a machine that converts mechanical into electric energy by rotation of copper wire coils in a magnetic field) that furnishes us with electric power.
29. The d———— (operation of extracting spirit from a substance) of whiskey from corn and other grains has been legalized.
30. The d———— (compactness) of iron is greater than air.
31. We will wait for the leaf mold to d———— (decay).
32. The c———— (shrinking) of rails on the railroad is caused by the cold.
33. Air is held in a liquid state by c———— (to bring within narrower limits of space).
34. An automobile has an internal c———— (development of light and heat accompanying chemical combination) engine.
35. The b———— (quality of floating) of the balloon enabled it to go a long way.
36. The b———— (apparatus that is essential to ignition) in an automobile is a new one.
37. The b———— (an instrument for determining the weight or pressure of the atmosphere) shows there is going to be a storm.
38. Along the coast of Florida, there are many a———— (wells formed

by boring into the earth till the instrument reaches water, which, from internal pressure flows spontaneously like a fountain) wells.

39. We find much a———— (one of a class of caustic chemical bases, soda, potash, ammonia, and lithia) in eastern Oregon.

40. Vinegar is an a———— (chemical that is sour, sharp or biting to the taste) derived from apples.

41. Spring is the time for the g———— (sprouting) of seeds.

42. The e———— (undeveloped) plant is in the seed that is put in the ground.

43. Alfalfa is a p———— (that which comes up year after year).

44. The c———— (green coloring matter) is the thing that makes the leaves green.

45. B———— (the science which treats of plants) should be interesting to a farmer.

46. We should s———— (make pure) the jars before canning.

47. We found the s———— (bony framework) of a bear in the woods.

48. The liver s———— (to separate, elaborate, and emit by natural process) bile.

49. S———— (liquid poured into the mouth) helps in the digestion of our food.

50. His r———— (act of breathing) was natural.

51. We shall p———— (sterilize by exposure to high temperature) the milk before using.

52. We need plenty of o———— (colorless, tasteless gas) to breathe.

53. Some things we eat do not have much n———— (food value) in them.

54. Do not i———— (draw into the lungs) the poisonous gas.

55. The i———— (that which poisons or corrupts) caused blood poisoning in his arm.

56. One of the vital organs of the body is the h———— (organ that serves to keep up the movement of the blood).

57. There are many g———— (tissue in animals or plants, producing some peculiar substances) in the body.

58. A bud is a g———— (portion of organism capable of becoming a new one) of a fruit or a leaf.

59. The g———— (fluid produced in the mucous membrane of the stomach) juice helps to digest food.

60. We shall f———— (to expose to smoke or gas as in cleansing clothing) all our old clothes.

61. People e———— (give off from the lungs) waste products in the form of gas.

62. We shall d———— (cleanse from disease) the house.

63. The d———— (breaking up and absorption of foods) is the work of the alimentary canal.

64. We have red and white c———— (minute discs) in the blood stream.

65. He has poor c———— (movement of blood through the body).

66. Each c——————— (a small closed cavity) in the body is a living organism.
67. The end of bone was covered with c——————— (a smooth, whitish, elastic substance).
68. When we breathe we take in air and throw off c——————— (a gas that contains impurities).
69. The water rose through the soil by c——————— (attraction by which liquid is drawn up) action.
70. The b——————— (microscopic rod-shaped vegetable organism) are found in decomposing liquids.
71. The a——————— (act of taking a substance through the tissues) by the plant is a wonderful process.
72. Wheat grown anywhere without attention to the selection of pure seed is likely to show many v——————— (deviations from a standard type).
73. The t——————— (a small mass of the roots of leguminous plants) on the roots of the clover are of the highest value to the farmer.
74. People now know that t——————— (cultivation of the soil is of greatest importance during times of drouth).
75. The farmer tries to enrich the s——————— (the bed of earth which lies immediately below the surface soil) when it is plowed.
76. G——————— (insertion of a small shoot of a tree into another tree) has improved our apples in the Northwest.
77. The farmer has a large s——————— (pit or airtight chamber for ensilage) near his barn.
78. Spring is the time for p——————— (lopping off, as superfluous branches of trees) of apple trees.
79. The p——————— (spreading or extension of anything) of plants from seeds is a form of agriculture.
80. The honey bee is a great help in the p——————— (conveyance of pollen to the pistil of the plant) of plants.
81. N——————— (an atmospheric gas) is necessary for plant life.
82. A mass of growing bread m——————— (woolly fungus growth formed on moist surfaces) is composed of many white threads.
83. We sometimes find m——————— (growth of minute fungi on plants) on the under side of grape leaves.
84. The youngberry is a h——————— (cross between two varieties of plants) between the loganberry and the blackberry.
85. Flowering plants are unable to flourish unless there is considerable h——————— (vegetable mold) in the soil.
86. H——————— (gardening) is a fundamental industry.
87. The fruit tree had fire b——————— (a kind of plant disease).
88. Plants that have food stored up in their roots during the first summer's growth and grow seeds in the second season are called b——————— (two year long).
89. Sugar cane is a s——————— (juicy) plant.
90. The mud was made by the s——————— (matter which subsides to the bottom) in the pond.

91. There is more n———————— (nourishing) value in cereals than in fruits.
92. We worked out the experiment in the l———————— (place for scientific experiments).
93. There is much e———————— (changing of water into vapor) on a warm day.
94. The c———————— (to cause to change into a curd-like state) of the food in the stomach is caused by the action of the juices on the food.
95. A part of the sugar is converted into c———————— (substance forming framework of plants).
96. C———————— (many heat-giving food stuffs—sugar, starch) form a large part of all plants).
97. Copper is a good c———————— (that which transmits) of electricity.
98. We can use this stone as a f———————— (point of support for a pry) when we pry open the man-hole.
99. Do you know of any s———————— (liquid in which a substance will dissolve) for rubber?
100. The p———————— (living substance, that of which all living things are made) of each living thing, from the daisy to the elephant, varies a trifle from any other in its chemical composition.

CANDIDATES FOR PROMOTION

How can you spot the scientific terms most likely to make their way into the common stock of words? One of the best ways is to note the terms regarded as usable without explanations by the leading science writers for the newspapers and magazines. Another and perhaps better approach is to discover what scientific terms a top-flight POPULARIZER in the field finds it necessary to employ.

A very versatile, sound operator in this field is Lancelot Hogben, author of *Mathematics for the Million.* He followed up this best-seller with an 1100-page book, *Science for the Citizen,* which has the sub-title, "A Self-Educator based on the Social Background of Scientific Discovery." Hogben not only puts science in its SOCIO-HISTORICAL setting; he also shows what science means for human life and thought: that at its best it appeals to the deepest and strongest drives which make us human. This philosophy, of the social and human significance of the scientific approach, Hogben calls scientific HUMANISM.

Since his purpose is to supply the reader with all he needs to understand and master the sciences, as well as to stress their HUMANISTIC appeal, it is natural that he should take special care about TERMINOLOGY. Above all, he must be intelligible, easy to follow. Too many learned scientific terms would defeat his purpose. The fact that his book on mathematics—to most readers a forbidding subject—sold by the hundred thousand, indicates that he is successful in reaching the wider public. Hence we should expect his choice of scientific terms in *Science for the Citizen* to be based on careful and prolonged inquiry into the number of scientific terms a student working by himself can be expected to master.

Ruling out the names of chemicals and everyday terms (such as those in the preceding quiz) which are a familiar part of the common language, there are about 400 scientific words not yet in the standard vocabulary that Hogben finds necessary in his 1100 pages. You could UNEARTH many more that are used in the 480 pictures and diagrams, drawn for the book by J. F. Horrabin, but for the most part these are self-explanatory when the picture is before you. The first time Hogben uses any of the 400 terms, he defines it UNOBTRUSIVELY, not in the formal logical language of a dictionary, but in an easy descriptive style, or in what is called OPERATIONAL language; that is, he tells what happens, or what the process or phenomenon is like in action.

59. Do You Know the Basic Terms in the Life Sciences?

The fifty terms from the life sciences which follow are among those most commonly used in Hogben's *Science for the Citizen* when he is dealing with topics from biology, psychology, and anthropology. The terms are grouped by tens. Match each term in the left-hand column with the proper clue in the right-hand column.

Familiar Terms from Biological Science

A

1. [ ] METAMORPHOSIS
2. [ ] MUTATION
3. [ ] NEURONES
4. [ ] NUCLEUS
5. [ ] ORIENTATION

6. [ ] PARASITES

7. [ ] PHOTOSYNTHESIS
8. [ ] PITUITARY
9. [ ] POLLINATION

10. [ ] STERILITY

[a] conducting nerve cells
[b] change of form
[c] carrying yellow powder from ANTHERS to PISTILS in plants
[d] condition of being unable to reproduce
[e] heritable new feature or change in plant or animal
[f] organisms living on or within another organism, from which they get food
[g] central core of cell
[h] gland at base of brain
[i] process of getting "located," to get directions straight
[j] plant manufacture of CARBOHYDRATES from CARBON DIOXIDE and water in presence of CHLOROPHYLL and light

B

1. [   ] CRETINISM
2. [   ] CURARE
3. [   ] ECOLOGY
4. [   ] ELEPHANTIASIS
5. [   ] ENSILAGE
6. [   ] EPIDERMIS
7. [   ] STERILIZATION
8. [   ] STIMULUS
9. [   ] SYNAPSE
10. [   ] VIRUS

[a] juncture where impulse passes from one nerve to another
[b] filter-passing organisms
[c] top layer of skin
[d] idiocy and failure to mature, due to extreme THYROID deficiency
[e] branch of biology dealing with relation of living things to environment and each other
[f] disease marked by enlargement of limbs and skin-coarsening
[g] arrow poison
[h] fodder stored in SILO to keep it fresh
[i] something that stirs to action, or effort
[j] DEPRIVATION of power to reproduce

C

1. [   ] CAROTIN
2. [   ] CARBOHYDRATES
3. [   ] CEREBELLUM
4. [   ] CEREBRUM
5. [   ] CHAMELEON
6. [   ] CHOREA
7. [   ] CHROMOSOMES
8. [   ] CILIA
9. [   ] CONSANGUINITY
10. [   ] CORTEX

[a] part of brain regulating INVOLUNTARY movement and lying below cerebrum
[b] layer of gray matter covering brain-surface
[c] blood relationship
[d] compounds of carbon, hydrogen, and oxygen
[e] plant pigment convertible by animal into VITAMIN A
[f] lizard that can change its skin-color
[g] part of brain that is seat of conscious thought and voluntary movement
[h] ST. VITUS' dance
[i] heredity-carrying microscopic FILAMENTS
[j] hairlike filaments

D

1. [   ] ALBINISM
2. [   ] ALGAE
3. [   ] ANEMIA
4. [   ] ANTHROPOMORPHISM
5. [   ] ANTISEPTICS
6. [   ] ANTITOXINS
7. [   ] ASEPSIS
8. [   ] ASTIGMATISM
9. [   ] BARNACLES
10. [   ] CAPILLARIES

[a] shelled animal that clings to ship bottoms, etc.
[b] hairlike tubes
[c] unequal CURVATURE in eye lens causing blurring
[d] water-plants minus roots, stems, leaves; often scummy
[e] lack of color PIGMENTATION
[f] deficiency of red blood corpuscles
[g] attribution of human form
[h] counter-poisons
[i] condition of surgical, germ-free cleanliness
[j] infection-preventatives

E

1. [   ] EUGENICS   [a] drug-like substances produced in body, which elicit specific responses when distributed by blood-stream

2. [   ] FUNGI   [b] masses or groups of nerve cells

3. [   ] GANGLIA   [c] non-starch-making PARASITIC molds

4. [   ] GENES   [d] cross-breeding

5. [   ] HYBRIDIZATION   [e] trance-like state induced by a MESMERISER, in which attention of subject is DIFFUSED and SUGGESTIBILITY heightened.

6. [   ] HYPNOSIS   [f] medieval botanical treatises about medicinal plants

7. [   ] HERBALS   [g] pre-formed EMBRYO ("little man") assumed by medieval thinkers to exist in SPERM or OVUM

8. [   ] HOMUNCULUS   [h] blocking or dampening down of response

9. [   ] HORMONES   [i] scientific improvement of stock by deliberate selection of mates

10. [   ] INHIBITION   [j] material particle in CHROMOSOME which carries hereditary trait from parent to offspring

Hogben interweaves material from the life sciences with his interpretive accounts of major developments in physical science and mathematics. He is not particularly concerned about the divisions between the different special subjects, preferring rather to give an over-all SYNOPTIC view of the whole of science.

For quiz purposes, however, there is a certain advantage in dealing with the terms separately. Many interpreters of science, unlike Hogben, prefer to narrow their scope to one area of the vast field. The late Selig Hecht, whose specialty in biophysics dealt with light and vision, wrote the finest popularization of a scientific subject produced in our time, *Explaining the Atom.* Working outside his own specialty, he yet combined narrative method with expository skill in such even measure that he managed with a minimum of scientific jargon. Apart from the names of chemical elements, only about fifty technical terms appear in the two hundred pages of his book. By thus limiting himself to the basic terminology of atomic physics, and the few other terms from the physical sciences that were necessary, he made good his claim to write for ". . . the complete layman" and to "make intelligent voters." The lay student of scientific terminology can well follow suit, and master new terms in small doses.

60. Terms in the Physical Sciences

Match each scientific term in the left-hand column with the proper clue in the right-hand column.

A

1. [ ] EQUINOX
2. [ ] EUCLID
3. [ ] FOOT-POUND
4. [ ] GALENA

5. [ ] GALVANOMETER
6. [ ] INDUCTION (ELECTRO-MAGNETIC)

7. [ ] INERTIA
8. [ ] IONS
9. [ ] ISOBARS

10. [ ] ISOGONAL

[a] equal-angled, as to compass variations
[b] instrument for reading voltage
[c] equal-pressure line on weather map
[d] production for electricity in wire by cutting a magnetic field
[e] electrically conducting submolecules
[f] when day and night are of equal length

[g] lead SULPHIDE
[h] tendency to remain in state of rest or motion
[i] first great GEOMETER, and the GEOMETRIC system he devised
[j] unit of work in British system of measurement

B

1. [ ] ANODE

2. [ ] BENZENE
3. [ ] BUOYANCY

4. [ ] CALCULUS
5. [ ] CATAPULT
6. [ ] CATHODE

7. [ ] CENTRIFUGE
8. [ ] COHERER

9. [ ] CONVECTION

10. [ ] DECLINATION

[a] tube packed with loose metallic particles which stick together when a high frequency alternating current is run through them
[b] DEVIATION of compass needle from true north
[c] coal tar DERIVATION, the molecule represented by six carbon atoms in ring, with six hydrogen atoms hitched on
[d] power to float
[e] launching or throwing device
[f] branch of mathematics dealing with variables and changing rates
[g] positive ELECTRODE
[h] whirling machine acting on cream-separator principle
[i] conveying of heat by movements of particles in gas or liquid
[j] negative electrode

C

1. [ ] DIELECTRIC
2. [ ] DIFFRACTION

3. [ ] DISTILLATION
4. [ ] DOPPLER EFFECT

5. [ ] DYNAMICS
6. [ ] ELASTICITY
7. [ ] ELECTRONS

8. [ ] ELECTROPLATING

9. [ ] ELECTROSCOPE
10. [ ] LODESTONE

[a] magnetic rock
[b] device to detect presence of minute charges of electricity, showing if they're positive or negative
[c] negatively ELECTRIFIED particles
[d] branch of PHYSICS dealing with action of force on bodies in motion
[e] breaking up of light or other ray
[f] INSULATOR
[g] heating a liquid and condensing the vapor thus given off
[h] pitch of sound from a moving source apparently growing higher or lower to listener
[i] resistance of matter to stretch or DISTORTION
[j] covering with a metal coating by ELECTROLYSIS

D

1. [ ] ISOTHERMS
2. [ ] ISOTOPES

3. [ ] MICROTOME

4. [ ] OSMOSIS
5. [ ] OXIDATION

6. [ ] OZONE

7. [ ] PROTONS
8. [ ] RADIATION

9. [ ] SILICON

10. [ ] TRINITROTOLUENE

[a] positively charged electric particles
[b] act or process of giving out rays,—light, heat, electronic, etc.
[c] element found most commonly as sand, which CRYSTALLIZES also into precious forms
[d] high explosive
[e] any of two or more FRACTIONALIZED forms of an element having similar chemical properties but slightly different atomic weights
[f] lines of weather map joining points of equal temperature
[g] device for cutting very thin sections
[h] combining with oxygen,—e.g., burning or rusting
[i] TURPENTINE—soluble oxygen that gives out stimulating odor
[j] mutual diffusion of gases or liquids at different pressures through POROUS membrane

1. [ ] VITRIOL   [a] work done to make a body at rest attain a
                                       given velocity if no heat is lost
2. [ ] ZENITH   [b] large stone pillars of CAIRNS used in measuring
                                       SOLAR SOLSTICE
3. [ ] VOLTAGE   [c] chemical DECOMPOSITION by electric current
                                       of substance in solution
4. [ ] ALCHEMY   [d] ancient QUADRANT for measuring angular alti-
                                       tudes above horizon
5. [ ] ASTROLABE   [e] SULPHURIC acid
6. [ ] CALORIE   [f] medieval PSEUDO-science which sought secret
                                       of turning base metals into gold
7. [ ] ELECTROLYSIS   [g] electrical potential determining direction and
                                       distribution of ELECTRIFICATION
8. [ ] KINETIC (energy)   [h] amount of heat required to raise one gram of
                                       water one degree CENTIGRADE
9. [ ] MEGALITH   [i] science of atmosphere and weather
10. [ ] METEOROLOGY   [j] point in the heavens directly overhead

Most of these terms which Hogben finds necessary in his self-educator
are scientific shorthand: words which pack a lot of meaning into short
compass. This drive for terms that can be taken in only one way finally
winds up in the use of letters and formulas, whereby words are further
reduced to arbitrary symbols. "The ratio of the circumference of a circle
to its diameter" becomes π, which the mathematician describes further
"an INCOMMENSURABLE"—not expressible in FINITE fractions. Undoubtedly with the new *Eniac, "e*lectronic *n*umerator, *i*ntegrator, *a*nd *c*alcula-
tor," π could be worked out to GOOGOL places, googol being the name
which Professor Edward Kasner's nine-year-old nephew obligingly supplied for 10 with 100 zeros after it (mathematicians write it 10^{100}). But π
expressed NUMERICALLY to googol places would still be only an APPROXI-
MATION.

Mathematicians have to use the concept INFINITY in some of their
calculations, too, and they've adopted a handy symbol for it, a figure
eight on its side: ∞, which looks as if it could work a lot of magic.

But no RUNIC character or magical ABRACADABRA ever worked such awe-
inspiring results as Einstein's formula for energy-mass EQUIVALENCE; that
energy equals mass multiplied by the square of the velocity of light. Lise
Meitner's reflections about the bearings of this formula, $e = mc^2$, on the
experiments in FISSION which she and Hahn performed in Berlin in 1938,
made her realize as she was on her way out to Denmark as a refugee

that they must have released 250 million electron volts of energy from each split nucleus—which is what makes an atom-splitting chain reaction so powerful (see p. 306).

Not since PROMETHEUS stole fire from heaven and brought it down to earth has anybody so stormed the ultimate secrets of nature as has Einstein with his pencil. He not only upset NEWTONIAN physics and astronomy, but he challenged AXIOMS that since the Greeks had been taken as the foundations of geometry, and since Newton as the basis for the laws of motion and gravitation. The explosions at Hiroshima and Nagasaki were implicit in that harmless-looking equation, though he would never have willed any such use of his work.

The symbols and formulas of science are not really words. But to a quickened imagination they may have some of the power of those COLLOCATIONS *of words* in a great poetic line that echo right up to the edge of Old Chaos and on into the Dark Night of Time of which Lucretius, the great Roman poet of science, wrote. These symbols interpreted enable us in an INTERMITTENT flash to see things under the aspect of eternity.

Newton's answer to the friend who congratulated him on having plumbed all knowledge expresses the scientist's humility in the face of the infinite: "I feel," he said, "like a child picking up pebbles on the shore of the unknown ocean of truth."

The symbols and formulas may look dry and abstract to those who cannot read them. But they convey a wealth of meaning and an AURA of history to anybody who can approach them with imagination. And surely the work of the atomic scientists (horrible as was its first FRUITION at Hiroshima, when control of atomic energy was taken out of the scientists' hands by the generals and politicians) makes it possible for man to envision in their awful majesty Lucretius' "flaming walls of the world."

TRANSLATING THE ATOMIC SCIENTISTS' JARGON

Hiroshima was still eighteen months in the future when agitated Military Intelligence officers paid a business call on the editor of *Astounding Science-Fiction,* a few days after that magazine published a story with the title "Deadline" in its March 1944 issue. This yarn told of a successful secret service mission to destroy an atomic bomb in the making. The spy, dropped by parachute, was captured and taken to the research headquarters of the physicist who had finally assembled a workable atomic bomb. To prove to the scientist that he was himself a nuclear physicist, the spy, when shown the bomb on its stand, describes its mechanism:

Two cast-iron hemispheres, clamped over the orange segments of CADMIUM alloy. And the fuse—I see it is in—a tiny can of cadmium alloy containing a speck of radium in a BERYLLIUM holder and a small explosive powerful enough to shatter the cadmium walls. Then . . . the powdered URANIUM OXIDE runs together in the central cavity. The radium shoots NEUTRONS in this mass—and the U-235 takes over from there. Right? [Actually, says Editor Campbell, this bomb would not have worked.]

All this supposedly happened on an imaginary planet, Cathor. But the bomb pattern was so close to the blueprint for the one Oppenheimer and his aides were starting to put together at Los Alamos, New Mexico, that the G-2 men wanted to know who *on earth* in the Manhattan Project had been talking. No one, the editor told them. The technical data on which the story was based came out of articles published in the learned journals in 1940—including abstracts of German and Russian material.

Well then, said the G-2 CONTINGENT, would he for godsake quit carrying these stories about atomic energy. The dean of science-fiction editors, John W. Campbell, countered with the argument that total suppression of all such stories, which he'd been running since 1939, would arouse more suspicion than would their continuance. His argument carried the day.

Had the G-2 men done their homework on the back issues of science-fiction magazines, they would have found some stories even more prophetic. One, published in 1940, "Blowups Happen," by Robert Heinlein, Annapolis graduate and plastics engineer, dealt with the psychological hazards of SERVICING an atomic pile. After one young engineer cracks up, engineers are required to work in pairs, and a psychologist is always on duty in a control tower, checking on them. The minute an engineer shows any signs, either on duty or off, of a change in his behavior pattern, the psychologist yanks him off the job for a PSYCHOMETRICAL check. Needless to say, the psychologists (the engineers call them "witch doctors") are about as popular with the engineers as political COMMISSARS were with Red Army generals. Finally feeling gets so bad that the general superintendent calls in his head psychologist, to summon the best expert to solve the dilemma. Lenz, who was a pupil of Korzybski, is called in. He is an expert in SYMBOLIC logic and PSYCHI-

ATRY who had checked the "PANDEMIC NEUROSES of the Crazy Years of Atomic Warfare." Lenz proves able to handle the problem, and also gives an "assist" when it is found that a mistake in the equations on which the safety factor depends necessitates dumping the molten metal in the pile, and RELOCATING the prime energy source on a space-ship 15,000 miles out. The private company which owns the pile objects, but Lenz forces their hand, and the world is saved.

Another fantasy describes the human sports (a sport in the biological sense is a deviation from the normal type—see page 239) called the "Baldies" who are the result of germ plasm MUTATIONS caused by exposure to RADIO-ACTIVE EMANATIONS in the great atomic wars. The "Baldies" are TELEPATHIC and can read the thoughts of ordinary human beings, though they can by practice shield their thoughts from each other.

Most striking forecast of our present wrangles, however, is a story published in *Astounding Science-Fiction* in 1941. It describes the struggle, domestic and international, over control of atomic weapons. A general is made Atomic Commissioner, when a woman scientist Dr. Estelle Karst (modeled on Lise Meitner) discovers how to make radioactive dust that will DEVASTATE an area a hundred miles square so it will not support life for a century. The general, though an enlightened liberal—a combination of Evan Carlson and General Marshall—finds he has to act as dictator. A weak president, in the hands of a JUNTA of Republocrats, tries to order the use of atomic weapons to collect big companies' claims in South America. The general refuses and decides to order all other countries to deliver their airplanes to a designated spot in the great plains area. They comply, but the long-range bombers of the Eurasian Union (now what country could that be?) apparently flying in to give up, pull a sneak attack with their own stock of atomic dust, and almost succeed. They are outwitted and destroyed, and the general establishes a PAX AMERICANA. The title of the story is an unbeatable critical comment on it: *Solution Unsatisfactory*.

All these stories—and forty-seven more dealing with various types of scientific adventure—are found in a collection called *The Best of Science Fiction*. Admittedly, science-fiction is commonly rated in the literary subcellar. Actually most of the good stories in the field are written by some scientist, to amuse himself and pick up pin-money. (Julian Huxley, Director-General of UNESCO, has one in this ANTHOLOGY.) The scientific assumptions on which the stories are based are usually plausible EX-TRAPOLATIONS of known science. (Extrapolation: finding by computation or curve-plotting, based on known terms of a series, other terms, whether preceding or following—more often the latter. This is a kind of legitimate scientific prophecy.)

In any case, whether it's respectable reading or not, science-fiction can prepare you to follow without too much difficulty *Atomic Energy for Military Purposes* by H. D. Smyth, the classic document on the subject. Anyone who wants to understand what is happening in the Atomic Age should master the vocabulary of nuclear physics sufficiently to read this book, until its sequel, *Atomic Energy for Peacetime Purposes,* is written —as it will be. And the most feasible method for acquiring this lingo, for most laymen, is to look at science-fiction.

61. MAKING A START ON THE LINGO OF ATOMIC ENERGY

The terms and sentence quotations which follow are from two famous pieces of science fiction. In context, you should be able to figure out what most of the terms mean. How many do you know when you see them isolated, as they mostly appear in this listing?

From *Solution Unsatisfactory*

artificially RADIOACTIVE materials
RADIOACTIVE FISSION products
CYCLOTRON
FRACTIONAL-RESIDUES technique
PHYSIOMEDICAL
RADIOACTIVE-dust
germ PLASM
half-life
ISOTOPES
MAXIMA
MINIMA
prime movers
MOBILES
APICES
BRONCHIA
Pax Americana
TELEVISOR
NONINTERCEPT
scrambler

From *Blow-ups Happen*
by Robert Heinlein

ATOMIC DETONATION
LINEAR RESONANT ACCELERATOR
squirrel sleuths
BERYLLIUM
NEUTRONS
elements
BARIUM
XENON
RUBIDIUM
ISOTOPES
DISINTEGRATION
chain reaction
two hundred million electron volts
eruption of KRAKATOA
self-perpetuating SEQUENCE of nuclear splitting, just under the level of complete explosion . . .
input-output
critical point

trigger
ALTIMETER
CONCATENATION
ELECTROSCOPE-discharge
GRID
direction finder
an occupational disease
stray RADIATION
DISINTEGRATION
sealed the GASKETED door
der Tag
FUGUE
witch doctor
OSCILLATOR
PSYCHOMETRICALS
the safety INTERLOCKS
the best industrial-temperament
PSYCHOMETRICIAN
PSYCHOSES NONLESIONAL and SITUA-
TIONAL
STIMULI
EMPIRICALLY
SYMBOLOGY
theory of ABSTRACTION
CALCULUS of statement
the PANDEMIC NEUROSES of the
Crazy Years
VISIPHONE
STRATOCAR
atomic fuel for INTERPLANETARY
flight
jury rig
RADIANT output
PITCHBLENDE
ANTIPODES
MOLECULAR energy
chemical reactions
radioactivity
mechanics of INFINITESIMALS
you were compelled by the "TRUTH
TROPISM" of the scientist
DATA
POSTULATES
radioactive series
group

mathematical PROBABILITY
theoretical mathematical prediction
a MOLAR scale
a VERNIER screw
a psychologically unstable condition
plastics, LITHICS
MISEVALUATION
SEMANTIC readjustment
The wrong meaning the patient's
mind has assigned to it
SITUATIONAL PSYCHOSIS results from
ADRENALIN exhaustion.
ADRENAL
AMELIORATIVE
PSYCHOANALYSTS
ANODYNE
equations
an associated group of mathematic
symbols
Dr. Destry included an assumption
valid in MOLAR PHYSICS, but for
which we have absolutely no as-
surance in atomic physics.
LUNAR theory
LUNAR BALLISTICS
TERRESTRIAL volcanoes
DYNAMICS of VULCANOLOGY
the meteor-bombardment theory
dwarf star
the gassy envelope
"Would you like to try to give a
congressional committee a course
in the mechanics of infinitesimals?"
You could create the damnedest
panic this slightly slug-nutty
country has ever seen.
Mass PSYCHOSIS
One taste of the Crazy Years is
enough.
radio-SYNCHRONIZED
CHRONOMETER
the controlled and CEREBRAL EC-
STASY of the impersonal seeker
for the ELUSIVE truth

field
curious CURLICUES of the calculus
of statement
mercury-steam-TURBOGENERATOR
ANTIRADIATION
cyclotron
CONCUSSION wave
King studied the paper. Lentz had assigned symbols to a great number of factors, some social, some psychological, some physical, some economic. He had thrown them together in structural relationship, using the symbols of calculus of statement. King understood the PARAMATHEMATICAL *operations* indicated by the symbols, but he was not as used to them as he was to the symbols and operations of mathematical physics. He plowed through the equations, moving his lips slightly in *unconscious* SUBVOCALIZATION.

the increasing INCIDENCE of occupational PSYCHONEUROSIS among the engineers

. . . you are none of you ATOMIC PHYSICISTS; you are not entitled to hold opinions in this matter. (Lenz to the Board of Directors of a privately-owned atomic pile).

SIMIAN
firing chambers, nozzles, fuel stowage, fuel metering
giant combustion chamber

THALAMUS
a sensuous OBLIGATO
flame of CORTICAL activity
escape-speed
his verbal shorthand
a fuel that would lift a rocket free of the Earth's gravitational pull.

He offered for their inspection the outline of a propaganda campaign on a national scale, such as any major advertising firm could carry out as a matter of routine. It was complete to the last detail, TELEVISION broadcasts, spot plugs, newspaper and magazine coverage with planted editorials, dummy "citizens committees" and—most important—a supporting whispering campaign and a letters-to-Congress organization. Every businessman there knew from experience how such things worked. [This is much what Leo Cherne, of The Research Institute of America, did for the Federation of Atomic Scientists when they came to him for help in getting their views before the public and Congress. The campaign Cherne outlined the scientists carried out, and it helped get the Army out of the saddle—so far.]

bugs
high reaction velocities
unease

Quiz Keys for Chapter XI

53. Page 254.
1. reshuffle
2. "say"
3. record
4. contact
5. order

6. sharing out
7. first call, second call, etc.
8. chore
9. levels
10. aides, staff

58. Page 266.

1. vibration	26. elements	51. pasteurize	76. Grafting
2. velocity	27. electricity	52. oxygen	77. silo
3. transmission	28. dynamo	53. nutrition	78. pruning
4. thermometer	29. distillation	54. inhale	79. propagation
5. solution	30. density	55. infection	80. pollination
6. saturated	31. decompose	56. heart	81. Nitrogen
7. resonant	32. contraction	57. glands	82. mold
8. resistance	33. compression	58. germ	83. mildew
9. reflection	34. combustion	59. gastric	84. hybrid
10. radiation	35. buoyancy	60. fumigate	85. humus
11. neutral	36. battery	61. exhale	86. Horticulture
12. negative	37. barometer	62. disinfect	87. blight
13. meter	38. artesian	63. digestion	88. biennials
14. magnetism	39. alkali	64. corpuscles	89. succulent
15. lever	40. acid	65. circulation	90. sediment
16. Isothermic	41. germination	66. cell	91. nutritive
17. insulate	42. embryonic	67. cartilage	92. laboratory
18. indissoluble	43. perennial	68. carbon dioxide	93. evaporation
19. incandescent	44. chlorophyll	69. capillary	94. coagulation
20. hydrogen	45. Botany	70. bacteria	95. cellulose
21. hydraulic	46. sterilize	71. absorption	96. Carbohydrates
22. humidity	47. skeleton	72. variations	97. conductor
23. filter	48. secretes	73. tubercles	98. fulcrum
24. fermentation	49. Saliva	74. tilth	99. solvent
25. erosion	50. respiration	75. subsoil	100. protoplasm

All but ten are in general literary use, though not always in the scientific sense.

59. Page 271.

A	B	C	D	E
1. [b]	1. [d]	1. [e]	1. [e]	1. [i]
2. [e]	2. [g]	2. [d]	2. [d]	2. [c]
3. [a]	3. [e]	3. [a]	3. [f]	3. [b]
4. [g]	4. [f]	4. [g]	4. [g]	4. [j]
5. [i]	5. [h]	5. [f]	5. [j]	5. [d]
6. [f]	6. [c]	6. [h]	6. [h]	6. [e]
7. [j]	7. [j]	7. [i]	7. [i]	7. [f]
8. [h]	8. [i]	8. [j]	8. [c]	8. [g]
9. [c]	9. [a]	9. [c]	9. [a]	9. [a]
10. [d]	10. [b]	10. [b]	10. [b]	10. [h]

60. Page 274.

A	B	C	D	E
1. [f]	1. [g]	1. [f]	1. [f]	1. [e]
2. [i]	2. [c]	2. [e]	2. [e]	2. [j]
3. [j]	3. [d]	3. [g]	3. [g]	3. [g]
4. [g]	4. [f]	4. [h]	4. [j]	4. [f]
5. [b]	5. [e]	5. [d]	5. [h]	5. [d]
6. [d]	6. [j]	6. [i]	6. [i]	6. [h]
7. [h]	7. [h]	7. [c]	7. [a]	7. [c]
8. [e]	8. [a]	8. [j]	8. [b]	8. [a]
9. [c]	9. [i]	9. [b]	9. [c]	9. [b]
10. [a]	10. [b]	10. [a]	10. [d]	10. [i]

VICE-VERSA QUIZ FOR CHAPTER XI

1. A "tagged" atom of carbon, or of some other element, which has taken on a change of sorts because of exposure to radioactive emanations from an atomic pile, is called an _____ of carbon.
2. Possible, as distinct from actual, current production is known as plant _____. It measures the degree to which output could be stepped up.
3. The cost-of-living _____ of the Bureau of Labor Statistics is based on the 1935–1939 average cost of a number of items of importance in a family budget, as they could be purchased in representative cities and towns in this country. Measured on this base, the _____ now stands at _____ per cent. (What is the actual figure shown on the business page of your newspaper, or in *Business Week,* at the time you read this?
4. Supply the missing words: Industrial standards are expressed in engineering shorthand; commercial standards are buyers' commodity _____; and consumer standards translate these into terms the salesman can use and the consumer can understand.
5. When there are too little goods and too much money, _____ usually sets in, unless government regulation and rationing prevent it.
6. If a manufacturer forces a customer to buy not only the pressure gun of the manufacturer's make, with which to shoot rock-wool insulation into walls, but also requires the purchaser to buy the rock-wool of the type the manufacturer makes, this is known as a _____ sale. It is illegal, under the present court interpretation of the Sherman Act.
7. Goods are of three types, depending on how they last: _____, _____, _____.
8. What is parity?
9. Governmentally-held supply of any commodity, as a reserve against emergencies, is called a _____.
10. A low-tax, high-profit, autarkic-aimed economy for the United States,

such as is promised by the Congressional chairmen for 1946 to 1952, may lead to a ——————— which will result in all of us who are lucky enough to keep our jobs and part of our savings, having to carry on our backs twelve to fifteen million unemployed, as we did from 1929 to 1933.

11. What are some of the derogatory terms trade union members apply to fellow-employees who will not stick by the union?
12. "Spreading jobs by limiting the amount of work a man may do in a shift," or "requiring the employer to pad the payrolls with extra job-holders"—either one is ———————.
13. What is the difference between a *stretch-out* and "stretching out the work"?
14. "Rejiggering the boundary lines of voting districts to give the party making the change a majority in the newly-outlined district" is ———————.
15. Put down the Communist jargon that you can remember.
16. What is the technical term in foreign office jargon for *annulment* of a treaty?
17. What is the single word which means "preponderant power, as among states"?
18. What is the diplomatic term for "reasons of state"?
19. What was Churchill's coined term to avoid admitting that somebody on his side of the House had lied?
20. When a court has a case under consideration, the matter is said to be, in a technical legal sense, ———————.
21. Professor Calway, a character in Galsworthy's play, *The Pigeon,* is arguing with another economist. Calway quarrels with his opponent's economic theory as conducive to a "hitty-missy cartload-of-bricks regime." What is the usual (uncolored) term for an economic theory of this type?
22. The alkaloids in tea are ——————— and ———————.
23. The coined word for "radio detecting and ranging" is ———————. Allied developments of the principle involved have given us ———————, ———————, and ——————— (other names made up of initial letters).
24. A device or substance which reacts to light is said to be ———————.
25. The highest magnification so far attained depends on the use of the ——————— ———————.
26. Are rubber and glass plastics?
27. Distinguish between *silica, silicon,* and *silicone.*
28. The Maya had a positional mathematics centuries before the Arabs introduced into Europe from India the concept of ———————, on which positional mathematics hinges—and would still hinge, even if a duodecimal system replaced our present decimal system.
29. The symbol for infinity is ———————.
30. The process of getting directions straight, so the location and "lay of the land" (either physical or mental) are known, is called ———————. How did the Army and Navy use the word in a specialized sense?
31. A disease marked by enlargement of the limbs and skin-coarsening is called ———————.

32. Heredity-bearing microscopic filaments are called ――――.
33. Counter-poisons are ――――.
34. The inducing of a trance-like state in a subject, in which attention is diffused and suggestibility heightened, is called ――――.
35. Can there be *inertia* upward, when a projectile is traversing the rising part of the parabolic curve that is its ――――? If so, what is the proper scientific definition of *inertia*?
36. A coal tar derivative, its molecule represented by six carbon atoms in a ring, with six hydrogen atoms hitched on, is called the ―――― ring.
37. Another term for an insulator is a ―――― substance.
38. The atomic scientists compared the force of the atomic bomb explosion to that of 20,000 tons of ――――, which spelled out is ――――.
39. The ancient quadrant for measuring angular altitude above the horizon, which Chaucer calls a Jacob's ladder, we now call an ――――.
40. A close-linked chain of events is sometimes called a ―――― of events.
41. Give the term for "two or more words that are identical in spelling, but which come from different sources and have different meanings." Also give the technical term for two or more words that sound alike but have different meanings. Are these technical terms? If so, to what technical branch do they belong?
42. The correct term for the actual events happening inside the atomic bomb when it explodes is ―――― ――――.
43. The instrument for measuring the height of a plane above the earth is called an ――――.
44. Where you have a graphic curve drawn according to a known equation, and calculate a value of the variable at a point behind or beyond the section of the curve which appears in the drawing, the process of arriving at this value is called ――――. (The word has appeared four or five times in the New York *Times* in a year.)
45. How soon do you think *allergic* will be accepted as a standard word in the figurative sense now commonly given it in ordinary talk: "antipathetic"? ("I'm *allergic* to middle commercials.")

[XII]

ONCE OVER LIGHTLY

Vocabulary-building is a game in which words are counters, and the player is always playing against his own earlier score. He needs, therefore, to take stock from time to time, to see how well his gains have been consolidated, and what his future prospects are. Such stocktaking calls for a review of old campaigns with words, even while planning new ones—all with a careful eye on the scoreboard.

There are many real-life situations in which it is possible to put to the test various methods for acquiring and retaining word-meanings. All Americans tell stories: how well can you pick out the key word in a joke, and remember it? When you run into a new word in your reading, how good are you at inferring its meaning from the context? How often do you hear over the radio a word that is new to you? How readily, in your own speaking and writing, can you solve tough word-problems— or their manufactured equivalent, word-puzzles? Take good cross-sections of experience in each of these fields of verbal problem-solving, and you have a rough-and-ready check on the efficiency of vocabulary-building methods. First, consider the humorous approach.

62. What Word Was Wrecked—and How?

Jot down the word or phrase which somehow got scrambled up in each of the following. Can you give a tentative label to the type of comic manipulation involved in each case?

1. In a murder mystery by Craig Rice, *Home Sweet Homicide,* the children who play detective are considering burning a lot of clippings and letters that had been used by the murdered woman for blackmailing purposes. The little boy speaks:
    "Let's have a bonfire," Archie said. "It's no fun burning stuff in the—*insinuator.*"
2. *The Smiling Ghost,* said the advertisement, is *mystorical.*
3. A bamboo is an Italian baby.
4. His hair waved a little like the statue of the *dinkus* thrower in the Vatican at Rome.—O. Henry.
5. A census taker is a man who goes from house to house increasing the population.

6. And I follows, like Delilah when she set the *Philip Steins* on Samson. —O. Henry.
7. A CRITERION is a most savage animal.
8. The bee-what of the tee-mother of the trotharooroo.—A. Huxley, *Point Counterpoint*.
9. An epicure is a poet who writes epics.
10. "Andy," says I, "the boys ought to have *dromedaries*. All colleges have 'em."
    "What's that?" says Andy.
    "Why something to sleep in, of course," says I.—O. Henry.
11. A Gael is a storm at sea. There was a gael in Shakespeare's *Tempest*.
12. The *horse-peculator* said, "This ain't no *debile* or *eleemosynary* business, though it's carried on at *vespertine* hours, and it's likely to lead to an *epicedian* fate via the rope."—Manufactured from O. Henry's elevated vocabulary.
13. God's Own Country is Heaven.
14. Strong drink is an adder and a *subtractor*, too.—O. Henry.
15. GORILLA warfare means when the sides get up to monkey tricks.
16. "Have you ever drunk from the fountain of this immortal poet, TASSO's, lines, Mr. Thacher?"
    "Not even a demi-Tasso."—O. Henry.
17. An IBEX is where you look at the back of the book to find out anything you want.
18. "I ain't particular," says Andy, "I'm equally good and VARICOSE on all subjects."—O. Henry.
19. ICONS are what you fatten pigs on under oak trees.
20. A MILLENNIUM is something like a CENTENNIAL, only it has more legs.
21. *Love's Last Shift,* by Colley Cibber, means, said the Frenchman, "La dernière *chemise* de l'amour."
22. Adagio is a kind of ANESTHETIC dancing.
23. "You say my boy is *illiterate*," Mrs. Shaughnessy said to the social worker. "It's a lie. I married his father three weeks before the lad was born."
24. An INCINERATOR is a person who hints bad things instead of coming right out and telling you.
25. I can't read nor write, and I see no reason why I ain't *illegible* for office. —O. Henry.
26. What disease did Oliver Goldsmith die of? The book said that he died of PECUNIARY embarrassment.
27. He was outwardly decent, and preserved his AQUARIUM, but inside he was IMPROMPTU and full of unexpectedness.—O. Henry.
28. A *lyric* is something written to be sung by a liar.
29. Odysseus tried to rescue his men from the *lettuce-eaters*.—O. Henry.
30. The Macedonian *phenolax* went straight through the Persian Army.
31. Pope wrote principally in heroic cutlets.
32. Wells' *Outline of History* is a veritable MILLSTONE on the road to learning.

33. "You catchee me one piecee Johnny Walker three dollar?"
    "Can do."
34. I had an *ample* teacher last term. He taught us to do three things. First how to write briefs and then to *exaggerate* them; second how to extract substances from novels, and last how to *interrupt* poetry.
35. Panurge tried to find out if he should marry or not by consulting the *virginal* lots.
36. Louis XIV had two wives and six *mattresses*.
37. Figurative language is when you mean a rooster and say CHANDELIER.
38. We had a lot of tinned food served on the *table d'goat.*—after O. Henry.
39. In quintessential triviality the shesoul dwelt . . .
    she-souls, he-souls, she-souls.—Joyce, *Ulysses*
40. The equator is a MENAGERIE lion running round the earth and through Africa.
41. Abracadadabra zib-zab-sum, tigna bina sesquipedalia, sesame, sedamy, Shadrach, Mashach and Abedwego.
42. The cuckoo is a bird that lays other bird's eggs in its own nest and "VIVA VOCE."
43. Persian cats is the chief industry of Persia, hence the word "purr."
44. Sound is a rapid series of ESCULATIONS.
45. The prevailing religion of England is HYPOCRISY.
46. Letters in sloping type are in HYSTERICS.
47. "Marden me, padam, you are occupewing the wrong pie. May I sew you to a new sheet?"
    "Cheautiful birch you have here."
    "Many thinkle peep so."
48. The boss was in *circumference* when the insurance agent came. Don Parker—New York *Daily Mirror*, January 21, 1933.
49. "In the last bundle, one rag failed.—Fritz Rundl, Ph.D." (A Swiss recently come to an American university as an instructor, notifies his laundry driver that something was missing.)
50. Go climb a tree up, and around chase yourself.

In any deliberate collection of jokes dependent on wordplay, it is easier to tell what word was pied up than to resurrect the laughter which once greeted the old museum pieces. Fashions in the comic change. But for the word-fancier there is a good deal more than meets the ear in the style of old jokes. Analysis can throw new light on the antiques, though it cannot make them any funnier.

THE COMEDY OF WORDS

There were gags long before the term was invented. Shakespeare called his own efforts in this line "witcracks" (*Much Ado About Nothing* V, iv, 102), but threw his best clown, Kemp, out of the theater for ad-libbing political gags during a performance.

In the gag family are several types of jesting that hinge strictly on wordplay: MALAPROPISMS, spoonerisms, Goldwynisms, macaronic lingos, and "double talk." And PUNS must not be overlooked, though many who have suffered from them may feel that the pun should be defined as the hit tune is by its DETRACTORS: Something you can't help remembering but devoutly wish you could forget. One of the charms of the malapropism, indeed, is that it is far from being a conscious pun.

MALAPROPISMS

An industrious German, Heinz Stallman, went through the whole body of English plays in print, from the beginnings to 1800, to collect all the malapropisms he could find. He got a good harvest, nearly three hundred. English is a punning language, and no mistake; it's probably richer in wordplay than any other, partly because it's so loose, rambling and ill-defined that it lends itself to comic effects; also it's fuller of HOMOPHONES than any other language except Chinese.

It wasn't until Sheridan's Mrs. Malaprop that the trick had a name, but there were plenty of malapropisms before her, and there have been plenty since—as witness the great ACCUMULATION of GOLDWYNISMS, most of which have been FOBBED off on Sam Goldwyn. The best malapropisms belie their name. For even if in theory they are "ill-befitting" (*mal à propos*) words, they actually have a kind of "shock logic" of their own, in that the PERPETRATOR, while he uses the wrong word, works it into a combination that makes a kind of gifted nonsense. So when Mrs. Malaprop speaks of the "contagious" countries (she means CONTIGUOUS) we chuckle over those Typhoid Mary areas, at the same time we relish the PRETENTIOUS DOWAGER's over-ambitious flight. When she says "INDUCTION" for SEDUCTION, "ILLEGIBLE" for INELIGIBLE, transforms HYSTERICS into "HYDROSTATICS," VERNACULAR into "ORACULAR," we feel these are PROVIDENTIAL errors. Mrs. Malaprop is always TEETERING on the verge of a really colossal slip into INDECORUM, and her minor verbal INDISCRETIONS fill us with hope.

63. A SCALE OF HUMOR?

Which five of the following MALAPROPISMS do you think the funniest?

	By mistake for	Source
LACONICALLY	IRONICALLY	Sheridan—*Rivals*
ILLITERATE	obliterate	*Rivals*

	By mistake for	Source
canary	QUANDARY	Shakespeare—*Merry Wives of Windsor*
FELICITY	velocity	*Rivals*
PUTREFACTION	PETRIFACTION	*Rivals*
COMMONTY (form of "community")	comedy	Shakespeare—*Taming of the Shrew*
perpendiculars	particulars	*Rivals*
INEFFECTUAL	intellectual	*Rivals*
LECHERY	LETHARGY	Shakespeare—*Twelfth Night*
extrumpery	EXTEMPORE	*Misogonus*
SUBSTRACTORS	DETRACTORS	*Twelfth Night*
upstantial	substantial	*Jonson—Tale of a Tub*
honeysuckle	HOMICIDAL	Shakespeare—*2 Henry IV*

You can go on making your own wordplay on these themes. A "honey-suckle" maniac would put any "commonty" writer in a decided "canary" —and it wouldn't be the wine from the Canary Islands that went into Falstaff's sack, either. Leonard Bacon may have been UNCONSCIOUSLY re-calling one of these malapropisms when he described a character in his *Ph. D.'s* as a "pale, ineffectual, Christian intellectual." Certainly we all have heard speakers whose content and delivery alike are wonderfully described by "extrumpery." And next time you hear about an "upstand-ing" and "substantial" young man, just substitute Ben Jonson's "up-stantial," and you can sit through the after-dinner speeches in a better humor.

Boners: Who's Stupid Now?

A special form of malapropism is the schoolboy boner—or "howler," as the British call it. For example:

> A CAUCUS is a dead animal
> An OCTOPUS is a person who hopes for the best
> A PLAGIARIST is a writer of plays
> A RUMINANT is an animal that chaws its cub.

Joke books have been compiled from these "boners," supposedly made by high school and college students who misunderstood or misused words. *It apparently never occurs to anyone that the examiner, teacher or school board should come in for part of the laughter.* Actually, the pupils are giving them away. Somebody made a mistake before the student slipped up. Examiner and student are engaged in the game of

291

cross questions and crazy answers. The crazy answers are funny enough but they also have an IRONICAL aspect.

Before a student pies up his words, somebody has slipped in estimating his COMPREHENSION *and his word range.* Often the student, not knowing what the word means, fuses it in his mind with a word he happens to know—or he confounds it with a word very like the original. But the error is not all his. *Some educational doctor made the wrong* DIAGNOSIS *and there was no way to bury his error.*

Our democratic DOGMA which insists on exposing all students to miscellaneous verbal learning should also come in for a little DERISIVE laughter. In fact, when we laugh at "boners" we should also reflect somewhat soberly, Who's stupid now?

The case is different with contrived verbal slips.

Taking Canon Spooner's Name in Vain

The spoonerism, which takes its name from Canon Spooner of Oxford, is a TRANSPOSITION of the initial consonants of two words: a special case of what is called METATHESIS, which involves altering the order of consonants anywhere in a word—as *calvary* for *cavalry,* ANENOME (pronounced like "an enemy") for *anemone.* But the spoonerism differs from an ordinary slip in that the pied-up combination usually makes a kind of NONSENSICAL sense.

By legend, the spoonerism was launched when by INADVERTENCE Canon Spooner read out a line of the hymn "Conquering kings their crowns shall keep" as "Kinkering congs . . . etc." Soon the story went around that he had greeted some undergraduates whom he had invited to tea, by telling them, "Gentlemen, I feel a half-warmed fish within my bosom." From these small beginnings—all but the scrambled hymn line probably APOCRYPHAL—a regular industry of manufacturing spoonerisms grew up in England. Volumes are still published, and the more nonsensical sense the initial METATHESIS makes, the better readers like it. In this country, radio announcers walk always in fear of making an unintentional spoonerism that will also be an IMPROPIETY.

Eponymous Hollywood Hero

A Goldwynism hardly needs definition for Americans. It's a piece of "shock logic," based on wrenching English IDIOM, at the same time using a twist of phrase that is decidedly outlandish. Probably the only Gold-wynism Goldwyn ever used was "Include me out," but ever since that got around, all the ODDITIES of speech PERPETRATED by Hollywood char-acters have been attributed to him. Actually, Goldwyn is a shrewd-spoken man, whose capacity for critical THEORIZING is well indicated in his famous APHORISM, "Sleep's a form of criticism, ain't it?"

Much of the humor of Yiddish-American stories—Lapidus' yarns, Arthur Kober's Bella series in the *New Yorker*—comes from the applica-tion of another layer of Teutonic influence to the already highly Saxon basis of English,—just as happened with "include me out," where a Saxon suffix is hitched on to a verb of Latin origin, that already has an ANTONYM from the Latin: *exclude.*

Folk Etymology

Another PERENNIAL source of amusement to the SOPHISTICATES is the havoc played with certain words by what is called *folk* ETYMOLOGY: a fanciful DERIVATION is invented to account for a word, and in accord with this home-made etymology the difficult term is approximated to some simple, understandable phrase or verbal compound—ASPARAGUS is trans-formed into "sparrow grass," or the battleship BELLEROPHON becomes "Belly Ruffian."

So in the slang PASTICHE (page 230), Mac translates the lecturer's term *substandard* as "sub-stander," which he thinks an ABBREVIATION for "subway-stander." He hears NONCE-*word* as "once-word"—which it is, *nonce* being the term for a LOCUTION found only once in print in all our literature. Mac's interpretation of the term *etymology* to mean "the science and art of eating" is itself a capital example of *folk* etymology. Dr. Pound's learned terms, few and simple as they are, are in effect a foreign language to Mac.

American exhibits a good many examples of folk etymology in the course of real translation. *Coleslaw* is from the Dutch *koolsla,* "cabbage salad." Often it is pronounced and even printed on menus as "cold slaw." *Woodchuck* has nothing to do with either *wood* or *chuck*: it's the pio-neer's way of naturalizing the Algonquin word for the creature: *wejack.* The principle of folk etymology is often FACETIOUSLY applied, and we hear of Hume Bogo, whose stories came to be called HUMBUG; or of Mr. Monk, inventor of the monkey-wrench.

Some real verbal potpies turn up when a writer, speaker, or singer deliberately mixes two languages. DUO-LINGUAL verse of this type is called *macaronic*—deriving from the Italian for "hash." The term seems a handy one to cover also prose mish-mash in two languages. In Pennsylvania Dutch (which is actually Low German and not Hollander at all) you can savor

Nix commen aus to the Deitcher's house, when the Deitcher ist nix zu housa. Have you the light gedoused and the cat outgeput?

In Yiddish-American, folk-ETYMOLOGY adds greatly to the macaronic effect. A *certificate* becomes a "stiff-ticket." Japanese-American, as it was used by Hashimura Togo, and on the air in the old program, "Frank Watanabe and the Honorable Archie," is necessarily a kind of PIDGIN-English, with phrasing based in part on Japanese word-order. So with the jumble of Texan and Mexican CONCOCTED by Tíntan, the witty Mexican comedian: what he sings in American, is *macaronic* with chile sauce added.

Orthodox language is left behind when we come to double-talk. Danny Kaye's is made to convey squirrely sense of a kind, through gestures and acting. It is the ultimate term of the patter song which Gilbert built up to such a high point in the Savoy operas. The classic example of the single double-talk word in English is of course the pseudo-Latin that Shakespeare put in Holofernes the schoolmaster's mouth in *Love's Labors Lost: Honorificabilitudinitatibus,* which the Baconians, regarding as a cryptogram, unscramble into

> Hi   ludi   Fr. Bacono nati,   se   tuiti
> (These plays, born of Francis Bacon, are their own protection.)

THE SUB-CELLAR OF WIT

In the realm of the pun proper, the best ones are IMPROMPTUS fathered by experts in patter-song lingo. W. S. Gilbert got off some good ones, usually out of RANCOR. Among his many aversions was Sir Charles Alexander, a well-known theatrical producer. Once in the newspaper room of his club, Gilbert came on an advertisement of Alexander's newest show, featuring strongly the charms of the leading lady with whom Alexander was generally supposed to have set up light-housekeeping arrangements. "Hm," Gilbert snorted, "Alexander is blowing his own STRUMPET."

Joyce's *Ulysses* is full of pied-up proverbs and puns, most of them heavily charged with SARDONIC commentary:

> God made the country, man the tune.
>
> Lawn Tennyson, gentleman poet.
>
> If others have their will, Ann hath a way . . .
> She put the comether on him, sweet and twenty-six.

> Whether these be sins or virtues, old
> Nobodaddy will tell us at doomsday leet.

Artful craftsmen can even achieve notable effects by translating a proverb from one language to another. The late Wu Ting Fang, when he was Minister to England, was invited for the weekend to the country house of the Duchess of Norfolk. When he came to leave, the Duchess asked him to write in her guest book.

"What shall I write?" asked Minister Wu.

"Oh, just some proverb or other," said the Duchess, "and sign your name."

"Proverb," said Wu, "what is a proverb?"

"Why, it's a TRADITIONAL saying, like 'penny wise, pound foolish,'" the Duchess told him.

Wu made some elaborate Chinese HIEROGLYPHICS, and left.

A month later the Duchess had as her guest the Keeper of the Chinese manuscript room at the British Museum. As he was signing the guest book on his departure, the Duchess said, "Now, Sir Frederick, you can tell me what Minister Wu wrote." Sir Frederick screwed his MONOCLE into his eye and as soon as he saw Wu's Chinese character his jaw dropped.

"How did he come to write anything so extraordinary?"

"Oh," said the Duchess, "I just asked him to write some proverb or other like 'penny wise, pound foolish.'"

"Ah," Sir Frederick said, "that explains it. He has written the Chinese equivalent of 'penny wise, pound foolish': 'What profiteth it a man if he go to bed early to save candlelight and beget twins?'"

Who would have the heart to apply to that anecdote (a true one) De Quincey's PETULANT GROWSING?

Of all the bores whom heaven in its merciful kindness and man in his utter folly have foreborne to hang, the teller of good stories is the worst.

If De Quincey's drastic remedy were to be carried out, most Americans would be hanged higher than HAMAN, with an especially high scaffold reserved for our modern Joe Miller, Bennett Cerf. But luckily there is little chance that anything could make Americans stop telling stories or enjoying wordplay.

64. SECOND THOUGHTS

And with this thought in mind, you may want to backtrack and take another look at the word-game on page 287, to try your hand at labeling the comic manipulation involved in each case as (1) a malapropism, (2) a "boner," (3) a spoonerism, (4) folk etymology, (5) macaronic mixture, (6) double-talk, (7) a pun, (8) an ordinary gag, (9) portmanteau word manufacture, (10) jocose use of learned words.

THE SERIOUS READER

More orthodox and traditional than the comic approach to words is the resort to wide and varied reading, as a way of enlarging vocabulary. Ideally, it would be admirable to meet all new words IN SITU—so you would first encounter them in the surrounding MATRIX of which they are a part, just as the archaeologist studies the objects which he digs up in the light of the strata where they lie, and in relation to other ARTIFACTS with which they are found. But time and space will not always permit of this leisurely procedure. When Casanova asked Voltaire, "Why not read only in the book of life?" Voltaire answered, "Because it's so unwieldy." This holds with words, too. To cover the ground, we often have to deal with them as isolated units. In what follows, you will find some such lists.

But in winding up an inquiry, we can well afford to be leisurely in making a final test of vocabulary to see how far new -found mastery makes it possible to avoid blackouts of meaning. And that calls for taking the words not singly, but in CONTEXT.

Here you should make a free-wheeling approach. Don't worry about the dictionary meaning until you're hopelessly stumped. Try to figure out, by all the devices at your command, what the meaning is. For, as Frank Colby remarks, in his *Confessions of a Gallomaniac:*

a word is not a definite thing susceptible of dictionary explanation. It is a cluster of associations, REMINISCENT of the sort of men that used it, suggestive of social class, occupation, mood, dignity or the lack of it, PRIMNESS, violences, PEDANTRIES or PLATITUDES.

Evidently, to sense words in this way, you must take them in place,— unless they are words so rich in historic, religious, or literary associations that even alone they convey the rich aura of meaning Colby had in mind. Hold his statement in SUSPENSION in your consciousness, as you work through the following passages.

On a first run-through of quizzes 65 through 72, (1) check only any blackouts of meaning which you experience, whether in the connected passages or in the special lists of isolated words.

Then (2) note how many of the words which puzzled you are in small capitals or italics. They are the key words in these examples. (3) See how many of them you can figure out by careful examination, and by using the Word-Analyzer, etc. In all, 250 test words are involved, and they are designated either by small capitals or italics. (4) How many did you miss?

65. POLITICS AND DIPLOMACY

1. *The Yogi and the Commissar*

. . . the European intellectual . . . now feels compelled to formulate human behavior at its two extremes. At the INFRA-RED extreme he sees the COMMISSAR, who believes in Change from Without and that the End justifies the Means. At the ULTRA-VIOLET extreme he sees the YOGI, who believes in Change from Within, that "the *End* is UNPREDICTABLE and that the *Means* alone count." They have no common meeting ground. The one is concerned with the individual's relation to society, the other with his relation to the universe.—Prof. F. O. Matthiessen, reviewing Koestler's THE YOGI AND THE COMMISSAR, New York *Times,* May 27, 1945.

2. Global Game of Anagrams

As one of the United States advisers remarked the other day, frequently ideas get so bogged down in words that it seems almost as though instead of building a World Organization for Peace and Security the representatives of 49 countries are out here playing a "GLOBAL game of ANAGRAMS.". . . The *destinies* of whole nations, whole peoples and of every man and woman and child on earth conceivably might hinge upon a single word written or DE- LETED here. There is the constitution of the *brave new world,* its declaration of independence. These are words upon which the international lawyers of future generations we hope will base their *professions* as America's constitutional lawyers do today. Therefore they are words to be chosen with care, to be weighed with PRECISION, to be polished with zeal.

And Country D in protesting that there's no equivalent in its language for such and such an English idiom isn't merely trying to gum things up. It's actually posing one of the most difficult problems that the conference will have to face in its final stage. Because all the documents eventually *adopted* are going to have to be translated not only into the other *working language* of the conference, French, but into three more *official languages of record*, Spanish, Russian and Chinese. The old League of Nations Conference was tied up for days by unexpected difficulties that didn't arise until the translation period was reached. And when the translators undertake to carry over all the NUANCES and fine shades of meaning written into *English texts* adopted here—well we may be in for some trouble, too.

—Vandevander and Player, in New York *Post,* May 24, 1946.

3. Which type of meaning change is Dr. Reinhold Niebuhr (quoted in *Time,* October 21, 1946) alluding to in the following:

. . . But if the real threat of war with Russia is understood it will become apparent to all but the willfully blind that there is no hope of peace in a policy which plays into the hands of Russia's IDEOLOGICAL STRATEGY. The program may also be a target for some American conservatives who do not understand that the American IDENTIFICATION of democracy with free enterprise is a luxury which Europe cannot afford. There is no possibility of saving freedom in Europe except by the support of political forces which stand to the left of American liberal thought. . . .

4. The following is a *Time* GALLIMAUFRY of terms from international affairs, economics, abnormal psychology, semantics (the science of meanings), and logic. What process of meaning change is involved in the case of the economic and political terms?

. . . never before had "The Hammer" so plainly and openly charted the cleavage between East and West. Molotov made it clear that the "iron curtain" is not a mere physical barrier, impeding free movement and free information; it is a partition between two world views, two kinds of morality, so that words, ideas, ideals, logic and precedents lose their meaning when they pass from one side to the other.

What Molotov had to say was logical and moral by the Soviet terms of reference. To Western ears it sounded like the elaborate logical structures of a PARANOIAC delusion.

Lexicography. The matter under discussion was the CRUCIAL Danube clause, Article XXXIV, of the Rumanian treaty. As they had since Potsdam, the United States and Britain were pressing for free trade on Europe's second longest river, now cut off along the Soviet line at Linz. Britain's Bevin used such words as "equal treatment for all" and "NONDISCRIMINATION." In Molotov's lexicon, these were not good words but bad. They meant "IMPERIALISM" and "dollar DIPLOMACY."

Senator Arthur H. Vandenberg reminded the peacemakers that the river had been INTERNATIONALIZED since 1815, controlled by an internation commission since 1856. IMMATERIAL, said Molotov. In 1856 the United States still had "slavery" and Britain was riding the crest of imperialism. It doubtless never occurred to Molotov that any mention of slavery nowadays makes a Western mind think of the modern totalitarian brand.

Vandenberg said that the United States has "no direct commercial interest of its own" in Danubia, but wants the river opened as a contribution to world unity. Words, said Molotov, who looks at the United States in the context of Marxist philosophy (developed in the dog-eat-dog phase of the 19th Century railroad barons and merchant COLONIZERS). Molotov clearly would not be surprised if a modern Jay Gould turned up on the Danube with a full bag of tricks. "I believe," said Molotov, "private capitalists can become the veritable owners of whole states . . . as a result of the power their dollars give to them." To prove United States INFILTRATION power, Molotov cited the UBIQUITY of United States movies and radio. So much for "one world." So much for "equality of treatment." Such phrases sound as HYPOCRITICAL to Russia as Russian "democracy" sounds to the West.—*Time,* October 21, 1946.

66. EDUCATION

1. The lingo of PEDAGOGY is a fearful and wonderful mixture of terms drawn from the other social disciplines, with a heavy INFUSION of half-understood mathematical and statistical concepts. This jargon is full of moral EXHORTATION and runs to wise saws as self-evident and boring as those of Polonius. But let a reformed educator tell the story himself. Criticism from inside the family is for once the best:

Gobbledygook Gagged
Back from three years in the Army, a New York University instructor named William Brickman took a look at the educational periodicals he used to write for. "The world," he found, "may indeed move, as Galileo once insisted, but educational writers . . . do not." To show what he meant, he wrote a paragraph for *School and Society:*

"The schools continue *to serve pupil and community needs.* The teachers *revitalize* the old methods, *stimulate interest* in the new program, and *implement the recommendations* of the curriculum experts. The latter envision a wider adoption of *vitalized* method and content, and are always striving after the *coordination of program* for the schools in transition. Under the *enriched curricula,* it will be possible for pupils *to achieve self-realization by meeting real situations, by being weaned from blind conformity to authority,* and by being *confronted with thought-provoking problems.* Above all, the school must be intent upon harnessing and *integrating the social and cul-*

299

tural forces within the structural framework of modern society. It is only through *pooling the resources* that the nation will be enabled to enjoy a generation of youth equipped with the desirable social behavior for this complex world."—*Time,* June 14, 1946.

First, what new meanings have the pedagogues run into the italicized words? Take the terms one by one, jot down their meaning in ordinary talk or writing. Then try to figure out what these pedagogical exhortations signify in the field of action. What is it they really mean to do?

2. By way of contrast to the ASBESTOS-gray texture of modern PEDAGOGESE, listen to a great Renaissance teacher:

To the illustrious Vice-Chancellor, professors, masters and doctors of the University of Oxford, greetings from Jordanus Bruno of Nola, doctor of a nobler divinity, professor of a purer and more harmless wisdom, the QUELLER of VAUNTING and kicking ignorance, feared and hated by POETASTERS, CRITICASTERS and all pretenders to learning! I do challenge you singly or all together in friendly fashion to a debate, upon any subject of your own choosing.

Which teacher would you rather try to learn from? Bruno was a follower of the old HUMANISM, which believed, in the words of his near-namesake Lionardo Bruni, that the young should study human nature in the great books of the ancients *and* in life around them. Humanists also believed a class was better off if it had two professors before it, of DIAMETRICALLY opposed views. Then truth and the student would have some chance!

67. RELIGION

1. Here are some terms from the Bible that are in the 20,000 commonest words. How many of them do you know?

PROCURATOR	SACKBUT	SHEKEL
BEATITUDE	SCRAPEGOAT	SOJOURNER
PSALMODY	SERAPH (pl. SERAPHIM)	SOOTHSAYER
PSALTER	CHERUB (pl. CHERUBIM)	SWADDLING (clothes)
	UNCIRCUMCIZED (Biblical for a non-Jew)	

2. A phrase from the Bible which is perhaps more frequently quoted than any other which the King James' translators kept in Hebrew, merely TRANSLITERATING it, is "Mene, Mene, Tekel, Upharsin" (rhymes with

"many many shekel too far, son"). Do you know what it means? Here is the fullest modern definition, in the words of a great swing spiritual by Harold Rome:

The King of Babylon, Belshazzar
He sat feasting on his golden PIAZZA
With his court and CONCUBINES
Stuffing in fried chicken and imported wines
Mene mene tekel, tekel, tekel,
Mene mene tekel Upharson.

They sat there at that banquet board,
Drinking from the vessels of the Lord—
Big swells of the neighborhood
Praisin' gods of gold and silver, iron and wood
Mene mene tekel, tekel, tekel,
Mene mene tekel Upharson.

That King of Babylon, Belshazzar,
Was a mean old razzer-dazzer,
Never paid no income taxes
The big shot of the Babylon-Jerusalem axis
He was a tyrant took delight in
Starting wars and doin' fightin';
Sons of Israel he called scamps,
Set them all to makin' bricks in concentration camps, Oh,
Mene mene tekel, tekel, tekel,
Mene mene tekel Upharson.

The tribes of Judah from below
Heard the SAXOPHONES and trumpets blow,
Sore and weary laid them down,
While Belshazzar's party kept agoin' to town
Mene mene tekel, tekel, tekel,
Mene mene tekel Upharson.

The guests were shaggin'; horns were blowin'
Lord, how gin and beer and wine was flowin'!
Of a sudden all was still
Ev'ryone stood frozen to the floor with a chill!
Mene mene tekel, tekel, tekel,
Mene mene tekel Upharson.

For through the plaster and the brick
Over by the candlestick
In Belshazzar's banquet hall—
A hand was writin', writin' slowly on the wall.
The King grew pale where he was sittin',
The fingers wrote and having written,
Vanished slowly overhead
And this is what the writing of the good Lord said:
Mene mene tekel, tekel, tekel,
Mene mene tekel Upharson.

The King called all his council table
To read the letters, but they weren't able
All his wise men, old and gray
Couldn't tell him what the writin' had to say.
Mene mene tekel, tekel, tekel,
Mene mene tekel Upharson.

Belshazzar off'red jewels and gold
If the meanin' of the words was told
In came Daniel, spurned them all
And for nothing told the bad news on the wall.
Mene mene tekel, tekel, tekel,
Mene mene tekel Upharson.

King, stop your frolic and your FLAUNTIN'
You've been weighed and you're found wantin',
All your days is numbered days,
The Lord don't like dictators, or dictators' ways.
Belshazzar cried out, "Man you're lyin'!"
But there was no use denyin'.
For he saw the words divine
Shinin' out just like a sanitaria sign·
Mene mene tekel, tekel, tekel,
Mene mene tekel Upharson.

The King of Babylon was slain,
But the children of the Lord remain—
All his idols turned to rust,
Crumbled are his kingdom and his powers to dust.
Mene mene tekel, tekel, tekel,
Mene mene tekel Upharson.

68. APPLIED SCIENCE AND TECHNOLOGY

HYDROPONICS is a word coined by Dr. W. F. Gerike, co-inventor of the process. Do you know what it means? Here is a passage from *Business Week,* which tells what happened to this word:

Wartime Experience—The Army coined the word "NUTRICULTURE" to describe this method for growing plant with NUTRIENT solutions rather than in soil. Considerable experience was gained during the war through Army installations on Ascension Island, a barren half-way point on the aerial route across the South Atlantic. (The term "hydroponics," first applied to this technique, has fallen into disfavor because it actually describes but one of three distinct processes for nutrient solution culture, that of growing plants in water solutions containing requisite plant foods. The other two methods are SUBIRRIGATION and sand culture.)—*Business Week,* April 27, 1946.

69. HIGHER LEARNING ON THE WPA

Here is a group of technical and special words from a passage containing a very high proportion of learned terms.

To do justice to the approaches to New York, in the opening chapter of *New York Panorama* by the Federal Writers' Project, Vincent McHugh, the author, employs technical words, for the most part in a FIGURATIVE or poetic sense, appropriate to travel in far-off places. Also he uses a good many unusual words. How many of these words do you know?

Technical Terms	*Unusual Literary Words*
LATITUDES	JEREMIAD
AGRO-BIOLOGICAL (theory)	APOCALYPSE
GERMINAL	APOTHEOSIS
BIOMETRICS	CAMERADOES (Whitmanese for *comrades*)
ARTIFACTS	SAFARI
ORBIT	AGGLOMERATION
SYMPTOMATIC	PANTECHNICON
VERMINOUS	PUEBLO
SIERRAS	SAMITE
AGRONOMIST	CROMLECH
RADIALS	HETEROGENEOUS
MERCUROCHROME	MELIORISM
PYLONS	PECULATION
SLIPSTREAM	DYNAMISM
WHORLS	INTRACOMMUNICATION

Technical Terms (Con.)	Unusual Literary Words (Con.)
CARTOGRAPHERS	PANEGYRICS
ALTIMETER	DAEMONIC
CHRONOMETER	INFRANGIBLE
ANEROID BAROMETER	AUTOCHTHONOUS
GYRO	REFERENTS
ANTENNA RING	TUMEFACTIONS
FATHOMETER	ARCHETYPES
ANTENNULES	UNORIENTED
GYPSUM	MAELSTROM
STALAGMITES	ANARCHIC
MASTODON (head·)	NASCENT
TECHNOLOGY	PREFIGURATION
SCHIZOID	INTERPENETRATING
PALEOTECHNIC	ANTIPHONAL
HYPERTROPHY	REORIENTATION
METABOLISM	CABALISTIC
ASEPTIC	GEOLATRY
MICROCOSMIC	
CROSS-RIPS	
CHLORINATION	
POLYPHASE (alternators)	
AUTOPSY	
SILICOSIS	
CORRELATIVE	
MESA	

"As Melville's Redburn indicates, the term *skyscraper* itself—a noun full in the homely tradition of the American VERNACULAR—was once synonymous with MOON-SAIL and CLOUD-RAKER as the name for a ship's topmost kites."— *New York Panorama,* chapter I.

McHugh's article runs roughly 7200 words. The technical words number 40, or about 1 in 180; the unusual words, 32, about 1 in 225. If all words over the 10,000 level were counted, the proportion would run four or five times as high as in *Newsweek*. This is really ERUDITE stuff; and delightful as well, perhaps because it is UNAPOLOGETICALLY learned without PEDANTRY or AFFECTATION.

To read this with any satisfaction, one needs a vocabulary on the order of 50,000 words, maybe more—the vocabulary of a learned judge, plus that of a top consulting engineer.

70. PURE SCIENCE

1. Atomic energy will turn up in the news very often in the next few years. See whether the homework you did on science-fiction vocabulary enables you to sight-read the following passage:

Piles for Power. The scientists who dominate the raw and REGIMENTED city (Oak Ridge) are not relying on missionaries alone. They are giving the Atomic Age a mighty shove by designing a *power-producing pile,* the most promising peacetime application of NUCLEONICS. Present piles (at Oak Ridge, Hanford and Chicago) are kept cool, but power piles will run at high temperature. Among the reacting URANIUM *rods* of a power pile will circulate a *chemically* INERT gas, hot as a dragon's breath, deadly with RADIOACTIVITY. This will heat a conventional boiler, yielding high-pressure steam, which, the scientists hope, will not be too radioactive to use in a TURBINE.

Isotope Rush. One group of Oak Ridge scientists is already doing a growing business in radioactive isotopes. Every week, with elaborate precaution, they pull a lead plug from a hole in the massive concrete shield around the Clinton pile. Out comes a GRAPHITE bar studded with little aluminum cans of chemicals which have been exposed to the storm of NEUTRONS raging inside the pile. These contain the ISOTOPES for which the world of science is clamoring. Sealed in heavy lead shipping cases, they are rushed to hospitals and research laboratories.—*Time,* October 26, 1946.

2. The passage which follows occurs very early in the definitive book so far written on *Atomic Energy for Military Purposes.* The passage is of particular interest because it states in language which is only semi-technical, the fundamental scientific principle on which nuclear fission is based. How far are the *italicized* terms in it familiar to you from your study of science-fiction vocabulary and from your recollection of material given in this book on p. 276?

THE CONSERVATION OF MASS AND OF ENERGY

1.2. There are two principles that have been cornerstones of the structure of modern science. The first—*that matter can be neither created nor destroyed but only altered in form*—was enunciated in the eighteenth century and is familiar to every student of chemistry; it has led to the principle known as the law of *conservation of mass.* The second—*that energy can be neither created nor destroyed but only altered in form*—emerged in the nineteenth century and has ever since been the plague of inventors of perpetual-motion machines; it is known as the *law of conservation of energy.*

1.3. These two principles have constantly guided and disciplined the development and application of science. For all practical purposes they were unaltered and separate until some five years ago. For most practical purposes they still are so, but it is not known that they are, in fact, two phases of a single principle for we have discovered that energy may sometimes be converted into matter and matter into energy. Specifically, such a conversion is observed in the phenomenon of *nuclear fission* of uranium, a process in which atomic nuclei split into fragments with the release of an enormous amount of energy. The military use of this energy has been the object of the research and production projects described in this report.

THE EQUIVALENCE OF MASS AND ENERGY

1.4. One conclusion that appeared rather early in the development of the *theory of relativity* was that the *inertial mass* of a moving body increased as its speed increased. This implied an equivalence between an increase in energy of motion of a body, that is, its *kinetic* energy, and an increase in its mass. To most practical physicists and engineers this appeared a *mathematical fiction* of no practical importance. Even Einstein could hardly have foreseen the present applications, but as early as 1905 he did clearly state that mass and energy were quivalent and suggested that proof of this EQUIVALENCE might be found by the study of radioactive substances. He concluded that the amount of energy, E, equivalent to a mass, m, was given by the equation

$$E = mc^2$$

where c is the velocity of light. If this is stated in actual numbers, its startling character is apparent. It shows that one KILOGRAM (2.2 pounds) of matters, if converted entirely into energy, would give 25 billion KILOWATT *hours* of energy. This is equal to the energy that would be generated by the total electric power industry in the United States (as of 1939) running for approximately two months. Compare this fantastic figure with the 8.5 kilowatt hours of heat energy which may be produced by burning an equal amount of coal.

1.5. The extreme size of this conversion figure was interesting in several respects. In the first place, it explained why the equivalence of mass and energy was never observed in ordinary chemical combustion. We now believe that the heat given off in such a combustion has mass associated with it, but this mass is so small that it cannot be detected by the most sensitive balances available. (It is *of the order of* a few billionths of a gram per MOLE.) In the second place, it was made clear that no appreciable quantities of matter were being converted into energy in any familiar TERRESTRIAL processes, since no such large sources of energy were known. Further, the possibility of initiating or controlling such a conversion in any practical way seemed very remote. Finally, the very size of the conversion factor opened a magnificent field of speculation to philosophers, physicists, engineers, and comic-strip artists. For twenty-five years such speculation was unsupported by direct experimental evidence, but beginning about 1930 such evidence began to appear in rapidly increasing quantity.

71. Sham Shaw

Bernard Shaw invariably refuses permission to quote from his works if the quotation is to be used in anything having a pedagogical smell. He is fundamentally averse to having any passage from his works employed for instructional purposes. He has threatened to lay his eternal curse on anyone who makes luckless school-children study his plays, saying that he would then be hated as Shakespeare is hated by those who have had to undergo a forced dose of him.

Although there is no possibility of quoting Shaw himself, yet a work on vocabulary-analysis would be incomplete without some near-encounter with the diction and style of the greatest living writer of English prose. So, in default of genuine Shaw, here is an imaginary speech that one would like to see him give. The occasion (decidedly in the future as this is written), is the FINALE of a week of half-hour broadcasts in which the most eminent atomic scientists, convoked by UNESCO, are able to announce the acceptance by the Security Council and the UN Atomic Energy Committee of a plan which the scientists have worked out for dealing with atomic energy. Here's the story and the patch of "Sham Shaw":

The presiding officer says, "Mr. George Bernard Shaw will now have the last word," and Shaw takes over the microphone:

I hope it's not my last word (Shaw said), since now more than ever I want to live to be a hundred, to find out if these artist-philosophers and showmen masquerading as scientists will know what to do with the world's ear now that they have got it. I am filled with envy, since I've been trying to achieve this feat for sixty years, and now at last do so only in the wake of a group of great actors who claim to be physicists. Their deadly quiet style of delivery alone must have administered a shock to American radio listeners from which they will be weeks recovering. Early in the week, indeed, I feared I was hearing my own UTOPIAN dreams come back to me.

But surely the results of this conference are in no way visionary. They are the first COMMONSENSICAL *and* imaginative findings to come out of an international conference in my lifetime. I attribute the result in no small measure to the fact that my friend Albert Einstein and his CONFRÈRES command a shorthand in the form of mathematics which enables them to work as fast as I do with my Pitman shorthand for words. They were able to CIRCUMVENT the massive stupidity of professional soldiers off the battlefield and to dominate the incorrigibly uneducable minds of politicians, and to confound dogmatic absolutists convinced they have ultimate truth by the tail, largely because as scientists they could agree so rapidly among themselves by using

307

their common language of mathematics, except for music man's only triumph over the Tower of Babel. I am glad to note that generals and politicians are alike excluded from this gathering, except for Mr. Trygve Lie, who as the first genuine world civil servant, is DISINFECTED by his position above the MÊLÉE.

I had thought, when I wrote *Back to Methusaleh* twenty years ago, that I had projected my vision so far into the future that nobody could catch up with me. Thirty thousand years seemed an ample time-gap to put between me and posterity. But the scientists at this gathering have proved themselves the adepts in pure thought that I foresaw as first emerging thirty thousand years hence. At the IDENTIC moment, they have also proved themselves far more practical than the economic black ANARCHISTS and scared PHILISTINES who were quaking with fear over the atomic bomb.

Surely the achievements of this gathering represent the most signal triumph in history for those who with me believe that civilization is a state of mind, not a collection of gadgets. Had these scientists done nothing else but make the politicians aware that they must henceforth reach the people through the truly international languages, music and mathematics, they would have performed an heroic feat. But they have done more: In Blake's mighty phrase, they have enabled man for once

To behold eternity in an hour, infinity in a grain of sand.

Your Listening Vocabulary

Shaw speaking and Shaw writing seem at first very much the same. But a check on vocabulary range in Shaw's BBC talks and recordings shows that like the experienced old showman that he is, he cuts down on his ration of highbrow words when he speaks. In his prefaces and essays, he uses long, hard words with the utmost freedom, whenever and wherever he pleases—and he makes them understood by the sheer head of steam he puts behind them. But he knows that this trick won't work so easily on the air.

Shaw's practice suggests a very practical test you can make of your vocabulary-building methods, and their effectiveness. If the proportion of hard words is likely to be less in radio, it should be even easier to check on your listening vocabulary, by seeing what proportion you know of long words actually used on the air over a fair range of programs.

72. Radio Vocabulary Range

The following words come from a wide variety of radio programs, highbrow, lowbrow, and middlebrow. Go through the list and check off (or note down) any which you cannot define. Then read the following discussion of vocabulary range in radio programs, in which all these words occur. In the case of any word you missed, see if the context helps to reveal its meaning. Here are the words from radio programs:

1. southerly	21. souvenir	41. synonymous	61. disrupted
2. cumulus	22. opiates	42. mobilized	62. foreboding
3. trawler	23. exploitation	43. annihilation	63. elation
4. fuselage	24. entrench	44. objectives	64. documentary
5. lariat	25. bludgeoning	45. compulsion	65. inexpressibly
6. ultimatum	26. drivel	46. unanimity	66. predominantly
7. stoats	27. lepidopterist	47. hectare	67. indomitable
8. avalanches	28. regimentation	48. preamble	68. centaur
9. gentians	29. tempi	49. plenipotentiaries	69. elusive
10. gerfalcons	30. contrapuntal	50. succumbed	70. invertebrate
11. germicides	31. fetish	51. dilemma	71. butt in
12. geysers	32. trite	52. tactical	72. hooked
13. stopes	33. bigoted	53. mobility	73. show-off
14. warder	34. pelvis	54. preclude	74. pay-off
15. fume	35. anesthesia	55. minutest	75. welcher
16. swinish	36. obstetrical	56. ensconced	76. yeah
17. humbug	37. pre-natal	57. stamina	77. tout
18. faker	38. realist	58. oligarchies	78. diagnosis
19. prehistoric	39. ordeal	59. prelude	79. insomnia
20. insatiable	40. inherent	60. category	80. fidgety

Now for some account of the programs in which these words appeared.

I. HIGHBROW PROGRAMS

In Archibald MacLeish's well known radio play, *Air Raid*, in spite of a generally simple and unforced diction, one finds a scattering of words well about the 15,000 level. Some of these are poetic words. MacLeish uses SOUTHERLY, which is in the twentieth thousand; CUMULUS (the type of cloud) which is somewhere between the 20th and 25th thousand; TRAWLER (20–25); FUSELAGE (20–25), but surely quite familiar from common talk about airplanes; LARIAT (20–25); ULTIMATUM (20–25); and a few others of like order of difficulty. But one may doubt if there are enough of these unusual words to create any appreciable "block" for a listener. The poetry of MacLeish is "public speech," BARDIC rather than COTERIE verse, and fairly understandable of the general, once they get over the shock of hearing poetic material on the air.

Auden's *Dark Valley*, a Columbia Broadcasting System Workshop play, contains a good many words over the 10,000 group. We find STOATS

(20), AVALANCHES (11), and in a *catalogue raisonnée* intended to SATI-RIZE BUREAUCRATIC file headings, a long list of words that would hardly be familiar to most listeners: GENTIANS (14), GERFALCONS (over 25), GERMICIDES (over 25), GEYSERS (12). STOPES (over 25), for step-like work-ings in the side of a mine-pit, would presumably be no more familiar to most American ears than it was to mine. STOATS (20) would not be IN-TELLIGIBLE to most city-bred listeners. Add to these stumbling blocks in the way of verbal difficulty the OBSCURE, SYMBOLIC nature of Auden's PSYCHOLOGICAL drama, and it is clear why it was never re-broadcast. Yet it is one of the few works in Wylie's *Best Broadcasts of 1939–40* that has genuine literary interest.

It is interesting to note what CONCESSIONS to the listener's vocabulary range are made in Eric Barnouw's masterly half-hour radio version of *Macbeth,* which is found as APPENDIX A in Barnouw's *Handbook of Radio Writing.* Barnouw uses patches from Holinshed's Chronicles for the CONNECTIVE narrative. He makes an interesting observation in this connection:

The effectiveness of this sixteenth century prose as radio NARRATION is probably due to the fact that it belongs to a period in which the ideals of written English were still, at least in many writers, closely related to those of spoken English. Holinshed shows no trace of "literary" prose style, which in later periods came to have only a faint relationship to spoken language. Holinshed's prose reads as if it were made for the human tongue. (Barnouw —*Handbook of Radio Writing,* page 192. Little, Brown, Boston, 1939.)

When Barnouw comes to condense the Shakespearean text, he takes almost no liberties by way of adding—that would be rash, indeed! But he EXCISES lines and parts of lines freely, where they contain ARCHAIC words. In the passage

> That memory, the WARDER of the brain,
> Shall be a FUME, and the receipt of reason
> A LIMBECK only; when in SWINISH sleep
> Their drenched natures lie as in a death . . .

he explains that he has dropped out the clause ". . . and the receipt of reason a LIMBECK only . . . ," observing that the word "LIMBECK" is not in *Webster's Collegiate Dictionary.* His note continued: "The adaptation makes small cuts of this type throughout, wherever the original would

be certain to cause the acute 'lost' feeling so disastrous to listener enjoyment and interest." (Barnouw, *op. cit.*, page 214.)

He drops out many of the ingredients of the witches' brew, because the
words are difficult, and others because they violate too markedly the
radio TABUS. Most of these TABUS are waived for Shakespeare productions, he says, but not all (*loc. cit.*, page 242).

With these EXCISIONS, the half hour script to which Barnouw has condensed *Macbeth*—and a superb job he has made of it, keeping all the
high poetic passages, and INTENSIFYING the tragic drama by FORESHORTEN-
ING—the half hour version has not more than forty or fifty words beyond
the 15,000 range.

To be sure, while I have included Shakespeare under the heading of
"highbrow" programs, his plays were considered mere popular entertainment in his own day; and the academic critics ranked his dramas as
of little more account than our professorial critics would esteem a movie
SCENARIO or a run-of-the-mill soap opera SCRIPT. Maybe there is a moral
here: that the critic must sift the popular art of his own time, even
though the task has now become HERCULEAN.

To sum up, then, on the vocabulary range of the "highbrow" offerings
on the air: Typical SCRIPTS include a very few words above the twenty
thousand range, a scattering of words above the fifteen thousand range,
and a good many above the ten thousand level.

II. MIDDLEBROW PROGRAMS

Under "middlebrow" programs, I group a very wide range of material:
such radio plays as Arch Oboler's, which use often devices from highbrow fiction and drama—even stream of consciousness techniques;
Orson Welles' productions; such "hit" dramas as *My Client, Curley,* by
Hermann and Corwin; the bulk of popular educational programs, such
as those fathered by Commissioner Studebaker, and by the Chicago and
Ohio groups; most forum and round table programs; political speeches
at a serious level; and most news broadcasts and COMMENTATORS' programs. The serious quiz programs belong here, and such "experience"
hours as Henry Lee Smith's prewar *Where Are You From?*

Arch Oboler, whether by accident or design, rarely goes above the
10,000 level of the man in the street, in his word choice. In *The Laughing
Man* I note only HUMBUG (15), FAKER (18), PREHISTORIC (12). In one of
Oboler's most ambitious attempts, *This Lonely Heart,* a stream-of-

consciousness play in which Nadedja Philaretovna is recalling her patronage and love for Tschaikowsky—whom she never met in person, 1 note only INSATIABLE (15), and SOUVENIR (17). And this is an hour script, which was performed with a full symphony orchestra furnishing background music. In the play *Bathysphere,* an anti-dictator tract in an underseas setting, there are only three words above the level of average comprehension, OPIATES (13), EXPLOITATION (17), and ENTRENCH (17). In a play *I Do,* there is only one word above the 15,000 level: BLUDGEONING (18). In *Mr. Pip,* we find DRIVEL (16), while in *The Man to Hate* there are no words above the average level; in this instance, when *denounce* (6) is used in talking to a child, it is immediately defined in simple action words. Even a CURSORY look at Oboler's work is enough to show that in spite of a certain literary drift, he has instinctively mastered Defoe's principles of simple diction in writing for mass consumption. That Oboler—or his typist—is ear-minded is shown by a curious slip in his preface: he writes—or dictates—*instance* for *incidence;* "The instance (sic) of originality and good sense in radio directing is no higher than it is in, shall we say, local politics" (Arch Oboler—*Fourteen Radio Plays,* Random House, 1940, page xxvi). Perhaps this is a stenographic error; but it is odd that it should not have been caught in proof reading. In general, however, Oboler keeps within the 10,000 range, and uses very few words indeed above the 15,000 figure.

The script *My Client, Curley,* about the rise to fame in New York of a caterpillar which would dance only to the tune "Yes, Sir, She's My Baby," is a rather curious instance of a departure from the norm usual in middlebrow programs. It has a large number of technical JARGON terms from the life sciences—even a good many Latin names of GENERA and species. It bandies about words like LEPIDOPTERIST (over 25); it brings in REGIMENTATION (over 25 by Thorndike's count, though I suspect it has grown more familiar now); TEMPI (14), CONTRAPUNTAL (over 25). It uses the jargon of the amusement world as found in the chaste pages of *Variety.* But all these departures from the vocabulary norm are easily accounted for: the big words are used for humorous purposes, and thus DISINFECTED. It makes very little difference, for the purposes of the script, whether the listener knows these words or not; it will be if anything funnier if he doesn't, since the scientists are brought in to be laughed at, and the satire on the methods of a New York "build-up" account for the jargon words. It might be well to add, however, that the unusual words are all used correctly, even if with no serious intent. There are a good many instances of this practice in other scripts that I have examined. Even the lowbrow programs, with wide mass appeal and Hooper ratings of 20 upwards, often use words in the higher frequencies in this comic fashion, with a BURLESQUE intent. This is part of the hangover from vaudeville technique.

Apart from the INTRUSION of these unusual words for comic effect, *My Client, Curley* keeps well under the fifteen thousand range—most of it under ten.

When we shift from these dramatic sketches in the middlebrow field to educational programs, we find a decided stepping up of the vocabulary level. In one of *The Human Adventure* programs put out by the University of Chicago, "The Story of Human Birth," included in Wylie's *Best Radio Programs of 1939-40,* we find a large number of words over the 15,000 level: FETISH (17), TRITE (16), BIGOTED (20), PELVIS (17), ANESTHESIA (over 20), OBSTETRICAL (over 25), etc.; and a good many over 10,000: PRE-NATAL (11), REALIST (12), ORDEAL (12), etc. There is a curious slip: *Mein Herr Doktors* (sic) for *Meine Herren Doktoren.* In spite of the best efforts to popularize, without talking down, the academic lecturer has a hard time to SLOUGH off his training in ABSTRACT and POLYSYLLABIC writing. Not but that some of these high FREQUENCY words are essential.

There is a wide range of variation in the vocabulary of political speakers on the air. Perhaps a few figures on White House English may be of most interest in this connection. Most of the late President Roosevelt's talks kept pretty well within the ten thousand commonest words, with just a sufficient sprinkling of words between the ten and fifteen thousand range to lend dignity and elevation to the discourse. In the speech which Wylie includes in his book, that delivered to the Pan-American Scientific Congress, we find, for example, relatively few: SYNONYMOUS (16), MOBILIZED (18—but surely now more familiar), ANNIHILATION (15), OBJECTIVES (14), COMPULSION (11), UNANIMITY (13). There are two words over the 20,000 range: HECTARE (put in right after acre, for the benefit of South American listeners used to metric system nomenclature); and DÉBACLE. As for slang and jargon, there is no instance of either in this speech. In the Boston address the Wednesday before the 1940 election, I noted *razz,* which the New York *Times* printed without quotation marks, no doubt following the handout. I was interested to see *razz* get into White House English; I predicted in print eleven years ago that it would get into standard American eventually. It is short, vivid, and expresses a shade of meaning for which there is no exact equivalent in the standard vocabulary; it sounds much like *raze,* which Charlie McCarthy would claim is SYNONYMOUS with his "mow you down,"—and it has a meaning not too different. And *razz* is the only word for a widespread American custom.

When we look at the news COMMENTATORS, we find of course considerable variation in practice. Elmer Davis, in spite of his Oxford classical training, keeps closest to the Defoe tradition. Except for the word PREAMBLE (14), I find in a typical Davis script no words over the 10,000 range. William Shirer uses PLENIPOTENTIARIES (17) and SUCCUMBED (14). Major G. F. Eliot uses DILEMMA (13), TACTICAL (20), MOBILITY (15), and PRECLUDE (14). Wythe Williams is fond of such words as MINUTEST (over 20), ENSCONCED (17), and STAMINA (15). Raymond Gram Swing is the most ERUDITE. In one broadcast he used OLIGARCHIES (19), PRELUDE (12), CATEGORY (13), DISRUPTED (20), FOREBODING (over 20), ELATION (over 20), DOCUMENTARY (19), INEXPRESSIBLY (13), as well as PREDOMINANTLY (10) and INDOMITABLE (10). The average listener must have a decided feeling of CULTURAL uplift as he listens to Mr. Swing.

To sum up on the middlebrow programs from these all too few samples, we find that in general they keep pretty well to the ten thousand commonest words, but allow a good deal of LEEWAY in the employment of diction in the ten to fifteen thousand range; and that with the exception of technical jargon words for comic effect, they are pretty CHARY of words about the fifteen thousand level, though they use a few.

III. Lowbrow Scripts

In the lowbrow scripts, it is rare to find a word above the ten thousand range. When one is used, it is usually for comic purposes, and it is very often worried to death, to be sure that no one misses the point. So Fred Allen compares himself to a CENTAUR (14), saying with that arch politeness toward himself that the old vaudeville MONOLOGISTS all have:

Allen—When the occasion warrants, I can give vent to the fawn in me and frisk about like a centaur.
Von Zell—What's a centaur?
Allen—A centaur is a fabled monster who has the body of a man from the waist up. From the waist down the centaur is a horse. Is the picture clear?
Von Zell—Yes. You're a centaur all right.

Again, Allen says to one of his visitors, a man who catches worms, "They tell me . . . you have made a profession of snaring the ELUSIVE (17) and legless INVERTEBRATE (13)." Surely in this context, ELUSIVE and INVERTE-BRATE would not create a block for any listener. This is the old minstrel show technique, using long and flossy words for FARCICAL purposes. It is the mock ponderous style.

The lowbrow programs are of more interest to the student of slang and COLLOQUIAL usage. In a single Jack Benny program, we note "butt in," "hooked," "show-off," "a cute kid," "burned up," "the pay-off," "welcher," "sure fire," "no kiddin'," "you've got a nerve," and "yeah" for yes. I note also TOUT, for a race-track hanger on—this is not in Thorndike's 25,000—but he may not have used the sporting page! I note also in this program DIAGNOSIS (15), INSOMNIA (13), and FIDGETY (19). As to the last, I think everybody would know the meaning; and the first two terms are employed for comic elaboration. Benny's gag-writers also show a high degree of skill in adapting the old raw burlesque and vaudeville jokes to a family audience. They have mastered the technique of sweeping the dirt under the sofa and sprinkling perfume on it, verbally speaking. Benny, for instance, sends this message to a FLIRTATIOUS nurse:

Jack Benny—Tell her that as a nurse, she doesn't know an aspirin tablet from a manhole cover. (Wylie, page 115)

This leaves the naughtiness in the mind of the listeners; and the network CENSOR, even if he is one of those who used to PATRONIZE the burlesque shows, can pass the clause with a good conscience, knowing that the script is working here on two levels—a method called comic irony in highbrow drama.

In this same script, there is one vocabulary feature perhaps calling for comment. That is the ADJECTIVAL CASCADE celebrating the charms of the SPONSORED product. The mixture of ghastly, forced gayety and jolly-doggism in this commercial makes it a comic example to read—however effective it may have been on the air as a sales-talk for the product. So far as range goes, the commercials keep SEDULOUSLY under the ten thousand level. But they overwork adjectives to a point where the law of diminishing returns would set in.

One would be NAÏVE to expect high literary merit in these lowbrow scripts, particularly the comic sequences, and the soap operas. But the critic should not be fooled by the absence of style into thinking these

315

scripts are easy to turn out. The wages of literary sin are very high in these fields; and a high order of craftsmanship is required. I find touches in the Allen and Benny scripts, still more in Charlie McCarthy's and the DEFUNCT Frank Watanabe's, which are marked by real folk humor; and without any trace of CONDESCENSION to the style of authors who compose in the American VULGATE, I may remark that I think it is harder to work in that medium than in standard literary dialogue. One needs an absolute rightness of ear. Ring Lardner, Sinclair Lewis, Dos Passos, Hemingway, and other writers of American have had that kind of ear. The gag writers have it too, but they don't step it up to a literary level.

To sum up, then, on the lowbrow programs: They keep very sedulously within the level of the ten thousand commonest words, but allow for a great deal of slang, and for popular jargon and cant words from the gangster, night club, race track, and amusement worlds. The lowbrow programs are on the whole more full of topical allusions, and can probably cover a wider range of meaning within their REPERTORY of familiar words and phrases, than we find in the middlebrow or highbrow programs which resort to higher-FREQUENCY words for fine shades of meaning or allusion.

73. Testing the Word-Analyzer

The high-frequency word, encountered either over the air or in print, is likely to be of classical origin. How readily, with the help of the word-analyzer, can you take the word apart?

Here are 100 words of Latin or Greek derivation, most of which have not so far occurred in the text of this book. Try your hand at analyzing them to determine the literal meaning, then, by what you know of the principles of meaning-change, trace the way each word has acquired its present sense. The number following each word indicates the Thorndike frequency number.

ANTITHESIS	[16]	AUTONOMY	[19]	CIRCUMLOCUTION	[20]
APATHETIC	[16]	AVOCATION	[18]	CIRCUMNAVIGATE	[13]
APHORISM	[16]			COADJUTOR	[15]
APOCRYPHAL	[16]	BEATITUDE	[16]	COEFFICIENT	[19]
APOTHEOSIS	[18]	BINOMIAL	[20]	COGNITION	[18]
ARCHIEPISCOPAL	[16]			COMMISERATION	[12]
ARCHAEOLOGY	[20]	CALORIMETER	[20]	CONDUCTIVITY	[20]
ASSIDUITY	[15]	CELERITY	[15]	CONFIGURATION	[18]
AUGMENTATION	[16]	CENTRIFUGAL	[13]	CONSANGUINITY	[15]
AURICULAR	[19]	CIRCULATORY	[16]	CONSTITUTIONALITY	[18]

CONSUMMATION	[12]	DELIQUESCENT	[20]	EXTRACTION	[15]
CONTRADISTINCTION	[16]	DEMORALIZATION	[16]	EXTRADITION	[16]
CONVALESCENCE	[17]	DEPRECIATION	[11]	FACETIOUS	[15]
CONVERGENCE	[20]	DESPONDENCE	[17]	FACTITIOUS	[15]
CONVOLUTION	[14]	DIAGNOSIS	[15]	FATUOUS	[20]
CRITERION	[15]	DISCOMFITURE	[12]	FELONIOUS	[20]
CUMULATIVE	[16]	DISINCLINATION	[18]	FELICITOUS	[18]
CUNEIFORM	[19]	DISINTEGRATION	[17]		
		DISSEMINATION	[18]	HYPERBOLE	[15]
DEBILITY	[16]				
DECADENCE	[16]	EQUIVOCATION	[15]	METAMORPHOSIS	[14]
DECLAMATION	[15]	EUPHONY	[19]	METROPOLITAN	[10]
DECLINATION	[15]	EVANESCENT	[15]	MONOLITH	[20]
DECOMPOSITION	[13]	EXCURSIVE	[16]		
DECOROUS	[16]	EXPECTANCY	[12]	PERIPATETIC	[20]
DECREPITUDE	[16]	EXPULSION	[12]	PERIPHERY	[19]

Over 20

ANTHROPOMORPHIC	ICHTHYOLOGY	GASTRONOMY
PLANISPHERE	ATHEIST	NECROPOLIS
STRATOSPHERE	HELIOGRAPH	STEREOTYPE
MISOGYNIST	HELIOTROPE	ANTHOLOGY
PSEUDONYM	AGORAPHOBIA	ANTARCTIC
HEPTARCHY	CLAUSTROPHOBIA	OMNISCIENCE
PETROGRAPHY	AËROLITE	ERADICATE
PERICARDIUM	MICROCOSM	BIPED
KALEIDOSCOPE	EXODUS	ALLEVIATE
ORTHOGRAPHY	HECATOMB	

74. TRY YOUR HAND AT A FABLE

Americans will travel a long way to learn a new funny story—a really new one. Try your hand at making one up in the way musicians often conjure up a new piece: by working over a well-known theme, to see if an interesting pattern will emerge. Use the fables beginning on p. 101 as patterns or starting points, but from there on, "roll your own," by COBBLING up a story using certain fixed words. This is no mean parlor game, if you're tired of bridge or Chinese checkers or chess. The easiest way to get a group of words that will really give your wits a workout, is to take the derivatives of some one Latin stem, in the combining form in which it enters English. Here is one which was "saved" out of the material in Chapter VI. It is one of the stems-of-all-work:

VERT, VERS, turn.

avert	ANIMADVERSION	VERSED	diversion
ADVERT	revert	VICE VERSA	pervert
convert	reversion	TRAVERSE	PERVERSION
INVERT	RE-REVERT	controversy	SUBVERSIVE
introvert	verse	controversial	SUBVERSION
OBVERSE	version	INCONTROVERTIBLE.	(and you can add
SUBVERT	VERSUS	VERSATILE	plenty more)
TRANSVERSE	conversion	VERSATILITY	
converse	RECONVERSION	divert	

If this game amuses you, turn back to the lists of Latin and Greek words in the Word-ANALYZER, pick out a likely stem and start making up a store of these fables. Leave the key words blank when you type up the copies in final form. A half-dozen or so copies of each on "flimsies" will furnish the makings for a speed contest, to see who can get to the point of the story fastest.

No matter how popular word-games become—and the crossword puzzle outrivals the old-time spelling-bee—there is no escaping the need for an accurate measure of *individual* vocabulary.

KNOW YOUR OWN VOCABULARY RANGE

Whether you are a writer, reader or speaker, it's a vital matter to know your own vocabulary range and how it stacks up with the average. The ideal is a wide vocabulary with a sufficient reserve of words for stand-by purposes, so that you can draw on the RESERVOIR at will; but you need a more limited and selected word list which is instantly ready on the tongue or pen, and under sure control.

75. COMPREHENSIVE VOCABULARY QUIZ

Here is a comprehensive test of your vocabulary. The test is in three parts. The first 100 words are from the eleventh- to the twentieth-thousand frequency range of the 20,000 words most commonly used—10 from each 1000. This is therefore a systematic test, built not on any HIT-OR-MISS or purely EMPIRICAL basis, but on the assumption that difficulty in learning word meanings ties in quite closely with how often you encounter words.

The second section of the quiz consists of 50 items given in context, as they occur in magazine material. The third section is 50 items picked from tests you have already encountered in this book, but in this instance only the clues are given: you are to supply the word. This third part is a test of readiness and sureness.

PART I

Of the four alternative equivalents given for each entry in the test, pick the one closest in meaning to the key word, and put its number in the parentheses in front of the key word.

1. [   ] ABASH [1] crush [2] toward the rear [3] shame [4] a metallic salt.
2. [   ] BIOGRAPHY [1] life science [2] a true life story [3] art of DEFAMATION [4] paul-prying.
3. [   ] CONVULSIVE [1] ugly [2] shaking [3] turning [4] upside down.
4. [   ] EDICT [1] banning of SACRAMENTS [2] ukase [3] decision of jury [4] tyranny.
5. [   ] GLOWWORM [1] flare-up from blast furnace [2] firefly [3] incandescence [4] radiance.
6. [   ] JAILER [1] someone in and out of prison [2] a jealous man [3] keeper of a prison [4] a cruel tyrant.
7. [   ] MUSTY [1] imperative [2] moldy smelling [3] dark [4] a cellar.
8. [   ] PERSPIRATION [1] breathing [2] state of despair [3] sweat [4] getting ready.
9. [   ] ROBUST [1] bursting out [2] sturdy [3] kind of oak [4] flying bomb.
10. [   ] SUBTERRANEAN [1] devious [2] underground [3] a disappearing river [4] wily.
11. [   ] WRY [1] raise a rumpus [2] askew [3] grain [4] woven.
12. [   ] TOBOGGAN [1] enter a swamp [2] long sled [3] steep place [4] slick.
13. [   ] SHEPHERDESS [1] kind of cloth [2] sheep without care [3] girl who tends sheep [4] kind of pie.
14. [   ] PROVOST [1] enraging [2] official [3] foresighted [4] a special kind of ceremonial gown.
15. [   ] NOCTURNAL [1] perpetual [2] night-time [3] furtive [4] kind of owl.
16. [   ] LAGGARD [1] enclosed within a compound [2] one who falls behind [3] a do-nothing [4] hard-up.
17. [   ] HAG [1] cut up [2] a kind of tobacco [3] sharp-featured old woman [4] bargain noisily.
18. [   ] EQUALIZE [1] agitate [2] bring to PARITY [3] raze [4] lower the level.
19. [   ] CRIMP [1] economize [2] collapse [3] crease [4] rascal.

20. [ ] BREAKWATER [1] an inlet [2] a kind of ship [3] seawall [4] device on prow of ship.
21. [ ] ADZ [1] a proverb [2] a cutting tool [3] sums up [4] rough.
22. [ ] BRICKLAYER [1] part of wall [2] mortar [3] oblong [4] one who lays bricks.
23. [ ] CREOSOTE [1] fumes [2] tarry substance [3] burn up [4] OPAQUE.
24. [ ] ENSHRINE [1] narrow [2] penetrate [3] put in hallowed place [4] make pilgrimage.
25. [ ] HAPHAZARD [1] lucky [2] risky [3] chancy [4] indifferent.
26. [ ] KNIGHTLY [1] properly [2] chivalrous [3] gently [4] wrongly.
27. [ ] NOISOME [1] clamorous [2] smelly [3] appalling [4] rascal.
28. [ ] PROMOTER [1] stockbroker [2] banker [3] developer [4] oxygen-furnishing apparatus.
29. [ ] SHELLAC [1] copra [2] RESINOUS varnish [3] punish [4] club.
30. [ ] TOLERANCE [1] breadth [2] forbearance [3] vision [4] wisdom.
31. [ ] AMMONIUM [1] portable organ [2] a chemical substance [3] groan of agony [4] smelly.
32. [ ] CANTO [1] half gallop [2] a singer [3] section of long poem [4] drinking room.
33. [ ] DEBATER [1] arguer [2] hairsplitter [3] collector of bait [4] SOPHIST.
34. [ ] EXPOSTULATION [1] explaining [2] remonstrance [3] losing patience [4] positing.
35. [ ] HOGSHEAD [1] top of barrel [2] a chest [3] cask of certain content [4] profane term of abuse.
36. [ ] LIMBER [1] one who trims trees [2] pliable [3] unfold [4] ELONGATE.
37. [ ] OPTIMISM [1] foolish betting [2] hopefulness [3] best odds [4] SENTIMENTALISM.
38. [ ] RASCALLY [1] a basement drinking place [2] wicked [3] PROVOCATIVE hat [4] a cheat.
39. [ ] SLUMBEROUS [1] waddling [2] ELEPHANTINE [3] heavy [4] sunk in sleep.
40. [ ] TURBID [1] muddy [2] upset [3] swirling [4] crowded.
41. [ ] ANTAGONISM [1] wrestling [2] word of opposite meaning [3] hostility [4] EMULATION.
42. [ ] CELIBACY [1] indifference [2] state of being single [3] a cause for celebration [4] living in a cell.
43. [ ] DECLAMATION [1] angle of incline [2] refusal [3] formal public speaking [4] thoughtlessness.
44. [ ] FANATICAL [1] air-conditions [2] mistaken [3] a head-hunter [4] frenzied.
45. [ ] HOVEL [1] remain poised over [2] squalid hut [3] a geometric figure [4] limp along.

46. [   ] LITURGY [1] sloth [2] repetition [3] ecclesiastical service [4] lead compound.
47. [   ] OVERARCH [1] church potentate [2] a kind of tree [3] meet above in middle [4] a coquette.
48. [   ] REASSEMBLE [1] look like [2] bring or come together again [3] quiet [4] a place where spare parts are kept.
49. [   ] SOLIDITY [1] inexpressiveness [2] obstinacy [3] density [4] fixedness.
50. [   ] UNACCOUNTABLE [1] innumerable [2] INEXPLICABLE [3] MYRIAD [4] predictable.
51. [   ] TURPITUDE [1] upside-down [2] disgraceful wickedness [3] CASUISTICAL [4] an axiom of conduct.
52. [   ] BEATITUDE [1] more than prettiness [2] blessed saying [3] saintliness [4] raising to sainthood.
53. [   ] COMPLAISANCE [1] a compliment [2] FATUOUS ACQUIESCENCE [3] a lovely meadow [4] self-satisfaction.
54. [   ] DROMEDARY [1] a beating [2] type of camel [3] bedevil [4] provoke by baiting.
55. [   ] GALA [1] a high wind [2] a star-cluster [3] festive [4] mare's milk.
56. [   ] INSUBSTANTIAL [1] strong [2] of one material with [3] wasteful [4] shadowy.
57. [   ] MODULATION [1] shyness [2] temperance [3] method of shifting from one key to another [4] admiration.
58. [   ] PLASH [1] splicing together [2] strike hard with thing [3] noise of water falling on something [4] joint between plastic substances.
59. [   ] SANITY [1] cleanliness [2] danger [3] healthy-mindedness [4] clarity.
60. [   ] SURCHARGE [1] rush upon [2] ship's financial officer [3] excess amount [4] warhorse.
61. [   ] WOBBLE [1] impede [2] sway unsteadily [3] wandering hobo [4] catch.
62. [   ] THRESHER [1] a bird [2] one who scrambles around [3] one who separates grain from chaff [4] gleaner.
63. [   ] SHARD [1] iron-clad hoofs [2] fragment of pottery [3] tough [4] point.
64. [   ] PROBLEMATICAL [1] argumentative [2] geometrical [3] chancy [4] workable.
65. [   ] NEGLIGIBLE [1] lounging garment [2] tending to forget [3] of little acount [4] wretched.
66. [   ] KINETIC [1] EGOTISTIC [2] wavy [3] pertaining to motion [4] attractive.
67. [   ] GUILELESS [1] heedless [2] without cunning [3] sweet [4] childlike.
68. [   ] ENCASE [1] in the event that [2] put into [3] a kind of cheese [4] a container.

321

69. [   ] COUPLET [1] married persons [2] two rhymed lines of verse [3] link [4] connective tissue.
70. [   ] BRAE [1] wide [2] article of apparel [3] hillside [4] sound made by donkey.
71. [   ] ASHY [1] veer off from [2] kind of wine [3] like ashes [4] find amount of metal in ore.
72. [   ] CHANTRY [1] sea song [2] chapel for singing Masses [3] music [4] wizardry.
73. [   ] DETRACT [1] take back [2] take away [3] withdraw [4] derailed.
74. [   ] FLASHY [1] powdery [2] showy [3] fat [4] small bottle.
75. [   ] IMMINENCE [1] quality of being outstanding [2] height [3] state of threatening [4] edge of cliff.
76. [   ] MAIDENLY [1] kind of fern [2] fine-grained [3] like a young girl [4] chiefly.
77. [   ] PATROON [1] one who subsidizes an artist's work [2] guard [3] landed MAGNATE [4] coward.
78. [   ] REPERTOIRE [1] VALISE [2] works that a musician, actor or company is ready to perform [3] witty BACKCHAT [4] assistant conductor.
79. [   ] SPONSOR [1] one who talks back [2] answer [3] one who assumes responsibility for [4] chanter in church.
80. [   ] UNEXCEPTIONABLE [1] unusual [2] picked out of a crowd [3] beyond criticism [4] a kind of bet.
81. [   ] BAIRN [1] heap [2] unfruitful [3] child [4] sheepfold.
82. [   ] COCKEREL [1] cheeky [2] feather in cap [3] kind of fish [4] rooster.
83. [   ] DISPUTABLE [1] quarrelsome [2] questionable [3] litigious [4] undrinkable.
84. [   ] FREEDMAN [1] advocate of liberty [2] a liberal [3] licentious person [4] manumitted slave.
85. [   ] INFANTILE [1] unspeakable [2] babylike [3] small [4] cunning.
86. [   ] MEDIATE [1] cut in two [2] run gantlet [3] act as go-between in dispute [4] statistical term.
87. [   ] PHAËTON [1] ghost [2] kind of airy [3] carriage [4] ancient ruler.
88. [   ] RIGMAROLE [1] conveyance [2] overturn a wagon [3] arranging ropes on mast [4] nonsensical sequence of statement.
89. [   ] SUBTRAHEND [1] lower tendency [2] number to be taken away from another [3] underground stream [4] drift below.
90. [   ] VAPORY [1] knavery [2] hangings [3] misty [4] distorted
91. [   ] YAW [1] yes [2] stretch [3] veer off course [4] marble.
92. [   ] TIDBIT [1] retaliation [2] quarrel [3] small delicacy [4] field mouse.
93. [   ] SHIBBOLETH [1] denunciation [2] catchword [3] sound made by reptile [4] keepsake.

322

94. [   ] PROPORTIONABLE   [1] ratio   [2] divisible   [3] corresponding [4] excessive.
95. [   ] NOMINATIVE   [1] of slight cost   [2] speech presenting candidate [3] case of the subject   [4] pointing out.
96. [   ] JINGO   [1] sound of bells   [2] fire-eating patriot   [3] rascal [4] jungle-dweller.
97. [   ] HANKER   [1] roll ball of yarn   [2] long for   [3] kerchief [4] hold ship stationary.
98. [   ] ENZYME   [1] commissioned officer in navy   [2] flag   [3] gland-produced CATALYTIC agent   [4] a paste.
99. [   ] COXSWAIN   [1] rooster-like strut   [2] steersman of boat   [3] over-confident person   [4] a small person.
100. [   ] BREAM   [1] breadth of a ship   [2] willow   [3] a kind of fish [4] a dim glow.

PART II

Jot down on a slip any of the fifty words in italics or small capitals which you cannot define in the following twelve passages. Guess at the meaning before you look up each word you miss. How far did each blackout of meaning affect your comprehension of the sense of the entire passage?

1. The region is studied from the standpoints of geography, ETHNOLOGY, ANTHROPOLOGY, ARCHAEOLOGY, *plastic arts, folk lore,* music, religion, CUISINE, textiles and costume, economics, *sociology,* politics, history. It must not be imagined that he handles all these aspects of Tehuantepec life with equal skill, completeness and understanding. Best of all are the archaeology, with its attendant comment on ESTHETIC styles and their *implications,* and the comment on folkways, costume, *folk arts, textiles* and what might be called the style of life in the region. Weakest are the chapters on history, INTERPRE-TIVE sociology and politics.—B. O. Wolfe, reviewing Covarrubias' *Mexico South,* in New York *Sunday Times Book Review,* October 27, 1946.

2. Can you accurately describe a SONNET, a cartel, a DEBENTURE, a *Wilson chamber,* a GENE, a PROTOCOL, NOLLE PROSSE and SCHIZZOPHRENIA [*sic*]? To each of the gents in these fields one of those words is everyday stuff. But since you do not and they do not know all these words, we are faced with what looks at first glance like the very birthplace and heartland of utter chaos.—Philip Wylie, column in New York *Post.*

3. The Supreme Commander last week also ordered seizure of members of Japan's Black Dragon secret society. You know what a dragon is, but can you define a DRAGOON? A DRAGOMAN?—Sunday New York *Times* Quiz.

4. *Radarange.* Most cooking methods—baking, boiling, frying—date from stone-ax days. They all heat food from the outside in. The Raytheon Co., prolific spawner of RADAR tubes, has shown short order cooks something new: a "range" which cooks food from the inside out.

The trick is done by shooting through the food a beam of ULTRA-HIGH

FREQUENCY radio energy from a MAGNETRON, the tube which powered many wartime RADARS. The waves make the MOLECULES in the raw food dance back and forth three billion times a second. Their motion generates heat. In seconds, the food gets hot. There is no waiting for the heat to seep in slowly, by *conduction,* from the surface.

Raytheon expects airlines to be the first big *"Radarange"* buyers. Quick lunch restaurants are prospects too. Radarange will grill a hamburger sandwich or a hot dog in 35 seconds. It bakes foam-light cup cakes, biscuits, or gingerbread in 29 seconds. It shuts itself off automatically.

Radarange is still too expensive for the home. But eventually, Raytheon hopes, a housewife will be able to slip a pot roast into the range and rush it to the table before her homecoming husband has parked his overcoat. For rare roast beef, rich brown outside, warm pink within, he will have to wait awhile: it is still beyond Radarange.—*Time,* October 28, 1946.

5. *What's a Psychoneurosis?* Later, because of the bitter feeling in Columbia, the trial had been moved to neighboring Lawrenceburg. But even in Lawrenceburg 736 talesmen had had to be questioned before twelve reasonably UNPREJUDICED jurors could be found. During this process, Judge Ingram struck a snag. One talesman's medical certificate, which reported a PSYCHO-NEUROSIS, set him frowning. After spelling the word out to himself, the Judge leaned forward and asked the man sympathetically: "Where does it hurt? What ails you?" One of the defense lawyers, a Negro, respectfully explained the term to the Judge.—*Time,* October 14, 1946.

6. ". . . any radical overhauling of the federal and state taxing systems . . . is CHIMERICAL in the period ahead . . ."—Leo Cherne, *The Rest of Your Life,* p. 142.

7. "Who gets *jurisdiction* of the cameraman who run the *iconoscopes* in the TELEVISION STUDIOS . . . ?"—*Op. cit.,* p. 172.

8. "PRECIPITRON . . . filters dust from the air electrically."—*Op. cit.,* pp. 197–198.

9. Lingo. The United Press correspondent with the British Second Army in Holland describes the type of German prisoner taken lately as "SCROFU-LOUS, ODOROUS, and PEDICULOUS." He quotes a British officer as translating: —————, —————, and —————.—*PM.*

What were the slang VULGARISMS in the translation?

10. A Bendix ad pictures the following branches of applied science as advancing in the crucible of war:

1. *Electronics*   4. *Optics*
2. *Magnetics*   5. *Carburation*
3. *Electro-Mechanics*   6. *Hydraulics*
                7. *Aerology*

Can you define them, with a little help from the Greek and Latin stems?

324

11. The holding-company act, which was passed to put a stop to just such BROBDIGNAGIAN JIGGERY-POKERY as USEPCO, put the headstone on V.E.'s empire.—*Time*, October 7, 1946.

Is *brobdig*—etc., spelled correctly? (See p. 192.)

12. . . . A radar comprises a *transmitter* that fires the BARRAGE of *pulses* into space—high-power chunks of beamed radio energy hurled skyward many times a second. The radar also comprises a highly-selective *receiver*, the ANTENNA of which is also aimed into space in the general direction that the pulses are transmitted.

As each pulse goes out the receiver catches a small part of it to start the *timing* process, then the receiver "listens" for the returning echo, which ends the timing. All this happens before another pulse goes out. The *sequence* of happenings is so rapid that it can only be observed on a *cathode-ray* screen similar to that used in a *television* receiver. A jog in a straight line indicates the start of the pulse, another jog, somewhat smaller, indicates the arrival of the echo from space. Beneath is a scale *calibrated* in feet, yards or miles. The operator reads off the answer painted by the returning echoes from space.

The radar cathode-ray screen also may be calibrated in micro-seconds or millionths of one second. Since a radio wave or a beam of light travels about 186,000 miles, or 327,000,000 yards, per second, in one micro-second it would go 327 yards. Thus, if a radar pulse returned as was pictured on the screen one *micro-second* later it would mean the "going" trip plus the "coming" trip of the wave was 327 yards, or the actual distance half of that amount, 163.5 yards. If 100 micro-seconds were indicated, the range or distance would be 16,350 yards.—"Theory of Radar," Tr. Kennedy—New York Sunday *Times*.

PART III—A TEST OF READINESS

The fifty clues which follow, from which you are to summon up the right words, are given just as they occur in earlier sections of this work.

1. half horse, half man
2. main dish; chief attraction
3. year for wandering or traveling
4. a sudden stroke to change REGIMES
5. your own ghost or divided personality
6. doom
7. MODERNIST music abounds in ——————— phrases.
8. French: Literally, "gluing" or "pasting," a method used by one school of SURREALIST painters: they glue odd bits of wood, glass, lace, egg-shell, and anything else handy onto canvas to form allegedly artistic designs and pictures.
9. A word that's so worked to death that it loses all specific meaning. The author's synonym for this is "omnibus" word.

325

10. . . . that branch of physics which treats of the emission, behavior, and effect of electrons, especially in vacuum tubes, PHOTOELECTRIC cells and the like.
11. colloq.: daffy: given a new vogue by the movie *Mr. Deeds Goes to Town* (1936)
12. (new meaning for word already in the dictionary) application of force or economic pressure to an AGGRESSOR
13. slang: a dilapidated motor car
14. . . . Motion Pictures (i.e., as used in movie jargon). Literally, the *mounting* (after cutting) of alternating sequences from two strips of film having CONVERGING lines of action, so that the moment of highest excitement will be achieved when the two trains of events link up. The excitement mounts, too.
15. familiar with many languages
16. act or process of spreading out from a center
17. mutual exchange, especially of trade privileges and concessions between two countries
18. clotting (of the blood)
19. Its (*Time's*) PORTMANTEAU or ———————— words are a virtual trademark.
20. Roman living room
21. the great artery
22. outer coat of eye
23. first aide (especially to a bishop)
24. main point (lit., cross)
25. spirits (the kind Aladdin summoned out of a bottle)
26. non-hen egg-hatcher
27. that seasick feeling
28. tiny nipple-like projection
29. referring legislature's act to people
30. overseer (of slaves or teachers)
31. naming the disease from the symptoms
32. plural marriage
33. beginner; raw recruit
34. plane figure with more than four sides
35. paper from pith
36. mark of disgrace
37. heat-conserver
38. Supply the key word that covers the widest swath of meaning for the following synonyms:
————————, joke, jape, quip, witticism, wisecrack, crack, gag
39. Supply the key synonym for
————————, ROCOCO, BAROQUE, FLAMBOYANT, FLORID
40. What's the business term which is defined as follows:
Keeping price levels steady (stable), particularly during war and its aftermath.

41. What is the technical term for the following?
    You let me use your patents and I'll let you use mine.
42. What is the diplomatic phrase for "the way things stood before"?
43. What are:
    . . . any of various substances that harden and retain their shape after being molded or shaped when softened by heat, pressure, etc.
44. What are:
    . . . semi-organic compounds, . . . not devised by atom-splitting . . . rather some slick chemist figures a way to cajole one of the hydro-carbon ring molecules into rearranging its internal housekeeping so that it throws out one of its carbon atoms and lets a —————— atom move in.
45. top layer of skin
46. deprivation of power to reproduce
47. deficiency of red blood corpuscles
48. electrically-conducting sub-molecules
49. Branch of mathematics dealing with variables and changing rates
50. 10^{100} was named a —————— by Professor Edward Kasner's nine-year-old nephew.

Quiz Keys for Chapter XII

62. Page 287.

1. incinerator
2. mystery-historical (blend)
3. bambino
4. discus
5. counting
6. Philistines
7. ?
8. (gibberish)
9. epicure: no connection with *epic*
10. dormitories
11. gale
12. horse-thief, weakly, almsgiving, evening, funereal (thus literally translated); all the words are used in their correct sense; it is simply that no one in his right mind would ever use these long, classical words in such connections.
13. All words rightly used; the mistake is taking literally a piece of Western bragging, which calls its section of the U. S. "God's country."
14. Pun on *adder,* a snake
15. guerilla
16. demi-tasse
17. index
18. various
19. Acorns
20. centipede
21. *shift,* stratagem, mistaken for (archaic) *shift,* petticoat
22. *aesthetic* is meant
23. illegitimate
24. insinuator (the reverse error from 1 above)
25. eligible
26. words used correctly; **error is in** the idea—or is it?
27. equilibrium
28. to a lyre
29. lotus-eaters
30. phalanx
31. couplets
32. milestone
33. Can you get me a bottle of Johnny Walker for three dollars?—Certainly I can.

34. admirable, expand, ? , interpret
35. Virgilian
36. mistresses
37. chantecler
38. table d'hote
39. words used correctly, though *shesoul* is a coinage for a "female soul."
40. imaginary line
41. phrases making up this incantation are standard words, or allusions, except *zib-zab-zum,* which is coined gibberish, and *Abedwego,* which is a pun on the name of the third member of the trio who went through the fiery furnace—*Abednego.*

42. vice versa
43. "purr"—etymologically no connection with *Persian*
44. oscillations
45. episcopacy (?)
46. italics
47. Reverse the initial consonants and reshuffle some of the syllables, and you can figure it out.
48. conference
49. *Ein Stück fehlt* is what the Swiss thought. In German, it means "One piece (item) was lacking."
50. *Up* and *around* are superfluous in standard American; but not in dialect talk affected by Pennsylvania Dutch.

64. Page 296.

1. malapropism	13. boner	26. boner	38. folk etymology
2. portmanteau	14. pun	27. malapropism	39. double talk
3. boner	15. boner	28. boner	40. folk etymology, boner
4. malapropism, folk etymology	16. pun	29. folk etymology	41. double-talk
	17. boner	30. folk etymology, boner	42. boner
5. boner	18. malapropism	31. folk etymology, boner	43. boner
6. malapropism	19. boner		44. malapropism
7. boner	20. boner	32. boner, pun	45. boner
8. double-talk	21. pun	33. macaronic	46. boner
9. boner	22. boner	34. boners	47. spoonerism
10. malapropism	23. malapropism	35. boner	48. Goldwynism, malapropism
11. boner	24. boner, malapropism	36. boner	49. Goldwynism
12. jocose use of learned words	25. malapropism	37. boner	
		50. macaronic	

75. Part I, page 319.

1. [3]	11. [2]	21. [2]	31. [2]	41. [3]
2. [2]	12. [2]	22. [4]	32. [3]	42. [2]
3. [2]	13. [3]	23. [2]	33. [1]	43. [3]
4. [2]	14. [2]	24. [3]	34. [2]	44. [4]
5. [2]	15. [2]	25. [3]	35. [3]	45. [2]
6. [3]	16. [2]	26. [2]	36. [2]	46. [3]
7. [2]	17. [3]	27. [2]	37. [2]	47. [3]
8. [3]	18. [2]	28. [3]	38. [2]	48. [2]
9. [2]	19. [3]	29. [2]	39. [4]	49. [3]
10. [2]	20. [3]	30. [2]	40. [1]	50. [2]

51. [2]	61. [2]	71. [3]	81. [3]	91. [3]
52. [2]	62. [3]	72. [2]	82. [4]	92. [3]
53. [2]	63. [2]	73. [2]	83. [2]	93. [2]
54. [2]	64. [3]	74. [2]	84. [4]	94. [3]
55. [3]	65. [3]	75. [3]	85. [2]	95. [3]
56. [4]	66. [3]	76. [3]	86. [3]	96. [2]
57. [3]	67. [2]	77. [3]	87. [3]	97. [2]
58. [3]	68. [2]	78. [2]	88. [4]	98. [3]
59. [3]	69. [2]	79. [3]	89. [2]	99. [2]
60. [3]	70. [3]	80. [3]	90. [3]	100. [3]

Part III, page 325.

1. centaur
2. pièce de résistance
3. Wanderjahr
4. coup d'état
5. Doppelgänger
6. Nemesis
7. dissonant
8. collage
9. counterword
10. electronics
11. pixillated
12. sanction
13. jalopy
14. montage
15. polyglot
16. radiation
17. reciprocity
18. coagulation
19. blend
20. atrium
21. aorta
22. cornea
23. coadjutor
24. crux
25. genii
26. incubator
27. nausea
28. papilla
29. referendum
30. supervisor
31. diagnosis
32. polygamy
33. tyro
34. polygon
35. papyrus
36. stigma
37. thermos
38. jest
39. ornate
40. stabilization
41. cross-licensing
42. status quo ante
43. plastics
44. silicones
45. epidermis
46. sterilization
47. anemia
48. ions
49. calculus
50. googol

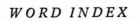

WORD INDEX

WORD INDEX

[NOTE: The words in this index include those printed in small capitals in the text to show that they lie in the range just beyond the ten thousand commonest in the Thorndike count, *plus* the words printed in italic in the text to indicate that they were words under discussion. See also Subject Index, p. 355, for the general index to the book.]

333

334

Chem., 41
Chemise, 288
cherub, 300
chesterfield, 11
chimera, 2, 10, 46, 132, 262
chimerical, 43, 324
chinook, 12
chirographer, 112
chirography, 48, 91
chiropody, 43
chiropractors, 192
chiseling, 224
chits, 71
chivalric, 170
chlorination, 304
chlorophyll, 271
choler, 132
choleric, 61, 155, 220
Cholmondeley, 219
cholor, 220
choral, 102
chordal, 223
chorea, 272
Christian, 161
Christianity, 219
chromosome, 273
chromosomes, 272
chroniclers, 211
chronique scanda-leuse, 256
chronological, 224
chronology, 83, 90
chronometer, 281, 304
chuckle-headed, 102
churl, 161
chute, 87
Ciceronian, 216
cilia, 272
cinema, 46, 72, 124, 132
cinemactress, 10, 72
cinemadaptation, 10, 73
cinemaddicts, 73
cinemadolescent, 10, 72
cinemagnate, 10, 70
cinemarmful, 72
cinematic, 69, 188
cinematograph, 91, 124
cipher, 169
circa, 71
circle, 173, 174

circuit, 190
circuitous, 32, 259
circulatory, 316
circumference, 289
circumfly, 174
circumlocution, 175, 316
circumnavigate, 86, 97, 173, 316
circumscribe, 32, 97
circumspect, 122
circumspection, 122
circumstance, 151
circumstantial, 118, 177, 258
circumvene, 107
circumvent, 121, 307
cirrhosis, 67
cite, 23
cityfied, 170
claimant, 105
clairvoyance, 193
clambake, 8
clandestine, 43, 177, 200
claret, 224
class, 153
claustrophobia, 89, 317
cleavage, 71
clichés, 68, 73, 225
clickeroo, 8
cliff-hanger, 8
clinic, 123
clinical, 67
clique, 181
closure, 104
cloud-raker, 304
clues, 212
clutch, 72
coadjutor, 93, 125, 316
cobbling, 317
co-belligerent, 71
cockade, 70
cockerel, 322
cockets, 181
cockney, 46
coed, 97
coeducation, 97
coefficient, 316
coequal, 108
coerce, 116
coerced, 6
coercion, 71
cofferdam, 258

cogent, 83, 101, 180
cogitate, 101
cognizance, 112
cognition, 112, 316
cognizant, 43
cognomen, 46
coherer, 274
cohesion, 71
coincide, 179
cole, 62
coleslaw, 293
colitis, 67
collaborationist, 71
collectivising, 257
collocations, 179, 277
collop, 62
colloquial, 10, 40, 61, 63, 69, 77, 97, 148, 216, 315
colloquialisms, 65
colonized, 148
colonizers, 299
colossal, 157
colossus, 125
columnists, 71
coma, 24, 188
combination, 5
come, 174
comeuppance, 70, 129
comic, 118, 214, 216, 217, 221
comfit, 95
comma, 24
commandant, 43
commandeer, 29
commando, 151
comme il faut, 256
commentators, 311, 314
commerce, 171
commiseration, 316
Commissar, 297
commissariat, 258
commissars, 278
commissary, 110
commitments, 69
commode, 113
commonsensical, 307
commonty, 291
communicant, 196
communique, 43
Communism, 98, 200
Communists, 152

compendium, 125, 193
compile, 202
compiler, 22
compiling, 54
complacency, 216
compactness, 83
complaisance, 114, 321
complaisant, 169
complete, 158
complex, 260
complexes, 190
compliant, 67
complicity, 114
compliment, 23
complimentary, 11
comport, 113
composite, 34, 95, 166
compost, 95
comprehensible, 257
comprehension, 115, 292
compression, 222
compulsion, 105, 313
comstockery, 215
comrade, 252
con, 132
concatenation, 32, 194, 281
concepts, 67
concern, 151
concerto, 43
concessions, 310
conchology, 90
conciliate, 195
concism, 217
concoct, 191
concocted, 294
concomitant, 258
concordance, 103
concourse, 186
concubines, 301
concupiscence, 43
concur, 104
concussion, 32, 282
condensation, 53
condescension, 316
condign, 105
condition, 151
condolence, 43
condottieri, 202
conduce, 96
conducible, 96

335

338

342

343

346

perpetrated, 293
perpetrating, 25
perpetrator, 93, 129, 290
perpetual, 61
perquisite, 116
persecutor, 93, 129
persona, 155
personality, 155
personnel, 20, 31
perspicacity, 122
perspicuity, 122
perspicuous, 31, 190
perspiration, 319
perusal, 121
perversion, 318
pessimism, 105, 177
pestiferous, 107
pestilential, 184
Petrarchan, 217
petrifaction, 291
petrified, 102
petrify, 85
petrography, 317
petrol, 76
petulant, 112, 295
phaeton, 133
phaëton, 322
phagocytes, 67
phalanx, 133
phantasm, 188
phantasy, 169
Pharisee, 12
pharmacist, 93
pharmacopeia, 192
pharynx, 133
phenolax, 288
phenolics, 263
phenomena, 133, 200
phenomenal, 72
philanthropy, 124
philharmonic, 124
philippic, 211
Philistine, 12
Philistines, 308
philological, 180
philology, 90, 124
phlegm, 220
phlegmatic, 220
phobia, 67, 84, 89, 260
phoenix, 13, 134
phonetic, 23, 53
phonetician, 45
phonetics, 124

phonic, 124
phonology, 124
phonophobia, 89
phony, 72
phosphate, 124
phosphorus, 124
photoelectric, 326
photogenic, 67
photographer, 91
photometer, 124
photophobia, 89
photosensitive, 263
photostat, 124
photosynthesis, 124, 270
phototube, 262, 263
phrasal, 154, 173
phraseology, 90, 181
phrenology, 90
physician, 167
physicist, 98, 111, 124, 239
physicists, 99, 186
physico-chemical, 190
physics, 275
physiognomy, 124
physiography, 124
physiologist, 190
physiologists, 220
physiology, 90
physiomedical, 280
piazza, 301
pic, 7
pictographs, 257
picturesque, 260
picturesqueness, 181
pidgin, 294
pièce de résistance, 15
pigeonhole, 29
pigmentation, 272
pimpernel, 62
pincers, 64, 71
pinchbeck, 215
pipestems, 105
pistils, 271
pitchblende, 281
pitfalls, 24
pituitary, 271
pity, 167
pivotal, 258
pix, 7
placate, 114, 195
placement, 20
plagiarism, 46, 119
plagiarist, 291

planisphere, 317
plash, 321
plasm, 280
plastics, 260, 263
platitudes, 73, 101, 215, 296
platitudinous, 215
Platonic, 13
plausibly, 149
play footie, 70
pleasantry, 114
plebiscite, 44, 65, 72
plebs, 93, 129
plenipotentiaries, 314
plenum, 252
plexus, 94, 114, 129
pliable, 114
pliant, 114
pliotron, 262
plugged, 66
plumule, 62
plutonium, 111, 265
podium, 30
poetasters, 301
poetic, 41
poignant, 211
pointless, 168
poison, 8
poisonous, 184
poker, 151
polemic, 73, 194
polemical, 73, 194
polemicists, 73
policer, 213
Politburo, 95
politician, 158
politico, 103, 158
politicos, 71
pollination, 271
Pollyannanias, 233
Polonius, 213
Poltergeist, 14
polyamides, 264
polygamy, 134
polyandry, 134
polygon, 134
polygonal, 86
polygyny, 134
polymerization, 258
polyphase, 304
polyphonic, 124
polysyllabic, 179, 217, 253, 313
pomposity, 73
poncho, 72
pontifical, 95, 198

pontoon, 64
pony up, 224
popularizer, 200, 270
popularizers, 223
popularizing, 119
porous, 275
portent, 120
portfolios, 72
portmanteau, 10, 70, 161, 326
portrayal, 217
posit, 200
positivist, 95
post, 97
postamputation, 68
postulate, 200
postulates, 281
postwar, 97
potash, 7
potentate, 21
pouter, 105
power, 153
praetor, 93, 129
praetorian, 13
pragmatic, 250
pragmatism, 183
preamble, 314
precedence, 46, 66, 256
precedent, 104
preceptor, 129
precipitant, 105
precipitation, 105
precipitron, 324
précis, 193
precise, 177
precision, 298
preclude, 104, 314
pre-condition, 254
precursor, 104, 129
predicate, 106
predilection, 111
predominance, 220
predominantly, 314
preëminence, 61
pre-eminently, 68
prefiguration, 304
prefixes, 52
prehensile, 115
prehistoric, 192, 311
prelude, 314
premeditation, 71
premier, 45
premise, 200
prenatal, 97
pre-natal, 313

347

preoccupation, 220
preponderance, 83, 168
prepped, 72
prepossess, 117
prerequisite, 65
prerequisites, 83
prerogatives, 246
presbyter, 134
presentiment, 114
prescriptive, 87
preservative, 119
prestidigitated, 68, 165
prestidigitator, 257
prestige, 52, 71
presumptive, 212
presuppose, 200
pretender, 120
pretentious, 8, 30, 290
prevision, 188, 193
previsions, 199
pre-war, 97
prima-facie, 65
primness, 297
priorities, 66, 73, 254
priority, 64, 65, 66, 258
pro, 132
probability, 186, 281
probe, 181
problematical, 321
proboscis, 129
procès verbal, 256
proclivities, 226
proconsul, 93, 129
procrastinator, 12
procrastinators, 157
proctor, 93, 129
procurator, 93, 129, 300
profanation, 86
profanity, 157, 179, 184, 222
professions, 297
proficient, 95
prognosticate, 32
prohibitionist, 98
prohibitive, 108
projectile, 83, 110
projection, 260
projectors, 72
prolate, 107
proliferation, 259

prolific, 94
prolix, 129
prologue, 90
Prometheus, 277
promoter, 320
promulgate, 45
propaganda, 47, 71, 73, 93, 129, 161
propagandists, 160
propitiate, 195
proportionable, 323
proposition, 151, 157, 165
propound, 95
propriety, 184
proscribe, 97
proscribere, 97
prosecutor, 119
prospector, 129
prostitution, 118
protagonist, 123
protean, 189
protocol, 9, 65, 124, 254, 323
protomartyr, 124
proton, 124, 262
protonotary, 124
protons, 199, 275
prototype, 124
protozoan, 124
protract, 121
Proustian, 217
proverbial, 109
provident, 122
providential, 290
provisional, 177
provocative, 65, 221, 320
provost, 21, 45, 319
proximity, 73
prussic, 218
psalmody, 300
psalter, 134, 300
pseudo, 68, 195, 213, 276
pseudonym, 195, 317
psyche, 134
psychiatrist, 194
psychiatry, 61, 67, 124, 278
psychoanalysis, 61, 67, 124, 281
psychoanalyst, 67, 89, 194
psychological, 49, 72, 201, 220, 310

psychologist, 20
psychology, 21, 49, 72, 90, 220
psychometrical, 278
psychometricals, 281
psychometrician, 281
psychoneurosis, 282, 324
psychopathologist, 194
psychoses, 281
psychosis, 124, 281
psychosomatic, 67
psychotherapy, 124
psychotherapist, 194
pub, 223
pueblo, 67, 303
pulchritude, 122
pulses, 325
punctuation, 105
Punica fides, 72
pundit, 148
punitive, 70
punning, 223
puns, 290
purists, 202
purport, 47
pursuance, 119
pursuivant, 62
purvey, 122
put, 174
putrefaction, 95, 291
Putsch, 15
pylons, 303
pyre, 192
pyrites, 124, 134
pyrography, 91
python, 134
pyx, 62, 134

quadrant, 276
quadrilateral, 71
quadrumanous, 109
quaestor, 93, 129
quagmire, 64
qualm, 85
quandary, 291
quarterdeck, 120
quarterly, 224
quasi, 129, 196
quay, 46
quean, 161
quebracho, 71
queller, 300
queue, 45

queued, 71
queues, 71
quid pro quo, 256
quietus, 129
quip, 197
quipped, 71
quire, 24
quirk, 220
quirks, 147
quisling, 71
Quixote, 211
quixotic, 211
quiz, 218
quondam, 129
quorum, 93, 129
quota, 61, 93, 129, 242

rabble-rouser, 72
rabblerouser, 112
Rabelaisian, 217, 226
raceme, 62
rachitic, 87
racketeer, 72
radar, 240, 262, 323
radarange, 323
radars, 324
radials, 303
radiant, 281
radiation, 72, 151, 239, 275, 281
radio, 223
radioactive, 151, 279, 280
radioactive fission, 280
radioactivity, 305
Radiological, 72
radium, 72
rail, 183
raison d'état, 256
raison d'être, 258
rajah, 192
ramifying, 91
rancor, 65, 115, 129, 179, 294
rancorous, 109
random, 168
range, 153
rank, 153
rant, 73
ranting, 213
rapacious, 115
rascally, 320
raspberry, 39
rate, 183

specialization, 150, 152
specialized, 240
specializer, 152
specie, 46
specification, 122
specify, 122
specious, 25, 46, 122, 194
spectacular, 89
spectrum, 61
speculator, 130
speculators, 71
Speleological, 90
spelunca, 90
spelunke, 90
Spenglerian, 203
sperm, 273
spermatozoon, 134
spheroid, 123
spine-chiller, 8
spiritualist, 196
splay, 62
splendid, 157
spondulicks, 226
sponge, 184
sponsor, 93, 130, 322
sponsored, 315
spoony, 226
sporadic, 32, 68
spurious, 73
sputum, 94, 130
squadrons, 102
squeal, 169
squib, 13, 182
stabilization, 73
stabilize, 46
stadium, 130
stalagmites, 304
stalemate, 71
Stalinist, 204
Stalinite, 152
stamina, 130, 314
stamped, 48
stanchion, 62, 118
Standard, 41, 156
state, 151
static, 81, 177
statisticians, 186
status, 45, 71, 93, 130
status quo, 254
status quo ante, 254
steals, 167
steapsin, 62
steatopygous, 2, 69

stenographer, 91
stentorian, 87, 200
stereoscope, 124
stereotype, 317
stereotyped, 157
stereotypes, 69
sterility, 271
sterilization, 272
sternum, 94, 130
stethoscope, 124
stichomancy, 55
stickler, 67
sticklers, 107
stigma, 134
stimuli, 281
stimulus, 272
stingy, 83
stipule, 62
stoats, 309, 310
stoic, 13
stolls, 64
stoma, 62, 134
stomach, 50
stomate, 62
stopes, 310
story, 61
stowaway, 86
strafing, 71
strainer, 118
straiten, 118
strata, 130, 225
stratify, 46
stratagems, 198
strategic, 66, 121
strategy, 64, 71, 72, 252, 298
stratocar, 281
stratosphere, 265, 317
stratum, 46
stereotyped, 215
stretching, 149
stretch-out, 248, 285
striated, 46
strictness, 118
stricture, 118
strident, 73, 87, 200
stringent, 65
strophe, 134
strumpet, 295
stupor, 94, 130
stylized, 109
stylograph, 91
stylus, 54
stymied, 28, 121
suave, 197

sub-conscious, 89
subirrigation, 303
subjective, 110, 155
sub judice, 256
subjugate, 46, 111
subjugated, 259
subjunctive, 111
sublimation, 260
subpena, 46
sub rosa, 256
subscriber, 97
subscription, 97
subsidiary, 259
subsidiaries, 73
subsistence, 11, 64
sub-standard, 293
substantial, 61
substantialize, 196
substantiate, 196
substantive, 118
substitution, 118
substractors, 291
substratum, 130
subtend, 120
subterfuge, 46
subterranean, 319
subtractor, 288
subtrahend, 21, 121, 322
subventions, 257
subversion, 318
subversive, 161, 318
subvert, 318
subvocalization, 282
succumb, 29
succumbed, 314
sufficiency, 95
suffix, 99
suffixes, 52, 87, 97, 98, 143
sugar daddy, 214
suggestibility, 273
sui generis, 256
sulfa, 67, 199
sulphide, 125, 274
sulfides, 134
sulphuric, 276
summative, 187
super, 130
superb, 157
supersede, 87
superhuman, 122, 216
superlative, 107
superlatives, 157
superscribe, 97

superscription, 97, 143
supervene, 87, 121
supervise, 122
supplemental, 173
supplementary, 52, 214
suprasensory, 186
surcharge, 321
surplice, 25
surprisal, 115
surrealist, 325
surreptitious, 115, 200
surrogate, 198
surveillance, 65, 122
surveying, 122
susceptibility, 73
suspension, 297
suture, 46
swaddling, 300
swart, 72
Swastikas, 116
swatch, 71
swath, 64
sweetie, 225
swell, 2, 156
swelter, 29
Swiftian, 217
swinish, 310
sybaritic, 198
sybarite, 215
sycophant, 184
syllabus, 193
syllogism, 61
symbolic, 67, 278, 310
symbolism, 187
symbolists, 190
symbology, 281
symmetry, 123
sympathizers, 251
symposium, 130
symptomatic, 258, 303
synapse, 272
synchronize, 66
synchronized, 281
synchroton, 262
syncopated, 216
syncopates, 223
synechdoche, 81
synod, 45
synonymity, 169
synonymous, 313, 314

351

353

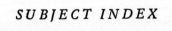

SUBJECT INDEX

SUBJECT INDEX

[NOTE: See also Word Index, p. 331.]

299, 303, 304, 312-314; specialized vocabulary of, 240 (*see also* vocabulary, special and technical); ordinary words specialized into, 240-245; radiation of everyday words into, 240; from labor-management relations, 246; from labor, 247-250 (*see also* jargon); from politics, 250–253 (*see also* jargon); in bureaucratic and United Nations jargons, 253-255; in diplomacy, 255-256; in the news, 256-259, 261, 262; in general use, 259-262; not in the dictionaries, 263-266; in popularizing books and science-fiction, 270-284

Tennyson, (quoted) 295

Thorndike, E. L., 52, 60, 61, 62, 63, 70, 77, 87, 312, 315, 316 (*see also* frequency numbers)

Thorndike's Century Senior Dictionary, 52, 63, 263

Time, 2, 8, 10, 32, 34, 40, 63, 67, 69, 70, 73, 74, 91, 182, 223, 255, 256

Tito, 92, (quoted) 93

Tintan, 293

Togo, Hashimura, 294

Toynbee, 70

Tschaikowsky, 312

Twain, Mark, 157

Typhoid Mary, 290

usage, 52; American, 40, 56, 60, 74-77, 158, 223, 314; British, 40, 53, 60, 74-77, 151, 158, 167, 223; Scotch, 40, 60; idiomatic, 166

Van den Bark, Melvin, 175

Variety, 7, 223

verbiage, 30, 100

Vergil, 54, 55

Vinci, da, 160

Vishinsky, 151

vocabulary, 56-57, 61, 69, 144, 146, 172, 173, 179, 185, 202, 304, 314; range of, 1, 22, 60, 70, 132, 312, 318; building of, 1, 10, 16, 22, 62, 70-74, 87, 144, 160, 234, 296; importance of, 20; analysis of, 60-69; importance of synonyms in building up, 166-210 (*see also* synonyms); richness in terms of

abuse, 179-184; epitomizing cultural history, 211-238 (*see also* words epitomizing cultural history); special and technical, 240, 246, 259, 280 (*see also* technical terms); modes of building technical, 239-286 (*see also* technical terms); in the news, 303-304; modes of building, 287-329; through analysis of wordplay jokes, 287-296; malapropisms, 290-291; boners, 291-292; spoonerisms, 292; Goldwynisms, 292-293; folk etymology, 293; macaronic lingo, 294-296

Voltaire, 296

Wallace, Henry A., 169

Watanabe, Frank, 316

Webster's Collegiate Dictionary, 52, 310

Webster's Dictionary of Synonyms, 176, 177, 178, 181

Webster's New International Dictionary, 11, 34, 52, 92

Weekley, Ernst, 46

Welles, Orson, 311

Welles, Sumner, 9

Wells, H. G., 211

Wilde, Oscar, 169

Williams, Wythe, 314

Wilson, Earl, 8, 166, 183

Winchell, Walter, 7, 39

Winston Simplified Dictionary, 52

Wodehouse, P. G., 75

word-analyzer, 100, 143-149, 162, 296, 316

word-detection, 16-19

wordplay, 1-19, 289, 290-91 (*see also* vocabulary)

words, in the news, 9-10, 39, 42, 63-66, 68, 74, 78-80, 84, 91-92, 148-149, 152, 162, 171, 184, 303, 305, 313; allusive, 10; stories behind, 10-13; foreign, 13-15, 53, 57, 70, 256; process and method of learning, 16-19, 73, 143, 296-297 (*see also* vocabulary); frequency of, 16, 22, 46, 51, 60-63, 70, 313; at work, 17, 19, 20-38; archaic, 40, 70; dialect, 40, 57, 61, 63, 65, 69, 77, 97, 148, 175; standard, 40, 41, 51, 61, 63, 70, 74, 78, 149, 223, 224; pronunciation of, 41-46; poetic, 41, 156;